SPIRIT

AND

FLESH

SPIRIT
AND
FLESH

Life in a Fundamentalist
Baptist Church

James M. Ault, Jr.

ALFRED A. KNOPF   NEW YORK   2004

Library of Congress Cataloging-in-Publication Data
Ault, James M., 1946–
Spirit and flesh : life in a fundamentalist Baptist church /
James M. Ault, Jr.—1st ed.
p.   cm.
Includes bibliographical references.
ISBN 0-375-40242-X
1. Baptists—Massachusetts—Worcester Region—Case studies.
2. Fundamentalist churches—Massachusetts—Worcester Region—
Case studies.   I. Title.
BX6480.W9A95 2004
306.6'8617443—dc22   2003065650

Out of concern for the privacy of individuals depicted here, I have
changed the names and identifying details of the church, church members, and others, while preserving relevant connotations and associations.
—James M. Ault, Jr.

To my parents,
James and Dorothy Ault

CONTENTS

Prologue   ix

PART ONE

1   Meeting   3
2   Frank and Sharon   17
3   The Shawmut River Baptist Church   36
4   The Old-Home Crowd   56
5   Phil and Jean   77
6   Reckoning   94

PART TWO

7   Spring   117
8   Fall   129
9   Winter   141
10 Bible Study   155
11 Prayer Life   173
12 Biblical Morality   186
13 Fundamentalism and Tradition   201

PART THREE

14 To Film?   221
15 Shooting   233

16 Marriage   246

17 Ben and Pam   260

18 The Wisdom to Manage   275

PART FOUR

19 "They've slandered my character!"   293

20 "Everybody could see it."   305

21 "The neck that turns the head"   316

22 "But what about you?"   332

    Epilogue   350

    Notes   371

    Bibliography   405

    Acknowledgments   413

    Index   417

PROLOGUE

If sin weren't eternal . . .

As I accompanied Pastor Frank Valenti down a corridor into the red brick labyrinth of Worcester City Hospital, built up piecemeal over the past century, the sounds of city traffic and the dim winter light faded away. As we stepped out of the elevator and turned the corner, I first caught sight of them through the thick glass windows of the waiting room outside Intensive Care: four women huddled in mourning. An eighteen-year-old boy had shot himself in the head, Pastor Valenti explained to me on our way there. His brain was liquefied and no brain waves registered. The doctors have spoken with his mother about donating his organs. If she agrees, he won't be "unplugged" from a life-support system until recipients can be found.

Sitting upright in the middle of the group and dressed in black, the boy's mother seemed dazed and weary as she went through the motions of casting consoling looks at the three younger women bent over sobbing around her. She nodded a look of recognition toward Valenti, as a spare, wiry man, wearing double-knit pants bagging at the seat, came up to greet us in the hallway. Vinnie, the boy's father, had known "Frankie Valenti" since growing up with him in the rural-suburban towns on the outskirts of Worcester in the 1950s. He and his family had never had anything to do with the fundamentalist Baptist church Valenti had founded in their hometown six years before. They were Catholics and, therefore, like me, "unsaved" in Pastor Valenti's eyes. Yet knowing Frankie Valenti was now a preacher, they had turned to him in their time of need.

Vinnie, his eyes fixed wide with terror and grief, asked Frank to walk down the hall with him to talk. Waiting behind, I noticed a large, muscular man, with curly black hair and tattoos on his arms, stalking tensely up and down the hallway. Valenti returned to the mourning women, placed his hand gently on the mother's shoulder and asked quietly, "Would you mind if I read some scripture?"

"What good will that do?" the curly-haired man suddenly snapped from the waiting room doorway.

"It will make *me* feel better," one of the young women responded in angry defiance. Valenti sat down, opened his large leather-covered Bible, dog-eared with use, and read a passage while the curly-haired man looked on in disgust.

When Valenti finished, he asked, "Do you mind if I pray with you?" The mother nodded her assent and Valenti bowed his head, clasped his thick hands together and quietly prayed aloud. Taking leave, he assured the boy's mother he would be in touch soon. We walked back to the elevator. As the doors opened and we entered, the curly-haired man overtook us, exploding in Valenti's face.

"You know, Vinnie hasn't been a father to him for years!" he snarled. As he continued his diatribe, Valenti lowered his head, occasionally raising his eyes in a look of tried patience. When the man finished, Valenti looked up and said calmly, "I'll talk with you later this afternoon, Rich." The elevator doors shut and we descended.

Rich is the mother's new husband, Valenti explained. Ever since his mother remarried, the boy had had terrible conflicts with his step-father. "That often happens in that set of circumstances," he observed sadly. Recently the boy had moved out of his mother's home and had been living in his father's apartment until two nights ago when he had put a bullet through his head.

"Everyone tries to undo fifteen years of sin and lousy living," Valenti said, grimacing as we slid back into his two-toned Chevy station wagon and left the hospital parking lot for our next destination. "They don't understand," he said, reflecting on the situation in matter-of-fact terms. "You can't undo sin. It's eternal. Either you take it to hell or to Calvary. If sin weren't eternal," he theorized out loud to me, "hell wouldn't be eternal. They're synonymous."

"Mmm, hmm," I muttered, as I often did when unsure of what my fundamentalist subjects meant by what they said. Although I had grown up the son of a Methodist minister, I had never heard the Christian Gospel applied in this way, like a law of thermodynamics, to such a familiar, yet grim, human reality. In the church circles I knew growing up in the 1950s, "sin" was not often spoken about in real-life terms and to use "hell" in a nonmetaphorical sense was seen as a sign of backwardness. Pastor Valenti, on the other hand, spoke of sin and hell as mathematical laws of the cosmos.

In any case, at this point in my life, whether sin and hell were synonymous and eternal was irrelevant to me. Ever since my freshman year at Harvard College in the mid-1960s, I would have considered myself an atheist if I thought about it at all. Having pursued a vocation as a scholar, I saw belief in God and the supernatural as a universal artifact of human society and, therefore, an important object of study. But there was no place on the horizons of my mind, accustomed, as it was, to adducing causes here and there, for the actions of God—or gods. In any case, it was not Valenti's religion that had brought me to follow him on his round of duties that February afternoon. It was his politics.

Valenti was vice president of the Massachusetts chapter of the Moral Majority, the most influential new-right organization at the time, founded five years before by Jerry Falwell. He was frequently called on by local television, radio and print journalists to represent the "Moral Majority point of view" at a time when popular mobilization of its conservative "pro-family" agenda was growing and transforming American politics beyond recognition. An ex-Catholic and Vietnam vet, Valenti had been among the first to graduate from Falwell's Liberty Baptist College in Lynchburg, Virginia, and, after returning to his hometown to plant a church, had become one of those thousands of politically aroused fundamentalist preachers who had made Jerry Falwell and the Moral Majority household words by the 1980s.

I had met Valenti a year before while beginning sociological research to better understand popular support for this new-style conservatism marching proudly behind the banner of "family values." As a sixties radical who had embraced the antiwar movement, feminism and other new-left enthusiasms of the day, I saw "pro-family" conservatism as so foreign to my own politics that I was convinced anthropological methods were the best way to understand it. And so I had begun interviewing members of grassroots groups and observing their activities: right-to-life demonstrations, the daily work of running a home school, a campaign against sex education in a public-school district, and so on.

But, among all the conservative groups I met, Valenti's fundamentalist Baptist church captured my attention from the moment I first walked through its doors. As a community enterprise, it made manifest a social world I had come to believe provided certain foundations for new-right conservatism as a movement with considerable popular appeal. It was also so different from the images of fundamentalist Christianity dominating the media at that time (and even now) that I felt Valenti's church would be a fitting subject for a documentary film for national broadcast. Several weeks before our hospital visit, I first shared this vision with Pastor Valenti and his wife, Sharon. I told them I had already interested a well-known filmmaker in the project and that we had applied for funding from the National Endowment for the Humanities.[1]

I was relieved when the Valentis responded positively to the idea, because I knew tough questions would undoubtedly be asked by some church members about the dangers of allowing an unsaved person to portray their congregation for national television. Since I was not saved and, therefore, did not have the Holy Spirit living within me, all their theological reasoning told them I could not possibly understand spiritual things or even the meanings of the Bible as God intended them for us.

Nevertheless, hoping this film would somehow materialize, I had intensified my research at Reverend Valenti's church, plunging myself more deeply into its day-to-day life as a participant-observer. I joined a weekly Bible-study group meeting in the home of a newly saved couple, practiced with the Christian Academy's basketball team, sang an anthem one Sunday with a men's quintet and accompanied Valenti on his round of duties the day we stopped at Worcester City Hospital.

The following evening when Pastor Valenti met his congregation for their midweek service, he briefly recounted our visit and asked his congregation to pray for the boy and his family. "What gripes me," he said, "is that they want the mother to give his organs, and they won't pull the plug until they find recipients." I flashed on the women huddled together in the waiting room. Shaking his head grimly, Valenti observed, "They've made that thing into a body shop over there!" He had a way with words, and, like others in his flock, he favored metaphor.

PART ONE

I

Meeting

You're either for God or against him.

I REMEMBER trying to muster the courage to first pick up the telephone to call the Reverend Frank Valenti. It was February 1983, the middle of Ronald Reagan's first term as president and a moment of ascending strength for a popular conservatism that was then transforming American politics. As a young sociologist having recently completed my Ph.D., I was several months into a research project to better understand what I called the conservative "pro-family" movement. By that I meant those groups struggling to defend what they saw as traditional family values through a constellation of enthusiasms including opposition to abortion, sex education, homosexual rights and the equal rights amendment. While the New Right as a political coalition also contained Libertarians and old-style Republicans, it was this popular movement animated by concerns around family and gender that gave new-right conservatism its mass base and political clout.[1]

My apprehension about calling Pastor Valenti stemmed from the suspicion and hostility that hovered over my first contacts with conservatives. I had sought them out near my home in Northampton, Massachusetts, a county seat on the Connecticut River in the western part of the state, where I had moved from Cambridge, Massachusetts, to teach sociology at Smith College. My first contacts had been with grassroots activists in right-to-life groups and in Birthright, an antiabortion counseling group. They were almost always wary and guarded, imagining that a sociologist—and one teaching at Smith College at that—

would be prejudiced against all they stood for. Since I often sensed among them the lurking suspicion that I was an enemy spy ultimately up to no good, I felt it important not to do or say things that would stamp me as an opponent. This constant vigilance was often more exhausting than making one's way in a foreign country where you do not know the language or customs. In that case, at least, ignorance did not mark you as the enemy.

I took care in dress, demeanor and speech not to do anything that would offend. Yet sometimes seemingly inconsequential things would trigger distrust. For example, I once asked a soft-spoken woman who counseled pregnant teenagers in a Birthright office about contemporary attitudes toward "sexuality."

"What do you mean by that word?" she snapped with an alarmed look in her eyes. "I can't stand when people use it. It always makes it seem more important than it should be!"

I had been referred to Pastor Valenti by Bill and Karen Fournier, a Catholic couple active in right-to-life and other conservative causes in the Worcester area. They reported to me with delight that Valenti's wife, Sharon, and her mother had just gained public notoriety by protesting a youth conference, "Dealing with Feelings," sponsored by Family Planning Services of Central Massachusetts. The conference had been held at a local Congregational church and had featured Dr. Sol Gordon, a noted sex educator. The Fourniers showed me an article on the protest in Worcester's *Evening Gazette*, in which Sharon Valenti's mother, Ada Morse, was quoted as saying, "This assault on our children's mores and morals is by an insidious humanist group hiding behind a veil of feigned decency, voraciously seeking to undermine patriotism, obedience, academics and morality and supplant them with subversion, rebellion, ignorance and sexual disorientation." This was the kind of conservatism I was looking for.

It had been the Fourniers' own campaign in their local schools against *Our Bodies, Ourselves*, the feminist health-care book, that had brought them to the attention of a correspondent I knew who interviewed them for a National Public Radio program on book banning. Though devout Catholics, Bill and Karen Fournier were unhappy with what they saw as the liberal and humanist directions of the Catholic Church. Two years earlier, Karen, a petite and energetic woman in her thirties, had asked a young priest teaching in her daughter's parochial school to reintroduce opening prayer in his classes. By then, only two teachers in the entire school were carrying on that practice, she reported. He refused, saying "It would upset some of the students."

What caused Karen greater distress was seeing her oldest daughter, then in seventh grade, come home from school wearing jeans and makeup and swearing. This caused "a heaviness in my heart," she said, which she carried with her to Washington, D.C., in 1980, to attend the first Family Forum, a conservative conference on defending traditional family values. There, she recalled, "God brought me to Raymond Moore's session on home schools." Soon after, she and Bill took their four children out of parochial school and, with several like-minded families, started their own home school, which they called the Holy Family Academy.

I made several trips to the Worcester area that fall to visit the Holy Family Academy, run in a renovated barn attached to the Fourniers' home, and to interview some of the close circle of parents involved. The Fourniers themselves took more easily than other conservatives I met to conversing with outsiders like me. This was not because they were less radical or militant in their conservatism. On the contrary. But they seemed more adept at articulating their positions in the face of opposed views, in part because they were able to notice and handle contrary assumptions underlying them. For example, though I felt comfortable describing *Our Bodies, Ourselves* as "a feminist health-care book," Bill, who had done graduate work in philosophy at Boston College, contested "the very word 'health.' "

"That particular book," he explained, "takes the word 'health' and calls 'healthy' the lifestyles it happens to agree with—like extramarital sex, homosexuality and masturbation—and 'unhealthy' or 'sick' lifestyles it happens to disagree with."

"They would like to change society's values totally," Karen explained quietly, "especially in the areas of sexuality and family. Using this book is one way of doing it, to get rid of the traditional family."

In retrospect, I realize, the Fourniers helped prepare me to meet the Valentis and their church. I remember walking a picket line with Bill Fournier one cold, sunny December afternoon in downtown Worcester outside a tall, turn-of-the-century office building that housed a Planned Parenthood clinic. As at other small demonstrations I had once attended as an antiwar activist, people came and went throughout the day, greeting and kidding friends. Some unloaded a pile of signs with stenciled slogans: STOP MURDERING BABIES, END

DEATH CLINICS and so on. Others carefully assembled more elaborate and well-worn homemade posters with photos of bloody "fetuses" (or "babies") and lengthier hand-printed text. Bill introduced me to those he knew by saying, "This is Jim. He's doing a book on pro-life."

"Great! We need that!" several offered in hearty encouragement for a book they assumed would affirm their cause. I felt strange about suddenly being taken for a fellow partisan, though I could not help appreciating the relief Bill's tact provided.

Later that afternoon some of the bolder demonstrators sneaked into the building and rode the elevator up to the Planned Parenthood floor. Bill and I went along. Soon after we arrived, in the reception area, a commotion erupted. A policeman arrived, and, as he herded us to the elevator, some took the opportunity to speak their views: "They're murdering babies in there! . . . Next they'll be killing old people and the handicapped!" I was unprepared for the icy looks and hateful stares from the Planned Parenthood staff as I stood there mutely looking on, now suddenly on the other side of a line of battle.

The Fourniers said that before I finished my research in the Worcester area I should go see "the Valentis' school." Just as it had been Karen Fournier's inspiration to start the Holy Family Academy, it had been Sharon Valenti's idea to start the Christian Academy attached to their fundamentalist church. What had moved her to do so, Sharon later explained to me, was picking up some textbooks from her children's public school and being "totally shocked at what the humanist view was teaching."

"It was sex education that really bothered me," she said, "because it was from a perverted standpoint. It wasn't abstinence. They taught about different contraceptives and how to use them, and encouraged the petting and the experiencing. The Bible says to abstain from all those things. They think they're not teaching any kind of morals," she allowed, "but you can't do that. You're either for God or against him."

In the wrenching reversal of American politics toward conservatism over the past quarter century, no institution has been more decisive than local fundamentalist or evangelical churches.[2] Week in, week out, thousands of such churches across the nation educate members on issues of the day, arousing and directing their political outrage and concern. Such churches have provided a ready-made organization for both Pat Robertson's Christian Coalition and, before it, Jerry Falwell's more radical Moral Majority. At the height of the Moral Majority's influence in American politics in the 1980s, most of its chapters across the country, like the one in Massachusetts, were headed by fundamentalist preachers trained at Jerry Falwell's Liberty Baptist College or at schools affiliated with the Baptist Bible Fellowship, a loose federation of rigorously independent fundamentalist churches to which Falwell had initially belonged. Moreover, fundamentalists in this independent Baptist tradition represented the harder-edged, more aggressive and tougher strain of conservatives on the American scene. This fact sharpened my fears as I first picked up my phone to call the Reverend Valenti.

I introduced myself, saying the Fourniers had suggested I call, and briefly described my study. Sure, he would be willing to speak with me, Valenti said, and we made an appointment to meet in his office. I did not take any notes of our conversation. I would soon get his story face-to-face. The only thing that stuck in my mind was something he said quite spontaneously toward the end. "You know something, Jim," he said, already quite personable with me, "I used to be in the garage business, and that was easy compared to running a church. I got eleven people working under me right now—you know, with the school and the church. And you know what? Managing people is one of the hardest things to do. It just flat ain't easy!" A mechanic-turned-preacher, I mused. His candor was refreshing, and I appreciated his observations about the challenges of managing people. Little did I know what role those challenges would play in the fate of his church, or how much change in my own life hinged on picking up the phone that day.

I KNEW VERY LITTLE about Worcester when I set out that cold, bright February afternoon to make the hour-and-a-quarter drive eastward from Northampton to meet Pastor Valenti. In time I would become more familiar with its leading industrial firms, such as Norton Company, with the 360-degree views from Mount Wachusett rising all by itself out of the Worcester plateau, and with the discrete neighborhoods making up that city: Leicester Square, College Hill, Quinsigamond Village.

Even though it is the second-largest city in the industrial state of Massachusetts, Worcester struck me as a museum piece, with its old craft-based industries, wire-pulling and machine tools, and its abandoned downtown. From an academic's point of view, the last time

Worcester made news was in 1911, when Sigmund Freud, on his first trip to the United States, chose to visit the then-prestigious psychology department of Clark University. Since then, it seemed, centralization and specialization had turned Worcester, like so many American cities flourishing at the beginning of the twentieth century, into a backwater—but a backwater that had changed, nevertheless, in many ways. Among other things, the crisscrossing interstate highways and the ubiquitous automobile had turned the rural towns and farm communities on its outskirts into ungainly suburbs, where old-time residents now complained about needing to lock their doors.

Following Valenti's directions, I exited the interstate in one such suburb on Worcester's perimeter and found myself in an eclectic area. In a short commercial strip, the common installations of mass society—an outlet for electronic banking, McDonald's, Bonanza—sat alongside establishments such as Danny's Lounge, the Valley Bait Shop and Mike Dukas' Diner, which looked like an Airstream caravan that had landed on cement blocks. On the residential streets, proper suburban homes with neatly trimmed lawns sat alongside idiosyncratic piecemeal constructions and homes with barns and horses. Commercial vans parked in driveways, derelict pieces of machinery in the yard and handmade signs—SEWING DONE or CURIOS 'N THINGS—suggested the presence of family businesses. It was an area where postwar suburban sprawl blended with older farm communities and long-stagnant mill towns of the New England hinterland, and where Frank and Sharon Valenti had grown up and founded their church.

As I drove along a wooded suburban road, the terrain suddenly opened to a large grassy field on my left. A small clapboard house sat close by the road, and behind it, surrounded by a macadamized parking lot, was a curious conglomeration of buildings. In the front stood an old rectangular building made of red brick with white clapboard dormers. Looming behind it was a large new warehouse-like building finished with gray aluminum siding. A wooden sign at the driveway told me I had arrived: THE SHAWMUT RIVER BAPTIST CHURCH—THE REVEREND FRANK VALENTI, PASTOR.

I found my way to Pastor Valenti's office on the second floor of the red brick building, which I learned used to house a bakery. It had been purchased with a large parcel of land for an extremely favorable price from two sisters whose family had worked at the Salvation Army. "The Lord's providence," those on both sides of the transaction had affirmed.

Valenti's secretary showed me into an office with wall-to-wall red-orange shag carpeting. Light from the one large window and from banks of fluorescent lights set in a drop ceiling glared off the faux wood paneling.

Pastor Valenti rose from behind his desk to shake my hand, and I sat down across from him. He was portly and about my height, five feet eight, and was wearing a snugly fitting three-piece suit, a thickly knotted tie and a large gold watch. He had short, neatly groomed black hair, which came down in full sideburns to frame the face of a comic: sheepish brown eyes, a slightly hooked nose and, set between two full cheeks, a restless mouth always ready, I soon saw, to smirk, grimace or smile. The olive green bookshelves covering the wall behind him held a library dominated by a half-dozen sets of like-colored volumes—Bible concordances and commentaries. A map of the area with markings and pushpins was Scotch-taped to the wall in the far corner of the room—an abandoned tool, I would learn, of earlier efforts at "systematic" evangelizing.

After some awkward small talk, we settled down to the purpose of my visit. I asked permission to tape our interview, explaining it was important to have things on record exactly as he said them. Pulling my tape recorder from my briefcase, I asked, "Maybe you can tell me how you came to start the church? Why this area? Why this community?"

Valenti paused and lowered his head, as if to find the thread of a familiar story, and then began in a low-key, deliberate voice. "In nineteen seventy-one, okay, I was what the Bible calls—John, Chapter Three—'born again,' okay? And I know Jimmy Carter has made that thing all out of context," he hastened to explain, "but what that literally means is that I've experienced what they call a second birth. The first one was when I was born, way back when I was an infant. The second one was when God regenerated my spirit. The Bible says that everybody is a trichotomy—body, soul and spirit—and when Adam sinned," he added, gaining momentum, "when each individual knowingly sins for the first time, their spirit is dead. The Bible says, 'You're dead and trespass in sin,' and God regenerates that spirit. They call it a rebirth, so you become a whole person again."

He came to a stop, and I was suddenly perplexed about where to go next. That everyone was a trichotomy of body, soul and spirit seemed irrelevant to my research. So, too, was religion, I believed. While some commentators might attribute views like "the father is the head of the

family" or "homosexuality is a sin" to fundamentalists' particular reading of the Bible, identical views were held by conservative Catholics
like the Fourniers, as well as conservative Jews, Mormons, mainline
Protestants and those with no religious commitments at all, all of
whom I met in the course of my research. Furthermore, the Valentis,
along with other converts in their church, I soon learned, had generally held such views *before* they were "saved" and become born-again
Christians. Their pro-family conservatism could not be explained,
then, by doctrines or practices found in any particular religion. In fact,
the neoevangelical movement, which separated itself from fundamentalism after World War Two to become more socially and culturally
engaged, had given rise to its own, albeit small, biblical feminist groups
in the 1970s.[3] The sources of conservative pro-family activism could
not be found, then, in any set of religious ideas or traditions. They had
to lie outside religion, I believed, but be present and observable in the
lives of the Valentis and those attending their church.

As it turned out, Shawmut River Baptist Church provided a rich
vantage point for understanding the kind of conservatism I set out to
study. As a community involving members and their families in an all-
encompassing round of activities, it brought more clearly into view a
broader social world in which new-right enthusiasms and fundamentalist theology flourished—and to do so, it had to make sense.

My research into the popular sources of new-right conservatism
grew out of a doctoral dissertation I had finished the year before on
why the women's liberation movement of the 1960s and 1970s had
taken root largely among white, college-educated women and found
limited support among working-class women and women of color. As
someone close to this movement, which came to be called Second
Wave feminism (to distinguish it from its nineteenth-century forebears), I knew that it had defined itself, above all, by its call to change
gender roles not just in public life but in family and personal life as
well—a cause that found expression in its popular slogan at the time,
"to make the personal political." The critical question, it seemed to
me, was why some women seemed relatively comfortable with traditional gender roles in the family, while others, including most of my
friends and colleagues, felt compelled to reject them.

Answers progressive academics often gave to this question at the
time were that working-class and Third World women had a "false
consciousness" about their condition, or that they were too pressed by

material problems to care about these other matters. These explanations seemed demeaning and did not square with either the noncomprehension or hostility with which these women often reacted to feminist enthusiasms. I had become persuaded, instead, that at least some women's commitments to tradition in family life had more to do with the ways their families actually worked—in particular, how the presence of extended-family ties affected the day-to-day experience of gender in families. At the same time, the relative absence of those ties among geographically mobile professionals could be seen to encourage certain breaks with tradition.[4]

I also realized that this way of understanding why some women continued to embrace traditional gender roles in the family might also shed light on why some might militantly *defend* them, like those women providing popular support for the rapidly growing New Right. While my dissertation had been theoretical, I had just received funding from the American Council of Learned Societies and from a new women's studies center at Brown University to carry out field research to see whether these understandings had any validity in real life. I was pleased, because my job at Smith College was ending and I was looking for something to do next.

Fifteen years before, in the summer of 1968, I had been disturbed by conservatives I met while canvassing working-class neighborhoods in Cambridge, Massachusetts, for a referendum against the war in Vietnam. I remember one woman with an American flag planted in her front yard angrily refusing to talk with us. Others recoiled in abhorrence, it seemed, from any contact with those they were apt to dismiss as "commie fags" or arrogant college students destined to become "pointy-headed liberals in Washington," as George Wallace mockingly identified "the enemy" at the time for his fast-growing national following.

In fact, it was Wallace's campaign for the presidency in 1968 that first registered on the national scene, much to the surprise of political commentators, the presence and power of vast reservoirs of righteous indignation and rage, which would feed the popular growth of new-right conservatism over the next thirty years.[5] By the mid-1990s this new-styled conservatism had not only swept the Republican Party to a congressional majority for the first time in forty years but also exerted such public force as to press a liberal Democrat like Bill Clinton to recast his presidential campaign in the language of "family values" and proudly take the lead in dismantling the federal welfare system. This political force had been created, above all, by impressive grassroots activism, starting with thousands of local campaigns across the nation for school boards, town councils and state legislatures, and involving the massive mobilization of born-again Christians into political life for the first time.

None of these reversals in American politics was remotely imaginable in 1968, in the midst of the Kennedy-Johnson era, when the steady stream of professors from Harvard University to Washington fueled the great liberal hope that the application of scientific knowledge to social problems would usher in a shiny new era of progress. Urban poverty would be eliminated and cities renewed, and progressive scholars convened at prestigious gatherings to discuss how we all would cope with the abundant leisure postindustrial society would inevitably bring.

However, as prosperity gave way to economic decline, and the years of the antiwar movement and the New Left gave way to the "Reagan Revolution" and the New Right, the issues animating the fresh wave of popular conservatism became more clearly focused on matters of family and gender. Even patriotic militarism, which seemed, on the face of it, not to have anything to do with gender, was powerfully charged if not deeply configured by it. After all, the most stinging epithet hurled against antiwar demonstrators was that we were "commie fags"—that is, not "real men." Anyone who ever saw a gang of right-wing toughs suddenly lunge into an antiwar demonstration and single out a long-haired marcher to beat up has witnessed the upset and rage galvanized by that charge.

Though men provided the angry muscle on such occasions, the majority of activists in the conservative pro-family movement were women. That these women were generally antagonistic to feminism was puzzling for those of us who identified with what we simply called "*the* women's movement." Clearly, there were now *other* movements of women, such as those marching behind the new-right banner, who, by and large, remained hostile to feminism. I wanted to better understand why this was so and, more generally, how people like me in the liberal middle-class intelligentsia could understand the popular appeal, the sense and meaningfulness, of this kind of conservatism to so many Americans. I believed this could best be done by looking closely at the lives of those representing the mass of local activists and supporters, rather than the New Right's more visible national leadership and organization. Without mass popular support, after all, those leaders and organizations would be unknown and irrelevant.

Though I began this study of pro-family conservatism with no interest in religion, I soon had to grapple with questions about the nature of Protestant fundamentalism, and its long-standing affinities with this kind of conservatism in American life. Why was fundamentalism originally an American phenomenon? And why were fundamentalist movements in a variety of the world's religions assuming ever-greater importance in the modern world? Though touching on these questions, this book aims, above all, to provide fresh understandings of new-right conservatism and fundamentalist Christianity in American life through the story of my relations with members of the Valentis' church against the background of our quite different lives. It is an ethnographic story, in which the development of characters and the dramatic unfolding of conflict-ridden and telling events serve as evidence for sociological interpretation. Here and there I draw out more explicitly what lessons these stories hold for understanding both fundamentalist Christianity and conflicts between conservatives and liberals on family-related issues, which still hold our nation in their grip. (Those interested in how these and other lessons relate to scholarly research on these topics can follow more detailed discussions in the Notes at the end of the book.)

My own sociological perspective is, of course, only one among many possible ways to see the events this book recounts. Other readers, like the Valentis or members of like-minded churches, are more apt to see in certain events the hand of God or, in the workings of their congregation, God's design for how a New Testament church *should* work. I have no reason to quarrel with such interpretations and do not see them to be incompatible with my own sociological ones.

As a story arising from our relationships, it is inevitably colored by my own background as well as theirs.[6] When I first began explaining to friends why my research had come to focus on a fundamentalist Baptist church among all the new-right groups I had encountered, I found myself adding wryly that it was not only because this community brought my central findings more clearly into view. It was also because it harbored "ghosts of my past," as I sometimes put it. Friends knew I had grown up in the home of a Methodist minister. But few knew what it had been like to spend every Sunday of my childhood sitting with my mother and two younger sisters toward the front of one of several churches my parents served in New Jersey and Massachusetts, and hearing my father hold forth about the ultimate things in life. Or what it was like to sidle up to my parents after worship as they exchanged pleasantries and vital information with members of their flock lined up to greet them. Or to stand around our dining room table with guests to sing "Be Present at Our Table, Lord" to the tune of the doxology.

My parents were both "convinced and committed Christians," as my father liked to describe the faithful. They met in the Methodist church of Sayre, Pennsylvania, a small industrial town in the north-eastern part of that state, when my father, as youth leader, gave my mother's family, who had just moved to town, a tour of the church building. It was laid out, I remember from childhood visits to relatives, in that square amphitheatre style reminiscent of late-nineteenth-century revivalism, with aisles radiating out from a central dais on the back wall. It was a monumental domed building of yellow brick with stone columns in Greek-temple style a block off the town park, where on summer evenings bands played from a gazebo. It represented quin-tessential small-town Protestantism with its distinct Methodist em-phases on enthusiastic worship, self-improvement and moral purity. My mother laughed to recall her own "taking the pledge" with other women in town at the time—that is, the temperance pledge to never kiss the lips of someone who drank alcohol.

My mother and father dated through high school, sharing a passion for education that led them to study vocabulary words together as they walked around town on dates. Both graduated at the top of their high-school class, my father in the middle of the Depression, when he took the only apprenticeship offered that year by a local tool-and-die plant. World War Two intervened, however, as it did for many Americans, and after the war it was my father's educational ambitions that advanced, while my mother's were put on hold. Having decided to enter the ministry, he attended Colgate University on the G.I. Bill while serving a small church in upstate New York. He went on to study at Union Theological Seminary in New York City during its halcyon years with Reinhold Niebuhr, James Muilenberg and Paul Tillich. During my school years he pastored several Methodist churches in suburban New Jersey (one in a working-class hamlet, the other in a commuter suburb) and then one congregation in the industrial city of Pittsfield, Massachusetts. From there he returned to New York City to join the faculty at Union as I left home on scholarship to attend boarding school and then college in New England.

At our very first meeting, Pastor Valenti made clear in passing what he thought of the kind of churches in which I had grown up. "What I mean by liberal," he said, describing a mainline Protestant church nearby, "is that they don't preach of the Gospel, they don't teach the blood, they don't teach inerrancy of scripture and the virgin birth. They just teach whatever they feel like, a bunch of wishy-washy garbage."

"Like what?" I asked. "What comes to mind?"

"A perpetual guide to how to be nice," he offered, adding in an effeminate voice to mimic a liberal clergyman, "'God is good, God is love, nice to your neighbor, neighbor nice to you . . .' You know, cute little stories," he continued, "a joke here or there. They never come across the part where it says it's a fearful thing to fall into the hands of an angry God. It's the same coin—two sides." Over my first few months of getting to know Pastor Valenti, apart from mentioning that my father was a minister, I spared him the fact that he was then a bishop helping shape the course of a denomination Valenti would dismiss in this way.

EVER SINCE I began writing this book during Ronald Reagan's second term as president, colleagues have urged me from time to time to get it out quickly before fundamentalist Christianity evaporated from public life. So poorly did they grasp its persistent appeal and relevance to many of their fellow Americans. These misreadings, I discovered, were not incidental but part of a long-standing pattern of misperception among intellectuals, who, ever since fundamentalism's "rise to notoriety in the 1920s," as one historian noted, had been repeatedly predicting its "imminent demise."[7] This pattern of misperception is one social fact we must elucidate as we approach more satisfactory understandings of new-right conservatism. As with other cross-cultural experiences, my coming to better understand conservatives involved coming to better understand myself and my own milieu. In fact, my experiences at Shawmut River Baptist Church ended up revealing things about my own background I had never even known.

Ethnographic fieldwork is a strange and, at times, transforming enterprise. You never know when insight will come, or how. Insight aims toward comprehending what people mean by what they say and do—meanings insiders in a culture find so obvious and unquestionable they would never think, or be able, to explain them to you. Since this research involved crossing boundaries of moral warfare in my own country, to question what others took for granted also threatened to mark me as a possible enemy. Insight often came, then, by accumulating slowly but surely the aspects of context that subjects took for granted whenever they spoke or acted. Never knowing in advance exactly what those aspects of context might be, I tried to remain attentive for hours, even days, when things happening around me seemed irrelevant.

So seemed Pastor Valenti's description of what his being born again meant—how God regenerates a spirit deadened by sin—when I first faced him in his office. Struggling to find a way to redirect his story to the sociopolitical questions on my agenda, I finally stumbled on a sufficiently mundane, practical question to move us forward. "Now, how did that happen?" I asked. "What actually happened?"

2

Frank and Sharon

*The best thing in the whole world for marriage
is the Lord Jesus Christ!*

Frank Valenti's search, as he came to see it, began in Vietnam. After graduating from high school in 1966, he worked in construction alongside his father and brother. It was natural. As a boy of fourteen he and his older brother, Kenny, were rebuilding engines, welding joints, hanging doors and helping their father, Joe, on jobs he contracted. "It felt good to keep 'em with me," Joe Valenti told me, " 'til they got all those things in 'em," he added, pointing his stubby index finger to his head and winking impishly. Joe was a stocky man, about five feet six, with strong limbs, broad hands and fingers that looked like "cut-off carrots," as Frank once described them. Joe and his wife, Marie, both Italian-American Catholics, attended their son Frank's fundamentalist Baptist church. They lived in a rural town that had in their lifetime become a suburb of Worcester, in a brick ranch house Joe had built and in which they had raised their four children. One daughter lived next door with several children and her husband, who had become a partner in Joe's construction business and then inherited it. Their other daughter was divorced and had a beauty parlor in the town center.

When I met him, Joe was seventy-three and had neatly groomed white hair, a pencil moustache and a ruddy complexion from working full days outdoors on construction. He had immigrated to the United States from Italy in 1920, when he was just a boy of nine. He had finished sixth grade in America at the age of sixteen and left school when, he said, "I just got to the point where I could speak English good. I didn't do no reading of books or stuff like that." Nevertheless, he had built up a successful construction business on the outskirts of Worcester during the postwar economic boom and took pride in the fact that, even without paid estimators, he was able to bid successfully for sizable jobs.

Like his father, Frank showed little interest in book learning. He once told me that, by the time he graduated from high school, he had never read a single book through. Yet his school had passed him from grade to grade. "That's sick!" he observed. But he counted it a blessing, he once told his flock from the pulpit, that he never got an education before he was saved. "They never had time to enslave my mind," he explained. In any case, evidently he had not given his teachers his fullest cooperation. Browsing through his high school yearbook one day, I came upon the "Class Legacy" section, where graduating seniors leave their good looks, sense of humor, and so on, to certain underclass students. I was amused by the following entry: "Frank Valenti leaves . . ." it read simply, ". . . and his teachers give thanks."

Without a college deferment, Frank was drafted for the war in Vietnam two years after high school. "In August you're sitting there funning in the sun," he chuckled, "drinking some beer and building a duplex, so you can make more money. Then, all of a sudden you're in Vietnam!" It was the summer of 1968. The Paris peace talks were deadlocked, the devastating bombing of North Vietnam raged on and the presidential race was heating up with bitter controversy over what was being called "America's longest war."

I was then in my senior year at Harvard College in Cambridge, Massachusetts, an hour's drive east of Worcester. That spring a handful of fellow radicals and I sneaked on to a bus carrying draftees to the South Boston Army Base and disrupted induction proceedings. We were thrown off the base, and those eligible were reclassified by the Selective Service as "1-Y," meaning prime draft material. This did not alarm me, however. That winter I had been knocked off my bicycle by a speeding car. When I awoke from surgery, with metal pins, plates and screws reuniting the bones in my left arm, the first thing the surgeon told me was "At least the army won't take you with this." I was soon reclassified with a medical deferment and felt a great burden lift. Like many young men at the time, I had given some thought to extreme measures, such as chopping off a toe or leaving the country, to avoid being drafted for a war with which I fundamentally disagreed. Now fellow students, seeing my cast, would come up and ask whether I was the one they had heard about who had had the marvelous luck to be liberated from the draft in this uncanny way.

In 1983, when I got to know Frank Valenti and other Vietnam veterans in his church, I realized that throughout my college and graduate student days I scarcely knew anyone who saw combat in Vietnam. Most people I knew got deferments of one kind or another, or, if they did serve, were spared combat. Frank's company, on the other hand, was assigned "eagle hops" in Vietnam's southern delta. Helicopters would drop them in a suspected Viet Cong area as "bait," he explained, to draw enemy fire. "Then they'd pull us back and bring the gunships in to flatten it. It was scary, because anytime you drew fire, somebody got killed or wounded."

It was a December night in 1968 when Frank returned to camp from a short medical leave in Saigon to find his company out on patrol. He fell asleep in his hooch, a two-by-four frame covered with a tent and mosquito netting. Suddenly the rat-tat-tat of machine-gun fire woke him. Bullets whistled over his head and slammed into his cot. Moments later an antipersonnel rocket hit three yards from him. "Blew me from one side of that hooch to the other," he said. "Took out the back of my leg and a couple of other things." He grabbed his M-16 and crawled to the door, when another rocket hit. "It was so close I could feel a wind of lead. I could feel all the shrapnel hitting me, and I was flying through the air, blown twenty-five feet away, sent crashing into the back of the hooch.

"I laid there. My legs were paralyzed. Shrapnel had gone into my side, lodged itself up against my spine. My Achilles tendon was blown out—and every major artery in your body (I mean for your lower extremities) runs through the back of your leg—they were all cut right off. Man, I laid there bleeding like a stuck pig. I had shrapnel going through my forehead. My scalp was sliced. My nose was laying over on the side of my face. And I laid there and said, 'God, nobody can live through this. Come and get me.'

"And that's the first time in my life," Frank mused, "that I ever recognized that there was a God—besides myself. Really! And I ran my hand down the back of my leg and it fell into a hole, and I said, 'Oh no!' And there wasn't anybody around. Nobody knew I was there. So I closed my eyes and passed out."

Frank was not expected to live. It took seventy-two pints of blood and many operations to put him on the road to recovery. He returned to the States "in a basket," he said, just before Christmas, 1968. He was nineteen years old.

WHEN FRANK TELEPHONED his high-school sweetheart, Sharon Waters, to tell her he was coming home, he said only that he "got a little shot up." Sharon was only seventeen, a senior business major at the regional high school serving the rural/suburban communities on that side of Worcester. Ever since her freshman year, she and Frank had dated. They always had a lot of fun, she remembered. She enjoyed the warm, boisterous, relaxed nature of the Valenti household. "It was cool to drink at their house," she said. "Their mother and father would never think anything about it. My mother, you know, she'd hang me by a rope!" Sharon's mother, Ada, had grown up in a Church of the Nazarene congregation in Indiana, and it was her formation as a Nazarene that provided the critical link connecting Frank and Sharon to a conservative Christian tradition.

Emerging from the holiness movement in late-nineteenth- and early-twentieth-century America, the Church of the Nazarene was formed by the merger of an assortment of groups, most of which had split off from Methodism. Like other popular revivalist movements at the time, including Dwight L. Moody's, the Nazarenes began with a more progressive ethos. They boldly endorsed women's preaching, for example, and only gradually, over the 1920s and 1930s, became more conservative. The Nazarene congregation of Ada's childhood in the 1930s required women to cover their arms in church.[1]

But during Sharon's childhood, Ada told me, she had lived far from church and far from God. Fleeing an unhappy marriage of thirteen years, during which she and her husband had both worked at factory jobs to make ends meet, she moved from Indiana to Washington, D.C., to work for an older brother, who had started a stenography business there. In Washington she struggled as a single parent to make a living while raising Sharon and her two older brothers. "I wasn't living where I should have been," Ada recalled. "I wasn't going to church and I wasn't asking God for his guidance and direction. I was just trying to do it myself. And I was really bitter about being divorced and having to support the children without any help."

Looking back on her upbringing, Sharon said, "My mother taught us morality, but never gave us the why." The "why," it turned out, was that this morality was given by God in his Holy Bible. In time Ada met and married a fellow stenographer, Tom Morse, who proved a loving and reliable husband and stepfather. Together they had a daughter. Tom eventually landed a position as court stenographer in Worcester, not far from—but also not too close to—his own family in New Hampshire, and they moved to the Worcester area in 1959, when Sharon was eight.

When Frank returned home from Vietnam a few days before Christmas, Sharon and her parents were shocked to discover the extent of his injuries. Sharon had planned to work after high school and pursue further education. Instead, she and Frank married six months later. "The sympathy kind of speeded it up," she explained. Four times each day Frank had to dress and rebandage his wounds. They moved into a ranch house right next to Frank's older brother, Kenny, and his family. Soon they had their first child, Timmy, and, two years later, Christie.

Frank was not expected to walk again. But the tissues regenerated enough so that, with the help of an artificial leg, braces and special shoes, he could walk with only a slight limp. But even then he suffered regularly from throbbing pain in his legs and feet, needed occasional operations on an ear damaged by the explosion and still had pieces of shrapnel working their way out of his body. Since he could no longer do construction, he began working as a mechanic to supplement his disability pension and keep busy. He ran a garage that specialized in souping up snowmobiles. Even this activity, however, caused such pain in his legs that it was difficult to bear. He began taking Percodan for the pain and, over time, became addicted to it.

Frank showed surprisingly little bitterness about his injuries from a war he saw "without a real cause." Sharon considered it a war for "political interests," while others at the Shawmut River Baptist Church saw it as a war for "big business." I was surprised to see that, at this time, at least none of these conservatives saw Vietnam as an honorable war in the national interest. Nevertheless, Frank affirmed that he had always been "very patriotic."

"I think I was more conservative than anything else before I was saved," he said. "My dad always taught me, whatever condition you're in, you put your right foot in front of your left foot in front of your right foot. You do the best you can with what you've got. So I came back from Vietnam and I was really searching, because for the first

time in my life, Mr. Wonderful—which I always thought I was—was a
zero, completely helpless and totally dependent on everybody and
everything else."

There is a photograph of Frank and Sharon at the time: he in his
uniform leaning against Sharon with his arms clasped around her; and
Sharon, with her light brown hair slightly teased and curled up at her
shoulders in that tight, bell-shaped Jackie Kennedy style popular in the
sixties, holding her arms loosely around Frank's waist. Their faces
seem set in worn resolve.

"It was terrible," Sharon said of their marriage. "We didn't know
each other. Frank's affections were at the garage and mine with the
children." Caring for her children also meant spending time with her
sister-in-law next door and her mother, who helped out regularly.
Meanwhile, Frank hung out at the garage with his father, and on weekends he worked on household projects or went fishing with a cousin.
As Frank summed up their marriage at our first meeting in his office, "I
was gettin' lost in making tables, hobbies, fishing, you know. We were
drifting, going our own ways."

As problems mounted, Sharon felt "cheated in life." Neither she
nor Frank had gone to college, and she felt stuck. "A garage mechanic
is a garage mechanic is a garage mechanic!" she said, laughing at herself. "At the time, I thought, 'Gee, if he could just talk right. If he could
stop swearing and just talk right. If he could not say "ain't," and
"should have went."'" Her stepfather, Tom Morse, as a court steno-
rapher, had what approached a fetish for proper English, and both her
parents had wanted her to go to college and "do differently," as her
mother, Ada, put it. "I'd cringe," Sharon remembered, "because I'd
know they'd be sitting there, and I'd know what they were thinking:
'You married a dummy.' . . . They were silent, but you could see it in
their eyes."

When problems mounted in Frank and Sharon's marriage, Ada
attributed them to their different "social backgrounds."

"We wouldn't have been sad," Ada admitted, "if they had been
divorced."

Feeling looked down upon by his in-laws may have fed Frank's tendency at the time to demean Sharon in public. He would berate her in
front of her parents and couples they played cards with. When she and
Frank played chess, he would overturn the table if he lost or, if he won,
yell at her for not trying. Sharon attributed Frank's rage to his growing

addiction to Percodan. However, the picture of a marriage frozen in mutual hurt and hatred was understandable in other terms. "She couldn't stand me," Frank recalled, likening his marriage to those of many couples he now counseled. "Typical, you know, the guy fakes the gal out, wins her over, gets married. Then, three years after the marriage, the wife's had a kid, maybe two, and all of a sudden she puts her fist up in the face of God and says, 'I got ripped off, I got cheated! Look at this slob you've gotten me!'

"Then the guy sits smugly in his corner saying, 'Boy, did I get ripped off. This woman is not like anything I've seen on TV.' He starts fantasizing . . . and the woman hates every minute of it. And when they have their relationship at the end of a long hard day, she walks upstairs—or wherever their bedroom is—and says, 'I hope he falls asleep with a can of beer and never bothers me!'

"The husband starts prostituting his wife," Frank continued, "buying her presents to get a little more zing out of life. Pretty soon they're both going out, buying new cars they can't afford, going deeper in debt, because they can't get any satisfaction out of each other."

"We had nothing in common except money," Sharon admitted, confirming Frank's account of a marriage mired in alienation and consumerism. "Frank would buy me the moon if he could. I was twenty-one years old and owned a house and a new Bronco!" While Frank would yell and scream, Sharon said, "I took out my anger in other ways, through the silent treatment. I thought I was pretty good, not understanding that that can be just as bad as the yelling and screaming. When a person treats you a certain way," she said, summing up their marriage at the time, "your natural response is to say, 'All right, you're going to be like that; I'll be like this, and we'll just exist.' And we did— we just existed." Both admitted they had been on the verge of divorce.

One day, in the midst of her misery, Sharon stopped by Tom and Ada's house to pick up her children and ran into the pastor of her parents' new church. Several years earlier Ada had found her way back to church. It was 1969, a year after Frank's injury and a time of turmoil across the nation. Ada was upset by the antiwar protests and "counter-cultural" movements at the time. "I've always been a person who loved the country," she said, "and when anybody'd spit on the American flag, that'd always burn me up and I'd want to get to them." Meanwhile, her older son had become a born-again Christian and begun studying for the ministry at Baptist Bible College in Springfield, Missouri (where

Jerry Falwell studied). He began proselytizing the family during holiday visits. Tom and Ada responded by looking for a church, but with disappointing results. "They were nothing—just liberal," Ada explained. "You just hardly heard the name of the Lord." Then a friend came by to tell her about a new church with a minister who "really preaches the word of the Lord." He was a Southern Baptist pastor from Kentucky who had gone out to start a ministry in New England as if it were a mission field.

"I knew that had to be what I wanted to hear," Ada thought, "not a social gospel." The pastor had been meeting with several families in a Bible-study group, which became the nucleus of a new church. Ada and Tom became founding members.

When Sharon ran into Tom and Ada's minister that afternoon at their home, she was embarrassed to be smoking. She herself was searching at the time, she recalled, and had even begun reading the Bible on her own. She had always been conscious of God, she remembered, but he was "fearful," not "personal," to her. "Does it bother you if I smoke?" she asked Ada's pastor. "I mean, does it put you in hell?"

"No, Sharon," he answered, "it doesn't. But it sure makes you smell like you've been there!" He laughed.

"That finally alleviated pressures," Sharon recalled, "and he had an opportunity to share with me a little bit about the Lord. It was something I wanted. I wanted to be cleansed from all my guilt. I think I added more guilt on top of what was there, because you can have a false guilt, too!" she observed of herself.

"And then, finally, one day it just all fell in place. The Lord must have really been speaking to me, and everything made sense. Just like lights turned on for me. I mean, Jesus died for me *personally*. I knew 'for God so loved the world,' but that's where it ended: the whole world, all at the same time. But, until I realized that 'for God so loved *Sharon*,' then I understood: God so loved *me* personally. And whenever I had that understanding, I think I just cried and just felt the sense of all my guilt gone, that Jesus died for all my sins. And from that point on I knew I had found what I had been looking for. Now my only problem was to deal with Frank."

Frank felt jealous of Sharon's newfound happiness and of the pastor she now quoted incessantly. "Being a Catholic," he said, "I felt, 'How dare you tell me!'" Out of spite, he even packed up the children one Sunday and took them to mass at his local Catholic church. But this only freed Sharon up while leaving him in church struggling with two young children on his lap.

Sharon then struck a bargain with God (though she later realized it was theologically wrong). "Lord, you know how much I love smoking," she remembered saying. "If you would just save Frank, I'll give up smoking now." With that, she broke up her cigarettes and never touched another one. "Some people who give up something for the Lord," she observed, "say he takes the desire away, but that wasn't the case with me. It was a struggle every minute, because I was almost a chain smoker. Every minute I would just want to go have one." A week later she asked Frank to come to her baptism at a nearby lake. She was astounded when he agreed.

Sharon remembered one moment of truth during their struggles at the time. Frank came home one afternoon to make up after a fight. "And the best way to apologize to me is through an Italian grinder," she explained, "so he brought one home. And I was just crying, to know he was going to hell, and that he wouldn't see the light, and I just saw no hope. And he came in to give me the peace offering and I said, 'I don't want it,' and just cried. And he threw it at me. But I ducked and it hit the wall." She laughed and then looked pensive. "And he said that was the time, when he was picking that grinder up off the floor, that he thought, 'You know, God, if this is real, I want it.'"

"Even in her miserableness," Frank recalled, "she had a peace about things that I never had before, that I really wanted."

Several months later, about the second or third time Frank accompanied Sharon to church, he recounted an event that I came to regard as a familiar kind of story told by members of the Valentis' church. It was invariably told with a distinct degree of specificity. "The sun was coming in the window over my left shoulder," Frank said, "and I don't remember a word about the message. All I remember is the preacher saying, 'If you want to go to heaven, you need only to ask Christ to save you.' And I said to myself, 'God, you know, if you want this life, you can have it. Because as far as I'm concerned, it's a waste.'" That was it for Frank and others: a moment in which salvation freely offered was freely received.

Frank found it hard to fathom what it meant to be "saved," he told me when we first spoke in his office. He was surprised to find himself soon "witnessing" even to hitchhikers he picked up. He didn't think Sharon totally believed it until they were at a prayer meeting at someone's home one night. "They asked for volunteers to close in prayer," Frank said, "and I accepted. Then I got down on my knees and led everybody in prayer."

Frank started changing in other ways he and those around him saw as dramatic. "For example," he said, "up to that point I worked construction, and all I did was swear. Ninety-nine percent of my vocabulary was F- and S-, all those slang and cuss words and filthy things that you can imagine."

"That's what guys did on the job," I allowed.

"But anyway, after I got saved, without even trying on my part, within three or four months I had completely stopped swearing!"

Other habits, like his addiction to Percodan, took painful struggles to break. Realizing God could not use him if he kept taking it, he gave it up one day and battled the ensuing withdrawal symptoms.

I had heard personal testimonies before, usually on television or from an occasional evangelist making a cold call at my apartment door. But Frank and Sharon's story had a different density and weight than those more formulaic accounts. "How did your life change," I asked him, "in more detailed ways? How did your family life change?"

"It was a progressive thing," he answered. "It didn't happen just all at once, *clunk!* Sharon and I started going to church together, and then we started reading the Bible together. Then all of a sudden we became interested in futuristic things together, prophecy." Mimicking their excitement, he recalled pointing out enthusiastically, "Look at what it says here in Proverbs about spanking your children!"

"I found out I was spanking my kids wrong. You shouldn't use your hand, the same hand that loves them, but, instead, a 'rod of correction.' And before you spank them you should explain that what they did was wrong and this is what God demands you do as a parent. This puts all the responsibility on God for what's right and wrong. God is the medium. He's the rules, the regulations." Instead of Sharon telling the kids "Daddy will spank you when he gets home," they started to discipline their children together, he said, "the proper way."

"So you and Sharon started discussing these things together in ways you didn't before?"

"Right, we had a channel opened up to us that was never open before. We had a channel opened up to God. If you didn't know how to live, the answers were always there."

"Can you think of an answer you found in the Bible for a problem in your family life?"

Frank thought for a moment. "For example, what man knows how to treat his wife right, if they don't know how God tells them to treat her?" He went on to describe how television "rapes your mind" by promoting sex as the basis for a good marriage, as well as unrealistic ideals that capture your fantasy. "Your wife can't compete with that garbage!" he exclaimed. "A woman is a human being. She's not up to snuff twenty-four hours a day any more than you are. So what I learned through the Word of God was—Proverbs 5:19, I think, says, 'Be thou satisfied with the wife of thy youth. Be thou ravished with her beauty always. Make her as a loving heart in a pleasant room.'[2]

"If you put your eyes on what God has given you and treat her like you would treat yourself, she takes on a whole different light. Now she appreciates you because you love her for what she is. And a sexual relationship is a natural outcrop of a good healthy partnership. We both want to please God, so we both talk about the scriptural thing that will please the Lord and we both get closer to the Lord and we both get closer to each other. Because Christ is the center of your activity, there's no pride in me to humble myself and say, 'Boy, this was stupid, what did I do this for?' And when she talks to me, she doesn't humiliate me and put me down because I've humbled myself and said, 'Hey, I'm wrong.' So dialogue opens up. You know, the best thing in the whole world for marriage is the Lord Jesus Christ!"

Frank remembered one decisive moment in this process of change. On his pastor's advice, he had promised God to practice self-sacrificing love toward Sharon and put the results in God's hands. He soon found himself with an agonizing opportunity to do so. He and Sharon were arguing about something, and it suddenly came to light that she was wrong. "And Sharon is seldom, seldom wrong," Frank explained gravely, "and she went flying down the hallway into the bedroom and started crying. And I sat back smug. I said, 'I got her! I know I got her!' And all of a sudden, what I said I was going to do for the Lord came to mind, and I said, 'Oh no, not *now!* Not *now!* I've got her, it's great! I don't know if I can do this. It's too much of a temptation!'

"But she came out about five minutes later," he continued, "and said, 'Honey, I'm sorry. I was wrong.'

"I bit my tongue and said, 'Hon', forget about it. Let me buy you some steak.' And I never brought it up again . . . and it *killed* me. But

I've never seen her respond like she responded. You know, forgiveness, *genuine* forgiveness, that's the way we operate our marriage."

I WAS INTRIGUED by the story of change in the Valentis' marriage. Being "saved" seemed to have been the crucial ingredient in turning a conflict-ridden marriage with little communication into a solid partnership. Even getting into prophecy together seemed to help. Figuring out how current events corresponded to biblical clues of the end times when they and other born-again believers would suddenly be caught up in the air in the Rapture—to be followed by the Tribulation, the rise of the Antichrist and the battle of Armageddon—heightened the urgency and confirmed the ultimacy of their newfound lives in Christ.

The story of the Valentis' marriage was not idiosyncratic, I soon learned, but was a common experience among members of Shawmut River and churches like it. The day-to-day business of church life had much to do with transforming and ordering family relationships, especially marriage. Those efforts were not always successful, I would see. And though the task was always seen as a matter of correctly aligning spouses with God's timeless plan for the family as set forth in scripture, it was couched in a commonsense realism one might readily appreciate from nonspiritual and nonbiblical points of view.[3]

But there was a startling paradox embedded in Frank and Sharon's story. Fundamentalists are often seen by outsiders to be rigidly opposed to change, even crippled by their fear of it. Yet in Frank and Sharon's story the whole point of being saved was the process of change it had unleashed in their lives. Frank would preach to his flock, "The name of the game is change: Either you accept God's call and change, or God sends trials to change you."

Some changes Frank mentioned, such as learning how to spank children correctly, were bound to disturb my liberal colleagues. But others, such as a husband and wife learning to discuss things together, would be seen as steps in the right direction, albeit surprisingly modest ones from some points of view.

As Sharon and Frank's story unfolded, however, the realities of change became even more striking. After about a year of what Sharon described as "gradual change constantly," Frank started teaching a Bible study with family members and close friends meeting in Tom and Ada's basement. His relations with his in-laws underwent a complete turnaround. He and Sharon now spent more time with them, and Tom and Ada saw it as a great testimony to God's miraculous work that Frank, as a born-again believer, was able to bring his Italian temper under greater and greater control and become more gentlemanly.

Then one day, as Sharon recounted it to me, she and Frank were driving down the road when he turned to her and asked, "What do you think about me being a preacher?"

"And I had been praying for six months that God would call him," Sharon admitted. "And I said, 'Well, Frank, I feel this way: If every man that was a Christian was a pastor, there still wouldn't be enough men.' And he thought about that, and I think that was basically the thought that moved him to go into the ministry." Within six months they left Massachusetts for Lynchburg, Virginia, for Frank to enroll in Jerry Falwell's Liberty Baptist College. "I was excited, I really was," Sharon remembered. "Not only had God answered my prayers about saving him, but here he is going into the ministry! Plus, he's getting an education! That's a bonus!"

It was August 1974 when Frank and Sharon packed up their car and with their two children drove twelve hours to Lynchburg, Virginia, to begin studies at Liberty Baptist College. The United States was just coming to grips with the impeachment of Richard Nixon. Amidst tumultuous change in their own lives, Frank and Sharon felt these events augured Christ's second coming and "the end times."

"We thought the Lord was going to come before we even made it to Virginia!" Sharon said, laughing to recall their naïveté as two new-born Christians "on fire for the Lord, our whole life involved in prophecy. The world was so bad, we never thought we'd see nineteen eighty!" I could sympathize with their apocalyptic imagination, having been part of new-left groups in which doubts were expressed about whether we would make it to 1970 before "the revolution."

When Frank and Sharon arrived in Lynchburg, Liberty Baptist College was in its pioneer years, founded just three years before as an outgrowth of Falwell's prosperous Thomas Road Baptist Church with its flourishing television ministry. At the time, Falwell's *The Old-Time Gospel Hour* was watched, according to some estimates, by four out of every ten households in the United States.[4] The year before Frank and Sharon arrived, only seventeen seniors had graduated from Falwell's

new college. Four years later, over four hundred would graduate with
Frank. For a few years students had met in whatever room they could
find at Falwell's church and in several rented buildings across Lynchburg. Now, during Frank and Sharon's stay, building had begun for
Liberty Baptist's new campus on top of Candler's Mountain in the
heart of this growing "new south" city. As new buildings of cinder
block and sheet metal went up, classes met in temporary trailers. Frank
and Sharon fondly remember sloshing to class through parking lots
turned by rain into seas of mud. In this heady atmosphere of growth
and change all around, Sharon recalled their excitement, "seeing
people just like Frank and me, who had similar lives—you know, miserable—and then God revolutionized their life. Some of the testimonies! We would be sitting in our seats saying, 'That's what
happened to us!'"

Falwell's vision for Liberty Baptist College, as he described it
grandly in his autobiography, was of a "great Christian educational
complex with its accredited university, graduate schools and a seminary." Young people from "across the nation and around the world,"
he wrote, would come to "study with us, be a part of America's fastest-
growing church, see it expanding, see it growing, learn how it's done,
catch the vision, carry the vision to their own hometowns, and trans-
late what God was doing in Lynchburg to churches in every state of
the union and every country of the world." It was a supremely practical
vision of education, linking it directly to what students might learn
from his own church and to the goal of planting like-minded churches
in their "hometowns" across the nation. This is what Frank and Sharon,
and many other Liberty Baptist graduates, would do.[5]

Furthermore, the Valentis' church and scores of other freestanding
congregations like it would, in turn, rely on Liberty Baptist for many
things. They would recruit staff from its graduates, draw speakers,
choirs and theatrical productions from it, send their leaders to its annual
Pastors' Conference or to its Bible Institute or seminary for further
training and look to it for leadership in the political struggles of the day.

In this way Liberty Baptist College fulfilled functions a denomination might, much like the Baptist Bible College of Springfield, Missouri, which Falwell himself attended in 1952. At that time, Falwell
wrote, Baptist Bible College was also in its pioneering phase, an unac-
credited school consisting of little more than a series of Quonset huts.
It had been founded just two years before as the training institute for

the newly formed Baptist Bible Fellowship, an association of staunchly fundamentalist and fiercely independent Baptist churches that had split off from the World Baptist Fellowship run by the domineering Texan fundamentalist J. Frank Norris. Norris, a colorful, caustic and controversial figure, was the South's leading fundamentalist in the early twentieth century, when fundamentalism was predominantly a northern phenomenon stirring little interest in the South.[6]

Indeed, when Falwell went off to study at the Baptist Bible Fellowship's new school in the provincial city of Springfield, Missouri, in 1952, it would have been impossible to imagine that this small offshoot of a relatively weak southern fundamentalism would by 1980 provide a *national* network of churches upon which the militant conservatism of Jerry Falwell's Moral Majority would be built. Yet, in the decades following World War Two, the Baptist Bible Fellowship was, by some estimates, the fastest-growing branch of Baptist fundamentalism in America, producing the largest organization of independent fundamentalist Baptists in the nation. The BBF now has six colleges affiliated with it, including a Spanish school in Miami and Baptist Bible College East in Boston, which I visited in 1983 as part of my research.[7] Founded a few years before and then housed in a former Catholic convent in the south-shore suburb of Milton, Massachusetts, Baptist Bible College East aimed to supply pastors for the growing number of BBF congregations in New England.

Perhaps the most distinctive feature of the BBF—apart from doctrines like biblical inerrancy and literalism, which it shares with other fundamentalists—is its radical view of the autonomy of each congregation from any wider church organization and its insistence on the absolute authority of a pastor over his flock. Baptist belief, in general, whether liberal or conservative, emphasizes the independence of each congregation, a doctrine that has helped contribute to the wild profusion of Baptist groups. Within each congregation, the BBF lodges authority *not* in a board of deacons or elders, but in the person of the pastor. Yet, in the absence of any strong denominational body to back them up, pastors in this tradition, I would learn, can be surprisingly dependent on their flock for economic, material and political support.

Jerry Falwell's practical approach to education at Liberty Baptist College, linking it directly with church experience, resembled the education he himself received at the BBF school in Missouri. Teachers of theology, Old and New Testament, pastoral theology and music held jobs in the growing assortment of ministries at Falwell's church or at other independent Baptist churches nearby. Few were full-time teacher-scholars. By the same token, few students devoted themselves full-time to study. Reading and writing assignments seemed modest. On my visit to a class at Baptist Bible College East, for example, the professor assigned only several pages of reading for their next meeting. Instead, students developed ministerial skills in apprenticeship fashion. They worked in various ministries at Falwell's church or others nearby, often in addition to "outside" jobs they held to put them through school and, later, sustain them while they built churches of their own.

Even though Frank Valenti lived off his disability pension from the army while studying at Liberty Baptist, he took a practicum in counseling, answering letters sent into the prayer ministry of Falwell's television show, *The Old-Time Gospel Hour*. There he gained a reputation for what his mother-in-law, Ada, affectionately called his "bold witness." She recalled with amusement the story of one young man who wrote in asking for help with a problem he had with masturbation. "And don't just tell me to lay it on the Lord!" the petitioner added emphatically. "I have, and he won't take it!"

The staff member in charge said, "Give it to Valenti!" Ada recalled.

Frank wrote back, "The problem is that you have a dirty, filthy mind; you won't get anywhere unless you change it!" He warned of graver things such thoughts might lead to—like rape—and suggested methods to avoid them. "The second look at a pretty woman is the most dangerous," he advised. "Don't do it!" Frank did not think highly of nondirective counseling. In fact, his course work in pastoral counseling at Liberty Baptist was organized around a stinging critique of that foundational ideal of modern psychotherapy. For Valenti and those who came to his church, there were clear moral imperatives in life—absolutes set down by God in Holy Scripture. It was a counselor's job *not* to be nonjudgmental or nondirective, but rather to remind people of these moral absolutes and help them live by them.

Given the emphasis on hands-on education rather than book learning at Liberty Baptist College, daily chapel counted as an important educational experience. It exposed students to a stream of like-minded preachers from the region and the entire country. Some were of national repute, like James Robison of Fort Worth, Texas, and Tim

LaHaye of El Cajon, California, author of *The Battle for the Family* and the currently popular *Left Behind* series on the end times. Chapel provided students with a variety of mentors and useful connections to a network of independent, fundamental churches throughout the country. It offered a steady diet of stories, anecdotes and testimonies, furnishing them with tips on how to start a church, see it grow, prepare a message, deal with church splits and so on—and all this through talk. Through this exposure in daily chapel, along with preacher-teachers in their classrooms and ministry jobs, students came to know what "a man of God" thought like, looked like and sounded like. In the Baptist Bible Fellowship model, that meant showing a plainspoken intelligence, avoiding fancy words and sprinkling speech with enough folksy, often southern, colloquialisms like "y'all" or "listen up, now" to assure listeners with little formal education that they were being spoken to directly.

Frank and Sharon's years in Lynchburg held such tough, change-inducing challenges for them that Sharon affectionately called those years "our boot camp."

"The first three months were totally devastating," she remembered. "Frank came home in tears—I mean tears—crying, 'I can't do it, Sharon, I can't do it!'" Whatever limited academic demands this practically oriented education imposed, even its modest reading assignments proved too much for Frank.

One night, Sharon recalled, "Frank literally got down on his knees and said, 'God, I just can't do it. I can't do it, I'm too stupid.' And somehow in God's providence," she remembered, "he walked by a room where a teacher was explaining to another student how to study. And God opened his ears—because he stood by and listened—and gave him a method of writing things down. But this was the thing that Frank needed and, from that point on, he was a straight-A student."

By the time I met him, almost five years after he graduated, Frank was an avid student, carefully reading books, making critical notes in the margins and taking notes for his sermons—a "method of writing things down," as Sharon had described it. Each week he prepared no fewer than three sermons and one adult Sunday school lesson by studying the Bible, concordances and other reference materials, and by doing "word studies" on biblical terms. He even drew on a smattering of Greek and Hebrew. This was quite a change for someone who described himself as having graduated from high school "functionally illiterate."

For Sharon, Lynchburg was a "boot camp" demanding changes of a different kind. "Frank and I were on our own for the first time," she recalled. "It was great and it was bad." Uprooted from their hometown, where the fabric of their married life was woven into ongoing relations with their own families, she remembered the first few months "going around and crying, 'I want my mom!' You know, just really so sad. I didn't think my little heart was going to make it. I went through this traumatic experience of not having any friends, not having Mom, and seeing all these girls out with their moms and enjoying it. Just the typical thing," she added. She was then twenty-five and a mother of two.

Despite missing her mother, Sharon came to enjoy Lynchburg, she said, because "Frank and I were drawn close now, and he was sharing things. I guess what happened," she continued, summing up changes in their marriage, "is that we learned that we were the best friends each other had. We started walking around the neighborhood, going out to eat. We had never done that before! It was just like falling in love all over again . . . this time the right way. Lynchburg," she said, "was the first time I learned about change."

Eventually Sharon studied full-time at Liberty Baptist until her third and youngest child was born. Her younger sister then came down to live with them, finish high school at Falwell's Christian Academy and help care for the children. Soon after, Ada and Tom followed, all attending Thomas Road Baptist Church together. During summers Frank and Sharon returned to Worcester and stayed with Frank's parents. Joe and Marie had mixed feelings about Frank's conversion. They were happy with the changes that getting saved had brought to his marriage, but resented being preached to. Frank tried not to be too "pushy."

"I wasn't going to be one of these religious idiots," he said, "that have great big long prayers at the dinner table to convert your father and mother while they're listening."

Still, there was tension. When Frank asked his father to lend him $300 for tuition, Joe called him a "turncoat" to Catholicism. In fact, Joe didn't think Frank would last long at college. "I says to her, he'll be back here in a couple months," Joe recalled when I interviewed him and his wife, Marie, over their kitchen table. "I says, he ain't gonna make it. I don't see how he could make it after bein' out of school since nineteen sixty-eight." When Frank persevered, Joe ended up helping him and Sharon out with money here and there, and Marie, who kept the money she earned working at a nursing home in her own personal account, bought Frank many of his books.

Then, the summer before Frank's graduation, as Joe and his older son, Frank's brother, Kenny, were working together on a job, a loader accidentally dumped tons of dirt on Kenny as he stood at the bottom of a ditch. Joe turned around just in time to see it happen. He scrambled into the hole and tried to dig Kenny out with his bare hands, but it was too late. Kenny's neck was broken in three places. He was twenty-nine—tall, muscular, with wavy brown hair, the golden boy of the family. His parents were devastated.

Looking back on it, Frank and Sharon felt Kenny's death "softened Joe's heart toward the Lord." Frank preached at the funeral and counted twelve people, mostly relatives, saved that day. He and Sharon saw this event as a "definite call" to return to Worcester and start a "soul-winning" church in their hometown.

3

The Shawmut River
Baptist Church

They like that close-knit stuff.

I T WAS WELL OVER A MONTH after first meeting Frank Valenti that I attended Sunday worship at his church. I had been occupied finishing up interviews with right-to-lifers and parents involved in the Fourniers' Holy Family Academy, and participating in our research seminar at Brown University. The seminar, the first offered by the university's new women's studies center, was made up of several other postdoctoral research fellows like me, who received funding to carry out research projects, some Brown faculty and a handful of graduate students and undergraduates. Our topic for the year was "Gender Representation and Politics." I was the only man regularly involved and imagined that, if the center's directors had inquired about me through the grapevine of feminist scholars, they would have been sufficiently reassured.

Since the feminist movement had arisen in the late 1960s, I had been an enthusiastic supporter, if not in certain ways a participant. During graduate school in the early 1970s, I lived in a commune with five other new-left partisans, including several young feminist scholars. Known among movement people in Boston as the Walden Street Commune, we tried, by working out differences and being present to each other at meals and regular meetings, to create an "intentional community" to overcome what we saw as the suffocating, isolating privacy of nuclear family life. I also participated in one of the early "men's groups," an effort parallel to feminist consciousness-raising groups to make issues of gender in family and personal life "political." More important, virtually all my women friends, colleagues and commune-mates were in consciousness-raising groups, the main organizational form Second Wave feminism then took. We were connected in various ways to the hub of feminist institutions in the Boston area at the time—Bread and Roses; the Boston Women's Health Collective, which produced *Our Bodies, Ourselves*; Nine to Five, a project to organize women office workers; and so on. In fact, it had been my close connection to the women's movement, in the first place, that had led me, as a sociologist, to address a question vexing it all along: Why are we white and middle class?

To attend our seminar at Brown, I made the drive each week from Northampton to Providence, Rhode Island, stopping in Worcester going or coming to move my field research along. It made for odd jux-tapositions of experience, shuttling from a right-to-life demonstration outside a Planned Parenthood clinic with the Fourniers, for example, to a seminar discussion on the recovery of "desire" in feminist theory. By this time, my initial excitement about finding new colleagues to share common interests with had dimmed. Our seminar was taken up largely with the study of theoretical works seen to represent advanced positions in feminist thought at the time—French structuralism and poststructuralism, deconstructionism, Lacanian psychoanalysis and semiotics. What linked these theoretical projects together as a family of enthusiasms was, in part, the notion that on the basis of some newly identified conceptual operation, existing ways of knowing could be transcended by being rightly seen as ideological, patriarchal and polit-ically retrograde.

Having already wrestled with the limits of objectivity in the human sciences from the perspectives of Marx, Max Weber and phenomenol-ogy, I was not greatly interested in these theories. And while they undoubtedly helped free some participants to think things afresh, they were not particularly conducive to free and open discussion. Seminar members seemed on edge about uttering things tainted with "histori-cism," "dualism" or some other regressive, patriarchal tendency seen to be hopelessly embedded in Western thought—except for those, of course, who named and shunned them.

In this climate, my efforts to understand new-right women without dismissing them—though fine in the abstract—seemed politically suspect. That I was the only man in the seminar did not help quell concern. The realities of the situation came home to me during one seminar discussion of a book on African-American women, when I commented on some implications of kinship in African-American life. One of our undergraduates, whose participation was normally marked by deference toward faculty and research fellows, commented with some satisfaction, "That sounds racist to me." Chairs rustled and knowing glances were exchanged, though our outside speaker that day treated my point as useful and thought provoking.

Before the semester was over, I had to present our seminar with initial results from my research. I hurried to finish up interviews with right-to-life activists in Northampton, Amherst, Holyoke, Springfield and beyond. They were an interesting and, in some ways, diverse group, mostly women. They ranged from homemakers married to men in small-business and working-class occupations, to a nurse and a college teacher whose brother had been a longtime mayor of a city nearby. As I talked with this nurse in the sunroom of her stately home in an old upper-class neighborhood, her husband, a banker who had grown up with her in that same neighborhood, walked through the front door into the foyer and merrily announced he had tickets to "the opera" that night. I felt I was watching a rerun of *Father Knows Best*, a television show from the fifties featuring a cheerful, prosperous family.

I also continued visiting Bill and Karen Fournier and others at the Holy Family Academy. Months later Pastor Valenti confessed to me that soon after my first visit, he had called the Fourniers "to check up on" me. "You know," he explained apologetically, "I had just been on TV on the homosexual issue and there were too many people out to dig up dirt on me. I had to be careful." The hate calls he and his family routinely received encouraged a certain vigilance on his part.

Frank reported that Bill Fournier had set him at ease. "Oh, Jim's okay," Bill had assured him. "It just takes a while to get to know him." We laughed, I in relief that I somehow had passed muster. And so my character had been duly checked up on by those on both sides of the culture wars at the time.

WHEN I FIRST TOLD Pastor Valenti over the phone that I would like to attend Sunday worship, he said I would be welcome. Then, after a moment's hesitation, he asked, "Do you have a Bible, Jim?"

Somewhat flustered as I tried to remember if there was one in my library, I responded, "Yes, I think I do."

"Well," he continued, disregarding my quandary, "bring it with you, 'cause all true scriptural Christians bring their Bibles to church." It was helpful advice, and I wondered what had motivated it. Rummaging around my bookshelves, I located a Bible and was surprised to find it was the one presented to me on my confirmation at age twelve. It had been inscribed, of course, by my father. It was the Revised Standard Version, a translation reviled as "liberal" by fundamentalists—and even burned—when it first appeared in the 1950s. I tucked it under my arm, hoping no one would notice.

Sunday Morning
March 20

As I pulled into the parking lot of the Shawmut River Baptist Church, a few parents were helping their children, bundled in wool coats, parkas and stiff polyester snowsuits, clamber out of the backseats of cars and vans bedecked with stickers like BOND-SERVANT TO CHRIST AND NEVER HAD IT SO GOOD and JESUS PAID IT ALL—APRIL, 33 A.D. Members called cheerful greetings to one another as they hurried toward the entry to the hall connecting the bakery building and the *gymnatorium*, the large new addition now almost completed. Inside, people were milling near the doors to the sanctuary on the bakery building's ground floor, gabbing, joking and looking for a place to put down their coffee cups. Children darted about or hung off their parents.

Inside, a piano was finishing the stanza of a hymn and a voice piped over the loudspeaker, "Please stand together and sing! Hymn number four hundred and eighty-four, 'Trust and Obey!'" I found a seat in the back as others scurried to their places. The room, only about sixty feet long and twenty-five feet wide, had low ceilings carrying banks of fluorescent lights. In the back, where the stairway climbed to the church offices in the eaves, a man wearing headphones adjusted levels on a small sound board perched on a narrow table amid boxes of books and other supplies used during the week by the church's Christian Academy. The room comfortably held seven pairs of dark, thickly varnished pews lined up in two sections with an aisle down the middle, at the head of which stood a simple wood podium. The congregation, including about seventy adults, nearly filled them up. Wearing ski parkas, Naugahyde jackets, flannel shirts, blue jeans and unfashionably long skirts, they sang forth:

> *When we walk with the Lord,*
> *In the light of his word,*
> *What a glory he sheds on our way!*
> *As we do his good will,*
> *He abides with us still,*
> *And to all who will trust and obey!*

They sang with enthusiasm and confidence, led by a strong tenor at the podium, singing mike in one hand as he vigorously directed the congregation with the other. They sang out with conviction, even the singsong high notes of the hymn's recurring chorus:

> *Trust and obey!*
> *For there's no other way!*
> *To be happy in Jesu-u-u-s . . .*
> *But to trust and obey!*

It was one of their standbys, I learned, and expressed something essential about their faith. In between verses, the song leader, "Brother Scott," announced exuberantly, "Shake hands with those around you!" As the piano played on, there was a burst of talk as people turned, leaned and stepped across the aisle to shake hands, greet and laugh with one another. In his dark suit, Frank Valenti stood out in the crowd. He was standing up front shaking hands with adults and children who walked up to greet him. There was no platform. Behind him hung a red velveteen curtain across the back wall, and two pews turned to face the congregation, where he and the music leader sat. On one side was a piano and on the other a small organ. Besides American and Christian flags, there was no cross, altar or sacred regalia of any kind.

Sharon Valenti made her way toward me in the back. She wore her short blond-brown hair curled loosely and a gray suit with a white blouse ruffled at the neck—the kind of measured modesty that bespoke someone well aware of her duties as the pastor's wife to set the proper tone. She smiled nervously but said with conviction, "Nice to see you out today, Jim." She introduced me to her parents, a pleasant-looking, gray-haired couple who leaned forward attentively to greet me over the din. "This is . . ." Sharon said, hesitating, ". . . Dr. Ault."

As the opening hymn concluded, the song leader and music minister said, "Let me ask Brother John Lukarilla if he wouldn't come up and lead us in prayer." A man standing in the front handed his Bible to his wife next to him and made his way to the podium. He began with bowed head: "Dear God, we just praise your holy name, Father, that we have an opportunity to be in this house." He spoke in a matter-of-fact, familiar, even tender way, as if God were simply sitting up there in the front pew. "Father, we come here—this is your house—to *praise you!* We come here, Father, to be fed, learn more of your word, to be exhorted, Father, that we might do more of your will. And we just pray that you touch the hearts of each and every one of us. And, Father, I pray you, bless the pastor. Give him the words to speak from on high. These things I ask in Jesus' name. Amen."

The congregation joined in his "Amen" and sat down. There was no printed program, yet people had no trouble knowing what to do next. The Reverend Valenti came to the podium, Bible in hand. "Brother John," he asked, smiling at the man who had led the prayer, "Lukarilla? . . . That's not an Italian name, is it?" (It was Finnish.) He laughed, and good-natured laughter rippled through the congregation. "Hello, Granny," he said, greeting a large older woman sitting near the front. "How are you, dear?"

"Just fine," she replied, smiling, taking the personal attention in stride, if not enjoying it.

Sitting next to me in the last pew, an older woman with white hair leaned over and explained cheerfully in a whisper, "That's really Sally Keener's grandmother!" She giggled nervously. "We *all* just call her Granny Gund. Sally Keener's playin' the organ," she added in a helpful afterthought. This, I later learned, was "Aunt Margaret." Since an injury and arthritis had forced her to retire from hospital work, Aunt Margaret had done "light housekeeping" at the church for $15 a week to supplement her Social Security benefits. Despite her modest recompense, Aunt Margaret took her duties as a call to keep things more generally in order around the church, and, by dint of her energy and talkativeness, made herself a notable presence at Shawmut River.

"Listen, folks," Pastor Valenti continued in a more serious tone, "we gotta start on time. Coffee and donuts keep encroaching on the service. I enjoy the fellowship as much as anybody, but we've gotta have some decency here!"

"All right, volunteers!" he announced with authority. "We need six men this Saturday morning at eight o'clock. We will feed you coffee and donuts, and we will feed you dinner, but we gotta get those classrooms done." (He meant the six new classrooms for the Christian Academy laid out on both sides of the gymnatorium.) "We'll have all the materials and everything to go, so all you'll have to do is dig in—with the exception of the aluminum drip edge. I still don't know what I'm gonna do with that."

Valenti announced that a "Growth Group" would be starting for young married couples to be "discipled" by him. "Cuddlecare," a preschool program, would also soon be inaugurated. It would be different, he declared: "We will have a male figurehead present, not just ladies. How many of you are honestly praying for Cuddlecare?" A few raised their hands and looked around sheepishly. He reminded them to pray since it was through prayer that the church's financial and material problems would be solved. Some jotted this item down on prayer lists in their Bibles. "Brother Dave, how much will Cuddlecare cost folks?"

"It'll be forty dollars a week for full-time," a man responded from the back, "twenty-five half-time, and twenty-five for each additional child." This was Dave Keener, a deacon and a teacher in the church's school. His wife was Sally Keener, the organist and "Granny Gund's" granddaughter.

Dave and Sally Keener were both from the Worcester area, I learned soon thereafter. They were saved in 1976, and after much deliberation and prayer, Dave had decided to leave his job as rotating foreman in one of Worcester's wire-pulling plants in order to teach at Shawmut River's school, even though it meant a drop in salary from $25,000 (including good benefits) to the $6,700 then paid the academy's full-time teachers. The Keeners had three young children, and Dave worried that his desire for more intellectually stimulating work was "my flesh talking to me"—that is, his selfish desires. Dave also had a taste for the nicer things in life. He confessed to "lusting after" things such as cars and stereo systems. (Now he drove a beat-up Honda.) So the prospect of not being able to afford such things might have weighed on him, too. But after praying about it and pondering a passage of scripture that instructed believers to "present your bodies as a living sacrifice," he decided God wanted him to become more involved in full-time Christian service and took a job as senior-high teacher at Shawmut River's Christian Academy.

The Keeners' drop in income had forced Sally to return to full-time work as a nurse. She enjoyed her work for a pediatric practice, but also had misgivings about working full-time. "I feel torn between two things," she said. "I feel guilty to be going to work because I feel like a woman should be a homemaker and take care of her children. On the other hand, my kids aren't here all day either; they're at school. I keep saying to Dave, 'God called you to do this, and why didn't he just provide enough money?'" It made sense to her, in this way, then, to work.

"Do we have some visitors here this morning?" Pastor Valenti asked, scanning the congregation and shuffling some cards on which some visitors' names were written. "What's your name, might I ask?" he said, addressing a young man, who responded in a muffled voice.

"Ed Jenkins," Frank repeated for all to hear, "who came with Leslie. What do you do for work, Ed, if I might ask?"

"I work in an abrasive factory."

"That's tough work," Frank commented. "It's nice to have you with us this morning, Ed. I hope you mingle and make yourself friendly and at home here. The Bible says, make yourself friendly and you will have friends. Most people who do that find they have a home here."

"Who else? . . . I know you," he said to a young woman sitting on the left. "You're a sister-in-law to Mike. That's a tangled mess of relations y'all have over there"—he chuckled, gesturing to where they sat—"but I'm gettin' it straight. Mike has been a champion for Christ in his family, and I believe Phil Strong has met his match." People laughed good-heartedly. Phil Strong, a successful businessman and important lay leader, had, together with his wife, Jean, brought fourteen adults—mostly Phil's relatives—to "know the Lord," and to Shawmut River. The "Strong clan" was the largest in church. In stimulating competition of this kind, Frank was pointing to a central fact about church growth in his congregation: New converts and members often came from the families of existing members, and a number of larger families made up the core of the congregation. The Strongs, along with the Keeners, Valentis and Lukarillas, made up almost half those attending. This was much like Jerry Falwell's own church in its early years, when, Falwell writes, by the time "Pop" and Bertha Johnson's family arrived, adding to his own, we had "a fairly good-sized congregation."[1]

Family was the backbone around which Shawmut River was built. When Frank and Sharon decided to start a church, beginning with a Bible study in their home and then meeting in a defunct social club in town, the fourteen who first attended were all relatives or close family friends. "Four families tithing," Frank admitted, "did help things along." But family members could be counted on to help in many, often less noticeable, ways: setting up for worship services, cleaning, handling correspondence, keeping the books, providing and running a sound system, taking the nursery during services, transporting people here and there and otherwise handling the infinite loose ends necessary to make such a venture work.

Pastor Valenti called on the ushers to "take God's tithes and offerings," and four men rose from the congregation and came forward to get wooden offering plates. All wore ties and a couple, sport jackets. No one, including ministers, singers or organist, wore a robe, which was a practice different from what I'd known growing up. Those who led prayer, read scripture and sang in the choir all came out of the congregation and wore street clothes, an outward sign of the radical sense in which Martin Luther's Reformation ideal of the priesthood of all believers was practiced in this congregation.

"We're gonna have to take a love offering this morning for the oil bill, folks," Pastor Valenti announced before the offering plates were passed. "We owe a hundred and fifty dollars. They won't deliver any more 'til we've paid this off, and we only have enough in the tank to last . . . How much you think is in there, Dick?" The soundman in the back shook his head; he did not know. "We might have enough to last 'til Wednesday, depending how cold it gets. So if you could please dig deep and give whatever the Lord lays on your heart . . ." The "love offering" was to be taken up later and was considered to be above and beyond members' normal tithes, which, according to Old Testament prescriptions, were to be 10 percent of a family's income (pretax income, as Shawmut River reckoned it). While not all members met this obligation, some did, including several successful businessmen like Phil Strong. This made several families major underwriters of the church. The church's weekly income from tithes and offerings hovered around $2,000 during this period, though it could fluctuate wildly, I would see, sometimes in disapproval of a particular decision by Pastor Valenti.

As the ushers passed the plates, the music minister and assistant pastor, Scott Sanderson, came to the podium with his wife and musical partner, Sue. He had a clean-shaven, boyish face and wore large tinted glasses. He spoke with a southern accent, which he seemed to exaggerate when he joked with the congregation about having once been a "doubting Thomas" himself, "like all you Yankees from New England."

Scott and Sue met at Falwell's Liberty Baptist College, where they sang in a traveling group called the En-psalm-bles. (Fundamentalists, I learned, have a penchant for puns.) They spent their senior year traveling across the country and to Australia. Like other groups touring from Liberty Baptist, some of whom passed through Shawmut River, their performances were "a faith ministry," meaning they depended on the benevolence of local churches for support. Each received $10 every two weeks for "extras."

Scott and Sue were both from fundamentalist families and had wider experience in the fundamentalist world than most at Shawmut River. Sue's father was chief financial officer of an evangelical college in Indiana, and her brother worked in the radio ministry of Moody Bible Institute in Chicago.

Scott's father, Wayne, had worked as a bookkeeper while he pastored a small church outside Greensboro, North Carolina, where he had grown up the youngest of twelve children in a family of tenant farmers growing tobacco. His family had attended a local Methodist church until one of his older brothers got saved and became a Baptist preacher. "He did some tent work," Wayne explained to me laconically, when I visited him and his wife, Peggy, years later. They met when Peggy's family, a traveling gospel music group from the Midwest, played at his church. A black-and-white photo hanging in the hallway of their brick ranch home shows her as a young girl among eight or nine family members sporting trumpets, guitars, a bass drum and other instruments. She is a little girl, about eight, standing in the front and holding a big guitar.

"Scott gets his sweetness from his dad and his silliness from me," Peggy explained.

Scott recalled the "retooling" required of him at Liberty Baptist to prepare him for music ministry in the new-style fundamentalist churches Falwell represented. He laughed about having the southern gospel music of his home church in North Carolina drummed out of him. In voice lessons he had struggled to eliminate the croon from his singing and learned to do without the steady *oompa, oompa* backup prevalent in churches in which he had grown up. In this and other ways, fundamentalists showed themselves ready to embrace "the new" while they celebrated the "old-fashioned" and defended "tradition."[2]

Scott signaled to the soundman in back, who popped a cassette into the tape deck, and soon the soft sounds of violins and electric keyboard filtered into the room, the sound track for Scott and Sue's morning anthem. Scott sang the first verse solo:

> *Long ago he blessed the earth,*
> *Born older than the years,*
> *And in the stall the cross he saw,*
> *Through the first of many tears . . .*

It felt very much like a romantic ballad from a 1950s musical, beginning in a pensive mood and rising, with full violins, to its resounding chorus, which Scott and Sue sang in unison:

> *Love crucified arose!*
> *The risen one in splendor,*
> *Jehovah's sole defender,*
> *Has won the vic-tor-y!*

Scott swayed slightly from side to side as he sang, and stretched out an arm or two at dramatic moments. Sue, a comely woman with curly brown hair down to her shoulders, stood upright and still, without any bodily movements except the discreet tapping of her right foot. She sang beautifully with a clear yet soft, breathy soprano:

> *Love crucified arose!*
> *And the grave became a place of hope,*
> *For the heart that sin and sorrow broke . . .*
> *Is beating once again.*

As they finished, a wave of "A-mens" and "Praise the Lords" moved through the congregation. Frank came to the podium as Scott and Sue took their seats in the congregation and, like some of the other young couples, curled up next to each other to hear the morning message.

Fundamentalists prefer the term *message* to *sermon*, wishing to emphasize that a pastor truly called by God acts merely as the vehicle for God's word. A preacher supposedly does not construct his own interpretations of God's word, however coherent, systematic or insightful they might be. Instead, giving himself over to the power of the Holy Spirit—that part of God working on and among people—he preaches "the word of God" in an almost unmediated sense. "Give him the words to speak from on high" was the prayer offered for the pastor by the layman opening worship this morning. This goal is best approached, it is felt, by sticking as closely to scripture as possible, finding out "what it says here" or "what he is telling us there." "He" in this case, as fundamentalists see it, is not the writer, but God himself, who through the Holy Spirit inspired these words to be written exactly as they are, as relevant, say, to second-century Christians in the Mediterranean world as to us in postmodern America.

"If you have your Bibles," Pastor Frank began this morning, "open up to First Kings." The sound of fluttering pages, the crispy thin pages of Bibles, filled the sanctuary. Many present took notes in their Bibles throughout the course of the message; parts of their Bibles were marked up with different-colored pens, highlighters or handmade tabs. But before Frank settled into his message, he still had other things to attend to.

"I see Donna has brought her mom with her," he said, smiling broadly as he looked over to the left row of pews. "She's over there smilin'. They've got you pinned in between Donna and Janice," he joked. "They're not going to let you out," he chuckled, "so you might as well make yourself comfortable."

"All right, we're going through First Kings," Frank declared, finally turning to his message. I learned in time that Pastor Valenti generally preached a series of sermons, each following one book of the Bible. While he would take the first book of Kings for Sunday-morning worship, he followed another for adult Sunday school, and others for Sunday- and Wednesday-evening services. He tried to balance, among other things, attention to the Old and New Testaments. "The New Testament is all doctrine," he explained this morning. "The Old Testament has all these family stories." The verses from First Kings this morning told one of these.

I COULD REMEMBER only bits and pieces of Frank Valenti's message that first Sunday when I sat down to take notes later. I did not yet feel comfortable taking notes during the service, which I soon began doing, discreetly, from my seat in the back-right pew. Without the church's own routine tape recording of each service—the only physical record of Frank's sermons since he preached rather freely and spontaneously from rough notes—I would have had a very limited account of it.

I could remember him hitting out on public issues like abortion and a bill before Congress that would permit a child to sue his parents at state expense. "If you raise your child scripturally," he warned them, "and make him go to church, when he gets old enough, he can sue you for forcing your religion on him. And that bill is in the House," he growled, "r-i-g-h-t n-o-w!" He banged his fist on the wooden lectern.

But when he spoke of abortion as "murdering and virtually butchering babies," I forgot his effort to quickly reassure those present "who have been in that situation before" that "God's forgiven you." Above all, I had trouble following how his points of social criticism connected with the story from the text that day, about King Jeroboam, who made molten images for his people to worship and turned his back on God.

Frank, in fact, took considerable time to bring King Jeroboam's story to life, reenacting the experience of his wife, who, following the king's orders, disguised herself to consult a blind prophet. Since God had already alerted the prophet before she arrived, the blind man recognized the wife immediately. "Can you imagine the look on this woman's face?" Frank asked us wide-eyed. "Instead of having her hair up all in braids like the queen, she had it all stringy, made it kinda greasy." He cuffed his hand around his own head as if doing up his hair. "She wore ragged clothes so she wouldn't be recognized." He turned sideways from the podium, lowered his head and shuffled a couple of furtive steps acting her part. "And she walks to the door, she knocks and steps through it . . . and this blind old prophet says [Frank paused, then declared with contempt], 'Whaddya doin'? . . . Whaddya look like that for? . . . I know who you are!'

"Can you imagine the look on her face?" Frank paused, cocked his head and grimaced. "She probably turned around and said, 'I'm gonna kill whoever squealed!'" The crowd howled with laughter.

But what did this story, as Frank brought it to life from the archaic prose of the King James Bible, have to do with abortion or the despised bill before Congress permitting children to sue their parents? Listening to his sermon again, I realized the connection simply was that, just as God destroyed Jeroboam for his sin, so, too, we would be judged for abortion or for neglecting our children. Here Frank pointed to his own "sin."

"I do not spend the quality time with my children that I ought to," he confessed, "and then, when I *do* spend that time with my children, it seems like they see it as a hurried time. You know," he said, rattling off the kind of attitude he took, the attitude of This-is-something-I-have-to-do-kids-so-hurry-up-and-let's-do-it-so-I-can-get-back-to-the-important-things.

"And I ask for their forgiveness at this very moment," he said, wrapping his two hands around the lectern and leaning toward the side of the sanctuary where the teenagers were sitting. "Pop's on the right road, Tim," he said, addressing his own son, and declaring he now had a plan to spend "good, pure, quality time" with his children.

I remember what odd mixtures of embarrassment, delight and mortification came upon me as a child when my father used us children to illustrate his preaching. Unlike Frank, however, my father used us as examples to make a point, not to offer the kind of personal confession Frank made here in front of everyone.

God destroyed Jeroboam even though "the Assyrian kings were far worse," Frank explained, because Jeroboam was "messin' with God's people." By the same token, children are God's property, Frank asserted, yet "the National Education Association says the child belongs to the state, and the state agrees!" The bill permitting children to sue parents was just another step in diminishing parents' ability to act as stewards of the children God has given them.

I soon came to see how readily any passage of scripture could be applied to the problem of building what members saw as a "godly" order of family life, and the forces seen to undermine or interfere with it, like feminism, the "homosexual movement," moral relativism and so on. If members of Shawmut River spoke of the Bible as "our handbook for life," it was, above all, a guide for family life. Under the formula that falling out of fellowship with a spouse is a consequence and sign of being out of fellowship with God, virtually every kind of marital problem could be discussed in these terms.

The church's abiding concern with the problems of family life was closely related to what impressed me most about its distinct atmosphere of worship. It was saturated with the personal, the familiar, the "at-home." Pastor Valenti's willingness to kid his congregation and recognize visitors in public, or to confess his own failures as a parent for everyone to hear, all helped set the proper tone. A familiar, personal atmosphere permeated every aspect of the service: the sentimental and romantic tone of Scott and Sue's anthem; the preference for familial terms of address such as "Brother Phil," "Aunt Margaret" and, simply, "Granny"; the personal idiom of prayer and the absence of any recitation of set-piece creeds or prayers (even the Lord's Prayer) that did not have the stamp of the spontaneous, the idiosyncratic, and the personal.

"The Lord's Prayer is given to us as a model," Phil Strong, an important lay leader, later explained to me, but the Bible says, "Don't pray with vain repetition." God is more interested in dialogue, Phil said, and it was daily dialogue with God that most marked what members had in mind when they spoke of "having a *personal* relation with Jesus Christ." Such a personal relationship was aptly expressed in the direct, informal, even tender way in which God was addressed in prayers offered aloud that morning.

Shawmut River's worship service was a gathering in which the personal was readily aired, in which the metaphor and mood of "family" prevailed, an atmosphere well served by the injunction Pastor Valenti gave to first-time visitors: "Make yourselves friendly and you will find you have a home here." Shawmut River was not the kind of church you could just walk into one Sunday morning without being introduced. That would be like walking into someone's living room and not being greeted. Once, Pastor Valenti failed to notice a first-time visitor in the crowd and was just beginning his message. Aunt Margaret, sitting next to me in the back row, became visibly agitated and vainly tried to catch his attention. Finally, no longer able to contain herself, she stood up and interrupted him in midstream. "Pastor! Pastor!" she sputtered. "Somebody's here who hasn't been introduced!"

I realized that one thing that makes television evangelists appear so untrustworthy to the uninitiated is their penchant for addressing their mass, anonymous audiences in such familiar ways, as if they were bosom friends and confidants. But experiencing a church like Shawmut River, I wondered how they could ever do otherwise if they sought to appeal to people churched in congregations like this.

Shawmut River had the feel of village life, yet its members were drawn from all over the Worcester area, some driving as much as forty-five minutes to attend. If it was a community, it was not one anchored in a neighborhood. Indeed, some members had been attending less than a year, and some, I would see, were just passing through. How was this villagelike atmosphere possible under these conditions? How viable, or durable, could such a community be in late-twentieth-century urban America?

While Shawmut River's village atmosphere appealed to me in some ways, it grated against my sensibilities in others. The intimate tone of spoken prayer, Frank's personal confession to his children and the sentimentality of Scott and Sue's anthem—all these, whatever emotional tugs they had, caused me to wince. For many like me, religion should be more formal and permit greater privacy in people's experience of God. But those who came to Shawmut River had no difficulty acclimating themselves to its personal, down-home atmosphere. Though they spoke of many life changes engendered by being saved and coming to a Bible-believing church, this was never one. Instead, most spoke of feeling right at home at Shawmut River, or at a similar fundamentalist church they had first attended, as soon as they walked through the door.

On the other hand, some who had happened upon mainline Protestant churches during their spiritual search spoke of being turned off by an atmosphere they found "phony" or "unfriendly," as one newly saved ex-Catholic described his experience at First Baptist Church on the town green. "Pastor," he explained to Frank at a Bible study in his home, "I hate to sound bad, but I saw your church as the poor man's church and First Baptist as the rich man's. I can sneak in there, but I can't into yours."

These experiences suggested that something quite distinct from fundamentalist or evangelical culture predisposed members to this kind of sociability, where the boundaries between public and private were drawn differently from in the churches I knew, where people had to be publicly recognized, or a pastor readily singled out members of the congregation to joke with, or an anthem took the form of a love song to Christ. Why did these people, whether raised Catholic, Lutheran or in no faith whatsoever, feel immediately at home at Shawmut River, while others found such a climate immediately distasteful?

WHATEVER ELSE I felt about the Shawmut River Baptist Church, it seemed a vital place at the time. Then only four years old, it was on the verge of moving into its new gymnatorium situated on a large parcel of land. Its Christian Academy, with seventy students from kindergarten through high school, met in a string of portable trailer classrooms stretching out to the woods behind. Above all, its members seemed enthusiastic, interested, committed and happy. They laughed a lot together.

None of this had come easily. Mesmerized by the striking success of Falwell's church in Virginia, Frank and Sharon looked back with chagrin on their goal of having five hundred in church their first year. "We thought all we had to do was advertise and say, 'Come on in,'" Sharon remembered. "But it was very hard and very discouraging because we were between two churches, both liberal. And I think we just wanted to cry every time we saw cars coming, and they would walk into *that* church, and they would walk into the *other* church. Every Sunday we'd worry whether we'd get anybody here at all."

Massachusetts was not Virginia, where rapid social change in a culture soaked with Baptist traditions fueled the growth of churches like Falwell's. Independent Baptists from the Falwell or Baptist Bible Fellowship tradition, on the other hand, looked on New England as a mission field, a foreign territory ripe for evangelizing. When Sharon Valenti's sister-in-law Judy Waters returned from Baptist Bible College in Springfield, Missouri, to her home in Worcester in the late 1960s, for example, she had trouble finding a church of this kind on this side of the city. Now, fifteen years later, she could choose from a dozen. But New Englanders' reserve, among other things, posed obstacles to certain fundamentalist practices. Pastor Valenti said it had taken an entire year of worship services before anyone had dared "come forward" to the altar rail to "get saved" or "get things right with God."

Now, as Frank closed his message with prayer, softening into tender pleas for his flock to repent and accept Christ, and floating entreaties out over the closing "invitational" hymn—"Are you here without Christ this morning? . . . If God is calling you, come . . ."—members seemed comfortable leaving their seats, singling themselves out publicly for all to see and walking forward to kneel down and pray.

At the end of Shawmut River's first year, when attendance was running about fifty, the congregation was turned out of the building in which they met. After praying for land, they found the bakery building on forty-eight acres with a two-story frame house and bought it from the Salvation Army sisters. But the bank wanted 50 percent down before financing the rest. One lay leader arranged to have his son buy his own house so he could put up $35,000 with the understanding that he and his family would live in the house standing on the land. Frank's father, Joe, put up an equal amount.

Renovating the bakery building had taken considerable work, much of it supplied by Frank, Joe, their relatives and other church members in the building trades. When they started a school, Sharon, her sister-in-law Judy, and Sharon's best friend from high school all taught. They held classes first in Frank and Sharon's basement and then in the bakery building sanctuary. For each worship service on Sundays and Wednesday evenings they had to break down all the classroom partitions and tables, carry in all the pews and then set everything back up again for school the next day.

As attendance grew, they decided to build an addition. But should it be for worship or for their school? Frank devised a plan to build a gymnatorium instead, a building to be used as both a sanctuary and a gym for their school. Two rows of classrooms would flank either side of the gym/sanctuary and would be used by the Christian Academy and Sunday school classes. Financed by a bond program, they began construction. Joe Valenti gave a backhoe and the use of other heavy equipment. Other church members donated materials, equipment and, most of all, their labor Saturday after Saturday. Even family members not involved in the church helped—Frank's cousin, for example, did much of the electrical work.

Now, with the gymnatorium almost done, the congregation seemed to be struggling financially. Without any larger denominational body to help, this was commonplace among independent Baptist churches, whose pastors, like Scott Sanderson's father, often worked at jobs "in the world" to support themselves. Shawmut River had the advantage of not having to pay Pastor Valenti's salary, since he relied on his disability pension as a veteran. But taking a "love offering" to pay an overdue oil bill was a sign of financial difficulty. The Christian Academy was not self-supporting and placed its own burdens on the small congregation. At the same time, the Valentis and other church leaders must have worried about how they would manage when payments on the bonds for the new building would come due. A larger number of tithing members would be needed to shoulder these burdens.

"There was a time when we were running one hundred seventy-five," Frank explained to me toward the end of our first conversation in his office a month before. "We had a church split last June," he added in a lower voice.

"What?" I asked, unable to catch his last words.

"A church split—some people just didn't like the way things were going, and they left. Took as many people as they could." Though Frank said the reasons behind the split were now "a little vague" to him, he went on to describe the logic of "church psychology" that leads to problems when a congregation grows from a small pioneering group to a church of one hundred fifty. "One faction doesn't want it to grow," Frank explained. "They like that close-knit stuff. They think the pastor doesn't have time for them and they take it as a personal insult." He also noted that when offerings grow, "People stop trusting you, but they don't say anything."

Whether these observations were rules of thumb learned from mentors at Liberty Baptist College or conclusions drawn by Frank himself, they struck me as worthwhile sociological perspectives on a perennial feature of independent fundamentalist churches like Shawmut River: their tendency to split. The story is told, for example, of a fundamentalist Baptist rescued from a deserted island where he had been marooned for many years. The rescuers saw he had built three huts for himself and asked what they were. "Oh," he explained, pointing to one after the other, "this one's my home. . . . This one's my church. . . . And this one's the church I used to go to."

Just as the Baptist Bible Fellowship emerged from a bitter split with Frank Norris's ministry, Jerry Falwell's own church began with a disgruntled group leaving a Baptist Bible Fellowship congregation in Lynchburg. Fundamentalism itself, which grew through supporters' willingness to separate themselves from established churches in defense of "the fundamentals of the faith," harbored a strong separatist impulse. It was embodied, perhaps above all, in the pugnacious masculine figure of the fighting fundamentalist unwilling to tolerate compromise with the evils of liberalism and modernism around him. (With his Italian-bred *machismo*, Pastor Valenti filled this role quite easily.) Moreover, the Baptist Bible Fellowship/Falwell branch of fundamentalism, with its extreme views of each congregation's autonomy providing no overarching denominational authority to resolve disputes, seemed to bring this splitting tendency to even greater heights. Yet Pastor Valenti's own point—that at some stage in church growth, people start missing "that close-knit stuff"—had something to be said for it. There are limits of scale at which the pleasures (and pains) of villagelike life are feasible.[3]

Falwell's extraordinary success in seeing his own church grow from its small beginnings to 18,000 members with sixty associate pastors depended not only on his charisma and organizational skills but also on the environment of a New South city like Lynchburg, and on his television ministry and Bible college, which provided denomination-like services to like-minded independent congregations around the country. In large churches like Falwell's, I learned, the kind of close, personal community of smaller congregations—that "close-knit stuff," as Pastor Valenti described it—tends to be found in members' Sunday school classes, where they become involved with one another in more personal ways.

During Shawmut River's conflicts the previous spring, Frank wished he had had counsel from a seasoned pastor. He felt that if he had not been so young and inexperienced, he might have prevented his congregation from splitting. His can-do attitude was admirable, but I would see such forces try him mightily again and again over the months and years to come.

4

The Old-Home Crowd

He'll make a good fundamentalist yet!

IN THE MONTH following my first visit to Shawmut River, I attended as many of its weekly round of services as I could, eager to see what insights the workings of this community held for understanding new-right politics. When I did not have the time to drive to Worcester, I sought out churches from the same tradition closer to home in an effort to see in what ways Shawmut River was typical or unique. And, in my travels around the country, I began collecting visits to independent fundamentalist Baptist churches as others do souvenirs. I became more adept at picking out the right kind of church from signs or advertisements in the Yellow Pages. "Independent," "Bible Believing" or "Bible Way," when combined with "Baptist," seemed a sure thing. "Baptist Temple" was also a good bet, summoning up the image of the first Christians, with whom fundamentalists liked to identify, who had gathered daily in the Jewish temple. "Full Gospel" or "spirit filled" meant something different, a charismatic or Pentecostal church claiming not to hold back any part of the *whole* Gospel as they charged other churches did. They meant, most pointedly, those miraculous powers given the disciples when the Holy Spirit came upon them at Pentecost, like speaking in tongues and healing by faith.

It did not take long to realize what sharp differences divided charismatic or Pentecostal Christians from more rationalist fundamentalists like those at Shawmut River, even though journalists covering the new Christian right at the time often did not recognize these differences.

Though sharing with Pentecostals much of the same biblicism (and its application to family life) and the same supernaturalism and critique of secular humanism in the society around them, Pastor Valenti, along with Falwell and the Baptist Bible Fellowship, took a hard line against charismatic practices. They argued that, though these spiritual gifts had been given to the disciples, they were not intended for our present age, an interpretation that drew upon the elaborate organization of the Bible into seven "dispensations," or periods, defined by God's various relationships to humankind, a standard tool of fundamentalists' interpretation of scripture.[1] Furthermore, some reasoned, if charismatic practices were not Christian, yet pretended to be, perhaps they were even the work of Satan.

Later, at the time of the devastating scandals rocking the empires of charismatic Christians such as Jimmy Swaggart and Jim and Tammy Bakker, Sharon felt it all made sense in the context of their Pentecostalism. "It's all emotion, isn't it?" she explained simply. And when Jerry Falwell stepped in to help resolve the Bakker crisis, many of his followers turned against him for involving himself with charismatics to begin with. But members of Shawmut River differed on Pentecostalism, and some ended up pointing to Pastor Valenti's hard line on this issue as a reason for leaving his church. I remember one vexing and inconclusive discussion among several church members about "crazymatics" (as they sometimes called charismatic Christians). At one point, Tom Morse, Sharon's stepfather, exclaimed in frustration, "I don't care what you say. You'll never get me to stand up and wave my arms around!" Something more than reading scripture seemed at work in arriving at these views.

Apart from the fact that Shawmut River was a "pioneer" church still pastored by its founder and made up mostly of new converts, it was otherwise fairly typical of churches I visited in the Baptist Bible Fellowship tradition—in worship, atmosphere, political outlook and even size. While larger than some, it was, given its reduced numbers as a result of the recent split, smaller than some older, more established churches. The median number of adults regularly attending mainline Protestant congregations is just under one hundred.[2] The median attending fundamentalist congregations, with their storefront churches and congregations meeting in homes, schools and other civic buildings, probably runs less. Very few reach the size of those megachurches that frequently capture media attention, and they, like

Falwell's church, often reach that size by fulfilling denomination-like functions for a host of smaller churches.

The number of regularly attending members at Shawmut River at the time was about seventy-five adults. (It would grow some over the next few years.) Despite media fixation on the large, mega-church movement, smaller churches like this represent the more common experience of fundamentalist Christians. It is helpful to remember, for instance, that if there are, say, two hundred smaller churches averaging one hundred members each for every large church with five thousand, the smaller church experience would outweigh the larger by four to one.

Though small independent congregations have been fundamentalism's main carriers, it is remarkable how little attention they have received in scholarly studies of Protestant fundamentalism in America, which I began to read after my research settled on Shawmut River. I discovered a new wave of historians taking issue with earlier generations of scholars, who, ever since fundamentalism's emergence, portrayed it as the last gasp of an obsolescent faith or as a rural phenomenon destined to fade away with the steady march of urban secularism and materialism. Instead, this new wave of scholars portrayed fundamentalism, quite rightly, as a new and distinctly modern movement that had arisen in the very heartland of modernity, in the large cities of industrial America at the beginning of the twentieth century.[3]

As one of the leaders of this new historiography, George Marsden, described it, fundamentalism sprang up in multiple branches of Protestantism out of "a mosaic of divergent and sometimes contradictory traditions and tendencies." These tendencies and traditions, Marsden wrote, included the American tradition of revivalism intensified by premillennial prophecy about the second coming of Christ; the Wesleyan holiness movement stressing a believer's progressive sanctification by the Holy Spirit (which fed into Pentecostalism); and intellectual efforts by Presbyterian theologians at Princeton to defend traditional American Protestantism, which, in the absence of an established church, anchored religious authority in personal experience and the Bible. The Princeton school's ideas about the Bible's infallibility and its intelligibility to ordinary believers without the guidance of clergy or tradition contributed to fundamentalists' distinct identity as "Bible-believing Christians."[4]

Marsden showed how these at times conflicting traditions coa-

lesced in the late nineteenth and early twentieth centuries into a movement defined, above all, by its militant opposition to modernism. That
meant opposing new, often scientifically justified, understandings of
the world that conflicted with what were seen as "fundamentals" of the
faith, often supernaturally governed events like the virgin birth or
God's creation of an inerrant Bible. Such antimodernism appealed to
popular adherents both inside and outside an array of mainline Protestant denominations. While many stayed within established churches,
others split off to form independent congregations or to join new,
more loosely knit associations that allowed greater local church autonomy. These various "fundamentalists," as they came to be called by a
Baptist journalist in 1920, took center stage in American life for the
first time during the fever-pitch battles they waged in the 1920s over
modernism in the church and evolution in the public schools.[5]

After these struggles climaxed in the Scopes trial of 1925 on the
issue of teaching evolution in public schools, the prevailing view had
been that fundamentalism had been put into retreat and had faded out
of existence. However, another new-wave historian, Joel Carpenter,
demonstrated that fundamentalism actually went on to experience
rapid growth in church membership throughout the Depression and
into the postwar period. Separating themselves from a world they saw
increasingly ruled by atheism and apostasy, fundamentalists created a
vast institutional infrastructure centered, above all, in the local church,
but also in Bible schools, Christian colleges, publishing houses, radio
ministries, Bible conferences and other parachurch organizations and
movements. Within this vital subculture, fundamentalism flourished,
providing fresh cadres for conservative Christian resurgence as my
own baby-boomer generation came of age in the last quarter of the
twentieth century.[6]

In a similar pattern of rediscovery, new studies of the legendary
Scopes trial have turned prevailing assessments of it upside down. The
dominant view had been that the trial's public humiliation of William
Jennings Bryan, the populist standard-bearer of the antievolutionary
cause, had turned the tide decisively against opponents of evolution.
Historians now believe that after the Scopes trial renewed energy actually flowed *into* the antievolution crusade, shifting the movement's
focus from changing legislation to influencing local school decisions.
This intensely local activism, historians now argue, created a powerful
climate around school administrators, teachers and textbook publishers

alike, which actually led to a *decline* in the teaching of evolution. It
was not until 1957, one notes, when the Soviet Union's launching of
Sputnik threatened American technological dominance, that federally
funded programs attempting to modernize public school science finally
brought evolution firmly into American public education.[7]

The tendency among American intellectuals to prematurely con-
sign fundamentalist conservatism to the dustbin of history until they
are shocked into disbelief by its startling resurgence suggested more
than the normal process of loss and recovery in historical scholarship.
It reminded me of my colleagues who kept urging me to get this book
out before Christian conservatism disappeared from public life. At the
root of this recurring problem, I believe, is the difficulty in simply
understanding how ordinary, right-minded people would believe what
fundamentalists and new-right conservatives avow, itself a result of
how far removed intellectuals generally are from the social worlds in
which these beliefs flourish. Recognizing that the sense and meaning
of any elements of culture can best be understood by considering them
in their typical context, I thought better sense might be made of fundamentalist beliefs by seeing them in the context of the key institution
accounting for their persistence in modern life: the local independent
church.

At the same time, I was struck by how often the local congregation
had been neglected in recent scholarship, precisely when it seemed
most decisive in understanding the nature of fundamentalist practice.
Revisionist historians went about describing fundamentalism's distinc-
tiveness as a religious movement by identifying and tracing the lineage
of its defining ideas: biblical inerrancy, for example, or dispensationalism as an elaborate scheme of biblical interpretation, or premillennialism as an interpretation of biblical prophecy about Christ's second
coming *before*, rather than *after*, the millennium of his personal rule.
But they rarely considered how these ideas actually worked in the day-
to-day life of local churches, even though Marsden, for one, was quick
to point out that fundamentalists' grasp of scripture took place more in
"small Bible study groups" than among fundamentalist intellectuals.
And another astute observer warned that we must "always distinguish
between popular fundamentalism, which is seldom scholarly, and
scholarly fundamentalism, which is seldom popular. What is true of
one," he noted, "is likely to be untrue of the other."[8]

The effort to understand fundamentalism through the history of its central ideas also has to reckon with the fact that these ideas were drawn from diverse religious traditions and, once congealed into fundamentalism's militant antimodernism, appealed to a variety of groups across a diverse array of denominations—Baptist, Presbyterian, Methodist, Dutch Reformed, etc.—each with its own traditions, ideas and practices. Moreover, even though many of fundamentalism's central ideas originated in England and were passed back and forth across the Atlantic in vital exchanges with North American colleagues, fundamentalism never became a popular movement in Britain. It was distinctly an American phenomenon.[9] Factors other than ideas, then, seemed necessary to understand its emergence and appeal.

The idealist approach to the study of fundamentalism also failed to bring into focus, and even missed altogether, certain aspects of its appeal that might help us better understand its emergence as a popular movement. The idealist approach led some to conclude, for example, that, unlike present-day fundamentalists, their forebears at the beginning of the twentieth century were not concerned with issues of gender and family life. However, another historian, digging into sources closer to the popular pulse of fundamentalism at the time, in newsletters and sermons from local churches, discovered a veritable torrent of criticism and commentary about family and gender. It swirled around issues such as divorce, which increased fivefold between 1870 and 1920, and the "New Woman," the college-educated woman of the city, whom fundamentalist preachers lampooned for being more interested in the dance hall than home, in Ibsen than the Bible or in having a pet dog than a baby. Though issues of family and gender perhaps became more pronounced in contemporary fundamentalism, similar preoccupations, it turned out, were present in its original phase. In fact, I noticed that in the discourse on family life articulated by First Wave fundamentalists, strong roles were played, in particular, by Shawmut River's own forebears, Frank Norris and his lieutenants, especially John Rice, whose book on the Christian home became a classic.[10]

Recognizing how weaknesses in existing scholarship stemmed, at least in part, from neglect of the local church, I wondered whether Shawmut River might hold some important lessons for understanding the very nature of Protestant fundamentalism in America. These questions began to percolate as my fieldwork at Shawmut River progressed. What can be learned about fundamentalist thinking and practice by seeing them in their natural context—in the local congregation with its weekly round of worship services, Sunday school classes and home-based Bible studies and prayer groups?

Wednesday Evening
March 23

My first Wednesday-evening service at Shawmut River was attended by thirty-some adults, about half the Sunday turnout. Others were in the nursery or with the teenagers who met separately on Wednesday nights. Those gathered made up what Tom Morse fondly called "the old-home crowd," mostly church regulars, many of whom were employed by the church or its Christian Academy and were required, as part of church discipline, to attend all three weekly services as well as adult Sunday school. When you add to these four weekly meetings Tuesday-night visitation (where members met and went out in pairs to evangelize), a weekly Joy Group for women, Saturday-morning work groups or prayer breakfasts for men and weekly Bible study or Growth Groups in individual homes, church regulars were involved in an all-encompassing round of weekly activities capable of having powerful effects on their lives. Pastor Valenti said you could gauge the strength of any fundamentalist church by how many turned out for Wednesday-night service. It was they—the "old-home crowd"—who seemed to set the tone and pitch of congregational life.

Wednesday-evening worship followed the same pattern as that on Sunday mornings, except that it was even more informal, spontaneous and familiar. Some churches devote much of their midweek service to prayer, breaking up into small groups, with each person taking a turn to pray aloud. At Shawmut River, Pastor Valenti treated his Wednesday-evening message like a Bible study involving considerable give-and-take.

"How many of you have heard yourself say, 'What are we fighting for?'" Valenti asked as he began a Wednesday-evening "study" on chapter 1 of the New Testament Book of James. "Why do we argue so much? Why do we bicker and clamor? . . . If you were a fly on the wall in the home of a couple that argued like that, what would be some of the things that you'd say to that couple?"

A young woman raised her hand. "To listen to each other," she said, quoting verse 19, which reads, "Let every man be swift to hear, slow to speak, slow to wrath."

"Excellent," Frank responded. "A good listener is a good counselor. Why would you tell 'em to listen, Cindy?" She thought for a moment. "Sharon," Frank said, calling on his wife.

"You can't pay attention when you're talking," Sharon offered bluntly, then threw her head back and laughed with those around her.

Frank concurred and went on to conclude, "What the scriptures are saying is 'Hey! Pay attention to God, that quiet still voice, and if you're talking and the voice from God is quiet and still, you're not goin' to hear it!'" Frank gave considerable weight to Sharon's views. Once he told his flock that "ninety percent of the spiritual things I've learned, I've learned from her."

In passing that evening, Frank took license to joke with members, and they responded. "I'd rather hear Scott sing than eat," he quipped about his music minister. "I've heard him eat!"

In a pattern I found common in other fundamentalist churches, Scott Sanderson as music minister and assistant pastor served as the principal object of the pastor's good-natured ribbing, a practice that drew upon and modeled the widespread banter, including ethnic jokes, with which the men of Shawmut River gingerly approached each other. Such humor seemed to make it easier for them, bred to be potentially aggressive, loyal defenders of their families, to approach men outside their own family circle.

After five years' experience, Pastor Valenti showed considerable skill in posing questions and fielding answers while leading members to a point he had in mind. With humor and enthusiasm, he drew on public and personal knowledge of members to encourage the shy, cajole the tentative and deflect the irrelevant or unuseful comment. "That's Phil; he's dumb," Frank joked, not wanting to go in the direction of one of Phil Strong's comments. But Phil, not at all offended, laughed along with the rest, and soon made another contribution.

The overall result reminded me of a college seminar, provoking spirited responses, concentrated effort and widespread participation by any academic standard. As a college teacher who taught in this manner, I knew how hard it was to make discussions flourish while pursuing lessons you wished to convey. Also, like any academic seminar, some sessions soared while others fizzled.

Along with a freewheeling discussion of the meaning of the text for

their lives, Frank tried to give his flock rudimentary guides to reading
scripture: attention to "thesis sentences" and paragraph organization,
and, here and there, the more precise meaning of the Greek word
standing behind the King James translation.

Sometimes he clarified what seemed to be elementary points.
"What do you do as soon as you see the word *wherefore*?" he asked. A
plump woman in a worn overcoat promptly raised her hand.

"It means all that he just said before," she answered.

"Right! It refers to all those things he just talked about."

He interjected reminders of previous lessons: "Remember now, the
word *perfect* means 'mature.' There's no such thing as a perfect human
being. We do not lose our sin nature when we get saved, okay?"

Or later: "What is the definition of *fool*? Remember, it virtually
means 'empty-headed.'"

"Jim, you can put that one in your book, if you want," he shot back
to me sitting in the last pew. "I'm sorry," he apologized for the second
time that evening. "I should refer to you as Dr. Ault, shouldn't I?" He
was, in this way, introducing me to the "old-home crowd." I was beginning to see that, while fundamentalists show great respect for higher
learning, making a point of such titles and displays of academic accomplishment, they are also apt to decry the "*phoolosophy* of the world," as
Frank went on to ridicule it that evening. And this ambivalence toward
higher learning, I came to appreciate, stands at the heart of the fundamentalist enterprise.[11]

In such discussions at Wednesday-night service and in the home
Bible-study group I would eventually join, techniques for reading
scripture were developed by teaching rudimentary methods of reading
and building up knowledge of a specific lexicon, which, like all jargon,
has a technical aura associated with its mastery. These exercises built
confidence in the congregation's own reading of a text they believed
contained absolute standards for their lives, our "handbook for life,"
they called it.

This same kind of Bible study also occupied adult Sunday school,
held an hour before worship every Sunday morning in one of the
Christian Academy's new classrooms flanking the gymnatorium.
Through Sunday school and three weekly worship services, apart from
whatever home Bible study or Growth Groups individuals might
attend, members of Shawmut River enjoyed a steady diet of reflections
on the Bible, all presented in speech. Imagining them to cover an aver-

age of one chapter a meeting, disregarding other passages cited in the course of any one study, this would amount to 208 chapters over the course of one year. At this rate, it would take a congregation more than five years to cover the entire Bible—*if* they read with comprehensive coverage in mind. But they did not. The New Testament books most commonly studied, for example, were the letters from the apostles to the early church, rather than the four Gospel books themselves.[12] And in the Old Testament, Shawmut River used Genesis far more often than, say, Leviticus, which details the variety of observances God handed down to the Jews through Moses.

The message this Wednesday evening had been drawn from the Apostle James's letter to the early church and was typical of Shawmut River's preoccupation with applying scripture to the practical problems of living a "godly family life." In passing, Frank hit out at things seen to threaten such family life. "The greatest wrath of God, the Bible tells us, came down on who?" he asked his flock. "On the Sodomites," he said. "Take away the *s* and the *o* and you have what they are: 'dumbites!'" he howled. "Did you ever see any group speaking out like homosexuals today? They've been out of the closets for a long time. They're growin' and you can't increase your numbers in the closet." The old-home crowd laughed.

"I don't hate homosexuals," Frank said, qualifying his outburst in dead-serious tones. "I despise their sin. . . . It's the most filthy thing!"

THE PEOPLE I FELT MOST COMFORTABLE with during my first months at Shawmut River were Scott Sanderson, the music minister, his wife, Sue, and Dave and Sally Keener. Their conservatism was less hard-edged and insistent than the Valentis', whose political vigilance was, at times, a source of discomfort. On one early visit to Sunday-morning worship, for example, I accepted the Valentis' invitation to join them for dinner afterward. Groups scattered here and there to a restaurant or home to eat and while away the few hours before it was time to return again for evening worship at 6:30 p.m. Some even went out together for supper after that, guaranteeing that the "Lord's Day" was fully that. The Valentis usually went out to eat with some combination of their parents and Sharon's childhood friend Barbara. Their children went off with the other set of grandparents or "Auntie Barbara," though Christie, their thirteen-year-old daughter, who liked adult company, often came along.

This one Sunday I accompanied the Valentis and Sharon's parents to a family-style colonial restaurant near church. This was a time when we might discuss the preaching that morning, and I was sometimes uneasy about what to say. When discussion turned to abortion, Frank asked me whether I knew that "America was founded as a republic and *not* as a democracy." What did he mean by this distinction in the context of abortion? I was never quite sure where failure to comprehend would be taken as a glaring sign of just how liberal I was.

In a democracy, Frank went on to explain, the constitution of government is totally subject to the will of the people, while in a republic certain things are taken as God-given absolutes that cannot legitimately be changed—like the sanctity of life or the nature of marriage. In this conversation, the Valentis took issue with many actions of the popularly elected government, and the word *democracy* seemed to stir up in them the kind of revulsion my progressive colleagues felt toward terms such as *family values* or *love of country*. Sharon once told me she could always tell whether someone was a secular humanist within moments of talking with him, because he would "soon say something that showed he didn't believe in absolutes."

On another occasion, Frank spoke of his passion to study history according to the word of God. "Secular scholars," he declared, "are really impotent when it comes to history." For example, he said, "Why did Napoleon do what he did when nobody was threatening him?" He went on to say that the Book of Daniel, though written two millennia before, explained why Napoleon's empire had come apart and been divided into four. "Because he was a pervert," Frank explained simply.

At such moments I would be stunned and not know how to reply. In these ways, casual conversation routinely threw up tests I felt unsure of passing. And all the while I felt under the skeptical scrutiny of, above all, Sharon. "Frank's more trusting of people than I am," Sharon told me early on. "I'm the skeptic." Two years later I was surprised to learn how acutely the Valentis read my face at those moments. By then Frank felt comfortable telling me how he used to notice my mouth drop open dumbstruck at something he said, and then watch me, with a vacant look in my eyes, write something halfheartedly in my notebook, as if to say to myself, he laughed, "Well, this one's for posterity."

However, after our initial conversations, it was rare for members of

Shawmut River to put me on the spot, at least intentionally. But some-times conversation would zigzag to that point where Sharon, Ada, or Frank might ask, "Don't you think the right to life is an absolute?" or "Don't you think the humanists control the public schools?" At those moments I would struggle to say something with integrity that, at the same time, would not provoke divisive argument. Above all, I hastened to turn discussion back to *their* views, not mine.

For these reasons, occasions for open conversation proved taxing if not exhausting during my first few months at Shawmut River. At times they gave me headaches. On Sundays, after spending several hours in adult Sunday school and morning worship—with all the socializing in between—and then participating in two more hours of conversation over dinner, I often did not have it in me to stay for evening service that night.

Spending a Sunday afternoon with the Sandersons and Keeners, on the other hand, was easier going. When Scott and Sue Sanderson first came to work at Shawmut River, it had been Sharon's parents, Tom and Ada, who became "our in-residence parents," as Scott put it. Tom and Ada had taken them out for dinner and had acted as grandparents to their newborn daughter. But when the Morses' own daughter, Kathy, returned to Worcester from Lynchburg with her husband and children, Scott said that had come to an end.

Since then, Dave and Sally Keener had become "family" to the Sandersons. They felt free to drop by each other's homes and encour-aged their children to call them "Aunt Sue" and "Uncle Dave." One Sunday afternoon I joined them for dinner at the Sandersons' small two-story apartment. It was in a white clapboard row house originally built for nineteenth-century millworkers near the center of town about two miles from church.

After a dinner of pot roast, brown rice and green beans, followed by butterscotch sundaes, we sank into the couch and easy chairs while the children played on the floor or out in the yard. This was the first time I sat down to talk with Sue or Sally. Socializing at Shawmut River was, to a significant degree, segregated by sex, and any private time between a man and a woman outside family ties was suspect. I remember Pastor Valenti feeling he could not drive a welfare woman home from church unless his daughter, Christie, went along. Therefore, as decorum required, I first got to know church men before getting to know their wives. Given these realities, a woman researcher at Shawmut River would have entered the community by different paths, with different vantage points along the way.

Dinner conversation my first Sunday with the Sandersons and Keeners was constrained at first. Sue, in particular, seemed watchful and distrustful until, during a discussion about secular humanism, I managed to successfully complete a point Dave Keener was making by finishing his sentence. Sue, sitting with her chair pushed back against the wall, looked at me and burst into a smile, exclaiming with relief, "He'll make a good fundamentalist yet!" Soon after the ice was broken in this way, Sue opened up. She confessed quite candidly that she had been suspicious of my taking notes during worship, worrying that I was taking down each and every "off-the-wall thing" Pastor Valenti might say.

The Keeners and Sandersons, I soon gathered, had differences with Pastor Valenti. Scott and Sue were sensitive, for example, about his tendency to rail against homosexuals. They granted that he often distinguished between hating the sin and loving the sinner but were not convinced that un-Christian attitudes were not at work.

Later that afternoon Sue spoke frankly about the problems of determining the Bible's true meanings, given its inconsistencies, something fundamentalists generally held to be theoretically impossible. She recalled her distress talking one day with a Pentecostal insurance salesman who came to her door. "After I quoted all the scripture we've been given *against* speaking in tongues," she said, "he quoted a bunch of passages supporting it, that we'd never read." She shrugged her shoulders in consternation at the dilemma this chance encounter had posed.

Shawmut River had not much in its budget to pay its music minister and teachers. At the time, Scott and Sue received $190 a week, supplemented, however unevenly, by a stream of benevolence from members who took them out to dinner, provided used furniture or hand-me-downs for their two-year-old daughter or left bags of groceries anonymously at their back door. And these were the good times. During one downturn in church finances, the Sandersons qualified for food stamps and Scott took on part-time work selling vacuum cleaners. Fortunately, that did not last very long. Scott was more artist than salesman.

Scott poured his artistic passions, above all, into his "cantatas," or musical extravaganzas, he produced each Christmas and Easter telling those sacred stories in drama and music. The music ranged widely, from Handel's *Messiah* and Gospel hymns to choruses reminiscent of 1950s musicals and pensive ballads sounding a bit like Joni Mitchell. Characters were costumed in burlap or old drapery material with sandals or cloth tied around the feet. Some men grew beards, and at Christmas Scott arranged for live goats, sheep and donkeys, all of which made a vivid impression hoofing up the center aisle of the sanctuary, skittish and wild-eyed.

The Sandersons and Keeners were mainstays of the church, among the core members carrying its business forward each day. Dave was a deacon and taught the senior-high classes—English, history and social studies. His brother Dan, a bachelor, taught history and English to the junior high. Scott taught Bible and Sue kindergarten. All the Keeners sang in the choir with Scott and Sue. Sally played organ and Sue piano. In a small congregation, participation in all quarters of church life was a priority and specialization limited.

As minister of music, Scott Sanderson acted also in the capacity of assistant pastor, helping Pastor Valenti in untold ways. Stopping by church any day, you might find Scott holding a piece of Sheetrock as Frank hammered it in place, running an errand to the hardware store or recording parts of a choral piece on audiocassettes so choir members could learn their parts as they drove about the city.

Each week Scott prepared various assortments of adults and children to perform musical numbers at the weekly round of services: sometimes adult choir, sometimes the "King's Kids," sometimes a mother-daughter duet, sometimes just Sue and him, or one of them singing solo. Scott said there were "three funnels," or tests, music had to pass through in order to be appropriate to carry a Christian message. Above all, the melody, which represented the *spirit*, had to be prominent, and the rhythm, which represented the *body*, subordinate. This ruled out rock music, he pointed out, because "it is mainly rhythm with some hypnotic harmony and very little melody." To test the rhythm itself, he advised people to "get alone and do what comes naturally. If the music makes you snap your fingers and tap your feet," he said, "it can *possibly* pass through this funnel. But if you are inclined to move around the midsection of your body because of the music, it *cannot* carry a Christian message." At this, he rolled his eyes and laughed.

On these grounds, Shawmut River took a strong stand even against *Christian* rock music. It often fell to Scott in his senior Bible class to press this issue with the academy's resistant teenagers, which he did with some misgivings. "It's almost like I'm doing to them what was done to me," he admitted with some frustration.

"When I was growing up, certain people expected Christian reactions to a lot of things, so much so that I was turned against Christianity." As an art student at a local technical college in the late 1960s, Scott became caught up in the euphoria on campus at the time. He recalled the first Earth Day celebration, when fellow students headed off to a rock concert in Woodstock, New York. "I didn't know *what* they were talking about," he confessed, but he readily joined the partying and revelry involved.

After graduating, he took off with a friend for Long Island, New York, to work as a commercial artist. There, in the heady atmosphere of sexual liberation in New York in the early 1970s, he quickly saw quite a bit of life. His involvement in a world where getting high, promiscuous sex and homosexuality were accepted and openly practiced deepened to a point of personal crisis. Finally, after considerable turmoil, he decided to return home and come back to God and back to church. He later learned that on the very night of this decision, his father had called upon his congregation to pray for his lost son in New York. Scott took this as evidence that, as the Bible promised, whenever two or three were gathered and asked something of him, God would answer their prayers.

Scott's experiences outside the fundamentalist community of his childhood helped him see the fundamentalist world around him as an outsider might. I remember Sue and him laughing heartily as they reported to me that whenever they attended a large fundamentalist gathering, they could always tell the Moody Bible Institute graduates from the Bob Jones ones, or the Liberty Baptist from the Tennessee Temple ones—by how far a man's hair came down over his ears, for example, or how long a woman's skirt was. It amused them that these details ended up mattering so much. Scott's outsider perspective made him a good informant, and I found myself often turning to him to help explain the inner workings of the congregation, especially in times of conflict.

Scott now took a firm stand against practices that he and his fellow art students had tolerated in the seventies. I remember one conversation we had about homosexuality during our first interview. "You can't say 'Jesus Christ is a part of my life, but I'm still homosexual,'"

Scott declared. Once you accept Christ and are saved, he continued, "you become a new creature" and the Holy Spirit would center in on that sin.

Unlike the mainline Protestant churches I was familiar with, Shawmut River focused on sin as an inescapable part of human life—the "blackness" or "dirtiness of your soul" is one particularly stark way Pastor Valenti described it. The template prayer that all people had to say in their heart of hearts to be saved was called the "*sinner's* prayer" and required each person to admit, "I am a sinner" and pledge to "repent," or turn away from, "my wicked ways." But that was never completely possible, according to church doctrine, and they believed that human beings, since they still "lived in the flesh," could not help but continue sinning. Furthermore, any progress they *did* make depended upon the help of the Holy Spirit dwelling in them to make them, as Scott had said, a new creature.

"But even though you're a new creature," I ventured to ask, "you still sin, don't you?"

"Yes," Scott replied, "but the name 'Christian' means to be 'Christlike,' and homosexuality could not be a part of being Christlike."

"But wouldn't that be true of any sin?" I wondered out loud. "I mean, even if you see it as sin, I just don't see why it would be incompatible with being a Christian."

"For some reason, though," Scott replied thoughtfully, trying to better address my quandary, "in fundamental circles, that particular sin is looked down upon as one of the worst."

"You say, 'for some reason,'" I continued, "but what is that reason? Is it biblical? I don't see why it's singled out."

"God singled it out," Scott replied emphatically. "An entire city was destroyed because of it," he said, referring to the Old Testament story of the destruction of Sodom, "and that particular sin, with a list of certain sins, is called an abomination in the first chapter of Romans. Do you want me to read that? I've got that with me," he said, reaching for the Bible at his side.

"No," I said, wanting to move on. But checking it later, I found the following passage in Romans, chapter 1, where Paul is discussing the fallen state of human beings "Who changed the truth of God into a lie, and worshipped and served the creature more than the Creator . . ." (verse 25). Paul goes on to describe the consequences of this fallen state in verses 26–30:

For this cause God gave them up unto vile affections: for even
their women did change the natural use into that which is
against nature:

And likewise also the men, leaving the natural use of the
woman, burned in their lust one toward another; men with men
working that which is unseemly, and receiving in themselves
that recompense of their error which was meet.

And even as they did not like to retain God in *their* knowledge, God gave them over to a reprobate mind, to do those
things which are not convenient;

Being filled with all unrighteousness, fornication, wickedness, covetousness, maliciousness; full of envy, murder, debate,
deceit, malignity; whisperers, backbiters, haters of God, de-
spiteful, proud, boasters, inventors of evil things, disobedient to
parents . . .

I still could not see why homosexuality had been singled out as a
particular abomination in the eyes of God, among the variety of sins
that God "gave over" to those who turned from worshipping him to
worshipping the creature—sins including backbiting, boasting and dis-
obeying your parents.[13]

However conservative the Sandersons and Keeners were
socially or theologically, I came to see them as the liberal wing of the
congregation. (Years later Scott reported that he and Sue, upon reading a Christian magazine, now felt they might be more accurately
described as "evangelicals" rather than "fundamentalists.") I was taken
aback, then, when Sally Keener said that when she had first come to
Shawmut River, she had found it "*so* liberal." She meant compared to
Heritage Baptist, the Baptist Bible Fellowship church she and Dave
had first attended after being saved. At Heritage Baptist they met Scott
and Sue, who had come to Worcester from Indiana to run the music
ministry. "It's not so much that Shawmut River's liberal," Sally
explained, "as it's not legalistic." The pastor at Heritage, on the other
hand, insisted women not wear shorts, Sally recalled in amazement,
and his wife—a woman from Oklahoma who "sort of ran the show
indirectly," Sally said—would tell her that her "ears should not show"
and that she "should not wear hoop earrings."

"Good grief," Sally declared in amazement, "these things were issues! Who cares? Seriously, if you develop the inward character, you don't have to worry about what's on the outside. That will fall into place later."

On the other hand, I was then surprised to hear Sally admit that she and Dave had *needed* such "external government" at that time in their lives. "We were footloose and fancy free," she remembered. "I never even *owned* a dress! Good heavens! Wear a dress? We were a bunch of freaks!"

Sally Keener impressed me as someone whose feet were planted so firmly on the ground that she could face even the most troubling circumstances in life in a calm and straightforward way. I imagined she was effective as a nurse. She was a slight woman, only five feet tall, who always wore her blond hair shoulder length and slightly curled under. She did not have the philosophical turn of mind that Sharon, Frank or her husband, Dave, had and showed an impatience with issues of church doctrine. She had a practical intelligence and, above all, seemed always ready to laugh and enjoy life.

Her husband, Dave, recalled that before they were saved, they had often spent weekends partying together with his brother, Dan, and Sally's sister and her husband. On Fridays, Dave said, the guys would pick up a case of beer and they would party. Dave and Dan had grown up in a close-knit Catholic working-class neighborhood of Worcester. It was the kind of neighborhood, Dave explained, where as children they had felt free to go into a neighbor's upstairs apartment to help themselves to the cookie jar. Though their father, who spent his career as a laborer for the City of Worcester, was from a Yankee Protestant family, their mother was French Canadian. Their mother's father lived with them in a three-bedroom house he himself had built. Their mother's two sisters and their families lived down the street.

When Dave and Sally started living together and then married, they first lived with Dave's parents. Sally's family disapproved, and a "cold war" between them and Dave ensued. Sally was from Swedish Protestant stock, among those who had immigrated to work in the wire-pulling mills of Worcester. Only Sally's grandmother on her father's side was a churchgoer. However, Sally's family lived near her mother's mother, Granny Gund, in a neighborhood in Auburn, on the south side of Worcester, where Sally remembered Swedish still being spoken. Sally's mother had been the oldest of four daughters and had taken care of the household while her mother, Granny Gund, worked as a nurse. Two of Granny's other daughters, who remained unmarried and still lived with her, carried on nursing as a family tradition. And so had Sally.

Sally and Dave, Dave's brother, Dan, and Sally's sister and her husband all got saved in a chain reaction started by one of Sally's sister's friends whom Sally had always admired. After they got saved, Sally's mother, Granny Gund and Sally's two maiden aunts living with Granny all followed suit. Sally remembered that when the pastor of Heritage Baptist had given the invitation one night, the whole entourage filling an entire pew went forward together to the altar.

"I can remember our first Friday night after we were saved," Sally said, recalling how they used to party on Fridays. "We all sat there and said, 'What do you do when you're saved? This is *boring*!' So we used to have little Bible studies. We'd have literature from church—things they had talked about—and we'd look things up. I can remember taking notebooks to church with me and writing, writing, writing. The first year we were saved, all I did was write!"

"It was like a hunger," Dave recalled. "I had to read the Bible, and we would read it together." The pattern of change in their marriage was very much like the one told to me by Frank and Sharon.

"Instead of two separate people going our own way," Sally said, "we became one."

The Keeners and Sandersons were open and kind to me. At the time I was going through a painful breakup with a woman I wanted to marry. I soon realized that it was impossible to hide this event from people at Shawmut River; they easily read the pain on my face. Scott, Sue and Dave, in particular, always asked how things were going "with your girlfriend" and assured me they were praying for us. Scott was the first church member to profess his "Christian love" for me. "I don't want you to misunderstand this," he hastened to add. "It's Christian love I'm talkin' about," he said, distinguishing *agape* from *eros*.

The Keeners presented me with a Bible, a King James version with Jesus' words in red lettering. And it was Dave Keener who first posed to me the community's most important question. He was a short, spare man, who walked with a springy step that conveyed dignity and energy. In his midthirties, he had sandy-colored hair and mischievous blue eyes always ready for a laugh or a prank. His brother, Dan, fit the same description. Though Dan was shy, both were quite emotional and given to talking excitedly about what the Lord had done for them. High on Dave's list, perhaps, would have been God's work in taking away his bad dreams from experiences in Vietnam.

He once told me about crouching in trenches at night and watching grenades flying overhead, deadly silhouettes against the dark sky, never knowing when one would land next to him. Or about the time he was squatting with his pants down over an outdoor latrine when a North Vietnamese soldier emerged from the woods downhill from him. Dave yelled, startling the man, who disappeared into the woods only to return moments later with a grenade. He threw it at Dave, and it rolled within yards of him. Luckily, it didn't go off.

What Dave felt was most horrible about Vietnam, he said, was "to see the look of hatred in that soldier's face and to feel there were people out there who wanted to kill you." After returning home, he found he could not go hunting with his father anymore. Simply walking through the woods was too scary. But, he said with enthusiasm and gratitude, the Lord had even taken those fears away from him.

Leaning back in his chair toward the end of our first conversation, Dave eyed me steadily, smiled invitingly and asked, "Have you ever had—in a scriptural sense—a born-again experience?" His eyes burned with disarming passion.

After explaining that I had been brought up by parents with a strong Christian faith, but a faith that I had fallen away from, I answered, "No." Dave then opened his Bible to the Book of Romans and set out to show me the "Romans road," what fundamentalists affectionately call the steps to salvation succinctly laid out in that book containing Paul's letters to the early church in Rome. "Have you ever heard there is just one way to heaven?" he asked. "It's like a gift," he said, reaching into his pocket and pulling out a ten-dollar bill. "It's like if I took this ten-dollar bill," he said, holding it up in front of me. "God says, 'I will save you and you can have eternal life; all you have to do is accept it.'" He smiled. Beads of sweat had formed on his forehead.

It would be months before this question was put to me again. Given how urgent members saw the matter of a "lost soul" among them, I realized that word must have spread through the congregation that, yes, Dave *had* given me the Gospel. Moreover, as long as I was still hanging around, listening to the word, participating in prayer and worship, there was less urgency than any momentary encounter posed. The question of my (or anyone's) salvation was, in any case, posed at the end of each service when Pastor Valenti gave "the invitation" over the closing hymn. But, in time, the matter of my salvation would be taken up more directly by those in charge.

5

Phil and Jean

It wasn't Leave It to Beaver . . .

Aﬁer the opening hymn, Pastor Valenti announced that we had to take a love offering for Mary Shepperson's van. "What seems to be wrong with it?" he asked a tall, middle-aged woman with fine, gray-brown hair pulled back in a bun.

"The brakes," Mary Shepperson replied, keeping her head slightly bowed and peering over eyeglasses that had slid down her nose.

"Are the pads gone?" Frank asked. "Can you hear metal on metal when you push on 'em?"

"Aye-up," Mary said, her accent betraying her up-country Maine origins.

"We're gonna take a love offering for Mary's brakes," Frank declared. "There's no more generous Christian lady here than Mary, God bless her." Mary's generosity was well known at Shawmut River. She and her husband and their first two daughters had migrated to Worcester in 1963 from a rural town in central Maine. Other members of her family had followed. "There was no work up there," she explained. "You had to travel thirty miles for a minimum wage." After working for twenty years in a factory making uniforms for Catholic clerics, Mary had taken a job teaching in Shawmut River's preschool. Now she often drove Aunt Margaret and other women without transport to and from school and worship services. She also let the Christian

Academy use her van for field trips and sporting events. During one of the church's deepest financial crises, when Pastor Valenti had felt it necessary to cut back what little was paid Aunt Margaret for cleaning, it had been Mary who "really carried me," Aunt Margaret said. "She used to take me home on Wednesday nights," Margaret remembered glowingly, "so I'd have the best meal."

The plate was passed for Mary Shepperson's van that evening. Mary got much of what she needed to have it fixed. "I like things like that," Sally Keener said. "I think it's great. It's a joy to help someone like that, too. You know there is a need, and you want to get that for them. You don't do it saying, 'Well, I know the Lord's going to bless us.' You just do it because you see a need." Members believed that if you gave, and especially sacrificed to give, God would shower you with blessings. Nonetheless, that should never be the motive to give, as Sally said, and God always knew what motives were truly involved.

Registering needs and recognizing how the Lord met them was the bread and butter of conversation at Shawmut River. But special time was taken at the beginning of Sunday-evening worship for testimonies and prayer requests. They represented two sides of the same reality. Testimony pointed to the perceptible evidence of God's work in the world—a job found, a marriage saved, an illness healed—and prayer requests brought these same needs to public attention in the first place and made them a matter of community prayer. If needs were prayed for by faithful and obedient believers, members assured one another, God would surely answer them—of course, they allowed, in his own ways and own time.

This evening Brother Duane rose to ask for prayer. "My wife is ill, and my mother-in-law is looking for an apartment," he said.

"You're sure it's not the other way around, Duane?" Pastor Valenti asked jokingly, and people laughed. Many knew that Duane and his wife had been struggling with problems in their marriage (and those who did not were thereby informed). Testimonies and prayer requests circulated briskly in the wider sphere of church talk, as members chatted when picking up their children at school, prayed at a Bible study or had their daily conversations on the phone with relatives or friends. Praying together over the phone was one of those practices that impressed me with how much members' faith occupied the day-to-dayness of their lives.

As prayer requests were given, members jotted them down on

prayer lists, which they slipped into Bibles or pockets, eventually to stick them up, perhaps, on their refrigerator doors alongside shopping lists and other items of household business. And many looked to those lists in the course of conducting their "prayer lives." It occurred to me at the time that these practices were probably an effective means to seeing needs met merely by social means. As faithful members meditated regularly on their prayer lists, I reckoned, they would be routinely reminded of specific needs and have them in mind when someone mentioned news, say, of an apartment becoming available, a job opening up or another member's unexpected windfall. In this way, needs and resources would be providentially brought together. Since members stressed that God always worked through people, this might be seen—even from a believer's standpoint, I imagined—as a socially effective means for God's seeing his church meet his children's needs. However, this theory, as I framed it, made no mention of God's work in answering prayer; it was purely sociological. And when I first broached it with Dave Keener, he immediately objected and pointed to a number of instances where answered prayer could not have worked this way.

In any case, when members gave me testimonies about how God had answered their prayers in concrete ways, they usually spoke about God working through various people, mostly relatives or church members. For instance, Dave Keener himself recounted praying fervently for a new muffler for his car, which he badly needed and could not afford. Then, one day his father turned to him and said, "You need a new muffler. How much is it? Go have it done. I'll pay for it."

And on another occasion, Dave was in an automobile accident when his registration had expired. He needed $200 to pay the fine. God answered his prayers, again through many people who came forward to help—his family, his wife's father and a number of church members.

During prayer-request time this same Sunday evening, Phil Strong, a businessman and prominent lay leader, rose to ask for prayer for his older brother Sam, who was "in turmoil," he said. Phil and his wife, Jean, had been witnessing to Sam and praying for him for many years, but it was this recent crisis in his brother's life, Phil felt, that now made him more open to the Lord.

Phil and Jean's evangelism among their families had not been without fruit. Fourteen adult relatives and a dozen children now in Shawmut River's pews were evidence of their effective efforts to win lost family members to Christ. But it saddened and worried them that Phil's brother Sam remained unsaved.

WANTING TO MOVE my research along at Shawmut River before presenting findings to our seminar at Brown, I looked for other church members to interview. Realizing how jealously Pastor Valenti guarded his flock with the shadow of last spring's split still hanging over him, I looked for people who, though outside the Valenti-Morse circle, were recognized leaders of the church. Phil and Jean Strong seemed a good choice. Though mainstays of the church like the Sandersons and Keeners, they were more independent lay leaders not employed by the church or its school. As proprietors of a successful insulation business, the Strongs not only were important donors to the church but also leaders of its largest family.

Phil and Jean met in 1971 in a dark, smoke-filled singles bar named Sir Morgan's Club in a strip mall on Worcester's north side—a curious but not unlikely place to find a couple destined to play leadership roles in both a Moral Majority church and, later, in Pat Robertson's Christian Coalition. To be born again meant, after all, to turn away from an old life of sin and begin afresh as "new babes in Christ." Phil was twenty-three at the time, studying electrical engineering part-time at Worcester Junior College and living at home. With money he had made installing aluminum siding, he had just bought a new Corvette. Most nights he met up with friends at one of a number of singles bars on the outskirts of Worcester, like the Peacock, the Chandelier and Sir Morgan's. One night while nursing a drink at the bar of Sir Morgan's, he saw an attractive young woman walk through the door and called out to her by name. She came over only to learn that, according to him, he had mistaken her for someone else. He had called out "Jane," not "Jean," he said.

But Jean suspected Phil had gotten her name from her workmates and would not admit it. For her part, she declared he couldn't possibly be "Phil Strong," because she had gone to school with a Phil Strong and he wasn't *him*. Phil showed her his driver's license to prove it. This is how the dance of their relationship began.

"I thought I was pretty macho at the time," Phil recalled. "I had a brand-new Corvette and invited her to go out and take a ride with me, but she wouldn't."

"Why would I want to go see a car?" Jean remembered thinking to herself and feeling Phil arrogant to suggest it. She was two years older than he and just embarking on a new phase of life. She had grown up nearby in what had become a suburb of Worcester. Her mother, who had been abused as a child, had been subject to mental breakdowns when she at times would not even recognize her own children.

At nineteen Jean "broke away," as she put it, and took refuge working as a live-in governess in the home of a doctor and his wife and their five children. "It was a good experience," she said. She enjoyed the warmth of their wider extended family and learned, she said, that "just because people are angry and yell, they don't really hate each other; they got mad but still loved each other."

After this two-year "retreat," as she called it, Jean moved into her own apartment and took a job as a nurse's aide with an eye toward becoming a nurse. "I decided to join life again," she said philosophically, "make my own mistakes—kinda plow through life whichever way I could." In this frame of mind she frequented some of the same singles bars Phil and his friends did. Though she brushed Phil off the night they first met, he managed to get her telephone number and called several times to ask her out. She refused.

Then one night their paths crossed at the Peacock Club and Phil was stunned when Jean ran up and threw her arms around him, gushing, "Phil! Phil!" She later told him it had been a ploy to get rid of another man. But now when he asked her out, she accepted. Then, shortly thereafter, on their second date, Phil asked her to marry him.

"He asked me to marry him," Jean chimed in during the first interview I conducted with them, "and I bet him two dollars he'd chicken out."

Phil grinned. "I said, 'Two dollars?' I says, 'You're on.' The next month or so we decorated the apartment, and as soon as the apartment was decorated, we got married. And this all happened *within a month!*"

"And I had to pay," Jean laughed about their bet, "but I got the better end of the deal. It was two dollars down on his paycheck for the rest of his life." It was a story they seemed to enjoy retelling. We were sitting across from each other at their rustic dining room table. The dining area opened onto a kitchen that was separated from the living room by a large stone-and-mortar chimney at the center of the house.

On the kitchen side, an electric stove was set back against it. Old cooking implements, needlepoint and other handicrafts decorated the chimney and kitchen walls.

Here on most Sunday afternoons Jean fed an impromptu gathering from church. At the close of morning worship, she and Phil spread invitations around as knots of people chatted and children raced about. Jean pulled herself away from the hubbub to get things started. In time she assembled an array of dishes—ham, macaroni and cheese, steamed vegetables, meat loaf, scalloped potatoes, mixed salad and pies. Her cooking, as well as her household decor, betrayed her Swedish heritage: lattice-crusted pies and wood furniture with kitschy embellishments. Sometimes other church women brought dishes. They always helped out, cheerfully recruited by Jean to the kitchen, where talk turned, among other things, to the morning message, answered prayers or scriptural truths and their application to life.

After dinner most stayed to laze away the afternoon talking, or taking turns riding Phil's snowmobile up the trails into the woods behind their house. Some of Phil's relatives might drop by. Several lived on the same road and his parents right across the street. Sometimes they joined in and other times begged off from a gathering too thick with church talk. As the afternoon wore on, choir members started looking for coats and ties or shoes and socks, and soon thereafter the rest piled into cars to get to Sunday-evening service.

Phil and Jean seemed to be thriving in this period of their lives. Phil was tall and medium set, and though his body did not appear muscular, he was quite strong and capable of hard physical work. His round face was prone to rashes from psoriasis, a skin disease from nerves that had gotten him a medical deferment from Vietnam. He wore a bushy moustache, and his short brown hair came down on his forehead to frame sparkling blue eyes.

Jean had calm, blue-gray eyes and a clear complexion. She was of medium height and had chestnut brown hair, which she wore either curled down to her shoulders or pulled up in a loose bun with wisps turning whimsically this way and that.

Phil and Jean seemed good partners. After many false starts and important learning experiences in construction-related businesses in Florida and Massachusetts, they had started an insulation company that had caught the wave of escalating oil prices in the late 1970s and taken off. Their company was doing $1.5 million in business annually and employed forty people, including a number of Phil's relatives and church members.

The Strongs lived modestly in a ranch house they had designed and built themselves across the rural-suburban road from the farmhouse where Phil had grown up. They had set their house back off the road on a large grassy plot bordered by woods and a pond. Finished in rough-hewn boards with a matching barn next to it, it was reminiscent of a pioneer homestead. "The little house on the prairie," Sue Sanderson affectionately nicknamed it. Over the next few years, they added three more children to the three they already had and, as the fortunes of their company improved, added a second floor to their house and an indoor swimming pool.

Phil himself had grown up the youngest in a family of ten children, most of whom still lived in the area. "My sisters pretty much brought me up," he said, but it was his older brother Sam, now in crisis, who "took on the father image and would discipline us. He'd come home during the daytime, and if we skipped school, we used to go hide in the barn and he'd catch us and whale the life out of us!"

"It wasn't *Leave It to Beaver*," quipped Jean dryly about both their families, invoking the wholesome family portrayed in that 1950s television show. As the youngest in the family, Phil often came home from school to find no one home. His father was rarely around. When he was not running his own small construction company, he was helping out nights in the family restaurant. "On Friday nights, I used to peel potatoes," Phil recalled. "It was fish-and-chips night, and I'd peel hundreds of pounds of potatoes."

After graduating from high school in 1966, Phil began hitchhiking back and forth to Worcester Junior College to study electrical engineering while working at various jobs. Most nights he went out drinking with his buddies. "I wouldn't get back until three or four in the morning, and there'd be just enough time to shower and get up and go to work. Then I'd go out again. I thought life was going out and getting drunk or feeling high and working, and that was it. I lost a few years there," he said of this period, shaking his head. "I got so fed up with everything I was doing that I decided to get married."

"Why did I marry him?" Jean said in response to my question. "I was tired of being single," she answered, pausing to think more seriously about the question. "And he was decent; he didn't swear or drink all the time and he wasn't abusive. At twenty-five," she mused, "you know the types of people that are out there. And as my mother used to say," she added with a laugh, "you don't know anyone until you marry them anyway."

ALONG WITH SHARON VALENTI and Sharon's mother, Ada, Jean Strong was a leader among the women of Shawmut River. She not only presided over get-togethers at her home each Sunday but also ran the church nursery, where during every worship service she sat with young mothers, often with an infant or two on her lap, overseeing a brood of young children and chatting about the "things of the Lord." Talk often turned to how to be a Christian mother and wife. Jean took seriously the duty of women "older in the Lord" to teach younger ones, and she hosted the only regular formal gathering exclusively for church women during this time: a morning Joy Circle, where a small group gathered each week for prayer, Bible study and sharing.

"You have to be taught to love your husband and children," Jean insisted. "After marriage you have your first fights and realize, 'Hey, this guy doesn't think the same way I do!'" That was true of her own marriage, launched after she and Phil had known each other for only a month. Though she and Phil now enjoyed an effective and prosperous partnership, their marriage had suffered from severe problems in its early years and the story they told resembled the Valentis' and Keeners'.

Just as abruptly as they had decided to marry on their second date, Phil and Jean moved to Florida nine months later, after visiting a friend of Phil's who had moved there from Worcester. Phil planned to find work installing aluminum siding but discovered that instead of earning the $7 to $8 an hour he had received up north, the going hourly wage in Florida at the time was only $2.25. He held a number of jobs, including one as a partner with a builder, who also hired Jean as receptionist and bookkeeper. "I learned all the bookkeeping aspects of the building trade," Jean recalled. "I even got to the point where I was a construction coordinator." But after she discovered the builder was cheating Phil, they quit and started a succession of businesses installing aluminum siding, windows and screens. Phil did the outside work of sales and installation, and Jean the bookkeeping and office work. They lived a quarter mile down a dirt road in the middle of the woods in a wood-frame house they bought for $10,000. Phil's father gave them the down payment. At times they earned a decent living, happy when they were making $500 a week and employing as many as nine installers. But when recession hit, they found themselves "saving pennies for milk," Jean recalled. During one of these downturns, problems in their marriage came to a head.

"In Worcester," Jean remembered, "Phil was out drinking every night, and if I didn't like it, well, too bad. He had his brothers and friends to stick up for him." For that reason, she said, "I was really looking forward to moving to Florida." At first they relied more on each other, she recalled, "but that was very short-lived, because Phil ran into some old friends, and the old patterns started all over again."

They found themselves fighting bitterly over even the smallest things. "I'd feel like I had a right to get angry," Phil said, "and I'd yell to get my point across. And she'd get hurt and she wouldn't say anything."

Jean admitted she had often given in to Phil with the attitude that "I really don't care, don't expect my help, and when it goes flump in your face, I'm going to stand here and say, 'I told you so!' I wasn't doing it to be heartless," she explained with a tone of regret. "I was doing it with the attitude 'Why should I do anything for you when you don't come home until ten or eleven at night, you don't even have the decency to call me and tell me you're going to have a drink with the boys, and when you do come home, you're so mean and miserable and hateful, I don't even want to see you around!'" Her voice gathered indignation along the way, as if she were reliving her anger at the time. After a moment's thought, however, she observed, "You're actually trying to punish somebody."

"And I felt that," Phil acknowledged with a twinge of hurt in his voice even now.

"And you become very cold," Jean observed. "You get to the point where you can't care about yourself, because if you stop to care even a little bit, you're going to get hurt, so you just don't care about anything. At this point, we both knew it was about over." Their first child had just been born. Jean said that if she had lived closer to family and friends or had had any money in the bank, she probably would have left.

It was during this low point in their marriage that Phil began "searching." He met some Jehovah's Witnesses on a job, and he and Jean attended some of their meetings. Though the couple did not take to it, these experiences prompted Phil to think more seriously about religion. Neither had a strong religious background. Phil's father, having been raised in a Catholic orphanage, which he had fled as a teenager, had a dim view of organized religion. Jean's parents had sent her to a Catholic church as a child, but they themselves had not attended, and when she was old enough, Jean stopped going.

Then Phil ran into an old friend who invited them to his wife's baptism. It was at an independent Baptist church much like Shawmut River. Its pastor was a graduate of Tennessee Temple Baptist Bible College, another staunch center of Baptist fundamentalism. At morning worship Phil accepted Christ as his savior. Always more circumspect, Jean held out until the service that evening.

Like the Valentis, what excited Phil and Jean most about their new faith was how their relationship with Christ and the guidelines provided in scripture helped transform their marriage and family life. Before, as Jean saw it, "there were no guidelines for the marriage. I had likes and dislikes and Phil did his thing and if I didn't like it, what could I do? There was no common denominator. There was nothing you could bring it to. And it would then become a battle of will: whose will is stronger and whose will is going to survive. It was chaos!'

"When we received Christ," Phil added, "all of a sudden we now had a rule book to go by, and when we had problems the preacher was right there to give us answers. He would open up God's word and say, 'Okay, here's what God has for you.'"

Their story reminded me of Frank's description of his marriage before he and Sharon were saved. "How would you like to play football without referees and without a rule book?" he had asked me, likening his marriage to such a situation. What rules did the Bible provide Phil and Jean, Sharon and Frank or others at Shawmut River to rescue their marriages from chaos and acrimony? Some mentioned biblical prohibitions against drinking and swearing, others an exhortation from Proverbs to be "satisfied with the wife of thy youth" and the more general injunction, central to Christian ethics at Shawmut River, to put "others" before "self." Jean quoted Proverbs, "It's a soft voice that turns away wrath . . . ," to suggest how she should react to Phil's anger, rather than retreating into a shell of spite. But what did the Bible say specifically about marriage?

The text Phil and Jean turned to that afternoon—and the one most often invoked at Shawmut River about marriage—was the well-known passage from Paul's letter to the Ephesians (5:21–28). It reads:

> . . . submitting yourselves one to another in the fear of God. Wives, submit yourselves unto your own husbands, as unto the Lord. For the husband is the head of the wife, even as Christ is the head of the church: and he is the savior of the body. Therefore as the church is subject unto Christ, so let the wives be to their own husbands in every thing. Husbands, love your wives, even as Christ also loved the church, and gave himself for it; that he might sanctify and cleanse it with the washing of water by the word, that he might present it to himself a glorious church, not having spot, or wrinkle, or any such thing; but that it should be holy and without blemish. So ought men to love their wives as their own bodies . . .

Members saw this passage from Ephesians, which compares marriage to Christ's relationship to the church, as setting forth God's "chain of command" for the family. "As the church is subject unto Christ, so let wives be to their husbands in everything." For their part, husbands should love their wives "even as Christ also loved the church and gave himself for it."

On the face of it, this passage requires that a wife be subordinate to her husband, who is "head of the wife." But members of Shawmut River, and especially women, were apt to qualify what this actually meant. Even though they felt this meant that husbands should have the final say in a decision, they would often cite the opening phrase—"submitting yourselves one to another in the fear of God"—to emphasize the fact that both husbands and wives had equally to submit themselves selflessly to each other in the "fear of God." Church women were also fond of citing the creation story in Genesis to point out that "God created woman out of man's rib, not his foot—not to be *walked on*, but to be *by his side*." Wives were to be partners, not servants.

The idea that wives should be subordinate to their husbands appeared incongruous in light of marriages like the Valentis' and Strongs'. About my own search for a mate, Scott Sanderson once joked over Sunday dinner that the Sandersons and Keeners would find me "a good Christian woman who would grovel at my feet . . . like Sharon or Jean," he added with a chuckle. Everyone laughed at the irony, because it was hard to imagine two stronger-willed, more formidable women. How did this biblical framework work for them? Since this framework was important to the biblical Christianity the Strongs, Valentis and Keeners had picked up, quite uniformly, in three different fundamentalist Baptist churches in Massachusetts and Florida, it seemed an important part of this tradition's popular appeal. So I was interested to question Phil and Jean further about it when I first interviewed them.

Jean emphasized that the "chain of command" set out in "God's plan for the family" in Ephesians could not work if all the links were not in place. Phil had to submit to Christ and show the "fruits" of that submission, she said, before she would consider submitting to him. As Phil told his story, his submission to Christ involved a basic reorientation in life.

"Prior to knowing the Lord and knowing God's word," he said, "I didn't grasp the responsibility I had for my family. I felt as if I was more responsible for myself and that the married life—the children, the wife, and the house and all this other stuff—didn't mean that much to me." Hanging out with his buddies, on the other hand, did. It was the social center of his life, which became all the more attractive as conflicts in their marriage grew. "I mean, with the baby crying and my wife complaining about something or other," he admitted, "I'd just as soon go out with the boys.

"But after I started getting into God's word," Phil said, "and the emphasis it placed on the husband bringing up the children and actually being the head of the home, that's when I decided it wasn't important anymore for me to go out with the boys and drink." Phil saw these changes as "maturing in the Lord," growing into what God had intended him and other husbands and fathers to be: the heads of their families. To *not* do what God wanted, Phil said, meant "hurting the person who first loved me" (meaning Jesus).

Such themes were found widely in fundamentalist churches of this kind in the mid-1970s and would be taken up years later by the "Promise Keepers" movement among more mainstream evangelical Christian men. But seeing these verses in Ephesians as a call to husbands to accept domestic responsibilities rather than go out drinking with the boys was not necessarily how this passage might be read. The Strongs, along with others at Shawmut River, did not arrive at this and other interpretations by reading the Bible on their own. Neither did they mention any Christian self-help literature that shaped their thinking in these areas. Instead, they learned "God's plan for the family" as set forth in scripture in the context of their deep and many-sided involvement in a church community. In their church in Florida, for example, Jean said that the preacher and his wife "adopted us."

"My kids used to call him Grandpa Mosher and stuff," Jean recalled. "As a matter of fact, I felt closer to them than I did to my own parents. And I could talk to them and get parental advice from them that was good, sound, wholesome, Christian."

"Ma Mosher," as Jean called the pastor's wife, also led the Joy Circle she joined, where, as she described it, "you were able to talk freely" about what submission in marriage means, or what love means "when physical attraction wears off."

For his part, Phil got involved in an almost endless round of church activities: men's fellowship in the morning, bus ministry on Saturday, visitation on Tuesday evening, and a ministry at an old-age home on Sunday night. "I was growing a lot," he recalled, "and I had an awful lot of time to talk to the preacher." As he began to take more seriously the church's prohibition of drinking, smoking and swearing, Phil found it increasingly difficult to hang out with his old pals. Beer and rough language were the necessary ballast for the smooth conduct of their socializing, and his friends felt uncomfortable with his abstinence. Such prohibitions, I soon recognized, represented more than simply a change in "personal morality." They served to dismantle a way of life and, in turn, lend greater cohesion to marriage and church relationships.

Only when Jean saw these changes in Phil—the fruits of his own submission to Christ—did she consider submitting to him. Even then, she recalled, it took considerable struggle. "I wasn't willing to give up my independence and say, 'Okay, Phil, you run the house.' . . . You're not going to turn over your life to a *drunk*! And no matter how Phil had changed, I still held that picture." When Phil stopped going out with the boys, she found it surprisingly difficult to cope with his being home. "*Whoa-o-o! Oh my!*" she hooted. "He's actually gonna carry on a *conversation* with me?"

Then she recalled one of their "biggest catastrophes," when their television was struck by lightning and blew up. "Now you had nothing you could bury yourself in. Good grief! You had to listen when he gave his opinion on things. At first it was kind of scary," she observed. "I found it really difficult to talk to him, and I found the only way I could talk to him was to ask him questions—to interview him. After a while we kind of got used to it and began to know each other as persons, and I began to understand how he felt about things." She began to see, for example, how Phil felt about problems he faced in business or about laundry piled on the dining room table. And she began to understand the ways her actions affected him.

Doing a "word study" on submission under the tutelage of Ma Mosher and other women "older in the Lord," Jean learned that submission did not mean obedience. "That's for children," she said. Instead, it meant supporting your husband "without grumbling. . . . It's an uplifting, an uncomplaining, it's putting your shoulder to the grindstone, right alongside him, and saying, 'Okay, together we're going to do it.'" She noticed that as she adopted a more supportive attitude toward Phil, he continued to change in positive ways toward her. "Every little change in me," she observed, "produced a little change in him. And the vicious circle that was going one way started going the other way. And anybody can do it," she said matter-of-factly. "It just takes . . . change."

However, coming to know each other as "persons," as Frank and Sharon first did in Lynchburg, did not change Jean's sense that men and women represent two essentially different kinds of human being. That continued to be one of her taken-for-granted assumptions about life, but now Jean had a new language to speak about it. "Men are logical," she told me. "Women are very emotional. They're like fractions with different denominators," she continued, summing up the process of change she experienced. "You can't add them together unless you have a common denominator, and that denominator is Christ."

IT WAS TEMPTING to see this pattern of change—especially its focusing men on newfound responsibilities to wife and children—as fully consistent with feminism, if not, as some writers came to interpret it, as de facto feminism, or "postfeminism"—that is, the result of feminism's influence. In fact, didn't the very gathering together of women in Joy Circles or Bible studies, as Jean and Sharon had done, where women could "speak freely" and teach and support one another, stand to empower women in some of the ways feminist consciousness-raising groups had? It was all the more striking, then, that Jean, Sharon and virtually all the women I came to know at Shawmut River showed such hostility to feminism and insisted upon upholding sharp differentiations in gender roles in family and church.[1]

"Feminism is an insult to my intelligence," Sharon charged, "and I'm tired of them speaking for me." Instead, Sharon held up the conservative Catholic Phyllis Schlafly, an outspoken opponent of women's liberation, as "a perfect example of what we fundamentalists stand for."[2]

"I don't go along with abortion," Sharon went on to explain, "with *Our Bodies, Ourselves,* with the divorce rate and leave your children to anybody to bring them up." Along with other women at Shawmut River, she asserted that "a woman's place is with her children." Nevertheless, Sharon, Jean and others did not object to mothers working outside the home, if circumstances permitted, and supported equal opportunity for women in economic and public life.

"Anybody that's qualified should work the same job for the same pay," Jean declared.

"I'm pro–getting the same salary that a man does," Sharon agreed. "I'm pro-respect. But, I think the Constitution already took care of that issue."

Issues of equality in the economy and public life, then, were not what Jean and Sharon objected to in contemporary feminism. In these areas, one could imagine them and other conservative women I met supporting certain feminist initiatives. Instead, they objected to feminism's critique of gender roles in the family, its "rebellion . . . against domesticity," as one feminist writer recently characterized the women's movement of the 1970s, the time when Jean and Sharon, grappling with marriage problems, had become Bible-believing Christians. Jean, for instance, charged feminism with "knocking the housewife and mother," and Sharon charged it with "taking any kind of value off the family. See," she explained, "they want everybody to be important individually. They don't want family units. And that's what's happening to our country."[3]

For Sharon and others at Shawmut River, feminism was part of a wider array of destructive forces tearing at American life, even her own, Sharon said, pointing to problems in her own marriage. "*I* was the most important thing to me," she explained. "And I think that's what's happened. We've become most important to ourselves, and the children have suffered."

The Valentis, Keeners and Strongs all came to fundamentalist

Christianity while wrestling with problems in marriage and family life after having children. The challenges they faced had to do with learning not only how to get along with their spouses but also how to bear the kinds of sacrifices caring for children required. It is not surprising, then, that they were attracted to a faith so taken with articulating "God's plan for the family," set forth in scripture as a framework to deal with such issues. They had not turned to feminism.[4]

When I once asked Sharon how she had seen feminism during those years, in the 1970s, she wondered whether it had even existed at the time. For her it evidently had not. By now, she, Jean Strong and others at Shawmut River felt that feminism held particular dangers for them as women. As Sharon put it, "While God's word puts women on a pedestal, feminism brings women down to be walked on."

I wondered how to reconcile church women's hostility toward feminism with a pattern of change somewhat in keeping with feminist interests. Were the women of Shawmut River feminists in fact but not in name, as some suggested? If not, what differences were involved and how should we understand them? I also wondered how church members might apply the doctrine of submission to situations where husband and wife were locked in conflict. Did not the teaching that wives should be subject to their husbands in everything relegate women to subordinate and relatively powerless positions in their families and churches? Was fundamentalism, as some feminist writers interpreted it, an effort on the part of men to control women? If so, how could we understand the interests of women such as Jean Strong, Sharon Valenti and Sally Keener, who were all committed to fundamentalism and its Bible-based "plan for the family"?[5]

When I asked Jean and Phil how the Bible helped them approach conflicts in their own marriage, I was interested to see them give quite different answers. Phil held that they could turn to their pastor, who had time to "search the scriptures" to know "where the answer was in God's word." So definite and straightforward were these guidelines in scripture, he felt, that "even if a person has not received Christ, if they use the rules and the order which God set up, they will have a happy marriage."

"You'll find, though," Jean added, adopting a less straightforward approach, "that most mature Christians, when they argue, it's not something you can open the Bible and say, 'Okay, dear, God says this, and you said this, and I said this, so we'll have to do it this way.'" Phil peered at her quizzically. "The things that it's telling a married couple," Jean continued, "are very subtle. Ninety-nine percent of the time it is that you are out of fellowship with the Lord and it's something you have to deal with between you and Christ."

For Phil the matter came down to relying on the pastor to know where to find the answer in the Bible. But for Jean, very little seemed cut-and-dried. Mostly it had to do with being out of fellowship with Christ, or out of God's will, a far more ambiguous and indeterminable reality but, in their terms, the ultimate one. How was it determined, I wondered, whether someone—husband or wife, member or pastor— was outside God's will or not? Certainly, appeals to the Bible would be involved, but in fundamentalist Baptist churches like Shawmut River, it was the pastor who was seen to have the final say in how scripture should be interpreted. Yet even a pastor's authority—in principle absolute—was routinely challenged; look how often such congregations experience splits. How could any faction legitimately turn against its pastor? Before my research came to a close, I would have opportunities to find out.

6

Reckoning

Like Amway or anything . . .

I T WAS ONLY TWO MONTHS after first meeting Frank Valenti that
I had to present my initial findings to our seminar at Brown. Over
the past six months of field research, I had gathered the life stories of
thirty-four individuals and observed the activities of groups they were
involved with, including Shawmut River and the Fourniers' Holy
Family Academy around Worcester, Birthright and right-to-life chapters near me in the Connecticut River Valley and most recently a
group fighting sex education in the public schools of Athol, Massachusetts, a run-down mill town near the New Hampshire border.

Though the Athol group recognized their young people's needs for
information about sex—especially AIDS and other sexually transmitted diseases—they were pained by the values they saw embedded in the
curriculum developed for their schools, especially its nonjudgmental
attitude toward sex outside marriage and, even more so, the "values
clarification" approach to teaching morality underpinning it. That
approach, they felt, encouraged students to see values as things individuals chose from competing possibilities, rather than as unchanging
givens they needed to accept. In their view, it denied the existence of
moral absolutes.[1]

As I approached my presentation to our seminar, I decided to focus
on Shawmut River to raise some of the larger issues involved. As a
community enterprise, it demonstrated in a more immediately appre-
hensible way the sense I was making of popular support for new-right
politics. At the same time, the life stories of its members resembled in

important respects those I heard from other conservatives I interviewed. As I listened to their stories and observed events in their daily lives, I began to see how new-right politics, as well as fundamentalist Christianity, easily meshed with lives so different from my own.

Virtually all the conservatives I met (with some exceptions discussed below) spent their formative years into adulthood involved in a circle of relatives and family friends on whom they relied to meet day-to-day needs. Prominent among those needs were help with child care and with the profusion of loose ends that domestic life necessarily involves. For those in wage work or small business, help also included basic economic needs like roofing a house, fixing a car or providing money to meet household expenses. For those better off—like the family of a local banker or medical doctor—help also involved the advantages and amenities "good connections" can bring. But nothing promoted stronger bonds within these family circles than sharing the love and care of children across generations. And in all these helping and sharing relationships, reciprocity was the governing standard of conduct and the willingness "to oblige," the prevailing ethos.

At Shawmut River itself, extended-family ties were the building blocks of church life. The Valenti-Morse clan provided the engine for founding and building this pioneer church. Furthermore, family ties provided the chain of relationships along which conversion and recruitment traveled and the backbone, the tensile strength, of its core membership. Five family groups, including the Valentis, Strongs and Keeners, made up more than half of the church membership. And those three individual families alone made up half of Wednesday night's "old-home crowd." This pattern was similar to Jerry Falwell's church in its early days and was evident in what I casually picked up about other like-minded independent Baptist churches around the country. Not infrequently they could be found to be copastored by a father and son-in-law, or two brothers. The president of the Massachusett's chapter of the Moral Majority at the time, for example, shared the pastorate of his church with his father-in-law.

Shawmut River not only incorporated existing family ties but also gave family relationships a privileged place in its symbolic order. Members were fondly addressed as "Brother Dave" or "Aunt Margaret," and Pastor Valenti routinely paid deference to elders in the congregation by greeting them from the pulpit on a Sunday morning or by inviting their stamp of approval on an accepted truth. "Am I right or wrong, Granny?" he would often shoot from the pulpit to Sally Keener's grandmother in her customary pew.

Even for members without relatives in church, I was struck by how much their lives were anchored in such extended-family relationships. Most, even those without any relatives in church, were wage earners or small-business proprietors whose families were rooted in the area. If they attended college, it was usually a local college, and, while attending, they continued to live at home. The church's one educated professional at the time—apart from teachers and nurses—was a veterinarian who, after schooling at the University of Massachusetts in Amherst, had returned to Worcester to set up a practice in his hometown.[2]

Some church members, however, were not from the Worcester area or for some other reason were now removed from daily contact with their own families of origin. They included Scott and Sue Sanderson, Aunt Margaret, two families who had immigrated from Taiwan and Northern Ireland, respectively, and Anne Sullivan, a single mother on welfare who had fled an abusive marriage in a nearby city. For these members, Shawmut River's climate fostered the formation of new family-like ties of mutual dependence like those they had been accustomed to rely on in the past.

Anne Sullivan and her three children, for example, were taken under the wing of a middle-aged couple in church whom they came to call "Granny and Grandpa Harding." The Hardings helped care for Anne's children, bought them things they needed and took the family out to dinner. At the same time, these relationships were a "blessing" to the Hardings. Though they lived right next door to their own son and daughter-in-law, a family feud had alienated them, at least for the time being, from treasured relationships with their own grandchildren.

Like the Hardings, Aunt Margaret had grown up in Worcester but had experienced a breach in her family network. She had been very close to her mother until she passed away but had had no children of her own. Most of her siblings had moved away, and after her parents and husband had died, she had few relatives to turn to. It was a niece, however, who had first brought her to Shawmut River and introduced her simply as "my Aunt Margaret."

"Very pleased to meet you, Aunt Margaret," Margaret recalled Pastor Valenti responding, and the title had stuck ever since. When her niece had stopped attending, however, Margaret had had no way to get back and forth for services.

"So Dan Keener came over," Margaret recalled with glee about Dave Keener's brother, "and said to me, 'Can I take you home, Aunt Margaret?'

"Yeah, you can take me home. I'd *love* it. So going home, he says to me, 'I'm not going into the details, but I want to not just *call* you Aunt Margaret. I've decided I'm *adopting* you.' He let his mother and dad know," she continued, savoring every detail in the progression of their relationship, "and he brought his mother over one day, and so we were introduced. And they had me over to the house one time, too." A bachelor in his mid-thirties, Dan still lived with his parents.

Now and then Dan would give Aunt Margaret a bag of groceries or help her out in some way or other. Sally Keener remembered the time he gave her a whole bag of "goody-type things—little canned hams, special cheeses and crackers—things you wouldn't buy for yourself, only if company was coming. And she's like in her glory for two weeks," Sally recalled, smiling broadly. "She'd call him up and say, 'Guess what I'm eating tonight!'"

This was not done as charity, carrying the stigma of receiving help without giving in return. Instead, it was part of a personal relationship knit by a chain of reciprocities between Margaret and Dan—how family members were expected to act toward each other. When Dan did a short stint at Liberty Baptist College in Virginia, for instance, he rented a one-room apartment with shared bath for $100 a month and found himself, at times, he said, with "one-quarter of a tank of gas and half a box of noodles to eat." During this period, it was Aunt Margaret who sent him a little money to help out.

"I don't know how that woman survives," Sally observed, "but she would be the first one to give somebody money." As other students of reciprocity have noted, those who depend most on help from others are often quickest to give in the first place.[3]

Pastor Valenti referred to this creation of helping relationships within the church as "the third stage of church growth," when "people start doing things for other people." It was a feature of the church that Phil and Jean Strong first attended in Florida. The pastor and his wife didn't "counsel us," Jean said, correcting my language. "They adopted us." Through "adoptions" like those between Aunt Margaret and Dan Keener, between the Sandersons and Keeners, and Anne Sullivan and the Hardings, Shawmut River helped repair and patch up a life of mutual dependence that members were accustomed to in their own family circles. These adoptions, or "fictive kinships" as sociologists sometimes call them, flourished in Shawmut River's villagelike atmosphere, where existing kinship ties were present and recognized, where the idiom of kinship reigned, and where the willingness to oblige and to think of "others" before "self" was seen as an absolute issuing from the very word of God.[4]

For their part, Dave and Sally Keener could rely on either set of their parents to help care for their children, or on Granny Gund (Sally's grandmother) and her two unmarried daughters living with her (Sally's aunts). This was part of the Keeners' ongoing round of social interaction. "I spend half my time at my relatives'," Sally told me. "We go there for supper a couple of nights a week." Sometimes Granny Gund would simply insist on taking their children for the day just to have them around.

Granny Gund was a huge woman in her early seventies who suffered from emphysema and heart ailments and wheezed uncomfortably when she walked. Her imperious manner made her known affectionately among her relatives for being able to "drive you nuts," as Sally put it. Still, Sally and Dave felt obliged to take her out shopping and on other outings. Then one day they would drop by her house, Sally reported, and Granny would say, "I just bought you a twenty-five-inch console TV," or, when she knew their car was failing, "Take my car. You drive it for a while. If I want it, I'll call you back." She beamed to report these reciprocities as if they were the fulfillment of what good living was all about.

Shawmut River invested such giving and the sacrifices it involved with sacred meaning: God wants you to give to those in need, even when it involves sacrificing self. They believed God would particularly bless the sacrificial giver, one who gives even when it hurts, and regaled one another with stories about how, after they made such sacrifices, God saw to it that their own particular needs were met through someone else's benevolence. Self-sacrifice was a virtue that gave expression to the predictable logic of life: Giving was, through reciprocity and God's almighty hand, a reliable way to meet needs and find fulfillment in life.

Dave and Sally Keener, even with their scant income, were particularly joyful givers. Sally claimed Dave was "forever giving our last five dollars" to a single mother they knew who did not have enough to eat, even though the Keeners themselves needed the money for groceries.

"Then somebody will turn around and give us a bag of groceries or a check," Sally said. "It works out that way."

Though a life of mutual dependence within a family circle was commonplace among members of Shawmut River and other new-right activists I met, it was foreign to people I knew in academia and the New Left, as well as to other educated professionals I knew. Most of us were prepared, from the moment we left home for college, to leave family dependencies behind and learn to live as self-governing individuals. This left us free to move from one city to another for graduate education or for those specialized jobs for which our training qualified us. In the process, we learned to piece together a meaningful life with new friends and colleagues alongside old ones. Our material security did not rest on a stream of daily reciprocities within a family-based circle of people known in common but rather on the progression of professional careers, with steadily increasing salaries and ample benefits to cover whatever exigencies life would bring.

These contrasting patterns of family life between my progressive friends and colleagues, on the one hand, and conservatives I met, on the other, encouraged me to consider new-right politics against the background of lives that worked quite differently from my own. If Shawmut River was busy repairing and infusing with sacred meaning a life lived through family obligations, what could be gained by looking at new-right enthusiasms as an effort to defend and strengthen such a life?

This perspective helps resolve some of the puzzles new-right politics pose to outsiders. For instance, considering Sally's readiness to give, it seemed incongruous that she was so hostile to public welfare. "I don't have any sympathy for people on welfare," she told me. "I think you should earn what you get." She felt only the disabled should qualify. Like other conservatives I spoke with, Sally objected to social programs where benefits were, as Sharon Valenti put it, "just handed over without any cost." That is, where benefits were given solely on the basis of an individual's right with no obligations attached.[5]

This vantage point might even help us understand the familiar charge that conservatives like Sally or Sharon frequently make: that Ted Kennedy (or some other liberal Democrat) is a "communist" and that "communism is undermining the moral fiber of American life." This was the kind of statement that might prompt us, as it did the historian Richard Hofstadter, to judge right-wing conservatives to be paranoid.[6]

But is it so irrational to think that people's greater reliance on government programs—the liberal Democrats' vision—might weaken their need to rely on other means to survive, like family? Is it not the expectation, as with Aunt Margaret, that you will eventually need help from others that compels people to sacrifice to help others out in the first place? Therefore, would not people's fuller dependence on a safety net of government programs threaten to dissolve some of the underpinnings of reciprocal obligation—or the "moral fiber" of American life, as such citizens experience it? Furthermore, recognizing that by "communism" many Americans mean, at least since the Bolshevik Revolution, the full-scale bureaucratization of society under a centralized state, can't we appreciate how someone like Sally Keener might see the vision of growing state welfare as a kind of "communism" bound to undermine the moral foundations of her way of life? In such ways, seeing conservative politics through the lens of life lived through family obligations governed by reciprocity helps make sense of conservative statements we might otherwise dismiss as paranoid or irrational.[7]

Or consider another puzzle new-right enthusiasms pose to liberals: that conservatives oppose abortion as murder yet support militarism. Liberals often see this pairing as evidence of conservatives' wanton hypocrisy or, at best, hopeless illogic. "Their so-called pro-life argument," one scholar charged, reflecting a commonly held view, "is deeply compromised by staunch support for increased military spending and for the death penalty. It seems clear that their pro-life position is not a consistent theological or philosophical stand."[8] (By the same token, conservatives I met seized upon the hypocrisy they saw in liberals' crusade to "save the whales" while championing the right to "kill babies.")

However, seeing right to life and militarism through the lens of a life lived through reciprocities within a family circle shows how extraordinarily consistent they are, for both express family-like obligations of an ultimate kind: for men, to take up arms and even sacrifice their lives to defend women and children; and for women, to risk their lives to bear and care for children and other dependents. In these idealizations, stirring the highest passions, family obligations appear as matters *not* of *choice*, but of unquestionable *duty*.[9]

That opposition to abortion aims to uphold the broader obligation to care for dependents in the family is seen in how readily right-to-lifers slide from one to the other in their political rhetoric. "If life isn't safe in the womb," they would typically say, "it isn't safe in the nursing home." Sally Keener, along with others at Shawmut River, was adamant about caring for older family members. Having worked in nursing homes, she was greatly upset to see people "dump off their relatives" there. If Granny Gund became bedridden, she said, "I would feel obligated to quit my job and take care of her. I would *never* put her in a nursing home."

Similarly, having antiwar activists refuse to bear arms because they disapprove of a particular war, or of war in general, makes men's obligation to protect women and children a matter of choice, not unquestionable duty. (This would be so even for a war like Vietnam, which conservatives I met often saw as senseless.) From this perspective, any contradiction between opposing abortion and supporting militarism melts away. Instead, they appear as part of the same vision of what life is all about: men and women being willing to sacrifice self for the larger good in ways defined by traditional gender roles in the family. In this vision, family obligations are cast in terms of sharply differentiated gender roles felt to express essential differences between women and men. To deny these obligations or these roles—or the essentialist views of gender underpinning them—means for many conservatives the dissolution of the family and the consequent collapse of civilization as they know it.

However sensible it was to see new-right politics in these terms, supporters themselves were not apt to interpret their politics in this way. They spoke simply of defending "the family" or fighting for "traditional family values" against, for example, the "do-your-own-thing mentality" of the sixties or "antifamily" forces they saw arrayed against them. This was so, I came to believe, because they took extended-family ties so much for granted that they could not imagine life without them. When I told members of Shawmut River that I was interested to see that family groups were the building blocks of their congregation, they would say things such as "Any fundamental church would be that way."

"It's like Amway or anything," Sharon's stepfather, Tom Morse, replied simply. "The first thing you do is get your family involved." So much did he consider a wider family circle the natural foundation of *anything* you might organize, including the remarkable marketing success of Amway.

The taken-for-grantedness of our own pattern of family life makes it a faulty lens through which to perceive the actions of others. The misperceptions it creates occur in both directions between conservatives and liberals in American life. When I mentioned to Sharon that some mainline Protestant churches I knew were not made up of larger family groups, she concluded that their faith must not matter that much to them. Otherwise, she assumed, they would have brought their wider families along.

And one day, several months into my fieldwork, Pastor Valenti turned abruptly to me and asked in puzzlement, "Where *do* you live out there in Northampton, anyway? You're still at home, aren't you?" He meant with my parents. Even though I had told him on more than one occasion that my parents lived in Pittsburgh, Pennsylvania, he could not help but imagine that, since I was not married, I would still be "at home." In fact, as I looked around, I realized that virtually all the unmarried men and women at Shawmut River—even those, like Dan Keener, who were well into their thirties—still lived "at home."

By contrast, by the time my friends and colleagues and I married—even if just out of college—we generally had established ourselves as independent individuals removed from daily cooperation with parents and other relatives. Rather than conform to an existing moral code shared by our elders, to whom we were bound in daily cooperation, we were encouraged and needed to fashion our own moralities within an environment where diverse and unreconciled ones jostled uneasily with each other and in which perhaps the only standard we might readily share was mutual tolerance for different values. We did not choose to be moral relativists; the lives we lived, in some sense, required it.

At the same time, when professional people like us married, we were free to explore a realm of intimacy—of couple privacy—unhindered by day-to-day involvements with our families of origin. My women friends and colleagues would never have found themselves several years and two children into a marriage lamenting, "I want my mom!" as Sharon did upon moving to Lynchburg. Or, like Jean Strong, after several years of marriage, finding it necessary to learn how to talk with Phil by *interviewing* him. Similarly, no one I knew began married life living under the roof of one set of parents or the other, as many at Shawmut River did, including both the Sandersons and Keeners.

At the same time, the unrestrained privacy and greater intimacy of our marriages carried their own particular strains, including the social isolation of housewives bearing the relentless responsibilities for child care and housework. These strains fueled our criticisms of traditional gender roles in the family and prompted numerous adaptations to relieve them, including our interest in a wife's work outside the home as something good in and of itself, our explorations of communal living and our reliance on "support" or "consciousness-raising" groups to help bridge the gap between public and private. A touchstone of the feminist critique of the family in the 1960s and 1970s was that because women were socially isolated in the private sphere of family life, they were removed from the discourses and power structures of public life.

But the role of housewife and mother did not isolate the women of Shawmut River socially. Instead, it bound them in cooperative relations with women relatives—cross-generational groups in which their common identity as women was collectively fashioned. That identity emerged in a world separate from men's, in which women as well as men appeared as distinctly different creatures, as "fractions with different denominators," as Jean Strong put it. These were some of the reasons, I had argued in my doctoral dissertation, why sixties feminism, which defined itself in terms of its critique of the family, had arisen and flourished among college-educated, professional women, rather than among working-class women or women of color. Wherever extended-family ties were vital, I proposed, much of that critique might assume less relevance and be felt even to undermine women's interests.[10]

Day-to-day cooperation among women relatives naturally involved different households in one another's business and made it people's business to know much more about one another's affairs than I or my colleagues would tolerate. These radically different standards of privacy came home to me in a story told by Sharon's sister-in-law Judy Waters about her experience in the 1970s at Baptist Bible College in Springfield, Missouri, Jerry Falwell's alma mater and the flagship school of the Baptist Bible Fellowship. Her husband was attending classes at the time, and Judy was at home with their one child. Each week a member of the faculty would stop by their apartment for a visit, Judy recalled, sometimes unannounced, just to see that everything was all right, including their marriage and her housekeeping. Judy did not find this inappropriate, even at a time when students at other colleges and universities across the nation were busy overthrowing the last vestiges of in loco parentis rules, permitting them to do almost anything they wanted to in their own private space.

These contrasting sensibilities of public and private, I came to see, were one reason why some people felt immediately "at home" when they first attended Shawmut River, even if raised in quite different churches or no church at all. Its villagelike atmosphere was simply an extension of the kind of sociability prevailing in their own family circles, within which the personal was readily aired, people stood ready to "oblige" and relationships were seen and acted upon as *given* rather than *chosen*. Members were immediately comfortable with and enjoyed the familiar, down-home atmosphere of worship at Shawmut River, where a stranger needed to be introduced, where someone openly asked for prayer for a troubled marriage, or where a pastor joked about his mother-in-law. While my colleagues and I might cringe at such violations of our own sense of privacy and propriety, members of Shawmut River saw the reserve and discretion of local mainline churches they had visited in the course of their spiritual search as "cold" and "unfriendly."[11]

This mirroring of misperception was something I became quite familiar with over the years. For the members of mainline Protestant churches were not, by and large, cold and unfriendly. Rather, their formality and reserve served, partly at least, to protect individuals' privacy, permitting them to *choose* rather than simply *accept* whom they might get to know. You choose friends, not family.

Misperceptions of this kind often leave people unable to truly comprehend what their opponents are saying. During a debate over sex education at an open meeting of the school board of Athol, Massachusetts, for example, a well-dressed man rose to say he had read the disputed textbook proposed for this sex education curriculum three times and did not find anything objectionable in it. It did not push *any* particular values, he said quite matter-of-factly. "It lets individuals come up with their own." It did not occur to him that seeing values as something individuals "come up with" on their own rather than *accept* as given—whether by parents, natural law or God's word—was *itself* a moral position. He was unwittingly giving expression to the very "moral relativism" conservatives around him were contesting. Such utterances were the kind Sharon Valenti had in mind when she said she could quickly identify a secular humanist by some remark that inadvertently revealed that he or she did not believe in absolutes.

IN MY TALK TO OUR SEMINAR, I did not set forth this interpretation of new-right politics in explicit terms or unravel any of the puzzles it allowed. Instead, I limited myself to describing what a fundamentalist church like Shawmut River did for its members as a first step toward understanding why churches like it have consistently supported conservative politics of this kind.

My reluctance to present this interpretation stemmed partly from my awareness that things were not as clear cut or straightforward as this. In any case, I was not trying to explain why this or that individual was moved to new-right activism. Too many particularities of temperament, life story and historical context would necessarily be involved to reduce political action to sociological factors of this kind. Instead, I was trying to account for the broad pattern of support for conservative versus liberal politics of the family across the American class structure and American public by employing these contrasting types of family life. Why some supporters get mobilized into political action and others not, and what conservative politicians make of this base of potential support, each with his or her own purposes and values, were different matters altogether. In addition, I wanted to show how these contrasting types help us interpret the meaning of conservative pro-family politics by permitting us, for instance, to see coherence where we might otherwise see contradiction.[12]

But my hesitation to present this interpretation arose, in part, from the life stories of a significant minority of new-right activists I met who had *not* grown up in circles of cooperating kin but ended up living within them. The fact that these included some of the most outspoken leaders of groups I observed was even more intriguing.

Jean Strong, for example, told me that her mother, because of her mental afflictions, had cut off her family's contacts with relatives nearby. Only by retreating to work as a live-in governess in another family had Jean experienced a model of what she took to be normal family life. Eventually she became an active participant in Phil's sprawling family network and in the life of fundamentalist congregations in Florida and Massachusetts. She nevertheless remained involved with her own family, taking a divorced niece under her wing, for example, and helping her father manage being back in his home after a hospital stay.

For different reasons, Sharon's mother, Ada, in fleeing a marriage of thirteen years, had left her family circle in her hometown in Indiana. She went to Washington, D. C., to join her brother and his family, on whom she had to depend more fully. Ada looked back on those as hard years. She had, I could see, all the more faithfully fostered and maintained ties of daily cooperation with her own daughters and even her former daughter-in-law, Judy Waters. Though Judy had been divorced from Ada's son for some time, she and her teenage daughter remained actively involved in the Valenti-Morse family circle. She was a founding member of Shawmut River and now taught in its Christian Academy.

But the most striking evidence of weak extended-family ties came from three leaders of a nearby chapter of Birthright, an antiabortion counseling organization for pregnant women served by about sixty volunteers, mostly women. These three leaders were praised by their followers, above all, for their ability to "say what I feel," as one volunteer put it. Two of them, the chapter's codirectors, were Irish Catholic nurses who had grown up in families with few relatives at hand. They both had then settled into the orbit of their husbands' extended families. At first they had resented their in-laws' intrusions into their domestic affairs, though they appreciated the help they received with child care. But overall, they felt it was good for their children to be part of such large, close families. "I realized what I had missed," one said.

The last of these three Birthright leaders, also a nurse, had grown up in an upwardly mobile family who had moved to a wealthy suburb of Boston, where her father taught in the public schools. She and her husband had similar backgrounds, she said. Each had grown up an only child and attended an Ivy League college. They had met in Boston, where she was training to become a nurse and he a physician. After marrying they had returned to his hometown, where he had always planned to build a private practice. "It was like walking into an enclave of people all looking at you under a microscope," she told me about settling into her husband's family circle. She recalled, in particular, being pained by her mother-in-law's habit of dropping by unannounced and commenting on her housekeeping or on her daughter's dirty fingernails. She eventually acclimated herself to this new life (after insisting her in-laws phone before dropping by) and summed up the experience warmly, like her two colleagues, by saying, "I felt I had come home."

I was struck by how many women leaders in Birthright and Shawmut River had experienced extended-family life as problematic in one way or another early in life—it was either cut off or never really present—before settling into their husbands' kin networks and building strong local ties with their own daughters. It was no wonder, then, that they more readily noticed and could more easily articulate what their followers took for granted: that "family life" of this kind could *not* be taken for granted but was under attack. It was threatened by a number of forces they saw tearing at it, including individuals' desire for upward mobility, the "do-your-own-thing mentality" of the sixties, the "welfare mentality" that individuals have a naked right to social support, and abortion and the "contraceptive mentality," which separated "sexual pleasure" from "sexual responsibility," as one of these Birthright leaders put it. "You're just breaking down society," she said, summing up the consequences of these forces, "and we don't seem to know how to stop that." She likened herself and her Birthright colleagues to the "last centurions holding back the barbarians—we're the only ones who see what's going on!"[13]

This pattern in leaders' lives pointed to something I had begun to think about new-right conservatism as a whole. If seen as an effort to defend and strengthen relations of mutual obligation in family circles, it would be called for only where such a life was undermined or threatened, yet still alive and relevant. This might be the case for rural or small-town migrants to a modern city, or for residents of a small town or rural hamlet overrun by the suburban sprawl of a growing metropolis. But it would not be so for, say, a rural community untouched by forces of urbanization.[14]

Later in my research, I met a young anthropologist who had just completed fieldwork in a rural white community in South Carolina, where a family-based economy was still so strong that land changed hands largely outside the marketplace, through family ties. She noticed that members of the Southern Baptist church in this community had so little comprehension of the conflicts then raging between liberals and conservatives in the Southern Baptist Convention that they had to have a special representative sent out from the convention to explain it to them. Where mutual dependence among kin was not threatened, new-right enthusiasms might not only hold little interest but even be incomprehensible.[15]

This perspective would also help us better understand fundamentalism's distinct historic trajectory, from its origins at the end of the nineteenth century in metropolitan centers such as New York, Boston, Los Angeles and Chicago, where the impersonal urbanity and individualism of the new industrial order first took told and to which rural migrants to those cities had to adapt. Boston's Tremont Temple, for example, a premier church of the emerging fundamentalist movement at the turn of that century, found a majority of its members among migrants to the city from the maritime provinces of Canada and rural New England.[16]

Only later did fundamentalism spread more widely and eventually reach the South. In the early twentieth century, it found little support in that most rural region of the United States. The South's principal fundamentalist at the time, Frank Norris, a man with rural roots in Alabama and Texas, ended up dividing his ministry between congregations in Fort Worth, Texas, then a booming cow-town-turned-city of one hundred thousand, and Detroit, Michigan, where his Temple Baptist Church was made up largely of southern migrants to the growing automobile industry.[17] A generation later, however, in the economic boom following World War Two, new fundamentalist centers sprang up along the rim of New South cities: in Virginia Beach, where Pat Robertson developed his charismatic Christian Broadcasting Network; in Charlotte, North Carolina, where Jim and Tammy Bakker established theirs; and in Lynchburg, Virginia, where Jerry Falwell planted his.

Falwell's church in Lynchburg, according to Frances FitzGerald, was made up of "the cusp of the new middle class," migrating from more humble origins in the countryside and small towns of southern Virginia and West Virginia (not unlike Boston's Tremont Temple three generations before).[18] For such people, fundamentalist congregations, with their folksy ambience, might help patch up and reinforce the sagging foundations of the kin-based dependencies on which members were accustomed to rely.

From these centers in the New South, fundamentalist and charismatic ministries spread in the latter decades of the twentieth century to receptive constituents in the Midwest, West and Northeast, part of a process social commentators would eventually refer to as the "southernization of America."[19] In this context of social transformation fueled by postwar economic growth and the spread of higher education and professional employment, we might better appreciate how a relatively obscure strand of southern fundamentalism—the Baptist Bible Fellowship split-off from Frank Norris's association—might connect with popular political impulses across the nation in defense of family and tradition.

In an early and influential article, Richard Niebuhr, dean of American religious studies, interpreted American fundamentalism as a movement "closely related to the conflict between rural and urban cultures," a movement he found most prevalent in "isolated communities . . . least subject to the influence of modern science and industrial civilization." Revisionist scholars criticized Niebuhr's view, pointing out, rightly, that fundamentalism first arose in cities. But if we consider fundamentalism as a defense of a rural *way* of life, a life organized in family-based networks of mutual dependence, whether in city, town or countryside, would not such a defense arise only where it was eroded and threatened—first, among rural and small-town migrants to the new urban centers of industrial society on the threshold of the twentieth century, and then, two generations later, in the burgeoning cities of the New South and, in the case of Shawmut River, in rural and small-town communities overrun by the suburban expansion of Worcester in the 1960s and 1970s?[20]

THESE COMPLICATIONS and considerations were more than I was prepared to set forth in our seminar at Brown University that afternoon. I limited myself to describing what I had witnessed up to then: the all-encompassing nature of congregational life at Shawmut River, the way its cohesion was strengthened by the barriers to outsiders posed by abstinence and witnessing, how its fellowship was made up of extended-family ties that set its personal, down-home tone and how its pervasive biblical discourses were preoccupied, above all, with regulating family life, especially marriage.[21]

But what guidelines did the Bible specify for marriage and family life? Given the range of meanings and the inconsistencies, ambiguities and contradictions the Bible might hold, as I saw it, how did fundamentalists arrive at relatively stable and uniform understandings of scripture's implications for family life? Fundamentalists insist, of course, that, if it is read correctly—that is, by a born-again believer guided by the Holy Spirit—contradictions and ambiguities cannot occur. But, I suggested to our seminar, members of Shawmut River had not generally learned that a husband was head of the family or that a wife's place was in the home or that homosexuality was wrong by reading the Bible. Though their Bible-based faith provided new meanings for these moral standards, they were notions they, for the most part, already held through tradition. Sharon Valenti told me, for example, that the Bible had given her the "why" for the morality her mother had taught her growing up. And looking back on my several years at Shawmut River, I never heard anyone cite scripture, for instance, to justify the traditional division of labor in the home. In fact, when the fundamentalist author Tim LaHaye in his book *The Battle for the Family* asserts the divinely ordained nature of those arrangements, he relies not on the Bible—which he otherwise cites profusely—but on a history of nineteenth-century America by the liberal scholar Carl Degler.[22]

As others have pointed out, the model of family life that conservative Protestants generally hold up as "traditional" harks back to nineteenth-century ideals. But, at the same time, I suggested, the traditional order of family life that church members held was not static. Like all traditional orders it was continually changing, though it disguised change to preserve the sense that its moral rules were timeless, unchanging and divinely ordained (see chapter 13). Among the specific changes encouraged by Shawmut River and churches like it, none was more striking than the effort to focus husbands more on family responsibilities, to encourage them, as Sharon Valenti saw it, to become "less self-centered and more God-centered" and to become "softer, more affectionate and more loving." At the same time, the doctrine of submission, which required men to sacrifice themselves for their families as Christ did for the church, also incorporated long-standing masculine ideals requiring men, as a condition of male honor, to sacrifice even their lives to defend their families.

Shawmut River also pressed men to take on church responsibilities, a departure from men's traditional aloofness from church life. At the close of the last hymn during one Sunday service, for example, Pastor Valenti asked all "the ladies" to sit down and leave the men standing. "Where in the church today in America do you see so many men?" he asked. "On Sunday morning most churches across America today are filled with women." Valenti's approach to these gender issues was very much in keeping with the style of Frank Norris, a forebear of Shawmut

River's fundamentalism, and Billy Sunday, the baseball-player-turned-evangelist, who railed against "sissified Christianity" and declared, "The manliest man is the man who will acknowledge Jesus Christ." Valenti saw Shawmut River championing a muscular Christianity capable of attracting men, even though a majority of the adults in its pews were women.[23]

In asking who was responsible for shaping the ongoing changes in tradition, I said it was tempting to look to the pastor, who in such churches enjoys the kind of unlimited authority outsiders are apt to deride as dictatorial. But pastors of independent churches like Shawmut River depend on attracting and holding a flock, I pointed out. To build Shawmut River, Frank Valenti had to depend on his wider family circle, and if he did not preach what his followers expected to hear, would they not simply withdraw their financial support or leave? The split that had occurred last spring had left the church in a precarious financial situation. If even two or three big givers—or simply the whole "Strong clan"—were to leave, might it not be difficult to survive?

I went on to suggest the importance of women's discourse in shaping the ongoing changes in traditional moralities of family life, in part because domestic life was seen, in the traditional view, as women's business.[24] Women's discourse took place in sex-segregated groups such as the Joy Circle, in which Jean Strong first learned what submission in marriage meant, and the women's Bible study Sharon led at Shawmut River. More important, perhaps, it took place informally in Jean's relationship with Grandma Mosher in Florida, for example, or, at Shawmut River, when church women gathered in the nursery or Jean's kitchen or spoke by phone on the church's prayer chain. At a deeper level, this exclusive domain of women's discourse at Shawmut River had grown up within, and been modeled on, patterns of daily cooperation and communication among women relatives defined by traditional gender roles in the family. It existed, I pointed out, "not despite the traditional family, but in and through it; not by challenging traditional gender roles, but by subscribing to them." In this way, I suggested, we might begin to understand conservative women's insistent defense of traditional gender roles in the family and their opposition to modern feminism's critique of those roles.[25]

My presentation to our seminar was politely but not enthusiastically received. Making sense of why some women do not identify with feminism and, instead, affirm traditional gender roles has not always been something feminist scholars have been happy to consider.[26] During the seminar discussion following my talk, I answered one question by referring to the presence of kin in church members' lives.

"What kin?" one senior colleague asked disbelievingly. At first I wondered whether her question showed how little legitimacy my observations now carried in our group. But then I realized how difficult it was for the kind of family life I witnessed at Shawmut River to show up at all on the radar screens of academic intellectuals. After all, in one study of American society that more recently captured the intelligentsia's attention about the state of the nation—Robert Putnam's *Bowling Alone*—the sort of life I observed at Shawmut River had not been taken into account at all in the author's analysis of Americans' relative degree of community engagement or social isolation. By Putnam's standards of measurement—that participating in voluntary associations represents community engagement—the members of Shawmut River, who were so taken up with day-to-day family involvements that they rarely participated in voluntary associations, would appear to be more individualistic or socially isolated than the classic suburban housewife volunteering for this and that simply to enjoy some adult company during her day.[27]

Family life, where we come to and depart from waking consciousness each day, is perhaps the most stubbornly taken-for-granted social reality we experience. Witness Pastor Valenti's assumption that if I was not yet married I must still be living at home. Patterns of family life shape our perceptions of the world and of issues arising in public life in ways that are enormously difficult to notice or control. Perhaps this is why it has been the sociology of the family, as opposed to other areas of study, that sociologists have continued to criticize for being unduly skewed toward middle-class experience. Even though ethnographic studies of family life outside the white professional middle class routinely reveal the presence of kin-based networks in the lives of many Americans, these realities have difficulty finding any secure place to lodge in academic intellectuals' perceptions of the world around them. Instead, looking at the world through their own assumptions about family life easily leads them to misread contrary realities staring them in the face.[28]

For example, though studies of poor African-Americans have shown that networks of kin sharing parenting responsibilities and household resources are key to their survival, these realities are overlooked even in much-praised portrayals of that world, such as Bill Moyers' award-winning documentary on poor black teenage mothers entitled *The Vanishing Family*. As an example of the frightening trend this film aimed to explore—that "single women and the children they're raising alone are the fastest-growing part of the black population"—Moyers and his producer presented the case of a teenage mother, pictured sitting with her baby and her own mother, age thirty-four, on the stoop of the house where they all lived together. Moyers and his producers, and media professionals praising the film, could simply not "see" the teenage mother and her own mother as *coparents* raising a child *together*, and with such collective misperceptions, the African-American family, with all its strength *across* generations, had, indeed, vanished from sight.[29]

PART TWO

7

Spring

How gossip sometimes overpowers reality . . .

MAY SPREAD an iridescent blanket of green buds across New England's winter-worn landscape as our seminar, along with the academic year, drew to a close. On Wednesday evenings, Shawmut River's two dozen teenagers, who met separately during that weekday service, now spilled out onto the large field adjacent to the church for a lazy game of softball in the twilight. As Pastor Valenti promised all newcomers, I began to feel more at home, especially in the place I found next to Aunt Margaret, Dan Keener and another bachelor in the last pew on the right—which I soon nicknamed, much to Aunt Margaret's amusement, "the oddball pew."

My position at Smith College had ended, and no teaching job had materialized for the coming fall. I still held a small grant from the American Council of Learned Societies to continue my research. I felt it had only begun at Shawmut River, yet held promise. The Moral Majority had become a household word across America, coming to stand in the public mind for the conservative pro-family movement as a whole. And in the televised debates accompanying the 1984 presidential election that year, which saw Ronald Reagan and George Bush (the senior) soundly defeat Walter Mondale and Geraldine Ferraro, Jerry Falwell was mentioned more than any other public figure.

Meanwhile, public attention was becoming increasingly fixed, through the media's selective eye, on the burgeoning empires of television evangelists, summoning up terrifying and often wildly inflated images of TV evangelists who seemed able, by means of power and wealth, to raise up armies to march in lockstep conformity to the battle lines or polling places. Such images arose in an intellectual universe unable to comprehend how masses of ordinary, otherwise sensible Americans would embrace new-right enthusiasms without being influenced by some powerful *external* force.

Yet it was ironic to note that Reverend Valenti and other pastors saw televangelists as "parasitic" on their local churches. Valenti himself routinely criticized TV evangelists for "spreading false doctrines," as he put it to his flock one Sunday. While some members might tune in occasionally—and a few regularly—to Falwell's or Chuck Swindoll's show or occasionally send a small check to one of their ministries, they were not avid or uncritical viewers. Moreover, they did not take political direction from them. Several I spoke with, including some core members, were not even familiar with the term *Moral Majority*, even though their own pastor served as vice president of the Massachusetts chapter of this most influential and highly publicized new-right organization at the time.

When I once used the term *New Right* in conversation with Sally Keener, for instance, she asked what it meant. "I don't ever watch TV or read the paper," she explained matter-of-factly. I said that journalists had coined the term to refer to the kind of politics Pastor Valenti put forward. She thought for a moment, then mused, "So wouldn't the New Right just be the old way that's been sort of tossed aside, forgotten?" For her, like other traditionally minded people, the good and the true were simply "the old way." She felt it had been not simply lost but "tossed aside," casually rejected, without much thought, consideration or respect.[1]

In fact, the Moral Majority itself, rather than being a powerful machine able to galvanize its members behind certain candidates or causes, represented little more than a loose network of like-minded pastors who kept one another abreast of relevant issues. Like the Baptist Bible Fellowship, it had no effective way to discipline chapters or indoctrinate members. Local autonomy and informal authority held sway.

The political outlook of Shawmut River's members was not created by TV evangelists or any other external force, though it might be refined or embellished here and there by the teachings of ideological leaders on local and national levels. Pastor Valenti, for instance, had a particular passion for preaching about evolution and the scientific basis of creationism, which received renewed interest during this period with the popular acceptance among conservatives of the Noachian flood theory claiming the world to be much younger than scientists believed.[2] "Science verifies the fact that the world can be no more than ten thousand years old," Valenti now preached to his flock, and creationism, he once told me, had been a major reason for his starting a church. While creationist teachings were new to many church members—and the veterinarian in the congregation disagreed with them—members' politics about family and gender grew more naturally in the soil of their traditionalism, nourished by patterns of extended-family life across generations.

Instead of fixing attention on television evangelists, I believed more accurate light could be shed on the new Christian right by portraying the inner life of one of the thousands of rank-and-file congregations, like Shawmut River, that had made Christian fundamentalism a popular and enduring feature of American life. This might be even more effective, I imagined, in a documentary film. Besides making vividly present the texture, feel and substance of its all-encompassing community life and its vital role in members' daily lives, it could make visible the kind of extended-family life that, however invisible and unreal it might seem to scholars, provided the social world in which fundamentalism and new-right enthusiasms flourished and had their meaning. Though always interested in film, I had no experience in making films of any kind and no idea where to begin. In any case, I knew I had to return to Shawmut River after presenting my talk at Brown. I had said I would.

Sunday Morning Worship
May 1

After the opening hymn, Pastor Valenti asked Brother Bill Tatum to come up and lead us in prayer. A young man with sandy hair, Tatum had come to Shawmut River with his family only five months before from Lynchburg, Virginia, to become principal of its Christian Academy. He had recently earned a master's degree in Christian education from Falwell's Liberty Baptist Seminary, and the Valentis had felt his degree would, among other things, add legitimacy to the academy's precarious accreditation in the eyes of state officials. This expectation may have heightened the disappointment Bill's accent and ungrammatical colloquialisms caused, especially among those set on correct speech, such as Sharon's father, Tom Morse.

As Bill reached the lectern, he turned to Frank and said in his Appalachian-colored Pittsburgh accent, "Hope you don't mind my white shoes." (He had on white patent-leather loafers.)

"I wouldn't have asked you if I had known," Frank moaned, rolling his eyes and laughing.

"They're imported from Virginia," Bill said, smiling with a take-me-on attitude that had a little edge to it.

At the evening service later that day Frank announced that a new "ladies' Bible-study group" would begin meeting, a "growth group" to be led by Sharon. "We're lucky to have someone who loves to teach and doesn't like gossip," he added emphatically. "Aren't I right, Ada?"

"Boring!" his mother-in-law groaned with laughter from her seat.

Frank returned to the subject of gossip during his message that evening. Taking his point of departure from a slim reference to "false reports" in chapter 6 of Nehemiah, he went so far as to offer his flock practical advice for how to combat gossip. "Try this," he suggested half jokingly. "Let them get halfway through—up to then you get all the good stuff—then ask, 'Did you talk with the person you're talking about?'"

He turned his body to play the other part in this imagined dialogue and gave a sheepish look. "Uh . . . no . . . I . . . uh . . . well, *I* got it from a reputable source, and *he* got it from a reputable source and *he* got it from *her*, and you know *she* wouldn't lie!" People laughed.

"Then," Frank proposed in dead-serious tones, "ask them to go with you and talk with that person. And make sure they don't swear you to secrecy either! In the case of gossip, silence is *not* golden; it's a wicked device of the devil!" This was not lighthearted commentary. I should have known then that conflicts were afoot, but I had not yet learned how to read the signs.

Gossip was a recurring theme at Shawmut River and churches like it. One independent Baptist church I visited at the time devoted the lead article in its newsletter to "gossip," and a picture of fundamentalist demonstrators accompanying a *New York Times* article showed them holding a sign that listed among familiar "evils," such as "homosexuality," "liberalism" and "immorality," that of "gossip." Sharon pointed out that gossip was listed in Proverbs 6 as one of the seven things God hates, chiefly because it is talk that, by its very nature, resists accountability.

"Most pastors," Frank Valenti once told me, "will not deal with gossip the way it oughta be dealt with—harshly. You deal with gossip in any other way than but stern, quick and whatever else you wanna call it, and you're a fool." In his mind, too, there was no doubt that in such congregations gossip was seen as a deadly serious thing.

Two weeks after Frank's preaching on gossip, his father-in-law, Tom Morse, opened Wednesday-night service in prayer by asking God to "bring your wrath on those attacking your fort here at Shawmut River. You have some warriors here who need strengthening." The image of an embattled garrison was ominous. Who was attacking Shawmut River? I thought Tom might be referring to the church's on-going feud with local town officials. Sharon traced this conflict back to a leaflet they had distributed to promote the opening of their Christian Academy. Titled "Why Johnny Can't Read," it criticized the quality of local public schools. But the freshest source of conflict with town officials was Frank's refusal to get an occupancy permit for the church's newly completed gymnatorium. The state had no right, he argued, to control the existence of God's church in such ways. Tensions had climaxed not long before I arrived on the scene, when a fleet of police cars had descended on Shawmut River one day and a building inspector had slapped the church with a number of building code violation citations.

Given these conflicts, I was surprised, then, when Frank came to the podium later that evening and announced that he had had "to relieve Bill Tatum of his position as principal of the school. We tried to be equitable," he said, speaking with a brusque casualness that betrayed some defensiveness. He then put off any further discussion of the matter. But the following Sunday he announced there would be a church meeting right after morning worship.

The meeting had been called, I was astonished to learn, to discuss "reconciliation with the Morgans," the couple who had been centrally involved in the split the previous spring. I knew the Morgans had sold their own house to help finance the church's purchase of this piece of land, with the understanding that they would live rent-free in the house sitting at the head of the driveway. But now I learned that they were still living there—twenty yards from where we were now talking! Nor had I heard anything about the charges Frank aired this afternoon, that the Morgans had "yanked on church members," he complained bitterly, continuing to invite them to a Bible study in their home a few steps away. "If you go to their home in fellowship," Frank warned sternly, "then you are out of fellowship with us!"

These were sharp criticisms of a couple Frank and Sharon had described as being "like parents" to them in the church's early years. Frank's father, Joe, had even told me, with a little embarrassment, that Frank's relationship with Herb Morgan had made him "almost a little bit jealous." Frank reported that the deacons had met and agreed on a letter to move toward what he called "a scripturally binding agreement" with the Morgans, and Phil Strong and another deacon had been chosen to go discuss the issue with them.

"Will you take them to court?" someone asked.

"If he takes us," Frank answered petulantly. "Otherwise we will follow scriptural principles. We shall not take a brother to court. But that doesn't say we can't bring three unrelated fundamental pastors to come in as our *own* court." Following Matthew (18:15–17), fundamentalist Baptists shun courts backed by state power in favor of scriptural procedures for dealing with conflict. According to Pastor Valenti, these involved the following progression of steps: first go to the party in a dispute; if that does not resolve the issue, bring two other believers with you to see them; and, finally, the step Frank referred to here, form a court made up of pastors from like-minded congregations. The latter was especially useful for independent churches such as Shawmut River, which was not part of any larger denominational body that might decide disputes. It was a device members would turn to again when conflicts threatened to divide their church.

Frank returned to the subject of Bill Tatum. Bill had been relieved of his duties, he said, because, according to him, Tatum had not run the school in "a distinguished, professional way," and they had lost some parents because of it. Moreover, Frank claimed that Bill was now starting a Bible study with the Morgans and inviting church members to attend. (Others later denied or discounted these charges.)[3]

"We've been through ten months of torture," Frank complained bitterly, "not knowing who was going to be yanked on next! If a Bible study is not sanctioned by me," he charged, pounding his fist on the lectern, *"don't go! It's disloyal!"* He gave members permission to "tattle on" those who did, giving us no fewer than nine citations from scripture to justify it.

· · ·

THE TATUM AFFAIR held important lessons. It was a humbling experience to suddenly discover powerful conflicts underneath the apparent calm of a community I had been observing for the past two months. Frank had spoken of "ten months of torture, not knowing who was going to be yanked on next," yet I had not heard a word about these ongoing tensions. And a key party to these conflicts was living a stone's throw away on church property. This demonstrated core members' remarkable capacity to control information despite the relentless publicizing pressures gossip and rumor posed in such a close-knit community.

The Tatum affair also brought into view the presence of a shadow community of ex-members, still so in touch with one another and still so focused on church affairs that they might readily be imagined to form alliances with newly estranged members such as the Tatums. It also showed how vulnerable Pastor Valenti felt in the face of the ever-present threat that his flock would be "yanked on" by enemies without, and how hurt, puzzled and, at times, angry he was about someone's leaving. Since church ties were seen and felt to be familylike, a person's decision to leave could be seen as a personal betrayal and was not infrequently felt as such. It could provoke charges and countercharges of the essential untrustworthiness of the other party. To have fellowship with them, as Frank said of the Morgans, means not having fellowship with us. To attend an "unsanctioned Bible study"—the potential nucleus of a new church—was, in his terms, "disloyal."

Bill Tatum was not the first principal of the Christian Academy to leave Shawmut River in a storm of conflict. His predecessor had been at the center of the church split the previous spring. I had wanted to interview Tatum ever since witnessing how animated he had become in one conversation I had had with him on situation ethics. "We need some absolutes," he had sputtered, his face close up to mine so I could feel the force of his statement, "or else everybody'd go nuts!" Unfortunately, now any dealings with him, it seemed, would jeopardize my relations with the Valentis.

It was not until I sat down to talk with Scott Sanderson that I heard more about what had happened with Tatum. Scott and I had escaped for lunch to the more confidential setting of Mike Dukas' Diner, where I sometimes retreated to take notes or have conversations off church premises. The subject came up when we were talking about the pattern of church benevolence that involved members in one another's lives. I mentioned that one prominent member had reported to me that when she had taken groceries to the Tatums, she had discovered a supply of Coca-Cola in their fridge. "Maybe we're from the old school," she had said, "but they just spent five dollars on Coke. I'm sorry, but they should have bought something like chicken. To me the Coke was just a waste." I told Scott that I wondered whether word about this had gotten around.

"I'm sure she made sure it got around," Scott said dryly, pointing out that there had been "too much personal input" in the Tatum situation. "With anybody else," he explained, "they would have gone out and bought the same thing, but it wouldn't have meant as much. It's almost like people were looking for problems. No one ever questions me as to what I use my paycheck to buy!"

"What were the Tatums gossiped about for," I asked, "regardless of the truth of the matter? I mean, you seem to be able to see how gossip sometimes . . ."

"Overpowers reality," Scott added to complete my thought. "Bill and Sally had accents from other parts of the country," he explained. (Sally was from Virginia, Bill from Appalachian stock in Pittsburgh.) "And the average New Englander has a tendency to look down their nose at a different accent, especially a southern one."

"Even if they drop their *r*'s," I offered, joking about the "Woostuh" accent prevalent at Shawmut River.

"Right," Scott agreed, "and for some reason they put that person in an illiterate category. On top of that, when Bill would talk with you, he would make some grammatical errors. And there were people who were extremely outspoken about being offended by that, especially with him being hired as the administrator of the school and teaching English. Some of the gossip stemmed from that. Some of the gossip was toward the pastor because he hired him. And then some things were just completely blown out of proportion."

"Like what?" I asked.

Scott seemed to search his brain for something he had worked hard to forget. As some adults had made their discomfort known, he recalled, it had influenced their children, and, "all of a sudden, it started showing up in the classroom."

"Authority undermined?" I theorized.

"Right! And then these same students started getting together and, taking some of Bill's personality—where he likes to get right up close to you and talk—started rumors about him getting too friendly with some of the girls. Completely tried to destroy his testimony. And these rumors got back to certain parents, and these parents met with the pastor. And so it was really blown way out of proportion. It caused one family to decide that if Bill was going to teach next year, they were going to put their kids somewhere else."

I remembered my one encounter with Bill when he had pressed up close to talk with me—a direct, confrontational style he attributed to growing up on Pittsburgh's working-class north side. I still asked Scott whether he felt there was any truth to these allegations.

"No," Scott answered with confidence. "It was just his personality misunderstood." ("Background" or "culture," Scott might have also said.) "These particular girls that made the accusations were supposed to apologize to him personally, but they said, 'I don't want to be alone with him!'" He shivered and pulled back to mimic their show of revulsion.

SCOTT'S ACCOUNT revealed some of the less pleasant aspects of the kind of village life Shawmut River represented. With the very same knowledge members drew on to meet your needs—even of what was in your refrigerator—they might also undermine or destroy your reputation and standing in the congregation. As with any community, what it does *for* you, and how it does it, provides the measure and means for what it can do *against* you. Though my new-left colleagues and I yearned for "community," our efforts to create it in communes, consciousness-raising groups and collectives were generally weak and short-lived. They demanded little from us and were not built up around family ties. I remember once reading that the average life of a feminist consciousness-raising group—the organizational backbone of the women's movement in the 1960s and 1970s—was only nine months.[4]

The events Scott recounted also demonstrated that behind any judgment uttered from the pulpit or elsewhere—such as Bill Tatum's not running the school in "a distinguished, professional way"—stood an immense and highly ramified social process. Such a statement represented the tip of an iceberg, supported by a vast body of determinations of fact—of what "we know"—added to slowly around original solidifications of "fact" now completely obscured.

Gossip is a particular form of talk known, above all, for its capacity to affect reputation, the commonly accepted identity a person carries in a community. Once reputation crystallizes, whether true or not, it provides a lens through which all members can legitimately see what that person's actions *obviously are*—such as Bill Tatum's habit of talking up close to you. In the quiet flow of normal conversation unruffled by dissent or controversy, ice crystals of "fact" gradually form, linking up slowly with others in a grid, which, as layer upon layer form, might eventually become solid enough to drive a truck across. Meanwhile, anyone trying to navigate the waters of life at Shawmut River had to beware these ice-formations-in-the-making hidden beneath its surface.[5]

Frank's preoccupation with gossip was understandable. Rather than the all-powerful commander of his ship, he seemed its frustrated pilot, nervously scanning the seas around him for signs of hidden icebergs whose creation and movement he was unable to control, things that would drive parents from his school or turn his flock against him. At this point, for two or three families to leave in a huff might spell the financial ruin of their church or their school. And all these forces of destruction could be created through mere talk.

In our conversation about the Tatum affair, Scott and I had touched upon key sources of power at Shawmut River, but neither of us had mentioned any names. Scott did not express any curiosity about the source of the one piece of gossip I had heard about the Tatums; perhaps he knew all too well. For my part, I took the opportunity to ask him whom he considered the most powerful people at Shawmut River, a question I began posing to members both in the core and on the periphery of church life. After Pastor Valenti, Scott first mentioned Sharon, her parents, Frank's parents and Sharon's sister-in-law Judy. This corresponded fairly closely to those figures other members first named as part of the church "power elite," as one welfare mother on the periphery of church life called it. Scott also named Jean Strong and Granny Gund, Sally Keener's grandmother.

None of these people was chosen because of any formal positions they held in church—for example, as a deacon or trustee. In fact, the women among them were not permitted to hold such positions. The deacons or trustees, I saw over time, played no decisive role in church life anyway. They met only haphazardly, and their makeup could shift without formal election or notification. Even a core church member like Sally Keener, whose husband, Dave, was a deacon, could not name those who served as deacons along with her husband. A board of deacons or trustees might be especially weak at a pioneer church like Shawmut River, still run by a founding pastor and his family. But a study of a similar fundamentalist Baptist congregation, now more than a century old, also revealed strikingly weak roles for its deacons.[6] Baptist Bible Fellowship churches held a "pastor-run church" to be a divinely ordained and biblically grounded ideal. But apart from that, formal positions of authority were not critical to the expression and resolution of conflict in churches like these, nor to the exercise of power. Conflict and power functioned on a more organic basis within the ever-flowing stream of talk carrying a vital oral tradition.

The fact that power at Shawmut River rested in informal processes of influence and opinion making rather than formal office and executive decision making was an important insight for my efforts to win the congregation's support for the documentary film I had begun to envision. That summer, through a close friend and colleague, I approached a well-known documentary filmmaker, and we applied for funding from the National Endowment for the Humanities. I did not yet share this with church members. I realized that for a sociologist educated at schools like Harvard and Brandeis, it would not be easy or straightforward to gain permission to film a candid portrait of their congregation for national television. Most members would have agreed with Pastor Valenti's judgment that "colleges and universities have become the religious synagogues and churches of America," working hand in hand with the government to promote "the secular humanist view."

Or as Sharon put it simply, "You go to humanist colleges, you come out humanistic in mind." By "humanist" she and other conservatives meant the belief that humankind itself provides its own standards for life. God doesn't. That this documentary would be funded by the National Endowment for the Humanities, the reputedly archliberal organ of the secular state, and slated for broadcast on PBS, another institution associated with "pointy-headed liberals" all over the country, might simply pound nails into the project's coffin.

But even more decisive, perhaps, fundamentalists believe that only saved people can understand the spiritual truths God intends for us in scripture. For them, the Holy Spirit dwelling within a born-again believer was the only reliable guide to understanding God's word. How could they ever expect a true and accurate portrait of fundamentalist Christianity from an unsaved, albeit well-meaning, sociologist?

Any person arguing against my project for these reasons would be on solid, incontestable ground, whatever their real motives might be.

Short of my getting saved, the only hope of success, I believed, rested in shaping how my project was initially perceived and interpreted by the community, and that meant by its key opinion makers. I had been disabused of the assumption that Pastor Valenti could effectively dictate the congregation's decision on such a touchy matter, despite the fact that there were, in theory, no limits on his authority. Nor did I feel it was the deacons or trustees I most needed to court. To succeed I had to extend a solid base of support among opinion makers strategically situated in the congregation's dense networks of talk. Before even broaching the prospect of such a film, I felt, such preparatory work had to be done.

Among other things, this required building relationships with key women in the congregation. The very fact that women were recognized power holders in a community resolutely defending a patriarchal model of the family, I believed, held the key to resolving the puzzle that had led me to Shawmut River in the first place: that women in such churches, and in the New Right at large, were among its most committed partisans, even in defense of traditional gender arrangements in the family. I realized that seeing how women exercised some power either in their families or in their wider church community would be a delicate subject to explore. Among other things, it would require relationships of trust with key church women.

In addition to an early interview with Sharon, I had already begun to build that groundwork by interviewing her mother, Ada, my first Sunday back at Shawmut River that May. It was she, on that occasion, who told me the story of discovering Coca-Cola in the Tatums' refrigerator two weeks before Bill Tatum left.

8

Fall

I really enjoyed that piece of meat.

THE TATUM AFFAIR faded with summer. The Morgans, leaders of the split the previous year, vacated the house at the end of the church's driveway, and Scott and Sue Sanderson, who were expecting their second child, prepared to move in.

One October morning that fall I found a letter in my mailbox, much to my surprise, from Pastor Valenti. It laid out in detailed terms, with biblical references, the "plan of salvation" found in Romans. He wrote that he was praying for my salvation, "even more than for anyone else," and called me "one of the most sincere, down-to-earth people I have ever met. For a lost person," he added, "that's quite a statement." He described accepting Christ as an act of "humbling yourself," of "not being ashamed to bow your head and ask him to save you from hell in Jesus' name." That October letter, I soon saw, was part of renewed efforts among his congregation to see me get saved.

It was remarkable how little pressure had been placed on me during my first eight months at Shawmut River, quite unlike the urgency I felt on those momentary encounters with born-again Christians I met at other churches I visited, who sometimes wanted to see me get saved right then and there. But in this case, I was coming to church regularly, hearing the word and talking at length with members about their experiences with the Lord. It was just a matter of time, most probably felt, before the Holy Spirit would move me to leave my pew, go forward and in my heart of hearts say the sinner's prayer and be born again.

The "sinner's prayer" meant saying to God, as Pastor Valenti often put it, "Lord, I am a sinner. I deserve hell. I'll turn from my wicked ways. Save me from hell in Jesus' name." Members felt so strongly that the conditions for saying and believing such a prayer would be sustained just by participating in their community that they spoke of failing to attend church as "backsliding" from faith itself. While they described someone attending Sunday school and both Sunday services as "spiritual," they would speak—albeit half jokingly—of someone who attended Wednesday evening, in addition, as being "*super*-spiritual." They felt that simply *being there* provided powerful conditions for belief, an observation whose truth I could readily appreciate.

As time wore on, some members lost sight of the fact that I was actually attending church to do research for a book. For most, it was too foreign a practice to keep in mind, and they had difficulty comprehending why I was still there yet had not made a decision for Christ. Ordinarily this would have been too uncomfortable a state for someone to remain in long. It meant being routinely reminded of people's concern for your condemned soul and your exclusion from those treasured experiences uniting those surrounding you—knowing they were all saved, living here and now in the knowledge that they would share eternal life together (the realities of which they occasionally discussed in matter-of-fact detail) and talking daily about the ins and outs of their "personal relationship with the Lord." Normally these tensions created discomforts that hampered relationships between born-again believers and "worldlies," a term they used for unsaved people, whose attention was necessarily focused on the world rather than on the kingdom of God. But for me, this outsider status was a normal and expected part of doing ethnographic research in order to understand the meanings binding a community together.

Members believed that it was ultimately only the Holy Spirit who could bring someone to Christ. Even though they saw accepting salvation by faith as an individual's decision—a voluntary act at a specific moment in time—faith itself, they would say, always came as a gift of God. Fundamentalists "got saved," as one commentator pointed out; "they did not merely learn to follow the Master. It was a miracle . . . an answer to prayer, a supernatural operation of the Holy Spirit. . . ."[1]

But this did not mean Christians were to sit back and wait. The Holy Spirit always worked through people, they reminded themselves, and the Bible demanded followers of Christ to spread the Gospel to all corners of the Earth. This requirement of "the Great Commission," as it was called, could be felt for every lost soul a believer might encounter, as well as those closer to home. In the case of Phil and Jean Strong's long-standing concern for Phil's father and his older brother Sam, it amounted to such a real and heartfelt desire to see them after death and spare them eternal suffering in hell that it became felt and spoken of as a *burden*. "I have a burden for his soul," members would say, and I would hear them chide themselves for not being bold enough in giving the Gospel to a relative, friend or coworker, or to let the issue languish too long. You needed not only to pray that God work in someone's life but also to "put feet to your prayers." You needed to take action, and God required it of you. But in the end, the effectiveness of your actions did not depend solely on your skill or timing. Ultimately, your efforts were meaningless without the efforts of the Holy Spirit working through you.

This tension between free will and determinism was not a problem members felt compelled to resolve theoretically, just as they saw no problem in believing the world must sink deeper into unbelief before Christ's second coming yet still worked for Christian revival in their day. It was part of the same posture toward life that required them to pray with the assurance that God would answer their prayers, while they applied themselves diligently to do all they could to achieve those same ends. Where putting "feet to prayer" left off and putting yourself in place of God began, and where consideration for lost souls gave way to offensiveness, had to be discerned on a case-by-case, if not moment-by-moment, basis. This was easier said than done, I would see, and members could differ sharply about which was happening at any moment. Their judgments in these matters necessarily involved dealing with a host of ambiguities, belying opponents' assumptions that it is their essential *incapacity* to deal with ambiguity that leads conservative Christians to insist on moral absolutes in the first place. But it is important to note (and a matter to which we will return) that in applying contrary maxims to the messiness of life, they did not feel compelled to resolve any resulting contradictions or ambiguities theoretically. Instead, in their best and most humble formulation, members saw their task, in the context of such ambiguities, to cultivate themselves as suitable instruments for fulfilling God's work on Earth, unhindered by fear or other concerns of self. That was one among many aspects of "the high calling of Christ" of which it was all too easy to fall short.[2]

That autumn other church members, in addition to Pastor Valenti, began asking about the state of my soul and said they would be praying for me. Some added my salvation to their prayer lists, kept in Bibles or elsewhere. One afternoon, while casually leaning against the refrigerator in one family's kitchen, I noticed, amid snapshots and shopping lists held by flowered magnets on the refrigerator door, a list headed "Prayer." Four or five items down I saw printed neatly: "Jim Ault—Salvation." These human acts certainly served to carry forward what members saw as the Holy Spirit's work; Shawmut River's collective concern became a presence in my life.

During this period I found myself sometimes responding to members' concern for my soul by describing the nature of my work as a researcher. Toward the end of my interview with Sally Keener, for example, she asked, "What do you think about it for your own personal self, I mean about becoming a Christian? . . . I've heard you say before you weren't a Christian."

I explained to her that my parents were Christians, though not fundamentalists. She readily likened them to her grandmother, who, she said, has never used the terminology "born again" or "saved," but "has a personal relationship with the Lord."

"She reads her Bible and lives by those principles," Sally explained, "so I consider her a Christian, and I would argue to the bitter end if someone said they didn't think she was a Christian because she never professed to be saved or born again."

But still, Sally wanted to know why *I* had not accepted Christ. I explained that my work involved "placing myself as an observer who's going to explain something to outsiders." I said, "You can't *observe* worship and *worship* right at the same time." In fact, I had come to notice in my fieldwork that what continually served to thrust me outside the community of believers at Shawmut River was my continual effort to notice and make explicit what members took for granted. Instead of seeing the Holy Spirit at work in the world, for instance, I busied myself noticing what members assumed about it as they spoke and acted. Since the Holy Spirit was that part of God seen to affect life by working, among other things, through people, I found it easy to replace "Holy Spirit" with "community" in many members' statements to arrive at worthy sociological observations. For example, when they saw the Holy Spirit, upon hearing a prayer request, move individuals to meet a fellow member's need, or when that member received church benevolence partly because he or she was known to be generous, I saw *communal* motivations at work.

Though I spoke truthfully to Sally about the way my research was continually building for me a standpoint outside the church's beliefs, I did not speak of other reasons I felt for not accepting Christ—that I felt these beliefs too preposterous to accept and that even to entertain them posed the specter of unthinkable rearrangements in life. At the same time, I also had not spoken to her about the other side of participant-observer research: participation. I sang Gospel hymns, bowed my head in prayer and discussed everything from the morning's message to people's personal "walk with the Lord," trying always to make myself understood through the common meanings particular to them as fundamentalist Christians. To do this smoothly and fluently required my taking more and more of their common meanings for granted, as the church's special lexicon became part of my working vocabulary. Through this process, the range of meanings I did not have to *take notice of*, but simply *experienced*, naturally grew.

The substance of born-again Christians' faith, one anthropologist has noted, is carried, above all, in their language—in the specific terms with which they address and interpret reality. Conversion involves learning that language and making it your own, something I would see close-up in a Bible-study group I would join that winter. And like learning any new language, that process takes place best through immersion—that is, through regular involvement in social contexts where that language is continually being used toward practical ends.[3]

One experience I did share with Sally that came from participating in, and not simply observing, life at Shawmut River was the experience of feeling "healed," I said, whenever I returned after an extended absence. I don't know where that word suddenly came from and was a bit surprised when I heard it later on the tape recording of our interview. In retrospect, I believe it had to do with my feelings of well-being and security as a result of being recognized, supported and cared for within the life of mutual dependence Shawmut River cultivated and sustained. Feeling "loved" may be as close to the mark. In any case, that very morning I had witnessed a striking reminder of the community's care.

As Pastor Valenti began to settle into his message, Aunt Margaret, sitting next to me, seemed fidgety and suddenly raised her hand. We were worshipping now in "the new sanctuary," the gymnatorium, which each week had to be converted back into a gym for basketball and other school activities. The work of moving some thirty heavy oak pews, as well as carpets and room dividers, and reinstalling a steel basketball post and hoop in front of the pulpit generally fell to the school's staff and teenagers. The pews were now arranged in three sections, not two as in the old sanctuary in the bakery building. Like others, Aunt Margaret, Dan Keener and I easily found a place in the new configuration for our "oddball pew."

It took everyone time to get used to this larger space, and as Frank began his message he did not notice Aunt Margaret's hand go up. Before I knew it, she was standing up next to me, clutching her Bible to her chest. "Pastor . . . pastor?" she implored, looking around her nervously and working the corners of her Bible. "Can I say something?"

"Sure, Aunt Margaret," Frank said.

"I want to thank whoever put that bag of groceries in Mary Shepperson's van for me last Sunday," she said, her voice faltering and her eyes welling up with tears. "I want you to know," she said, smiling nervously, "I really enjoyed that piece of meat." She quickly sat down. There was complete silence.

"I'll do it again, Aunt Margaret," Frank said, breaking the silence with a joke. He went on to thank Aunt Margaret's anonymous benefactor, adding, "May the Lord bring blessings to you."

Meeting people's needs was seen to be one of the central tasks of church life. "Our job as a local New Testament church," Sharon said, summing it up for me, "is to give the Gospel, to disciple those that are saved and to spread the love of God abroad—to be benevolent. It's not the government's job," she emphasized. "It's the church's job and it's the individual's job to be benevolent—to support those that can't work and to take care of our parents. Our church sees the need to support widows—the Bible commands that, by the way—and if they have no family around, then it's the church's responsibility to take care of that widow, to make sure she doesn't go hungry, or she doesn't go without oil in the tank or any need that she might have." So it was with Aunt Margaret.

Sharon, like other conservatives, objected to the government's role in welfare and placed responsibility for caring for the needy on "the church" and "the individual." Later on, when Phil Strong campaigned for state Senate, one of his proposals was to turn welfare over to churches, fifteen years before the federal government's program to

contribute funds to the charitable work of "faith-based communities." Giving at Shawmut River generally took place in the context of
personal, face-to-face relationships. It was quite different from the
abstract appeals for "refugee children" or "disaster victims" that characterized giving in the mainline suburban churches I had known as a
child—aid that ultimately would be dispensed by impersonal, bureaucratic organizations.[4] At Shawmut River, while giving was consumed
largely by the needs of members and their families—including welfare
mothers, widows and the unemployed—it extended quite readily, on a
personal basis, to strangers as well.

One day a mother and her grown daughter arrived at the church
office seeming a bit worn down by life. They said that they had just
been stranded and did not have money to get home. Frank called
Sharon at home to see if they could put these two women up. Duane, a
church member whose wife had recently thrown him out of the house,
had just spent a week at the Valentis', and Sharon was tired. She also
suspected, quite rightly, that Frank would be off doing something else,
leaving everything on her shoulders. Nevertheless, she agreed. This
was the kind of service to others that being Christlike demanded.

The mother and daughter settled into the Valentis' home for a few
days, but suspicions about them grew. They refused to sleep in the
same queen-sized bed and requested two rooms. They helped themselves to what was in the refrigerator, taking the best steak out of the
freezer and cooking it up. They did not clean up after themselves or
help in any way. Sharon was stewing about the situation when Duane
arrived to pick up some of his things. A few minutes after he left,
the phone rang and Sharon answered. "You ran out of gas?" she asked
in a confused manner while listening intently to the person on the
other end.

"Who is it?" her teenage daughter, Christie, asked. It turned out to
be Duane, who was calling to say he had seen those same women at
another fundamentalist church two weeks before with the same story.
Once off the phone, Sharon packed her children into the car and drove
to meet Frank and me at a restaurant to decide what to do. As they
shared observations over coffee at an Abdow's Big Boy, Christie bub-
bled forth with her own revelations. "Whenever you'd go out," she
said, "they'd watch *Love Boat, Three's Company*—even *Dallas*!" These
were programs Frank and Sharon condemned for adults, let alone children. When *Dallas* came on, Christie reported with relish, they'd say,

"It's all right, hon'. . . . It's nothin' you won't know about when you're grown, so you might as well know it now." Frank and Sharon grimaced at each other, while Christie's eyes lit up as she reported these scandalous facts, which she had somehow spared mentioning to them before.

Sharon returned home and told the two they had to leave. When they marched upstairs to get their things, Christie and her younger brother, who were listening from the top of the stairs, scattered.

"They knew all the lingo," Sharon laughed to recall. "They started wavin' their arms and saying, 'Let the Holy Spirit be a witness to this!' and 'Call yourselves Christians!'"

WHATEVER ITS POTENTIAL DISCOMFORTS, members saw giving as a sure path to a bountiful life. "It's a law of nature! A law of thermodynamics!" Frank declared one Sunday morning from the pulpit. "You'll reap what you sow!" he said, paraphrasing Galatians 6:7. Members also sometimes quoted the folk saying "What goes 'round, comes 'round" as a lawlike regularity describing life both inside and outside their church. For them it was a natural law ensured—and even animated—by God's almighty hand. They saw living life in mutual dependence with others as not only practically effective but also morally preferred. "The 'world' teaches independence," Frank preached, "but what does God teach? Total *de*-pendence!"

When the brake pads on my Volkswagen Rabbit wore down to metal and I mentioned I was finally taking it to my mechanic, Frank offered to do the job himself. When I said I would not want to impose on him, he cringed as if he had heard a screeching violin. *He* should do it for me. Why pay someone else? So one afternoon I picked up the parts he said we would need, drove out to Worcester and was soon out on the macadam in the church parking lot assisting him with the job. It took more time than we anticipated. We had some laughs at the unexpected stubbornness of some of the rusted bolts and at the parts mysteriously left over when the job was done. As we worked, we chatted about various things. I saved $200 I desperately needed, learned something about cars and saw our relationship grow.

As fall gave way to winter that year, I became more acutely aware of the caring power of the congregation as my grant money and savings were exhausted and I found myself for the very first time standing in line for unemployment benefits. During this period, the Valentis and others always insisted that lunch or dinner was their treat, and Phil Strong vainly tried to imagine some way to employ a sociologist like me in his insulation company. One afternoon when my car had a flat tire in the church parking lot and none of us could get the lug nuts on the wheel to budge, Phil dropped what he was doing at work and drove over with some tools to help.

As the months of being without work wore on, I began to notice that as soon as I drove into the Worcester area, I felt a sense of security settle inside. I knew help was at hand. If my car broke down or was impounded for a lapsed inspection sticker because I had put off getting my brakes fixed, or if I suddenly became ill or did not have money for gas, there were people there I could count on to help. Whatever my need, they would never see my calling on them as inappropriate. They would never say it was inconvenient. In fact, they would probably *welcome* the opportunity. Once in the Worcester area, I felt the safety net of their moral impulses spread out securely beneath me. This, too, amounted to more than merely *observing* life at Shawmut River.

If such material support mattered to me, someone only peripherally attached to the congregation through professional interests and living in an entirely different area, how much larger did it loom for someone like Aunt Margaret, or for the welfare mothers in church, or for members who had lost jobs, gotten divorced or experienced other sources of need?

Another experience I came to notice was how members' care and concern for my soul had a tendency to become most fully present precisely at those moments when Pastor Valenti gave the invitation at the end of each and every worship service. One good observer of fundamentalism has pointed out that, while for some mainline churches, celebrating Holy Communion is the central moment in worship when participants are prompted to meet God, for fundamentalists this comes at "the invitation."[5]

I have a vague recollection from my years at Shawmut River of taking communion once or twice—cubes of ordinary white bread and grape juice in small plastic cups being passed out rather unceremoniously to us in our pews. (The Methodists of my childhood were only slightly more ceremonial.) Communion was rarely celebrated at Shawmut River and did not figure importantly in worship.

But at the end of each and every message, Frank would ask us to bow our heads, come to close in prayer and "deliver the invitation."

Summing up points he had been preaching—often hard-hitting criticisms of sin—he would then soften his tone as he turned these toward personal questions. "Have you got the helmet of salvation on?" he asked softly one morning. "You know, a lot of people have prayed a simple little prayer and think they've been saved because of it. It's more than just saying, 'Oh, God, save me.' You know what salvation is? . . . It's a commitment to righteousness, a turning away from sin. It is not enough just to say, 'Oh well, I prayed this silly little prayer one day. I was really having problems, and things straightened right out in my life.' Have they?" He spoke gently, intimately. "Are you lying to yourself? Are you really saved, or have you fallen for some religious trick? Examine your soul this morning, dear brother or sister. Let me give you the plan of salvation, that there's no mistaking it."

As Frank quietly outlined the plan of salvation, Sally Keener began to play the organ softly underneath his rhythmic exhortation. She played bars of the invitational hymn we would soon sing together. "And now the hard part," Frank continued. "Are you willing to give up that little sin in your life? God's speaking to you right now, isn't he? If you want me to pray with you about it, quietly raise your hand. I see it here . . . and there," he said, taking note of hands raised as our heads remained bowed. This practice of calling for hands while heads were bowed permitted a degree of anonymity and discretion around how needs were registered. Yet much of the time, it seemed, in the back of the sanctuary, Dave Keener as deacon would be carefully noting who raised a hand for what purpose. This might prompt him or Pastor Valenti to inquire further of these people after the service or even approach them during the invitational hymn to ask if they wanted to go forward to the altar or to a quiet room to pray. These practices had evolved to help the Holy Spirit do his work. (Fundamentalists insist on speaking of the Holy Spirit as a male person, rather than an impersonal force, as some liberal theologies have it.)

"If you are here this morning without Christ," Frank continued his invitation one Sunday, "and want to accept him as your savior, don't hesitate, don't put off the decision before it is too late. The Bible says you will not be ashamed. If God is leading you, will you come . . . as we sing 'Just as I am.'" We rose to sing one of the somber, reflective hymns often chosen for the invitation:

> *Just as I am without one plea,*
> *But that thy blood was shed for me,*

"If God is calling you, come," Frank now entreated us over the hymn.

And that thou bidd'st me come to thee-ee,
O Lamb of God, I come, I come.

"Don't harden your hearts, come," Frank gently pleaded as people made their way forward to the front of the new sanctuary to kneel at the railings against the dais. Going forward meant singling yourself out publicly as a needy person and bowing before God in the presence of all. It was intrinsically a humbling act, and Frank often assured us we would not be ashamed to do it. It represented part of members' essential posture toward God. However, like all virtuous acts, it could easily be turned into its opposite, say, by those who prided themselves on how often they submitted to God's call in this way. And, like initiation ceremonies into a particular club or group, "going forward" heightened a person's vulnerability and separateness just before he or she would be warmly welcomed as a full and valued member of the community. Then the joyful announcement from the pulpit that so-and-so had accepted Christ would be met with a chorus of "Amens" and "Praise the Lords," followed by warm, congratulatory handshakes and hugs from a line of church members.

Since I was often the only unsaved person present at a worship service—especially on Wednesday or Sunday evenings—most people responding to Frank's altar call did so for matters other than salvation: to rededicate themselves to God or to surrender more fully to him by, for instance, "surrendering for baptism," or, as Frank invited members this morning, to pray "for a certain sin" in their life or otherwise "get things right with God." So whenever Frank addressed his invitation to someone "without Christ," as he invariably did, I could not help but feel everyone's attention on me. That awareness itself, I imagined, contributed to a charged atmosphere of expectation: the sense that God might act at that very moment to lead, prompt or convict. These were moments, I thought, when the Holy Spirit's "work"—moving someone to go forward—could also be translated into the language of community encouragement and pressure. They were times when miracles were expected to happen, and partly for that reason, I imagined, often did. Though I noticed this pressure, I was not prompted to believe.

But I was aware that the more common way new souls were won at Shawmut River was not simply through the invitation or altar call, but through Bible-study groups in the homes of relatives or friends. It was, above all, in those more intimate conversations, I would see, that people acquired the language, or discourses, of a new faith. That winter, I experienced such evangelism in a small Bible-study group being started in the home of a young couple Pastor Valenti had recently led to the Lord.

9

Winter

I never know where you stand on things.

A s winter settled in, I heard news from the National
Endowment for the Humanities that our film proposal had made
it through the first round of cuts and was being looked upon favorably.
My excitement quickened at the prospect of not just a great project to
work on in an exciting new medium, but simply any paid work at all. I
had by now spent some time doing groundwork among the church's
key opinion makers, and it was time to broach the idea with Frank and
Sharon. I told them there was something I wanted to discuss and suggested we have lunch.

On Sharon's suggestion, we went to the Atrium restaurant at a
nearby Hilton Hotel, a more upscale venue for us and one dominated,
it seemed, by the midweek business lunch. As Frank offered prayer for
our food and fellowship, I noticed our waitress had arrived with our
salads and was irked, then indignant, about having to wait for Frank to
finish. That, along with the routine stares of onlookers, had ceased to
faze me by now. I had come to accept the fact with complete equanimity that I was being identified by any and all around us as "one of those
religious nuts."

I began by recounting to Frank and Sharon the genesis of my idea
to make a documentary about Shawmut River. My experience among
them, I said, had persuaded me that a true-to-life portrait of such a
church would help correct some of the misperceptions of fundamentalist Christians prevalent in public life: among them, the fixation on
the empires of TV evangelists, the failure to recognize distinctions

between charismatic and other fundamentalist Christians and a lack of appreciation for the practical consequences they experienced in being saved and ordering their lives according to God's plan for the family found in scripture. I told the story of becoming connected, through a close friend, with a well-known documentary filmmaker who took surprising interest in the project partly because of the indelible impression left on him by his Bible-quoting grandmother, a staunch Calvinist from Nova Scotia. It was not lost on me that they and others at Shawmut River might readily see in these events the Holy Spirit's uncanny ways of putting this project together.

The kind of film we intended to make, I emphasized, would be in *cinéma-vérité* style, that is, it would tell its story not through voice-over narration but, instead, through real-life events and the stories members themselves told to the camera. I told them that we had applied to the National Endowment for the Humanities for funding and would hear the results soon.

I was relieved by how positively Frank and Sharon responded to the idea. Frank began by saying he had been praying God would use him in new ways to effect change in public life. He had been thinking about pursuing an advanced degree in Christian education. But now he wondered whether this project was the answer to his prayers. Neither Frank nor Sharon expressed doubts or misgivings on this occasion, though I suspected they had them. On the contrary, Frank asked me to present my proposal to the entire congregation the following Sunday.

As Sunday approached, my anxieties grew. Scott groaned with delight that I would be the first unsaved person to speak from their pulpit. "But you'll do all right," he said encouragingly, "as long as you don't speak in tongues." Afterward I wondered whether he also meant the strange tongues of academia.

"Over this past year," I told the congregation the following Sunday, "I have been impressed with how local fundamentalist churches help restore and defend traditional family values, how they help people change and order their lives according to God's plan for family, how church fellowship brings people to do things for others and how much sacrifice and hard work it takes to build a church." It was a remarkable story, I said, and a significant one. Reminding them that I had first come to do research for a book, I said my desire had grown to tell this story to a wider audience to help correct some of the distorted views of fundamentalism at large. I reminded them that right here in town Pastor Valenti had a reputation for being "a communist with two wooden legs." People laughed at mention of this oft-cited rumor, reportedly overheard in a local store, as an example of the kind of frightening things told and believed about churches like theirs. I had heard some frightening rumors myself. When children in the church's neighborhood had come across some animal bones that had been used in its annual Halloween production and then disposed of in the woods out back, rumors of animal sacrifice had prompted a police investigation.

In closing, I took the occasion to thank the congregation for its kindness, openness and good humor during my stay. "I have a deep affection for this community," I said. "You've taught me much, not only about fundamental Christianity, but also about life. I have faith that whatever you decide about this project, the Lord will work through this body for the best."

Whatever qualms I had about speaking in these terms as an unbeliever were assuaged by my sense that I was merely conveying my sociological understandings about how their community worked in their own theological language. Given their faith, how their community functioned and my relationships with them, I *did* believe things would work out for the best. Though I did not share, in the main, the community's faith or politics, I had come to trust in its basic goodness, although I could also see how, as in any human community, it could go awry.

After my announcement, Frank, Sharon and I went out to dinner to celebrate at Vallee's Steak House in downtown Worcester, a place the Valentis turned to for special occasions. In the prayer he offered before we ate, Frank asked God, among other things, to "be in this film you have led Jim to do."

Later, in the midst of a free-ranging and increasingly enthusiastic discussion of the film's potential, Sharon paused, took a deep breath and, looking steadily at me, said, "You know, I never know where you stand on things." I looked down and busied myself cutting a piece of steak, hoping she was not going to put me on the spot. I was relieved when she closed by adding simply, "But somehow I think you understand."

HOPING OUR FILM PROJECT would materialize, I delved more deeply into life around Shawmut River. In addition to attending a new

Bible-study group, I sat in on teachers' meetings and observed classes in the Christian Academy and, on Scott's invitation, even sang once in choir: five men, including Dave and Dan Keener, singing a love song–like ballad, in barbershop harmonies, called "More of You."

I began taking greater pleasure in my drives to Worcester, having found more direct routes along back roads through Amherst and Belchertown to Route 9, the old post road traversing Massachusetts from Boston to Pittsfield. Skirting the Quabbin reservoir at its southern end, I drove through old farm communities and long-abandoned mill towns such as Ware and Hartwick. One shortcut took me across cornfields frozen solid in midwinter. It was a narrow road lined with tall maples whose bare trunks cast long shadows across the roughly patched road parched white with salt.

During the week, the rhythm of life at Shawmut River was relaxed and unregimented. Try as hard as I could to determine by phone the day before what would be happening the following day, I would arrive to find that something else had come up. Someone's car had broken down, so Frank had gone to help get it started. Lumber had been delivered for the new nursery, so Frank had had his father come over to advise him about framing a door.

Frank always seemed to be building something. I often found him out on a backhoe or in his carpenter's apron working on some part of the building. Scott or Brother Duane, a machinist who worked nights, would be assisting him or acting as gofer, amid idle talk of things of interest: a course for memorizing scripture, how doors used to be hung, how scriptural principles of time management could help someone's new plastering business and so on. These were occasions when talk about faith and life took place exclusively among men.

Sometimes Frank was dressed in a coat and tie for an appointment or holed up in his office preparing a message. Once I came upon him in his office, concentrating fully on a telephone conversation with a man who had called anonymously because he was upset about homosexual acts he had committed. "Don't worry," Frank assured him matter-of-factly. "Just because you commit those acts doesn't mean you're a homosexual." They are just some sins, he said, like any of us might commit, which you can turn away from as part of coming to Christ.

Meanwhile, next door, in the church office in the eaves of the bakery building, Sharon and Janice Wooden, who had recently taken over as church secretary, could be found making phone calls, paying bills or dealing with the regular stream of needs from the school. Kids came up with cut fingers, no lunch or wanting to call home to see if they could go to a friend's house after school. Parents dropped off lunches or medicine or came to pay a bill, taking time to talk over church or school matters: what's behind a certain teenager's behavioral problems, how a woman who just left her husband is managing, how the Lord taught me to handle my two-year-old and so on. Here a parallel discourse among church women was being elaborated day in and day out.

At lunchtime, Frank and Sharon might run out for a bite to eat, meet Tom and Ada at a restaurant or go out with Janice. "We've struck up a real kinship with Janice," Frank announced warmly from the pulpit one Sunday morning, as a progress report on her work. Sometimes Sharon's childhood friend Barbara would come by and race Sharon by car to a lunch spot, the two of them later laughing like schoolgirls over the ploys each had used en route to outfox the other. A lighthearted, fun-loving atmosphere generally prevailed, unless problems were at hand. And they came with the steadiness of spring rain: the town wanting to close down the gymnatorium over the issue of occupancy permits, creditors threatening to cut off services because of overdue bills or a family suddenly pulling its children out of the academy.

Making problems a matter of prayer, and hence common concern, readily lightened them. Internal conflicts of a divisive kind represented tougher problems, and those were never far off either. Someone thought Scott's choice of people to sing in choir showed favoritism and poor taste; someone threatened to leave because of the pastor's judgment against "speaking in tongues"; and so on.

Teachers drifted upstairs when they had time and joined in talk. Sue Sanderson taught kindergarten and Mary Shepperson preschool for four-year-olds. In a school of only seventy-some students concentrated in the younger age groups, upper-level classes were shared by a number of grades. Dave Keener's high-school class included ninth- through twelfth-graders; his brother, Dan's, junior-high class, fifth- and sixth-graders; and Judy Waters, Sharon's former sister-in-law, taught third- and fourth-graders in the same class. A boyhood friend of Frank's served as coach, athletic director and youth minister. Ministers and office staff also taught courses: Sharon, social studies; Janice Wooden, who had a career as a nurse, biology; and Scott, Bible.

Evolution was a principal topic in biology and science classes. In Dave Keener's senior-high class I was surprised to see how much of the theory of evolution was taught in order to refute it. Dave presented the theory of random mutation, for example, as the way evolution explains "how you can form other kinds of life from one particular kind."

"But look at mutants," Dave argued, following a science text from Beka Book Publications, a "ministry" of Pensacola Christian College. "There are *very* few mutant forms and most are in bacteria, and ninety to ninety-five percent of mutants die early or are sterile." He reminded the class that science rests ultimately on faith. Above all else, evolution makes one claim, he said, "that things are steadily getting better."

"What evidence do you see that disproves that?" he asked.

"Well, New York City," one teenage girl answered, half in jest.

The academy relied on what was called the "principle approach" to Christian education. "The whole idea and philosophy behind that," as Sharon explained it to me, "is every subject points to God, not just the Bible one hour a day, but how does math relate to God? How does English relate to God? How does science relate to God? If he's the creator of all, then each subject ought to relate to God." Even in mathematics, Pastor Valenti pointed out, a system of numbers based on odd, even and zero represented the tripartite nature of God. Apart from these theological assertions, Dave Keener's senior-high math class concentrated on consumer math, stressing practical uses of math in daily life.

If the level of academic rigor at the Christian Academy seemed low to me, given the standards I was accustomed to in schools devoted to preparing students for college, I realized a more relevant standard of comparison might be the local high school, which almost twenty years before had graduated Frank unable to read a newspaper. In any case, teaching at Shawmut River's Christian Academy was more strongly geared to building character and instilling values—of course, values the church itself stood for. In her class of third- and fourth-graders, for example, Judy Waters read a book about a wild horse who, because he was so fast, thought he could go on his own without others in the herd. Lessons of life taught him otherwise. "Remember," Judy concluded, drawing class discussion to a close, "we're going to help each other."

Frank routinely declared that "academics without character building is stupid." The academy's ability to shape the inner life of students was strengthened by how much they knew about students' families and home lives. A majority of the students' parents attended Shawmut River, and many had a parent, aunt or uncle teaching at their school.

As I attended teachers' meetings held regularly in Pastor Valenti's study, I was impressed with how much time was taken up discussing particular students' needs and problems and how much information about them was marshaled from diverse sources. Information included, say, what a second-grader had inadvertently divulged about what was going on at home or what a mother's comment at a church service revealed about her *real* concerns. Through the children at the Christian Academy, church leaders learned much about members' lives at home.

"In public school," the Valentis' teenage daughter, Christie, observed with her characteristic realism, "nobody knows your home-life business and they don't butt their nose in. Whereas here, everybody's like a family—everybody knows everything!" While Shawmut River's teenagers chafed under the closely integrated supervision of parents and teachers, they also appreciated the individual care and attention it permitted, as well as the less regimented nature of school life compared with larger public schools run tightly by the clock and buzzer. Teenagers harbored stories of the care shown by teachers, such as one girl's recollection of Dave Keener going out to the pharmacy during his lunch hour to get medicine for a rash that was troubling her.

In any case, the academy's curriculum was not dedicated to preparing students for college. "Many of our kids aren't interested in going to college," Frank reminded teachers at one of their weekly meetings, "and I can't blame them." The school's handbook declared that students would be encouraged to attend only an approved Christian college and warned that the school would not send transcripts to a secular one. (I do not know whether this rule was enforced.) What I had witnessed of fundamentalist higher education on a visit to Baptist Bible College East outside Boston, with its heavily practical orientation and the very limited required reading, suggested that Shawmut River's Christian Academy probably prepared its students quite well for that kind of education.

The academy, however, did provide an extraordinary range of practical learning experiences for its students. In such a small school specialization was unknown. The same girls who played on the basketball team served as both cheerleaders and scorekeepers for the boys' games. The domestic science class would take on projects such as sewing costumes for church productions or culottes for the girls' basketball team. (Shorts were insufficiently modest.)

After school, or sometimes even in a free period during the day, boys would work on school or church buildings alongside Frank, Joe Valenti or Duane, who taught them carpentry, plumbing and how to operate backhoes and bulldozers. Through these "brothers in the Lord," some teenagers got summer jobs in those trades, opening up career opportunities that, by contrast to college and professional education, would tie them more firmly to family, locality and church. It also taught them the people skills involved in managing relations of reciprocity.

The Christian Academy was Sharon Valenti's special concern, founded on her own initiative. "It's part of my blood," she once said. Because I had had little one-on-one conversation with Sharon since first interviewing her a year before, I made it a point during my more regular visits now to attend her American history class for senior-high students. She was teaching about the Puritan settlers in the Massachusetts Bay Colony, whom she described as the "fundamentalists of their day." Like us, she said, they had stood up for "higher moral values" even against government and church leaders of the time.

The students were on their best behavior. A year later, when I got to know them better, they felt free to do things high-school students are prone to do in class: whisper, make sarcastic jokes half under their breath and pass notes. But even then, of all the academy's teachers, Sharon commanded their highest respect and best behavior.

Sharon traced the Puritans back to the nonconformist tradition and to the "Ecclesiastical Reformation," which she wrote on the board. "What does *ecclesiastical* mean?" she asked. No one raised a hand. "That's a fancy word for church," she explained. Not everyone in the church was a Puritan, she pointed out. "What does that tell you?" In the give-and-take that followed, she brought them, in Socratic fashion, to conclude that the Church of England was not abiding by the higher moral values to which the Puritans subscribed. Likening it to the present-day situation, where religious and government leaders sanctioned abortion, she imagined the government saying to the Puritans, "You can't disobey!" And the established clergy saying, "Hey, who are you? *I've* studied theology!" She mimicked their huffy indignation, drawing evidently on her experience of those attitudes being turned against her own views.

"Was it the church God had ordained?" she asked, going on to characterize the Church of England at that time as "ritualistic," "superstitious" and dominated by an "impersonal, cold atmosphere." The Puritans studied the church, she explained, and saw it was wrong for not holding values they knew were right.

"What are values?" Sharon then asked. Students took stabs at answering a question that I knew from teaching sociology was not easy. As the discussion floundered around "goals," "wants" and so on, I finally raised my hand.

"It can be helpful to look at values as ultimate ends," I offered. "Something is a means to an end up to a certain point where there's nothing beyond. It simply is. It's an ultimate end."

Sharon looked skeptical. "They must be of God," she cautioned.

"Well," I said, "that's how some people's values might differ from others." She did not seem wholly satisfied but returned to her lesson. Later, when we chatted about the class, she said appreciatively, "and you helped me with 'values.'" She also showed me a history text she found helpful in preparing her class. While some teachers relied on lesson plans taken directly from Beka Books or some other Christian publisher, Sharon fashioned her classes more idiosyncratically, using various texts. The volume she showed me had been published in 1890. She had gotten it in a thrift store and found the author's frank Christian perspective on colonial America refreshingly compatible with her own.

That same week I played a scrimmage game with the boys' basketball team. Like most players, they showed a tendency to dribble and shoot themselves rather than pass the ball effectively to one another in order to get the best possible shots. It is invariably a hard threshold to overcome to bring a group of players to a higher level of play as a team. I mentioned to Sharon that you could see the challenge of developing effective teamwork in terms of the Holy Spirit's effect on individuals, bringing each to think first not of him- or herself but instead of the team and to pass the ball to others, having faith in their collective strength as a team. "That's right," she said. "I never looked at it that way before."

During Sunday worship a couple of weeks later, Frank attributed the basketball team's latest victory over its rival, Valley Christian, to the "principle approach" in Christian education. "Faith is giving the ball to the guy open, even if we aren't sure what he'll do," Frank explained. "Our guys were the epitome of selflessness yesterday." Sharon's evident influence on Frank was one topic I wanted to raise with her the next time we sat down to talk. Their own conversations were just one circuit, though a critical one, in the vast machinery of talk making up the life of church and school.

Church and school interpenetrated each other in many ways. Frank and Sharon often took money out of church petty cash or their own pockets to buy something for the school, and vice versa. When they had time off, teachers drifted upstairs to the church office to join in talk, and church staff made their way downstairs, through the sanctuary and gymnatorium, to teach their own classes. Amid this ebb and flow, people would catch each other in passing for more private conversations, while Aunt Margaret roamed about keeping tabs on everyone. And in moments of free time during the day, people paired up to pray together, often with the same regular partners. Aunt Margaret and Mary Shepperson, who taught preschool, prayed together daily, in the pattern generally practiced around Shawmut River, with each taking a turn to pray aloud while the other offered up an occasional "Amen" or "Yes, Lord," in a rhythmic expression of support, affirmation and unity.

In these ways a bubbling stream of news, conversation and prayer steadily bathed every quarter of life at church and school, lending events and persons the recognizable features of *common* knowledge and a *shared* moral landscape—a landscape that everyone, then, would have to negotiate. This moral landscape included designations of what God commands, who's a good Christian wife, what's good Bible preaching—and their opposites.

Within the steady stream of talk forming a body of common knowledge, the mass media—press, television and radio—assumed little importance. Like Sally Keener, many members paid little or no attention to the press, and more than a few were not familiar with terms such as *New Right* and *Moral Majority*. Even when a major press story was mentioned, it was not further discussed or elaborated on with facts from other sources.

This was a culture, then, not generated or controlled by the mass media, but instead by the spoken word, either in face-to-face talk or by telephone. It was a distinctly local culture, yet fed regularly with news from, say, the Strongs' old church in Florida, from relatives living out of state or from the latest news about a recent scandal at Falwell's church in Lynchburg, Virginia.

This relative uninterest in the media did not necessarily leave members woefully ignorant about facts surrounding issues of the day. Some, of course, did follow news in local papers and on television and shared it with others. But, in the main, what facts did circulate in their talk came more from personal sources: an uncle who worked in the welfare office and witnessed its bureaucratic irrationalities; a sister who went to the Planned Parenthood office for counseling; a brother-in-law who, as a court bailiff, knew how plea bargaining worked; and so on. The scope and adequacy of this knowledge were uneven. It was far more accurate about domestic matters than foreign ones (a weakness perhaps reflected in the fact that foreign policy is often not the strong suit of the national political leadership Christian fundamentalists have embraced). Growing up in a family-based circle of people known in common is not a natural vehicle for developing cross-cultural acumen. When I mentioned an upcoming trip to Spain, for example, one church leader asked me if they spoke "American" there.

However, despite its holes and lapses, talk at Shawmut River otherwise assumed a realism and relevance that often surpassed the standard fare of cocktail and dinner-party conversation familiar to me in professional circles, which was quite predictably fed by the latest article in the *New York Times* or *The New Yorker*, or a story on *60 Minutes* or CNN. By contrast to these urbane professionals, members of Shawmut River could not be described as creatures of the mass media.

It may seem paradoxical, then, that fundamentalists were far quicker than mainline churches to use radio or television to communicate their message. Jerry Falwell began his local television ministry in 1957, and fundamentalist schools such as Bob Jones University have been quick to use satellite transmission of televised classes to provide curricula for homeschoolers across the nation.

Fundamentalists take so readily to television and radio, I believe, precisely because they are more at home in the spoken than the written word. At Shawmut River, people were always passing around audiocassettes of books, sermons, political addresses, inspirational music or the entire Bible read by the sonorous voice of Alexander Scourby. Each week, Scott Sanderson received audiocassettes by mail of the Sunday service at his father's church in North Carolina, and others received tapes from churches to which they were personally connected.

The preeminence of the spoken word was manifest also in the absence of a written program for Sunday worship and the preference for hymns with recurring choruses sung easily from memory. It also appeared in the remarks of an African-American preacher educated at Liberty Baptist College, who mentioned offhandedly to one of Shawmut River's sister congregations that he had been "*listening* to some of his sermons the other day." That is, instead of reading, if not skimming, a text, he was in the habit of listening to tapes of his own sermons in real time.

Critical knowledge of church affairs at Shawmut River, including weekly and monthly news and events, was carried by word of mouth. One evening I made the hour-and-a-quarter drive to Shawmut River in order to attend a "Family Life Seminar" given by a husband-and-wife team from Liberty Baptist College. When I arrived, I was shocked to find the church pitch-dark. I went inside—its doors were always open—and phoned the Valentis. They were surprised I had shown up since the program had been canceled some time before. Though it had originally been advertised in a printed circular and listed on the monthly church calendar sent to all those on the church mailing list, no written notice of its cancellation had been sent out. Even so, I was the only one to show up—the only one to whom the written word mattered.

So secure was the transmission of news by word of mouth that if I had not been at church for a while, I often found it difficult simply to find out what had happened in the intervening period. I would call the church office and ask in passing, "So what's happened in the last couple of weeks?"

"Oh, nothing," the person answering would say. But later in the very same conversation, something I said would prompt the puzzled query, "Oh? You didn't hear so-and-so passed away . . . left church . . . [or] had twins?" The conveyor of the news seemed momentarily stunned, having difficulty relinquishing the unshakable fact that everyone *must* know this. Evidently, these newsworthy events had already swept through the congregation like forest fires quickly spent. Their factual residues had sunk so thoroughly into the soil of what members assumed everyone "must" know that it was hard for anyone to call them up from memory as something worth mentioning.

This might have been mistaken for weak memory, but members were apt to keep a host of phone numbers in their heads rather than ever consult an address book and routinely committed an impressive store of Bible verses to memory. However, since each person's active memory of community events readily gave way to the collective store

of things known in common and, hence, taken for granted, it was difficult for individuals to distinguish and place past events with any degree
of historical accuracy. This provided fertile soil, I realized, for traditionalism to prosper. There was no documentary historical record to
turn to in order to challenge people's traditionalist claims that this was
simply how they had always done things "time out of mind."

The power of such an oral culture is evident also in the remarkable
continuity it has achieved in the life of churches like Shawmut River.
For if you walk into any Baptist Bible Fellowship or Falwell-related
church from Maine to San Diego, you are apt to encounter a familiar
pattern of worship, liturgical language, rules of church organization,
approaches to reading and interpreting scripture and a distinct lexicon
for describing Christian life. All these uniformities have been achieved
now for more than three generations, across great variations in regional culture and conditions and among fiercely independent local
churches, largely without the use of any documents prescribing these
practices. The firm sense of appropriate patterns of worship and
church life has been achieved over time and space largely through talk
and experience.

This stands in contrast to some mainline Protestant denominations
or other organizations I know, where it can be said that if you do not
put a grievance or proposal in writing, nothing will come of it. Even
after my father gave away many of his books upon retiring as a United
Methodist bishop, he still had shelves full of volumes containing minutes of governing meetings, "Books of Discipline" updated annually
and no fewer than three copies of *Robert's Rules of Order.*

The power of the spoken word in ordering church life within fundamentalism is closely related to the life patterns of the congregation
and its members. Shawmut River was made up not of individuals or
individual households living independently of each other but, instead,
of people embedded in ties of mutual dependence in wider family
circles. Such clusters of kin—like the Keeners, Strongs and Valentis—
were the building blocks of congregational life, setting its social tone
and moral outlook and providing a template for the multipurpose flow
of daily talk . . . and daily prayer. When divisive conflicts later erupted
at Shawmut River, these family-based networks would delineate the
lines of conflict.

Even those without family in church brought to Shawmut River
habits of thought and communication formed in such family circles,

which made them feel readily at home in its folksy, familiar atmosphere, with its more porous boundaries between public and private.
Made up of people who share household needs and child care in an
interlocking chain across generations, life in a family circle naturally
transcends the privacy of the nuclear family in many ways. Beyond
this, the all-encompassing round of church activities served to
strengthen the power of talk within the congregation by increasing its
density and weight in terms of *common* concerns, *common* situations
and *common* persons.

That Shawmut River was so impressively a community of the *spoken*
word, I came to see, shed light on how precisely it was also a community of "the Book." It helped resolve some of the puzzles fundamentalists' use of scripture poses to outsiders—for example, how they can
find in the Bible, with all its apparent inconsistencies and divergent
interpretations, a set of moral absolutes practically effective in dealing with the inevitably messy problems of life. Ways to resolve such
puzzles came more clearly into view that winter while I participated in
a Bible-study group in the home of a newly saved young couple, Doug
and Terry Laverne.

Bible Study

Prove what you think *and* prove *what you feel!*

W HEN PASTOR VALENTI first suggested I join a Bible-study group being started in the home of Doug and Terry Laverne, I was not sure whether it was because he thought it would be good for my book or would help get me saved. Home-based Bible studies were a prime means for winning new souls to Christ and teaching them what it means to be Bible-believing Christians. They provided formative experiences for many at Shawmut River, such as the Valentis, who started Shawmut River out of a Bible study in their home, and the Keeners, who found in theirs new ways to spend Friday nights.

If Bible-study groups often provided the seeds for new churches, it was because they embodied some of the same essential practices as weekly worship and Sunday school class—Bible teaching, prayer and testimony—yet in smaller, more intimate settings. It was around the Lavernes' dining room table, then, in one corner of their living room, that on Thursday evenings over the next year we learned the elementary discourses, the language, of fundamentalist Christian life.

Our Bible-study group would be a means, first of all, for "discipling" newly saved Christians like Doug and Terry. That meant to help them learn how to follow Christ, embarking on what was seen as a lifelong process of change, of "maturing" or "growing in the Lord." But our study group would also be a means of winning new souls to Christ among Doug and Terry's family and friends. In this way, a new family circle, not just an assortment of individuals, would become incorporated into Shawmut River, like the Valentis, Keeners and Strongs before them. Bible study at the Lavernes', therefore, pressed me closer to the social base of churches like Shawmut River and provided more intimate observation and experience of fundamentalist Christianity's elementary practices.

The effort to win souls among the Lavernes' family circle was not without its challenges and strains, for some were deeply committed to the Roman Catholic Church, which Pastor Valenti typically criticized from the pulpit as "the biggest cult in America today." Half of his congregation, in fact, were ex-Catholics, roughly equivalent to the proportion found in the population of Massachusetts or Worcester at the time.

Doug and Terry Laverne both grew up in families of French-Canadian descent in a historic, largely working-class neighborhood of Shrewsbury, Massachusetts, just across the narrow finger of Lake Quinsigamond from Worcester proper. "The village," as residents called it, was made up largely of one- and two-family ranch and clapboard homes, and walk-up apartment buildings straddling Route 9 as it winds its way out of Worcester eastward toward Westborough, Framingham and Boston. On the north side of Route 9 Doug Laverne's family ran a mom-and-pop grocery store and owned a three-story walk-up next door, where Doug's grandfather, brother's family and sister all had apartments.

Doug and Terry were then in their early twenties and expecting their second child. They had just bought and renovated a two-bedroom house a couple of blocks from Terry's family home on the other side of Route 9, where Terry had grown up the third of six children. Terry talked with her mother regularly by phone and often picked up her younger sister at high school to come over, help with the children, hang out and chat about what was happening "at home."

Terry and Doug first met in the neighborhood Catholic parish where they and their brothers and sisters had been raised and confirmed. As teenagers they hung out with the same gang in a neighborhood park and started "going together." It was from this long-standing circle of family and friends that most participants in our Bible study were drawn. And within this circle, I soon saw, Doug Laverne was known for his thoughtfulness, integrity and fun-loving spirit, qualities that made him a natural leader among his peers. He was the kind of person who, in Frank Valenti's eyes, might be effective in leading others to the Lord.

I had met Doug Laverne at the very first Wednesday-evening service I had attended at Shawmut River a year before. Pastor Valenti had him stand up that night and introduced him to the old-home crowd as a new Christian who had just "stepped out on faith" to start his own plastering business. Standing about six feet tall, Doug had a gangly frame and a long, angular face with warm hazel eyes and a friendly, disarming smile that revealed a jumble of teeth. After the service I noticed that Pastor Valenti made a point of introducing him to Phil Strong, suggesting that Phil might help out this "new brother" by directing some business his way. Doug's relationship with Phil would become important to him over the years.

Dropping out of high school at the age of sixteen, Doug had entered the plastering trade through his uncle, who took him to a work site one day and had him sweep up and mix plaster. After several weeks of these chores, the boss said, "He's okay," and started paying him ten dollars a day. Over the years Doug mastered the trade to the point where he now felt he could make a good living from his own business.

Doug first met Pastor Valenti while plastering the walls of Shawmut River's new gymnatorium. When Doug saw Frank approaching him, he muttered to himself, "Uh-oh, here comes a crackpot." He had heard guys on the job joke about how Frank Valenti was a "Holy Roller" after being "such a rowdy." But it was at their second meeting, Doug said, that Frank had made a strong impression on him by asking outright if he ever talked to himself. "Aw, that was a stupid question," Pastor Valenti added knowingly. "You talk to yourself all the time."

"He picked right up on that one!" Doug told me, his eyes sparkling. "I talk to myself a lot!"[1]

Doug had begun his "search," he told me, several years before, when he and Terry had discovered she was pregnant. He was twenty and she eighteen. Though they had become engaged casually three months before, Doug had imagined that marriage was still three to five years away. Friends suggested that "we do what everybody's doing," Doug recalled, "get an abortion, get rid of the problem and go on with life." One afternoon he rode his motorcycle to a quiet spot on a hill overlooking the city to think about their dilemma. "I got kinda alone with myself," he said, "and started wondering about God, and if I was just going to continue the way I was going—you know, self-centered and 'party Doug'—or if I was going to start thinking about getting serious and doing something.

"I started wondering if God really was real. You look across the city, and there's churches and cathedrals everywhere. At that point I started wondering, 'Can all these people be wrong? Is it possible that they're doing all of this for something that isn't even there, just a figment of their imagination?'" For a builder, these were impressive facts to ponder.

Doug vowed to "search it out," and after he and Terry married they became more involved in the Catholic parish of their childhood. For a time, Doug even attended mass every weekday morning before work. He also began praying for his family's needs (an apartment, a car, a house) and for things for his business (a van, a garage to store things in) and noticed, albeit gradually, God's concrete, uncanny answers to those prayers. Sometimes these answers came through the intervention of fellow parishioners, such as his neighbor, who let him know about a house for sale on his block. It was a run-down, unsightly two-bedroom clapboard house. Terry remembered walking past it as a child and thinking it was definitely *not* a house she would ever live in. But before sharing a word about it with her, Doug looked at it and made an offer of $15,000, which was accepted. Terry was upset when she found out. However, with help from friends and family in the building trades, Doug renovated it from top to bottom, making it a home Terry was pleasantly surprised to be happy to live in.

Meanwhile, problems mounted in Doug and Terry's marriage. Both told me they had never communicated much, but what they meant by that came home to me only through incidental details of stories they told—such as Doug's not telling Terry about making an offer on the house. He also had not shared much with her about his spiritual search. In the early years of their marriage, after the birth of their first child, Terry found herself "always unhappy," she said, and "yelling at Doug all the time." He was rarely at home. He was working crazy hours, and given the rising frictions at home, Doug, like Phil Strong, found the pleasures of going out to drink with his pals after work increasingly attractive. Terry found it hard being "home alone all the time with the kids," she said. "I was bored, so I just drank."

For his part, Doug found himself praying fervently at the time "that God would cause me to love her, because I didn't want to be another divorce statistic." They sought counseling from a Catholic priest, which proved disappointing. He tended to put Terry down, they said, and focused on behavioral tasks, such as Terry getting her driver's license. (At twenty-three, she was afraid to learn to drive, and because this kept her homebound, it had become an issue between them.) Doug and Terry contrasted this counseling experience with the help they found for their marriage at Shawmut River, where the pastor, Doug pointed out, could advise them from his own experience as husband and father. But it was not Shawmut River's framework for dealing with marriage that attracted Doug most to fundamentalist Christianity.

When Doug first met Frank Valenti on the job, Frank put a question to him that had been occupying him for some time. "Where will you go when you die?" Frank had asked.

From his Catholic background, Doug thought, "I'll never know until I die whether or not I'm going to heaven. All's I can hope for is to do my best, be a good person and try my best not to hurt anyone, and when my turn comes up, the Lord'll give me a fair shake. The thing that got me," Doug noticed, "is that Frank came in and brought a Bible, whereas I've talked with priests before and they never cracked open a book. And he started preaching to me directly from scripture. He'd open up the page and he'd point his finger at it, and say, 'Right here!' And he showed me in Romans where it says, 'If thou shalt confess with the mouth Lord Jesus and shall believe in the heart that God raised him from the dead, thou shalt be saved.' And I went, 'Wow!'"

Soon after, Pastor Valenti wrangled an invitation to stop by the Lavernes' home on the pretext of delivering Doug's check for the gymnatorium job. Terry was "up in arms," Doug said.

"We weren't great on entertaining," Terry explained. "I offered him a beer," she remembered with a laugh as the three of us talked one afternoon in their living room.

"He sat right here and I was right there," Doug recalled, sitting next to Terry on the couch. "He gave us the plan of salvation, and I prayed. And as I was praying the prayer, I knew what I was doing, I knew the commitment I was making. It wasn't just, you know, 'I'm gonna say this prayer and get up and walk away and know that heaven's in the bag,' you know." He chuckled and, taking on a serious look, continued: "When he left, I felt a peace. It was kind of spooky—I don't know how to explain it—it was better than any drugs I ever did. I wanted to go outside and do some screamin'. And as the days and weeks went by, I started realizing how real it was, that it was to heaven from this point forward, because of what Christ had done. And I was filled with joy." Doug found himself thinking, "Give me some more of what's in that book!" and began attending services regularly at Shawmut River.

Though Terry also said the sinner's prayer in front of Pastor Valenti that night, she later admitted it had not been heartfelt—a matter of decisive importance for being saved. "I didn't know what was happening, really," she confessed. "I was just hoping he'd leave." But not long thereafter she made a profession of faith, and several months after that, in July, both she and Doug "surrendered" for baptism.

It was the first baptism I witnessed at Shawmut River, and because Frank had not yet installed the church's own baptistry—a pool large enough for immersing an adult—it was done on a Sunday afternoon at Heritage Baptist, the church the Sandersons and Keeners had once attended. Heritage Baptist was housed in a solid brick building. Scott and Sue sang "Standing on the Promises of God" and "Calvary Covered It All," and five people, including Doug and Terry, lined up to enter the baptismal pool sunk into the dais behind the altar.

Baptism was not done to ensure or effect salvation in any way. Salvation was seen as a free gift, which had only to be accepted by faith in the knowledge that Christ died for your sins. Following Baptist teachings, members of Shawmut River believed that this view ruled out infant baptism as practiced by Catholics, Methodists and others, which is done before a person is old enough to recognize sin and make a decision for Christ. Yet, they affirmed, once salvation had been accepted, nothing could change it one way or another. Pastor Valenti distinguished this teaching from that of the Nazarenes or Jehovah's Witnesses, who taught, he said, that you could *lose* your salvation. Instead, baptism was seen as an outward sign of the inner decision to accept Christ, "like slipping a ring over your finger when you get married," Doug Laverne said, repeating an analogy commonly made. "It's just a symbol."

All five candidates for baptism carried bags of fresh clothes onto the dais and were dressed casually in jeans and T-shirts. Pastor Valenti met with the group beforehand, assuring them they had nothing to worry about. Wearing army green fisherman's waders, Pastor Valenti climbed down into the pool, which was about nine feet long and four feet wide. Unsteady without the metal braces attached to his specially made shoes, he took each step cautiously. One after another the candidates climbed down into the pool, up to their chests in water, and responded to his questions. "Terry, have you received Christ as your personal Lord and savior?" he asked Terry Laverne. She was a slip of a woman, with pitch-black hair and blue-gray eyes.

"I have," she replied.

Frank put a handkerchief over her nose and mouth and said, "I therefore baptize you in the name of the Father, Son and Holy Ghost. Buried in the likeness of his death"—he dipped her backward under the water as he spoke and, lifting her back up, continued: "and raised in the newness of life." Terry sputtered and blinked her eyes open to see. Dripping from head to toe, she climbed up the steps and took her place on the stage next to Doug, who smiled broadly and gave her a reassuring hug.

Despite these steps, Terry did not embrace the new faith with anything like Doug's conviction and zeal. As a fresh convert "on fire for the Lord," Doug reminded the Valentis and Strongs of their own excitement in the wake of conversion, and they happily watched him move forward to embrace each new step required of "a new babe in Christ": to attend weekly services, "get into God's word," witness to the unsaved and even tithe 10 percent of his income.

"I never wanted to be a slave to money," Doug said about tithing, "but some way or another you always feel it. You say, 'Do another job! Yeah! Build that checkbook up! Build it up!' When it came time for me to tithe, I said this is to prove that I'm not enslaved to that, just to do the opposite of what 'the world' tells you to do: to write a check out and give it to the church." It impressed me that Doug actually found tithing liberating.

None of these acts of obedience, however, and none of what was entailed by the larger vocation of following Christ, was required for salvation. Instead, they were usually undertaken out of a sense of obligation to Christ. As Doug put it, "because of what he done for me." For Doug, like others at Shawmut River, what connected being saved with following Christ was not the desire to achieve any ethical good or to show love to others for its own sake but, instead, simply the obligation to do things for Christ because of what he had done for them on the cross. Their relationship with Christ, like their relationships with one another, was modeled on the ethic of reciprocity.

Burdened by this sense of obligation, Doug even managed to overcome his pronounced shyness with strangers in order to engage in bold acts of witnessing. He recounted going into a coffee shop with a workmate who pretended he had just picked up a Gospel tract and was reading it aloud to him. When he came to the part that says a man must "repent," Doug, playing the straight man, asked, "Repent? What's that?"

With that a man sitting next to them jumped out of his seat and exclaimed, "Are you serious? You don't know what repent is?" and launched into a fuller discussion of the Gospel for all around them in the coffee shop to hear.

Witnessing closer up to family and friends, however, proved more difficult. Doug thought that telling his father about the "good news" preached at Shawmut River would be like telling him about an "excellent fishing hole" and that the very next Sunday his father would be up there with him. He was puzzled, then, when his father and other family members seemed uninterested. Finally, his father leveled with him.

"What are you doing up there anyway?" Doug recalled him asking indignantly. "You have a church right down here," he said, referring to the Catholic parish of Doug's childhood.

When Doug and Terry were baptized, Doug was surprised at how badly both sets of parents took it. "I didn't realize it at the time," Doug said, "but the pastor pointed out that by getting baptized we were telling them that their way was no good. I guess my father kind of felt I thought he had failed."

Friction over these issues grew. Doug and Terry's refusal to attend a niece's christening—which Shawmut River deemed an unscriptural, cultish practice—sent shock waves of hurt and resentment through the family. Family members saw Doug and Terry as "brainwashed" and "self-righteous," and Doug recounted being needled at one family gathering about all the bad things he and Terry used to do as teenagers, as if their claim to be saved meant to deny they had done wrong. "That ain't it at all," Doug explained to me. "I'm a sinner just like them—but a sinner who's been saved by grace." At that point, however, he felt they did not want to hear any more. "As soon as they say their piece," he observed, "they just turn you off."

Amid such conflicts and hard feelings, the news that Doug and Terry were starting a Bible-study group in their home, to which family and friends were invited, undoubtedly provoked suspicion. One of Terry's uncles, a theologically minded bachelor much involved in his own Catholic parish, attended for a while, in part, I imagined, to keep watch on behalf of Terry's family. I had come to see fundamentalist

churches as affirming and strengthening family ties. Yet here and elsewhere, becoming a born-again believer also threw up divisions and
discord.

Apart from Terry's uncle and a younger sister, who attended occasionally, most members of our Bible study were drawn from Doug's
side of the family. His two younger brothers attended. The older one,
Jeff, came with his wife, Sandy, a rugged woman who had been trained
as an auto mechanic but currently worked at a McDonald's. Jeff, by
contrast, was of slight build. When he worked, it was on plastering jobs
with Doug or in the Laverne family's store, where Doug and his siblings would help out—and *be* helped out, with groceries and other supplies. A downturn in the fortunes of one sibling or another could
suddenly push up the "grocery bill," as they called it, at the family
store. When we went around the table at our Bible study asking for
prayer requests, Jeff would mention needing some work to pay his rent
and wink Doug's way.

Doug's youngest brother, Gene, also attended. Like Doug and Jeff
before him, Gene had dropped out of high school, and he was still living at home. He usually came with his girlfriend, Amy, who was in her
senior year of high school and thinking about college.

Others from Doug and Terry's circle of family and friends came and
went for different periods of time. Some, such as Gene, Amy and Jeff,
got saved and began attending Shawmut River. Others, such as two of
Terry's sisters and friends Doug and Terry knew from their neighborhood gang, accepted Christ but never joined. They continued to
attend their own Catholic parishes (as did a number of Frank Valenti's
relatives whom he had originally led to the Lord).

The only member of our group from outside the Lavernes' circle,
besides me, was Ben Kachudnis, whose marriage crisis we would eventually follow in our documentary film. Pastor Valenti encouraged Ben
to join our group to help hold him together during a wrenching crisis
in his life. Several months before, Ben had come home one day to find
his wife, Pam, had left, taking their three sons with her (two were from
Pam's previous marriages, and one was theirs). For months he had no
idea where they were. During this period, Ben told me, he would walk
by his stove and think, "Well, just turn on the gas, blow out the pilots
and go to bed—a piece of cake."

Instead, Ben returned to Shawmut River, which he and Pam had
attended until Pastor Valenti had insisted they stop smoking if they

wanted to continue working at the Christian Academy, where Pam taught and Ben coached. Instead, they had left, and now Ben, with his wife and children gone, had returned. It was "like coming home," he said. "I could breathe there; I could actually sit and someone was here to comfort me." Many church members helped comfort Ben at the time. Pastor Valenti was continually counseling him. He took phone calls from Ben in the middle of the night, prayed with him before each service and often singled him out for attention during services with a joke, prayer request or call for an affirming "amen."

Frank felt our Bible-study group would help strengthen Ben and keep him from doing something rash, even tragic. In January, soon after we started meeting, his sons' local school received transfer papers for them, and Ben discovered they were in Florida and Pam was with a man they both had known in Worcester. Ben began obsessing about going to Florida to see them, joking on one occasion about taking a .38 pistol along. "If I hadn't come back to church," Ben once told me, "I really think I would have gone down to Florida and killed them— that's how hurt I was."

Our Bible study was to be led by Fred Webber, who had recently become an assistant to Pastor Valenti. A big, burly man with a deeply tanned face, hazel eyes and wavy brown hair, Fred was a jack-of-all-trades who had spent stints working as a detective, as an assistant to an escape artist (he was good with locks) and as a truck driver. It was while driving a truck and listening to Jerry Falwell's radio broadcast one afternoon that he had stepped out of his cab at a busy intersection in Saugus, Massachusetts, got down on his knees and accepted Christ. Soon after, he had called Liberty Baptist College. Someone had directed him to Shawmut River, an LBC-related church near his home in Worcester. He had enrolled in a correspondence course at Liberty Baptist and, under Frank Valenti's tutelage, had begun preparations for the ministry.

Bible Study
February 21

"Okay, it's not a long chapter," Fred Webber said to begin our study of the twelfth chapter of Genesis after our customary small talk over coffee and our opening prayer, "but there's a whole lot in it, so, Doug, why don't you start." We began each week by taking turns reading

aloud from one chapter, beginning with Genesis, chapter 1. Doug
Laverne read haltingly:

> Now the Lord had said unto Abram, Get thee out of thy coun-
> try, and from thy kindred, and from thy father's house, unto a
> land *that will suit thee . . .*

"No," Doug interrupted himself, seeing he had misread the last
phrase. Fred helped by reading the actual text over with him slowly:
"*. . . unto - a - land - that - I - will - shew - thee.*"

"Wow, I skipped a whole bunch of words there," Doug said, laughing at himself to make light of the embarrassment he felt on this and
other occasions when his poor reading skills showed. Reading itself
proved a challenge for others around the table, too, especially the men,
whose time and attention at school had often been more limited than
the women's. Doug had already come a long way since getting saved
and starting to read the Bible—or *anything*, for that matter. Before
then, he told me, he had been in the habit of just opening his mail and
throwing it away. Reading was just too difficult. Such reading habits,
however, jeopardized his new plastering business, as he struggled to
keep track of a growing stream of small jobs, each with its own estimates, costs, supplies, bills and payments, all recorded in piles of paper
accumulating next to the family phone, in his van and on a desk in one
corner of their basement. In this context, it was amazing to see the
archaic prose of the King James Bible become the raw material with
which Doug and others were learning to read.

Doug returned to Genesis, chapter 12, and with renewed concen-
tration continued to read, slowly but surely:

> And I will make of thee a great nation, and I will bless thee, and
> make thy name great; and thou shalt be a blessing: And I will
> bless them that bless thee, and curse him that curseth thee: and
> in thee shall all families of the earth be blessed. So Abram
> departed, as the Lord had spoken unto him; and Lot went with
> him; and Abram was seventy and five years old when he
> departed out of . . .

Doug paused in the face of the place-name "Haran," and Fred helped
him "sound it out," relying on the phonetic approach to reading naturally favored by those steeped in oral culture.[2]

Others in our group had even more trouble reading than Doug. And all of us experienced difficulties reading the lengthy genealogies in Genesis, including names such as Abimael, Arphaxad and Hazarmaveth. Once Terry emerged from reading a forest of such names and came upon the simple sentence "But Sarai was barren; she had no child." She laughed with relief.

"Thank God!" someone exclaimed to make her feel better. "Otherwise she would have named 'em something real bad!"

IT SEEMED we were always reading Genesis. At a chapter a week, it would have taken us a full year to get through just the fifty chapters of Genesis alone. That would have caused a vain tedium none of us could have stomached for long, had it not been for the various asides, detours and commentaries that peppered our study. "Rabbit trails," we called them with relish. They reflected the realities of our method, starting with an initial text and departing from it to pursue relevant questions, often of practical significance: such as what a "covenant" is; how we could "prove," Fred said, turning to II Timothy (3:16–17), that the Bible was "inspired by the Holy Spirit"; what "submission" in marriage means; why speaking in tongues is unscriptural; how to pray and what prayers God answers; how Christians are to settle disputes if the Bible prohibits them from taking a "brother" to court; where the Bible stipulates believers must attend church; how to know if Pastor Valenti, or any pastor, is "called of God."

To discuss these points "scripturally," which was always our goal, Fred would say, "Keep your finger in Genesis and turn over to Hebrews . . . Romans . . . First Peter," or wherever the relevant passage could be found. Learning how to find our way around the Bible in this fashion was one competence in which all of us could take satisfaction. And through Fred, members would order new Bibles, deciding on an edition with tabs, a "red-letter edition" with Jesus' words set in red italics or a hefty deluxe leather-bound one in a zippered case. It was always the King James Version, though I later learned that Pastor Valenti, as a Liberty Baptist graduate, did not insist on that translation.

We were encouraged to take notes in our Bibles. "The Bible's written on paper," Fred would remind us to overcome any reluctance we felt to write in this most sacred book, "and what's the one thing paper's good for?"

"Writing," we learned to answer in unison.

To live by the word of God, Fred assured us, the only things we'd ever need were "the Bible, a concordance—Strong's is best—and a dictionary." Yet he warned us that we should take whatever we read in the dictionary with a grain of salt—"It's not divinely inspired." Above all, he emphasized, "our study needs to be guided by the Holy Spirit." Since the Holy Spirit was ultimately the "author" of the Bible and came to dwell in the heart of a born-again believer, he stood to be our only sure teacher, enabling us to discern meanings God intended for us. That meant not just a passage's meaning in general but its specific meaning for us right now, in this context, given our particular dilemmas or needs. Members of Shawmut River often expressed their wonder that a pastor's preaching from the word of God would normally hit a variety of listeners with different meanings specifically targeted for them. This was one of the mysterious—even miraculous—ways God's word would be seen to profit those who believed in Jesus and turned to the Bible for help. Other ways included simply opening a Bible at random, after prayer, and seeing what answers to a certain dilemma God provided on that page. If, after invoking the Holy Spirit through prayer, we still could not understand a passage, Fred asked us, "What was the last resource I told you to turn to?"

"The pastor," we responded.

"Right," he said, affirming the authority fundamentalists invest in a pastor to determine correct interpretations of scripture for his flock.

Our rabbit trails, or digressions, were governed, above all, by the practical interests and felt needs of our group. Sometimes passages were turned to in order to address mundane problems—with a business, a child, a marriage—or an obstacle preventing someone from accepting Christ, or questions about the biblical rationale for certain elements of church life. Our habit of searching scripture for practical answers to concrete problems became, at times, a source of humor. Once when Doug was frustrated with his brother Gene's unkempt appearance at work, he thumbed through his Bible and asked Fred, half jokingly, "Hey, where are the haircuts in this thing?"

Compared with some of the long genealogical chapters our Bible-study group slogged through, chapter 12 of Genesis held a more pointed lesson this evening. Abraham (who was called "Abram," we learned, until God changed his name upon forming a covenant with him)—had obeyed God's commandment to leave the place called

Haran, Fred pointed out, but only *partly*. He had *not* removed himself from his kindred, as God had commanded in verse 1, but had brought Lot, his uncle's son, with him. So, Fred explained, "Abraham got into all kinds of trials," including a famine that forced him to go into Egypt, where further troubles befell him. But because Abraham had faithfully obeyed *two* of God's commandments, Fred explained, "God continued to work with him, because God's trustworthy, he's faithful. He made the promise and he's not going to go back on it."

Like popular biblical commentary reaching back to the Puritans, we read Old Testament stories such as Abraham and Sarah's as, above all, conveying to us vital facts about the "promises of God."[3] If God told Noah he would never again flood the earth, we learned, he would stick to that promise and find other ways to discipline Israel. God was not arbitrary or capricious, we were taught, but faithfully kept his promises. So, too, would he keep these promises to us now, often in as fantastic and miraculous ways as he did in Old Testament times.

We read this Old Testament pattern of promise making and promise keeping in light of God's ultimate promise of salvation through Christ, following the dispensationalist approach to biblical interpretation embraced by fundamentalists in the late nineteenth century (see chapter 13). Since this was God's *eternal* plan for humankind, evidence of this plan, and even actual appearances of Christ, we were taught, could be found in the Old Testament itself. From this New Testament perspective, we learned to recognize that Abraham "received his salvation" at the moment he first obeyed God. We also learned to recognize various appearances of Christ in Old Testament references to the "Angel of the Lord" or the story of Melchizedek (Genesis 14:18–19), who, as "priest of the most high God," brought forth bread and wine to bless Abraham. We learned to call these Old Testament appearances of Christ "Christophanies," employing the kind of technical jargon that carried the aura of specialized knowledge. Showing us how to recognize and decode such clues in scripture in order to reveal its hidden meanings also served to give us confidence in the authoritative character of the knowledge we were gaining.

However, there were distinct limits, we were instructed, in how much specialized knowledge was needed to understand the Bible. Though our study was guided by practical, not theoretical, concerns, theoretical reflection regularly came into play when we approached important doctrinal issues. For example, on one of his periodic visits to our group, Pastor Valenti chose to study the Book of James because Doug had told him someone new was coming that evening. Fundamentalists turn most often to the Letters of the Apostles to find and teach doctrine, and Frank had chosen the Book of James because of its discussion of salvation by *faith* rather than by *works*. This issue had been central to Martin Luther's critique of the Catholic church during the Reformation and was bound to stir up controversy in the Laverne family circle.

"Let's do this first," Pastor Valenti proposed to begin our study. "Define 'works'—speaking spiritually."

"Doing something physical in the name of Jesus," Doug Laverne offered.

"Anything you do is a work," suggested Ben Kachudnis.

Explaining that the Greek word for "work," *ergon*, meant "a person doing something," Frank said that, in approaching the Book of James, we were talking specifically about "works that save" and "works that condemn." This prompted a response from Terry's uncle Peter, a devout Catholic.

"When we're not with Christ," Peter theorized, "then we're coming from the flesh and we're doing the works of the flesh. And when we're converted to Christ, then we're doing God's will."

"Right," Frank affirmed. "That's exactly what I'm alluding to." Whether works were good or bad, he went on to teach, depended on whether one was saved or not. Having us turn to James, chapter 2, Frank read verses 8–10, ending with "For whosoever shall keep the whole law, and yet offend in one point, he is guilty of all."

"So he's setting up a standard of righteousness," Frank pointed out, going on to liken the Ten Commandments to a chain. If we break just one link in the chain—any link—the whole chain breaks, the whole law is broken, cutting off our relationship with God. No one can meet this standard of righteousness, Frank argued, turning for support to Romans 3:10, where Paul says, "As it is written, there is none righteous, no, not one."

Not only did this mean our own works could not get us to heaven, he continued, but to believe they can is, in fact, deeply "obnoxious" to God. "Why does God hate works prior to salvation?" Frank asked.

To answer this question, he then proposed one of his favorite hypothetical illustrations: the little old lady who is so good that we are tempted to think she, if anyone, deserves to go to heaven. But she most certainly has committed at least one sin, Frank pointed out, and hence broken the whole law according to James (2:10). And now, he continued, if she comes before God on Judgment Day believing she deserves heaven because of her good works, "what she's literally saying to God is 'God, you see, I didn't need Jesus. You were a fool to give Jesus! All these works I did made me, in and of myself, worthy to come into your heaven.'

"Now, can you imagine what God is going to say to that little old lady," Frank said, his eyes widening at the thought of telling God he sacrificed his only son for nothing. "Her works of self-righteousness are going to be more of a stench in the nostrils of God than Al Capone, who knows what a filthy wretch *he* is. They're saying there *is* another way to get to heaven. God, you *were* a fool to give Jesus!

"And the worst part of the whole thing," Frank continued, "she says she has faith in God. She says, 'I'm a good Catholic. I go to church every Sunday, I say the rosary up and down.' Or 'I'm a good Baptist. I go to church every Sunday. I even read the Bible once in a while.' Can that faith coupled with her works save her?"

"No," several around the table responded.

"It can't!" Frank affirmed. "It's impossible! Why? Because she has still ignored Jesus. Because 'in him, of him, to him and through him,' according to Romans, chapter eleven, verse thirty-six. You can't bypass him. The minute you try to be good to get to heaven, you're done."

These conclusions troubled Terry. "How do you know the old lady is condemned?" she asked Frank tentatively.

Frank turned back to Romans 3:10 to read again, "There is none righteous, no, not one," and went so far as to say that the blood of all those people this little old lady led astray by her wrong thinking would be required of her on Judgment Day.

"Is she conscious of it?" Terry asked.

"Probably not," Frank replied. "Most little old ladies are a byproduct of lousy religion—a religion that doesn't take the time to find out what God wants from them."

"'Doesn't take the time'?" Terry asked incredulously, perhaps thinking of her uncle Peter sitting next to her, who as a Catholic conducted as rigorous and time-consuming a religious life as anyone she'd ever known.

In sympathy with her deepening puzzlement, her husband, Doug, offered an example to help "put it into perspective."

"I can't say that my grandmother wasn't saved," Doug began, measuring his words. "She's dead now—the Lord rest her soul—but when she was in the hospital for the last time, I had brought her up a Christmas gift. And it was a statue of the Virgin Mary. And she was cryin' and sayin' how that was her favorite person, her favorite saint or whatever." His eyes watered to recall this tender moment with someone he obviously loved and respected. "And that was just the sweetest little old lady that you'd ever know . . . just misled." This last phrase Doug added in such a low voice that it might not have been heard. But it was not missed by Terry's uncle Peter.

"Excuse me," Peter interjected moments later. "I was a little offended here because I'm Catholic and I believe in my religion. When Doug mentioned something about the Virgin Mary, it struck me wrong because I feel he gave the impression that his grandmother was worshiping the Blessed Mother—who is supposed to be the Mother of God!" He went on to defend the practice of holding Mary in high esteem, noting, "This does not mean we're saved through Mary—we're saved only through Jesus."

Frank promised to consider these questions on another occasion when "we'll take up the study of 'idol worship.'"

"No, no, wait a minute now!" Peter objected. "I'm not talking about statues . . ." He pointed out that Catholics don't worship statues. "They are just a help to remind us of the person they represent."

Frank accepted his point and promised to devote our study next week to "worshiping images and all the peripherals of that."

"Yeah," Doug said thoughtfully, rubbing his chin, "that really would be interesting." He then turned to Peter to explain that by saying his grandmother's favorite saint was the Virgin Mary, he hadn't meant to say she didn't believe in Christ.

Discussion then turned to whether one could ever determine, in retrospect, whether Doug's grandmother, or anyone, was "a confirmed believer in the Lord Jesus Christ," as Frank put it, and therefore saved. Though the discussion remained inconclusive, Frank's thinking on this question turned on whether someone relied on the Bible as the foundation of his or her faith. "Can you believe in Jesus without believing in his book?" Frank asked rhetorically.

Our visitor that evening was still troubled, she said, by the fact that the little old lady thought she was doing the right thing, but, according to Frank, that was only bringing herself deeper into hell. "I don't think that's fair," she complained, "I don't feel that's right."

"You said the magic word, *fair*," Doug noted immediately.

"God isn't *fair*, he's *right*," Ben Kachudnis added knowingly.

"God isn't *fair?*" our visitor asked, shaking her head in bewilderment. The rest of us knew all too well from earlier discussions that, for fundamentalists at Shawmut River, judgments about what is "fair" or not represented human opinions that did not count in the face of what God says in the Bible. Meanwhile, Frank wrote four words on a piece of paper and held it up to our visitor.

"See those four words?" he said. "You said 'I think' and 'I feel.' The key is to *prove* what you think and *prove* what you feel!"

11

Prayer Life

God is a God of specificity.

Pastor Valenti's injunctions to "*prove* what you think" and "*prove* what you feel" expressed something essential about fundamentalists' use of the Bible. Apart from its colorful, even poetic, uses in personal exhortation and preaching, it was also used to "prove" matters of doctrine and morality revealed by God. This was often done by moving around the Bible to make use of various passages to define terms and fashion general propositions related to them—a method critics came to call "proof-texting." It sometimes bore a resemblance to that kind of scholarship where arguments are fashioned by stringing together citations from established sources. However, for fundamentalists there is only one essential source, the Bible. It is, however, a monumental one, offering rich and diverse materials for such an enterprise. It is made up of texts written over the course of twelve centuries by diverse writers in various languages and literary forms, some of which were derived from long-standing oral traditions whose origins cannot be traced. And its exact composition, including which existing accounts of Jesus' life and teachings were included and which excluded, was not fixed until Christianity became the state religion of the Roman Empire under Constantine.[1] Nevertheless, fundamentalists have no trouble believing that it was within the Holy Spirit's power to create, through this highly ramified and convoluted process, a text wholly without error or contradiction and perfectly suited for all peoples at all times, including us in twenty-first-century America.

Like the scholarly usage of established texts, our use of scripture

was guided by certain interests at hand that were not always prominent, or even very evident, in the passages we took up. For example,
while we approached chapter 2 of the Book of James with an interest in
the question of why "works" cannot get someone to heaven—a Reformation issue—the passages we used were more intent on establishing
the fact that "faith *without works* is dead" and that for Abraham "*by
works* was faith made perfect" (verses 20–22). We read this passage,
instead, through Reformation eyes. On other occasions, I could imagine Pastor Valenti reading it to suggest how we might know by a person's deeds whether he or she was genuinely saved.

In our more routine study of Genesis, however, we spent most of
our time drawing out practical lessons about God from the many
"family stories" Pastor Valenti said the Old Testament contained—
from the story of Abraham and Sarah, for instance, how God would
make and keep promises to us contingent on our obedience to him.
But more important than any of these interpretive exercises, perhaps,
were the ways in which our Bible-study group enacted some of those
very lessons in our own "prayer life" together.

Members of Shawmut River spoke of their "prayer life" the way
other people speak of "social life," "family life" or "professional life"—
that is, as an important, abiding, integral part of life. It was in our Bible
study that new converts from the Laverne family circle learned how to
pray and how to have a prayer life. That involved not only "communicating with God," as Fred Webber defined prayer in its simplest terms,
but also communicating with one another. Jesus told his disciples, Fred
reminded us again and again, citing Matthew 18:19, that "if two of
you shall agree on earth as touching any thing that they shall ask, it
shall be done for them . . ." Praying *together* about something made a
difference.

Each Thursday evening we went around the table to take prayer
requests, to check if everyone had prayed during the week about things
members had requested and to see how God had answered our
prayers—or, if not, how we should wait upon him faithfully to answer
them in his *own* time, not ours. As an unbeliever, I was not expected to
pray. But I was invited to request prayer on my own behalf, something
I came to genuinely welcome, especially for my film project or some
other employment. It was a comfort to have our group pray for my
needs, and I had come to reckon, like Pascal, that if there were a God
who answered prayer, I would not want to pass up the opportunity to
avail myself of that power.

We usually took prayer requests at the end of our meeting, unless issues erupted in the middle of our study or pushed themselves to the fore in informal conversations at the beginning. That talk often gave direction to both our Bible study that night and our prayer requests.

One evening as we first gathered and settled into conversation over the coffee, soda and cake Terry served, Doug and his brother Gene resumed an argument that had begun on the job that afternoon. Maintaining work discipline among the family members he hired was an ongoing annoyance for Doug and a recurring source of tension in our group. Employing his brothers was part of the web of reciprocities linking the Laverne family members together, a reality that naturally constrained Doug's freedom to enforce work discipline by hiring and firing whomever he pleased. For example, at the end of a beautiful day that summer, Doug told us with amused exasperation about driving to a job at 6:00 in the morning with his eighteen-year-old brother, Gene, following reluctantly behind in his truck. "I kept him right in my rearview mirror," Doug said, "then suddenly I looked up and he was gone." Gene had veered off to go spend that hot summer day at the beach. Yet this, even on top of other derelictions of duty, was not sufficient cause for Doug to fire his brother.

On this particular afternoon, Gene had yelled at Doug on a job and refused to pick up some drop cloths. Doug had thrown them in his face. That evening at Bible study, Fred had each vent his feelings and then settled us down to make prayer requests, saying that *he* would pray for patience for Gene, and for Doug "growth on all fronts," including "being more communicative with his guys at work."

On other evenings, conflicts in marriage pressed for attention. If Doug and Terry had argued that day—say, about Doug's not letting Terry know his schedule—our Bible study that night might gravitate to problems of communication in marriage, and Fred would elicit from Doug the request that our group pray that he be more sensitive to his wife and communicate better with her.

What Terry appreciated most about their new faith were the changes it had brought in their marriage. Instead of going out after work to drink with the boys, she told me, "Doug came right home, and we started talking to each other more." Over supper, Terry and Doug reported, they had begun comparing notes to see how their prayers of support for each other during the day had been answered. In this way, too, their communication improved.

Other needs our Bible-study group regularly committed to prayer—apart from the salvation of specific relatives and friends— were for Ben and Terry to quit smoking (Terry had already quit drinking), for Ben to find work and see his family reunited, for Jeff and his wife to find work and for me to have my film project funded or find other employment.

"When does your unemployment insurance run out?" Fred asked me, to determine what the group should specifically be praying for in my case. "God is a God of specificity," Fred never tired of reminding us, instructing us (as did the famed nineteenth-century evangelist Charles Finney) to make our prayers as specific as possible.

"In April," I replied. He then urged the group to take responsibility, as Christians should, and redouble their prayers on my behalf.

Whatever else this might have accomplished, sharing our problems, desires and needs put us into one another's shoes and knit us together as people who knew and cared about one another. Sympathy naturally flowed from this sharing and was evident in words and gestures of genuine concern and encouragement. It was evident, for instance, in the way the group enfolded Ben's three sons when they sometimes attended meetings after Ben had brought them back from Florida. One night we simply dropped our study for the evening to play with Ben's boys a rousing game of "Bible Trivia," a board game modeled on "Trivial Pursuit," popular at the time.

In our Bible-study group we felt we were not alone facing the problems of life, even those of us from outside the Laverne family circle. This intimacy was not created from scratch with obligatory hugs or other gestures of care and familiarity that one sometimes finds in upper-middle-class churches or secular self-help groups. Rather, it was built upon the premise of familiarity already present in the Lavernes' circle of family and friends, into which Ben, Fred and I had entered, and of which we partook. Even a rare creature like me, an observer having no previous connection to anyone in the group, felt irreversibly bonded by this experience to those in the Laverne family just joining Shawmut River. And it was this bond that prompted us to speak about *our* Bible study, as I do here, before I had come to speak about *our* church.

Shawmut River's premise of familiarity, signaled in Frank's sermons and in members' personal testimonies during worship, was now confirmed by those sitting in the pews around me whom I had come to know in our Bible-study group. Through sharing, praying and finding solutions to life's problems in scripture, Bible study at the Lavernes wove several strangers into its circle of familiarity and trust, and by so doing incorporated us all into church in a new way. In the pews around us we now had people we could count as "church family." Being incorporated into the "body" of the church seemed a fitting way to speak of the experience. The ties of intimacy that knit us together, as a small family-based group, into the larger congregation made us feel bound to one another in mutual dependence, like the body's organic unity among its various parts: hands, heads, legs. Like parts of a body, we had not chosen to associate with one another; we now *belonged* together. And if such parts of the same body were to turn against one another, would it not be an act against nature itself?

As the year unfolded I received notice from the National Endowment for the Humanities that our film grant had been approved. I dropped what I was doing, called my close friends and invited them over for a dinner party that evening to celebrate. The days of waiting in unemployment lines would soon be over, and just in time. My unemployment benefits would soon run out. I myself did not thank God for this development, but I did share this good news with our Bible-study group, which took it as an example of answered prayer.

In fact, after hearing the news, Fred told me that as the National Endowment's decision had approached, he and Pastor Valenti had actually fasted for it—for only three days, he explained, because the state of the pastor's inner ear, stemming from his war wounds, made a longer fast inadvisable. It was only now that he could tell me, Fred explained, because one condition for a fast to work, as laid down in scripture, was that it be done in secret. Another, he said, was that the person fasting should "profit nothing" from it. "If we had prayed that prayer for the benefit of *our* ministry," Fred explained, instead of for my project, "the prayer would never have been answered."

"I'm glad you didn't make a mistake," I said wryly, poking fun at a notion I tended to find troubling: that if you prayed right, God was *obliged* to act. Fred also told me that a group of men in church calling themselves Prayer Warriors had also been praying secretly for my project. Despite my skepticism, I had to ask myself: Had all these prayers, indeed, been answered?

In addition to sharing needs in prayer requests, our Bible-study group was learning how to discern God's answers to prayer and his other manifold ways of "working" in our lives. This was neither straightforward nor unambiguous. Difficult, knotty decisions, such as Doug's quandary about whether to go into business partnership with Fred, were put to prayer. (Doug eventually decided against it.) Praying and discerning answers to prayer were at the heart of developing a "walk with the Lord"—that is, of passing through time and space with God himself, in close communication with him and following his lead. Statements such as "The Lord led me to this job . . . this church . . . this person"—the kind of thing readily heard around Shawmut River—naturally occurred to someone who had, in this way, developed "a walk with the Lord."

But ambiguities about anyone's "walk" might easily arise from countless sources, including the ever-present potential for self-deception. When two separate individuals each gave Ben Kachudnis fifteen dollars to help him out, for instance, Ben saw this as God providing the finances for him to fly to Florida to see Pam and his sons. Some in our group, however, suggested that the money might have been intended, instead, to pay for his long-distance phone calls to them. Ben flew to Florida anyway and was surprised when Pam agreed to let him bring the three boys back to Worcester to live with him. He praised the Lord for answering his prayers but later wondered whether it might have been really Satan's doing, he said, because it had given Pam "one more thing to be angry at me for."

"Maybe God wanted them left there," he theorized, "so that they would, in turn, cause her to come back. . . . I mean, you can think that you're following God and be following Satan!" He laughed and rolled his eyes at this devilish conundrum.

When the boys returned with him, they all lived with Ben's mother. Then Ben began in earnest to look for a job and an apartment. When he reached a point of frustration in these efforts, he explained to our Bible study that he had told God, "Lord, I've been banging on doors for two weeks now and you haven't opened one for me yet, so you must want me to sit back and let *you* do it."

"But you still put *legs* to your prayer," Fred remonstrated. "If you say, 'I'm gonna sit here and wait for you to do something,' then God is not gonna bless it. As long as you put feet and legs to your prayer, then the Lord's gonna act." But where "turning it over to the Lord" meant being irresponsible and lazy and where not doing so meant trying to "do it all on your own" without faith in God's providence was often difficult to judge. So, too, was deciding if untoward events were the work of God or Satan.

When Doug Laverne heard that a fellow builder, to whom he had been witnessing, had accidentally shot a spike from an air gun through his leg, Doug knew immediately that "it was the Lord talkin' to him." Just as God stood ready to help us in so many ways, we learned, he also would work in our lives by punishing or reprimanding us. But later, when problems suddenly arose in my film project, the view Doug and Pastor Valenti took, I was relieved to see, was that it must be Satan "trying to get in the way." If Satan was seen to be "wily" or "cunning," it was precisely because members learned to be ever vigilant about the ways he was able to make his own doings appear to be those of God. This was another manifestation of the profound ambiguity members recognized about divining the will of God from observable events in life.

In whatever ways these interconnected discourses of prayer, testimony and spiritual discernment were applied to life, they cultivated in our group a radically supernatural view of the world and a keen consciousness of the close presence of God (and Satan) in everyday life. It encouraged us to recognize, as Fred put it, that "nothing happens by chance," or, to quote a familiar rejoinder around Shawmut River to anyone speaking about luck, "There's no luck with the Lord." In every presumably "lucky" or "chance" occurrence we could see, instead, the hand of God—or Satan.

And it was these discourses of prayer, testimony and discernment that Sharon Valenti singled out as the most important thing about the ladies' Bible study she had led at Shawmut River years before: "constant communication," she said, "not among ourselves, but with God. Every week we had answered prayers and we could see God alive in our lives." But seeing prayers answered every week depended on sharing these events, on communicating *with one another* in these ways. "Sharing," Sharon continued, "encouraged us as individuals in our own separate homes to be ever conscious of God and to keep on keeping on with the faith." In these ways, she said, we helped one another "prove" our faith.

This supernatural outlook provided the context in which other things seemed plausible. If God could hear our prayers and work in our lives through uncanny concatenations of events, and do this for each and every believer across the globe all at the same time, it did not seem unthinkable that he could have Sarah bear a child at ninety-two, could flood the entire earth or cause to be created, through an immensely complicated chain of events, a Holy Bible completely without error. The daily miracles of life routinely hoped for and witnessed made more elaborate achievements plausible.

By the same token, encountering supernatural events in the Bible made our own daily miracles comprehensible. Bible study and the discourses of our prayer life reinforced one another and infused one another with meaning. Bible stories mirrored the unfolding stories of our own lives, making biblical characters vivid, relevant and familiar. Just as God worked on Abraham, Sarah, Noah and Job, so, too, he was working on us.[2]

To deny such supernatural events was what fundamentalists objected to most about higher criticism, the modern movement of biblical scholarship—or about the scientific outlook itself. For example, simply to infer from evidence including style or emphasis that the books of the Pentateuch were not authored by Moses or that the creation story in Genesis was taken from Babylonian legend—all based on scholarly arguments excluding *supernatural* causes—seemed to deny the life experiences of the faithful. The "fundamentals" of Christianity held up as a test of faith by those who came to be called "fundamentalists" in the early twentieth century featured key miraculous events in the story of Christ: his virgin birth, deity and resurrection, as well as the inspired and infallible character of the Bible.[3]

In this dual movement of prayer and testimony, on the one hand, and Bible reading, on the other, our Bible study was training us in the essential discourses of faith at Shawmut River. Sharing needs in prayer and talking about God's answers to prayer took place day in and day out around the church and its Christian Academy: in small groups of men before each worship service, at staff meetings, at Saturday-morning men's prayer breakfasts, in groups of Prayer Warriors and in home-based Bible studies. It was also done every day with more intimate prayer partners, including husbands and wives, mothers and daughters and good friends such as Aunt Margaret and Mary Shepperson, who prayed regularly together during the school day. It was done through the "prayer chain," made up of church women organized to mobilize prayer quickly for any purpose over the phone or face-to-face through a chain of prearranged contacts. And it was done in all those informal conversations that bathed everyone's comings and goings at Shawmut River, conversations readily gravitating to issues such as "how the Lord's been leading me" or "getting my attention" as standard answers to questions like "How are you?" or, as Fred Webber would say, "How's the Lord been treatin' ya?"

Where prayer was shared in small groups or pairs, it usually took the form of each person praying aloud one after another around a circle with a leader drawing the series to a close. In larger groups this kind of public prayer might give rise to the tendency Sally Keener deplored of individuals trying to show off "how good they prayed." But in the smaller gatherings around Shawmut River, where people came to know one another's problems and needs, this was not common.

In our Bible study Doug Laverne led the way, as he did in many things, in learning how to pray and in developing a prayer life. It was Phil Strong who first encouraged Doug to pray aloud when they met for lunch during the workday, as they sometimes did. "I can't," Doug replied, "not in a public place or anything like that."

"Why not?" Doug recalled Phil asking him. "Jesus is sittin' right next to you, so just thank him for what he's puttin' on your plate." Since then, Doug had developed his ability to lead in prayer—to, as he put it, "try and think on something that's going to get everybody to lead in one direction."

This effort, as Doug described it, to direct fellow supplicants in "one direction"—to lead people to pray as a "we-group"—gave public prayer its potential political dimensions. After all, simply to pray "We thank you, God" for something makes that thing something everyone hearing that prayer apparently endorses as being in God's will. For his part, Scott Sanderson observed how easily public prayer could "get out of hand," and Sharon's mother, Ada, how easily it could descend into gossip. In times of congregational conflict it could be used to press one side of an issue—for example, during the Tatum crisis, when Sharon's stepfather, Tom Morse, prayed to God to "bring your wrath on those attacking your fort here at Shawmut River."

But all these public performances of prayer rode on the surface of more pervasive, private ones. Doug Laverne, like others, found that driving his truck around the city provided some of the best times to pray. Fred described the fluid communication any of us might develop with God with an illustration drawn from Pastor Valenti's preaching. Wondering in which direction his sermon should go, the pastor, Fred told us, would throw up a prayer so quickly that the Holy Spirit could instantaneously give direction to his preaching.

One Thursday evening, much to my surprise, Fred asked me to open our Bible study in prayer. On impulse, I agreed. I was in all other ways, after all, a participant as well as an observer in our group. I did a decent job, I guess, though as a nonbeliever, I spoke *as if* talking to God. Still, when I finished, I was pleased when Doug Laverne offered an affirming "Amen!"

Learning to pray right meant learning to believe right. I once heard a member make the judgment that someone else must not be saved because "she doesn't pray right." That winter Pastor Valenti devoted one message to giving more elaborate instructions about praying, citing biblical verses helter-skelter to demonstrate his points. "You cannot pray in doubt," he warned. "If you don't go to God believing he can unscramble eggs, don't go. Second, you can't have sin in your heart. You must pray in innocence toward God and your fellowmen.

"You also need to do something for your condition," Frank continued, pointing out that "Jesus' miracles always required the beneficiaries to do something to make them work"—such as requiring a blind man to wash mud from his eyes. In conclusion, to pray effectively, he said, you need to be saved, to pray in an attitude of thanksgiving and to pray in the will of God. These strictures made praying quite a different matter than putting wishes to a genie. Among other things, the very act of praying correctly required distancing yourself from sin in what you asked—that is, in the state of your intentions. To sin in your heart would distance you from God and from his willingness to answer your prayers. Yet once these conditions were met, Pastor Valenti and others affirmed, God would grant anything in his divine will. Like fasting for my film project, there was a disquieting sense in such practical advice, that if one fulfilled *x* conditions, God would *have to* act, and you could count on him even to unscramble eggs.

This issue once came up pointedly in our Bible-study group when Fred explained that though God *might* answer the prayers of someone who was not born again, he was not *obligated* to do so. "You haven't put yourself under obligation to him," Fred told an unsaved friend of Doug Laverne, "so he isn't under obligation to you. Now, when you ask him to come into your life as Lord and Savior, then you've obligated him. Now he's answerable. Now he's gonna do something."

Such talk about "obligating" God troubled me. "What holds God to an obligation?" I asked Fred.

A bit frustrated, Fred struggled to find an answer. "Because he's all-powerful, he's all-trustworthy and he's proved himself faithful," he began. He went on to say simply that God had set up his kingdom this way. In this and other theological matters, it was not surprising that when members imagined themselves in a "personal relationship" with God, they did so in terms of the paramount ideals of the world they knew, a world in which all security, satisfaction, love and fulfillment depended upon family and family-like relationships governed by reciprocal obligation—like Doug's sense that he needed to do things for Christ because of what Christ had done for him. By the same token, the more you see God's work in your life and the blessings he bestows, the more you are obliged to serve him, and the more you serve him by giving selflessly to others and in tithes and offerings to his church, the more he blesses you. "To whom much is given, much is required," members would say, paraphrasing Luke 12:48.

The binding character of reciprocal obligations, members believed, was an absolute that God himself had ordained for all time, and they cited biblical verses such as "whatsoever a man soweth, that shall he also reap" (Galatians 6:7) or folk sayings such as "What goes 'round, comes 'round," to describe the laws of the universe God himself had set up and would abide by.

This cultural lens also sheds light on fundamentalists' firm embrace of the doctrine of substitutionary atonement held in such disfavor by liberal theologians. It sees Christ's death as an unavoidable necessity to reconcile—or to make *at-one*—God with a sinful humanity. There was no way around it. God could not simply say, "Let there be redemption." Instead, "there was something in sin" that made Jesus' death "a divine necessity," wrote a contributor on this doctrine to *The Fundamentals*, those foundational writings helping launch the fundamentalist movement at the beginning of the twentieth century.[4] According to laws of the cosmos, which even God the Creator could not breach, a price had to be paid, the reciprocal balance of gifts, services and wrongdoings had to be restored. (By the same token, to deny the legitimacy of capital punishment—a life for a life—is seen by some to deny this same principle of the universe as God ordained it.)

Fundamentalists' doctrine of substitutionary atonement, which they share with conservative Catholics, is often criticized by liberal theologians as "legalistic," but it is not legalistic in a narrow modern sense. Instead, it reflects the mainspring of reciprocity at the heart of *all* social relationships that mattered to members of Shawmut River. Reciprocity was also the common denominator of relationships of mutual dependence in the tribal, nomadic society of the ancient Hebrews. It was also central to household relations under the paterfamilias in ancient Rome, and to relations between vassal and lord in medieval Europe. All these social worlds contributed to developing and sustaining a doctrine now so objectionable to modern urbane theologians, who, by contrast, see the world around them, as one colleague put it, as being made up of "separate individuals, joined in temporary, voluntary association."[5]

To members of Shawmut River, on the other hand, living in close-knit ties to family, the doctrine of Christ's substitutionary atonement seemed sensible, if not self-evident. It is what "any man with sense today" understands, wrote the above-mentioned contributor to *The Fundamentals* on this topic, even if how Christ's "work" on the cross redeemed humankind forever was, from another point of view, an inscrutable mystery where "all human language breaks down."[6]

By the same token, if the social world the members of Shawmut River took for granted emphasized the personal, concrete and particular, was it not fitting that they would imagine God as a person—a father—rather than as a "higher power" or an "immanent principle," as H. Richard Niebuhr once characterized liberal theology? Or that they would see the Holy Spirit as a person rather than a "force"? Or that they would see evil not as an abstract force but as a "person," Satan, whose biography they could recite matter-of-factly—as the angel Lucifer, "the fairest of God's angels," as Sharon Valenti once explained to me, until he fell by trying to usurp God's position? Fundamentalists' recognition of the personal character of a supernatural world alive and present in all around them is what makes them so dead serious about condemning any efforts to play with those realities, for example, in rock-and-roll lyrics or in children's literature, where some fundamentalists have recently denounced the currently popular Harry Potter books, which tell the story of a boy who attends an illustrious school for magic and wizardry.[7]

In recognizing a world of spiritual beings—angels, demons and spirits—which they find amply demonstrated in scripture, American fundamentalists share much with the growing number of Christians in Africa, Asia and Latin America (now more than two-thirds of the world's Christians) who have been steadily building a Christianity outside the post-Enlightenment worldview of the educated West, which boxed off the realm of spirits as being irrelevant to understanding material realities.[8] Along with people living in villagelike settings throughout the world, the members of Shawmut River imagined God and the entire personified spirit world, including Satan, in terms of the logic of the social cosmos they knew. How could their ideas be seen as false according to standards taken from outside that culture? If some academic theologians insist that the Holy Spirit is a force or it is bad theology to think that Satan works on us or that God required his son to be sacrificed on the cross to pay for our sins, I had to wonder whether this did not partly reflect the social world these critics inhabit and its remove from the workaday worlds of masses of ordinary Christians around the globe.[9] Like others, the members of Shawmut River saw the Gospel through their own culture. And, from a believer's point of view, is it not likely that a merciful, all-knowing God would speak and relate to them through this same culture—that is, in terms they would understand?

I 2

Biblical Morality

It doesn't break up families . . . or sink ships.

Rᴏɢᴇʀ's ʜᴇʀᴇ!" Doug Laverne exclaimed as we sat around the dinner table chatting about prayer and fasting one Thursday evening—"All right!"

"Does he have a beer can?" Fred asked gingerly.

Roger was a friend of Doug's and a fellow plasterer. His wife was expecting their third child, and he was working feverishly on the side to finish building a new home for his growing family. He was grateful to Doug for finding time to help him out despite Doug's own hectic schedule.

Roger felt comfortable dropping by the Lavernes' any time and often arrived in the middle of our Bible study, usually with a beer or six-pack in hand. Apart from his coming early, tonight was no exception.

The struggle to see Roger get saved, which tended to preoccupy our group whenever he came, usually gravitated to the issue of whether he would admit that drinking alcohol, even beer, was a sin and repent of it. To establish drinking as sinful in God's eyes, Fred, Doug and Pastor Valenti would cite, among other Bible verses, "Be not drunk with wine . . ." (Ephesians 5:18) and ". . . your body is the temple of the

Holy Ghost" (I Corinthians 6:19), which was taken by extension to mean it should be kept clean of tobacco, alcohol and other unhealthy substances in order to glorify God. No one at Shawmut River referred to passages such as Deuteronomy 14:22–29, which commands the children of God, on occasion, to buy "whatsoever thy soul lusteth after," including "wine" or "strong drink," in order to rejoice and give thanks to God, or St. Paul's prescription to "use a little wine for the stomach's sake" (I Timothy 5:23), or even his stricture for deacons, according to I Timothy 3:8, that they "not be given to *much* wine." Whenever scripture did speak of wine in connection with Jesus—at the wedding feast at Cana, when he changed water into wine, for example—Fred informed us that if we went back to the Bible's original language, we would find it was always "new wine" or unfermented grape juice being talked about. No one was moved to question the improbability of grape juice being kept from fermenting in the Middle Eastern heat.

But Roger remained unconvinced. "Why do you say alcohol is sin? I don't think he says that in here," he said pointing to his Bible.

Roger was apt to question biblical proofs others in our group would accept uncritically. Once, in the midst of a long verbal struggle with Fred about life after death, he asked, "Now, how do you guys know that for a fact?"

"The book tells me," Fred replied.

"But a *man* wrote that," Roger countered.

Fred then quoted II Timothy 3:16: "All scripture is given by inspiration of God and is profitable for doctrine, for reproof, for correction, for instruction in righteousness," and added, "It was the Holy Spirit that breathed into a man's ear to write it."

Roger objected, "But someone could've said, 'Well, somebody's gonna question this book, so I gotta give 'em a reason . . .'"

"Aw-w-w!" Fred exclaimed in exasperation.

But Roger had little interest in pressing such theoretical points further. "You might think I'm tryin' to be a pain in the neck," he offered apologetically, "but I'm just tryin' to be logical—a little bit. 'Cause you hit me with things, Fred . . ." He looked off as if contemplating the troubles he faced. Then his eyes turned back to Fred. "You know I believe in God! You *know* I do!"

This was one moment when the depth of Roger's afflictions suddenly came into view. More than drinking beer seemed to be involved, but our group observed a degree of discretion around the facts of one another's personal lives. Now, this evening, as part of a movement of growing candor, Roger expressed a more stubborn obstacle he felt to accepting Christ. "The only reason I haven't," he said, "is because I'm afraid I won't be able to hold up my end of the bargain. What if I just couldn't change my ways?" (Roger already took seriously the prospect of embarking on a relationship of reciprocity, a "bargain," with God.)

"You *are* going to fail," Fred concurred, "'cause you're *not* good enough."

Roger gaped at Fred in disbelief. "All right, can we hold it there for a minute? Dougie," he said, looking plaintively at his friend. "When you said the prayer, did you feel in your heart you would be able to hold up your end of the bargain? . . . I bet ya did."

"Naw," Doug said, shaking his head.

"Awe, com'on! Doug?"

"Roger," Doug said lovingly, "what makes you think I'm better than you are?"

Recounting his own helplessness in the face of sinful desires, Fred assured Roger that no one is strong enough on his own to defeat sin and Satan.

"Try living up to the Ten Commandments," Doug interjected.

But once Roger accepted Christ "into his heart," Fred explained, he would have a powerful ally in the Holy Spirit, who would come to dwell inside him, as he did in every person reborn in Christ.

"Where's it say God gives a man a new heart?" Doug asked Fred while thumbing through his Bible to I Corinthians. There, to help make the point, he read, "If any man be in Christ he is a new creature."

"I just can't believe he's gonna help me change my ways," Roger confessed in earnest. "I want that peace of mind that Doug's got. I have a lot of bad habits that I'd love . . ."

"But you don't wanna give them up," Fred interrupted.

"No, no," Roger objected. "There are some things I'd love to give up . . . but drinkin' beer is not one of them." Discussion turned to Roger's drinking, and a long argument ensued in which Roger held that he drank beer solely for its taste, just as Fred ate shrimp or drank coffee. For a while Roger managed to get the upper hand by exploiting caffeine's effects on the body.

"I'm not gonna defend it," Fred finally conceded about coffee, "but it doesn't give me cirrhosis of the liver, it doesn't kill the cells in my body . . ."

"And it doesn't break up families," Doug interjected softly. But to soften the blow his comment had evidently landed, he added quickly with a lighthearted chuckle, ". . . or sink ships."

Several months after this evening's discussion, in June, I heard that Roger had accepted Christ and begun attending Shawmut River. But over that summer he backslid and fell away. And by fall Doug confided to me that Roger was in jail, convicted of stealing to support a drug habit. His wife and three children had left him.

ROGER'S STORY, among others in our Bible-study group, laid bare a basic fact about all biblically based moral discourse at Shawmut River: It always took place against a background of much that people knew in common about a situation, knowledge that could remain tacit even while it informed all that was said. This might be done, as in Roger's case, to maintain discretion where illegal activities were involved, or simply to avoid embarrassing someone. But in addition, it might be done because making explicit the massively detailed reality of any moral situation was more than people would care to undertake—especially, if they could, instead, rely on much already known in common by all those involved.

The presence of such tacit knowledge in Roger's case became clearer as I looked back over the transcripts of our discussions. For example, when Roger mentioned a second time some bad habits he would "love to give up," Fred had asked gently, "Well, what are they?" and then, reconsidering his question, added quietly, "We know what they are. Go ahead. It doesn't matter what the bad habit is."

The point here is that all that was known in common about Roger's situation brought meaning to each and every turn of conversation about it. Now, I myself had learned *some* of what those in Doug and Terry's circle knew all along: that Roger's drinking beer, even during the workday, was part of a larger life of being addicted to getting high; that it was jeopardizing his family life; and that his arriving at our Bible study with a can of beer in his hand might even be seen as a cry for help. All this and more were known in common by most around the Lavernes' table, and the meaning and truth of every utterance about Roger's situation were furnished in large measure by the wider context of that common knowledge others could be counted on to know, and to assume others knew as well. To be sure, these things were not uniformly known. Doug had kept some details even from his wife, Terry, for a while, and Ben Kachudnis and I, as outsiders, were "out of the loop."

Roger himself was on the edge of the Lavernes' circle of family and friends, and what was true of his situation was even more the case for each and every life situation to which our moral discourse was applied within the Lavernes' circle. Moreover, this was true for all the family circles represented at Shawmut River, whose members had grown up accustomed to this kind of epistemological situation and the kind of moral discourse it supported. Since those closely involved could be counted on to share much about the particularities of any situation, the moral ordering of daily life sailed on the surface of an immense sea of things that could effectively be taken for granted. Its course could therefore be guided by an implicit common sense, or collective intuition, rather than by explicit reasoning or by applying general moral rules to individual cases.

In villagelike contexts, no one has to fashion workable rules to go by. It did not matter, then, in our considering Roger's situation, whether the Bible totally forbids drinking alcoholic beverages or how we might reconcile passages that seemed to contradict one another about drinking. Instead, what mattered was what members knew in common about Roger's situation—that his addictions were threatening to break up his family. It was these circumstances of Roger's life, not the precise clarification of abstract rules from a text, that implicitly gave meaning and warrant to the Bible-based tools of moral discourse applied to his situation. Resting on the firm ground of such tacit knowledge held in common, there was no need to qualify or clarify the scope and meaning of these rules any further.

This was the characteristic form of moral discourse at Shawmut River and, more broadly, in the social world of its members. It was part and parcel of the dense oral culture within which they moved and had their being. The texture and logic of such a moral discourse had enveloped them from the dawn of social consciousness in childhood and followed them through their emergence as adults, fashioning in them habits of thought and expression they naturally brought to their faith. People, not principles, mattered, and people whose relationships and life circumstances were known in common by relevant parties to any moral discourse regulating family and personal life. This is a central feature, I suspect, of moral life in any organic, close-knit community based on face-to-face relations. As the antithesis of modern bureaucracy, which demands that people be treated impersonally according to explicitly defined rules, this deeply personal and implicit moral discourse underlies popular conservatives' instinctive distaste for programs administered by large federal government bureaucracies and their implacable hostility to Big Government.

It is also a source of that small-town morality according to which, for instance, people might judge homosexuality as wrong in some absolute sense yet accept "Uncle Ned" as "queer" and love him to bits. While modern, urbane people are apt to judge this as galling inconsistency or self-serving hypocrisy, at the very next moment they are apt to dismiss small-town traditionalists as "rigid" and "inflexible," unaware of any contradictions these judgments involve. For there is a certain flexibility built into the very nature of this kind of moral discourse that the members of Shawmut River had grown up with.

On the other hand, for me and most of my friends and colleagues, the fragmentation of personal relationships into separate sectors—of relatives, friends, colleagues, as well as old and new friends who might not know one another—meant that we could not rely on any such concrete, organic consensus to guide us in grasping and acting upon a moral order of life. Unable to draw on an immense sea of *common* knowledge about particular situations among our loose-knit, even fragmented, network of relationships, we had to rely on more explicit terms to grasp and express moral notions. Abstract rules mattered more to us, realistically speaking, than they did to those at Shawmut River. And if such rules proved unwieldy in the face of the conflicting actualities of life, we might need to be explicitly reminded to consider the particularities of any "situation" in order to correctly apply moral principles to that case.

Similarly, if people like me could not rely as heavily on stories shared face-to-face against a background of much known in common about the persons and situations involved, we turned to more explicit, generalized and categorical expressions of moral knowledge, for instance, in literature—either in fiction or in nonfiction of a self-help or social-commentary kind. Most of us were prepared, step by step as we came of age, to comprehend the moral order around us more in these terms.[1]

However, if we view fundamentalists' Bible-based moral discourse from our own quite different social standpoint, we are likely to misjudge it sorely. While fundamentalists' timeless, God-given absolutes may appear rigid from the outside, within the organism of a close-knit community where much is known in common about persons and situations, they can be surprisingly supple and flexible over time and place. Moreover, to judge this moral discourse as being lower developmentally than one based on manipulating abstract principles, as some students of culture have done, represents a blind and vaunted projection of our own moral methods onto the alien context of villagelike life everywhere, whether it be in a rural community, small town, tight-knit working-class neighborhood or fundamentalist congregation.[2]

To better understand fundamentalists' use of scripture, then, and resolve some of the puzzles it poses, it is necessary to consider it in terms of the moral discourse fundamentalists are accustomed to. At Shawmut River, as in our Bible-study group, certain passages of scripture were used repeatedly in talk and took on a familiar, if not unforgettable, feel. They were the workhorses of theological and moral discussion. Passages such as "Your body is the temple of the Holy Spirit" (I Corinthians 6:19) were used to inveigh against drinking or smoking; "None is righteous, no, not one" (Romans 3:10), to argue for the necessity of salvation through Christ's sacrifice on the cross; "If any man be in Christ, he is a new creature" (II Corinthians 5:17), to assure people that saved persons will have the Holy Spirit's help in changing them; "I can do all things through Christ which strengtheneth me" (Philippians 4:13), to persuade people that they can endure any suffering; "All things work together for good to them that love God" (Romans 8:28), to assure them that something good can come from suffering, or from their own weak and imperfect ways; and "Whatsoever ye shall ask the father in my name he will give to you" (John 16:23), to convince them that God will answer prayer.

There were many such verses ranging from the most recognizable to those fading into the penumbra of the dimly known. But there were not too many to become familiar with and commit to memory over time, especially by those actively using them over the years in daily talk. Bible education was not undertaken for scholarly reasons but was inextricably bound up in the day-to-day practical discourses of evangelizing the unsaved, discipling new believers and, through testimony and discernment, recognizing God's work in one another's lives.[3]

The form these biblical passages took made them suitable for extemporaneous use in conversational situations. They were not too numerous to overload an otherwise accessible storehouse of sayings, and they were framed in suitable lengths so that they could be more easily memorized and uttered in a single sentence. Even their cadence and sound made them easier to remember . . . and more satisfying to say. "I can do all things through Christ which strengtheneth me," for example, or "All things work together for good for them who love the Lord" have a eminently repeatable, reassuring cadence. (The latter's cadence is actually improved by a slight departure from the actual text, as I normally heard it around Shawmut River: that is, "who love *the Lord*" rather than "love *God*," as the King James Version has it.)

Life at Shawmut River, and in the larger fundamentalist world, is replete with memorization exercises, games and contests to help children and adults know the word of God "by heart" (or to "hide it in their hearts"—not their heads—where it will shape their motivation to yield the visible "fruit" of spiritual life).[4] But the most effective way members came to know verses of scripture by heart was through their repeated use in sermons, Sunday School lessons and Bible-study groups, or in informal conversation at Shawmut River and its school. It was far more through talk than through reading that members developed a working knowledge of the Bible. While most core members read a little—and some, such as Fred Webber and the Valentis, quite a lot—those portions of scripture that became familiar, telling and authoritative did so through the spoken word.

In this way, the Bible became used and known largely as a body of stories and sayings—aphorisms or maxims—which are the characteristic tools of moral discourse in an orally transmitted culture. This discourse was metaphoric rather than categorical, narrative rather than discursive, concrete rather than abstract. While the Old Testament furnished many of the stories members called to mind, the New Testament, and particularly the apostles' letters, were the main source of doctrine, which took the form of maxims or sayings.

It had struck me early on that members found evidence for the Bible's moral authority in the familiar folk sayings it contained—sayings such as "There is no new thing under the sun" and "Don't count your chickens before they hatch." Once, when Pastor Valenti quoted from the pulpit the nonbiblical maxim "Familiarity breeds contempt," he hastened to explain, "That's not a scriptural truth, but it *contains* scriptural truth." That is, in his view, "scriptural truth" was this kind of stuff.[5]

Fundamentalist communities are in the habit of using such sayings—even nonbiblical ones—to express all their teachings. "Take the *whole* book," Fred Webber always taught our Bible-study group, "not a book full of *holes*," to insist we not explain away what the whole book teaches by sticking to one passage here or there. Or, to understand the relationship between the Old and New Testaments, we were taught to repeat the poetic couplet "The new is in the old concealed, and the old is in the new revealed."

These sayings bear the quintessential features of an oral tradition: metaphor, pun, rhyme and cadence. They are meant to be said precisely in the way they have been said before. To say, for example, "What you actually have is worth more than what you may hope to get" does not satisfy like "A bird in the hand is worth two in the bush." The authority of such folk sayings derives from the very fact that they have been passed down, just as they are, by those who came before us. Their artful, pithy, poetic cast makes them eminently repeatable and, hence, memorable, and this is the sign of their unassailable character as traditional folk wisdom. It is an important reason, I believe, for fundamentalists' persistent preference for the King James translation of the Bible, even though some, such as Falwell's school, have recognized other translations to be closer to the original texts. In addition to its having been written in an age dominated by the spoken word, the King James version expresses sayings in old-fashioned language with words such as *smite*, *cubits* and *strengtheneth*. It has the sound and feel of ancient, time-honored truth—the ring of tradition.[6]

In taking from the Bible an array of sayings to be used in talk, fundamentalists have little reason or need to worry about making them logically consistent with one another. This is one source of the radical disjunction between fundamentalist communities, on the one hand, and their scholarly apologists, on the other, who are often pressed to advance absurdly convoluted arguments to resolve apparent inconsistencies in scripture. Logical consistency—or inconsistency—is much more determinable and relevant when dealing with the fixity of a text than with the undocumented flow of talk, and problems regarding inconsistencies in the Bible rarely came up in conversation around Shawmut River.[7] Nor have I ever heard from any fundamentalist pulpit the kind of sermon popular in liberal churches where a preacher begins by contrasting, say, the Gospel of Mark's account of a particular event with apparently contradictory ones from, say, Luke or Matthew—an approach that highlights the human, historical authorship of the text rather than its supernatural and presumably unerring one.

In a sense, the array of sayings used in fundamentalist discourse becomes relatively detached from the book itself—though speakers may be more or less knowledgable about their place in the text. But that does not mean that these sayings are without context. Rather, the context comes from the occasions of their use. There are occasions when "an eye for an eye" seems right and others when "turn the other cheek" is good counsel; occasions when a person needs to be reminded of God's boundless love and others when he or she needs to be reminded of his wrath and judgment; times when spouses need to be reminded that a husband is "head of the wife" and should take more responsibility for his family's religious life and times when they need to be reminded to "submit one to another in the fear of God." And on most occasions when Bible verses were applied to life, members of Shawmut River could count on those involved to know much in common about the relevant particularities of the situation at hand—to know how these sayings should be correctly applied. This means that collective moral judgment could be arrived at without relying on the explicit application of abstract rules.

Given the logic of this procedure, there is no reason for determining an aphorism's precise meaning outside the particular context of its use. Half-truths and even vague, loosely suggestive terms of reference such as "The body is the temple of God" and "Eve was made from Adam's rib" can be invested with fuller meaning over various occasions of use. This permits flexibility, among other things, across diverse situations and diverse cultures. While a passage such as "The body is the temple of God," for example, came to be seen by many fundamentalists to prohibit, among other things, smoking, it was not so historically for fundamentalists in the South, where using tobacco was so entrenched in local culture that, as one southerner put it to me half in jest, if a smoker died of lung cancer, it was seen to be as honorable as dying for your country.

By the same token, there is no need to qualify an aphorism's meaning to accord with its varied uses. It does not need to be said, for instance, "an eye for an eye, except under conditions x, y and z." Whatever qualifications are relevant derive from the particularities of the context in question, a situation known in common by relevant parties, which provides a maxim's scope, meaning, sufficiency and truth. Moral order does not take the form of abstract rules framed in general, categorical terms to be realistically applied to individual cases but, instead, in the concrete particulars of human situations themselves.[8]

These realities affect the nature of the moral absolutes fundamentalists champion. When Pastor Valenti preached that spring, for example, that "God hates divorce!" he did not try to reconcile his position with Old Testament passages detailing how a man should properly go about divorcing his wife.[9] Instead, he took on the role of a courtroom judge facing a couple routinely pleading an uncontested divorce. "Lemme see here," he said gravely to the imagined couple, consulting his Bible in front of him. "It says in here you can't." This brought peals of laughter and a chorus of "A-mens" from his flock, even from the many, including his mother-in-law, Ada, and his sister-in-law, Judy, who had gone through divorces. Furthermore, none of those who had experienced divorce seemed troubled in the least by his blanket judgment. Was this wanton hypocrisy? If not, what sort of absolutes was Frank preaching?

Moreover, Pastor Valenti and his congregation had no difficulty accepting divorce. If called upon, they were perfectly capable of justifying divorces among people they knew. When a woman married to one deacon's nephew left him, for example, Pastor Valenti and the family involved approved, even though the wife had had an affair with someone at work. Her husband was lazy and not a faithful provider, I heard it said later, and she herself had to work full-time to help make ends meet. In this context, as Pastor Valenti explained in response to my questions, it was understandable why she had responded to the "sympathetic ear" offered by her fellow worker. Only later did I incidentally learn more about what all involved already knew: that the husband had drunk, smoked pot, ridden his snowmobile and "had a great time" at the expense of meeting his family's needs. Or when another member left her second husband, the Valentis took her in, and other church members helped her get a job and furnish an apartment. "He was a selfish man," I heard it said later about her husband, and when questioned, another member told me the husband had bought a new rifle when the family needed a washing machine.

These facts emerged only retrospectively, in a haphazard way, when I questioned people about particular occurrences. They did not come up as members sought to justify this or that departure from any general rule against divorce. And these judgments did not prompt anyone to consider qualifying the community's commitment to the black-and-white, absolute and unchanging prohibition of divorce. God *still* "hated divorce," and to follow him meant we should hate it, too.

Fundamentalists are dismissed by liberal critics, most of all, perhaps, for championing moral absolutes etched in such uncompromisingly black-and-white terms that they would seem unviable in real-life situations. Liberals accuse fundamentalists of being rigid, uncompromising, intolerant of ambiguity, hopelessly out of date and unable to accommodate change. It is easy to see how critics arrive at these views, confronted by fundamentalists' insistence on moral absolutes to combat the tide of moral relativism and individualism they object to in the culture around them. Yet if all this were true of fundamentalist practice, it would be hard to imagine how it could attract to itself, as it has generation after generation, masses of Americans who find in it, above all, practical help in dealing with the tough and messy problems of life, such as marriage.

This paradox can be resolved by seeing fundamentalists' absolutes against the background of the kind of moral discourse their lives support. The moral absolutes members take from scripture achieve their flexibility not in any explicit qualification but, instead, in the occasions of their actual use, guided firmly yet tacitly by a collective sense of the particularities of so many situations at hand. This was a source not only of their flexibility from case to case, we might note, but also of their adaptability to change over time.

Fundamentalists have been able to accommodate the growing incidence of divorce in American life, for instance, without abandoning their general prohibition of it. And they have been able to accommodate the growing incidence of mothers working outside the home, another one of those brute realities critics mention in arguing how outmoded and unrealistic fundamentalists' model of the family is. More than half the mothers of young children at Shawmut River worked outside the home (comparable to the national average at the time). This was in response mainly to the economic pressures caused by declining real incomes, and roughly a third of these working mothers were employed at Shawmut River itself, as teachers, secretaries and day-care workers. Yet, over my several years at Shawmut River, I never heard any woman being taken to task for working. Nor did I see any evidence of public pressure, or the fear of possible public disapproval, affecting a woman's decision to work outside the home. Indeed, when I first arrived at Shawmut River, the church was inaugurating its own day-care program to offer Christian care to deal with the unfortunate yet unavoidable reality of more and more mothers working. If parents need day care, make it *Christian* day care, Pastor Valenti reasoned.

At the same time, accepting the fact of mothers working outside the home did not lead members to jettison or qualify the model of God's plan for the family they relied on to order their lives. It did not make them feminist or necessarily evidence feminism's influence on their attitudes or practices. They still affirmed that men and women were essentially different and assigned by divine plan to essentially different roles in the family. In God's plan, a woman's primary responsibility was to care for her children. And they did not speak of the importance of women's work outside the home as an end in itself or something a wife's well-being or justice required.

Neither did this mean a mother's commitments to work were beyond criticism. Sally Keener, for example, who had agonized over her own decision to go back to nursing full-time when her husband left his job to teach at the Christian Academy, criticized one of the doctors she had once worked with. She had young children, Sally said, and did not have to work for financial reasons. "She's come to me," Sally recalled, "and said, 'I hope my kids can be like yours when they get to be older.' . . . And in the back of my mind I'm thinking, 'How can they be, because you're obviously not teaching them anything?' She's always at work and her kids are always with baby-sitters, so she's really not bringing her children up."

Though no working mother I knew at Shawmut River would have fit Sally's description of her colleague, Frank would warn his flock from the pulpit, "I am greatly feared of the increasing number of women going to work because they idolize their jobs. . . . Be careful!" But he did not say mothers should not work.

This pattern of flexibility and adaptability by tacit exception does not mean that rigidity, intolerance or hypocrisy do not occur in fundamentalist communities. In what human communities do they not? But they are not endemic among fundamentalists in the ways their critics assume, simply because of the moral absolutes they endorse. When rigidity or intolerance do occur, rather, they are apt to arise from particular circumstances involved: from conflicts and struggles for power;

from personal animosities toward an individual; or in those sprawling empires of television evangelists that have become increasingly detached from the tightly knit congregations from which they arose.

At the same time, those familiar with business corporations or academic institutions, where grounds for action need to be put into writing in terms of general *policies*, or abstract rules, know full well how intolerance, bigotry or injustice can be achieved through those very mechanisms designed to ensure impartiality and fairness. And that is to say nothing of the particular kinds of rigidities and inflexibilities characteristic of bureaucracy itself. Members of Shawmut River seemed to fasten on instances of such bureacratic irrationality as evidence of the very foolhardiness of that approach to dealing with social needs in the first place. And when Phil Strong ran for State Senate the following fall, one of the recurring proposals of his campaign was to remove social welfare from federal government bureaucracies and put it into the hands of local churches.[10]

At Shawmut River, by contrast, flexibility, tolerance and fairness were achieved simply in the informal, day-to-day collective acts of regulating family and personal life against the firm background of things known in common. They were achieved in the doing of them, not in any explicit accounting of them. In fact, this mode of ordering social life works best if participants are generally unaware of this disjunction between moral maxims, on the one hand, and the flow of concrete judgments, on the other. It requires the kind of collective unconsciousness and consciousness that taking things for granted necessarily involves.[11]

This does not mean that fundamentalists are completely unaware of the ever-present work of tacit common sense among them. At moments it might sail by unnoticed, as when, for example, I heard a Baptist Bible Fellowship preacher mention, when exhorting his flock to greet one another warmly, that the Bible had instructed early Christians to greet one another with "a holy kiss." "Not in modern-day America!" he quipped quickly to the crowd's laugh, dispelling any tensions they might feel about disregarding a biblically sanctioned practice tinged for them with the horrors of sexuality, or homosexuality. At other moments, this tacit common sense might come more explicitly into view, as in one conversation I remember with Sharon Valenti. That summer Phil Strong's father, who had always had a testy relationship with the church, suddenly died. There was no time for the luxury of final conversations. Was he consigned for eternity to hell? What would his family members think if Phil and Jean declared that judgment? But as silently as mist clears to reveal a sunny day, the supposition arose that Phil's father might well have been, and probably was, saved. It was something he had said recently, some recalled, that warranted such speculation, and no one spoke against it.

Curious about how such a collective judgment had been arrived at, I put the question to Sharon: "Was he saved?"

Always the theorist, Sharon replied, "Well, you know, you *always* think they *aren't* before they go, and they *are* after. If you had asked a week ago, the answer probably would have been 'no.' But he said something to Phil, like 'We are brothers in Christ.' And he's been softer in the past two months." So it was with the congregation's most critical judgment: whether a person was saved or lost. Quite soon, I would see such latitude toward the probably damned applied to me.

13

Fundamentalism and Tradition

Time out of mind . . .

Mᴄ ʀᴇsᴇᴀʀᴄʜ had begun as an effort to better understand pop-ular support for new-right conservatism—a movement that had transformed American politics—but my explorations had brought me into a fundamentalist Christian church. While the Shawmut River Baptist Church addressed the politics and ideology of the wider soci-ety, it also involved the politics and theology of Christianity, which raised other kinds of questions.

Noticing differences between the lives of new-right activists I met, on the one hand, and those of my liberal friends and colleagues, on the other, helped make better sense of their conflicting politics. Looking at popular conservatism as an effort to defend family obligations as sacred duties against the tide of individualism and individual rights unleashed in the 1960s and 1970s made sense and helped resolve some of the puzzles it poses for outsiders—why right to life coheres with militarism and capital punishment, for example, or why government welfare programs are seen to undermine the moral fiber of American life.[1] Why new-right women defend a model of family life that reserves positions of authority for men was a puzzle subsequent events at Shaw-mut River would illuminate.

The leading sociological studies of these conflicts in American life had explained them in terms of conflicting "worldviews" or concep-tions of "moral authority": the conservative one holding moral author-ity to be fixed and transcendent, the liberal one holding it to be relative and conditional. However helpful these studies were in making better sense of these conflicts, they did not explain why some people hold one worldview, others the opposite, or why these conflicting views happen to be developed and embraced by different groups in American life—in loosely predictable ways, at least. Neither could they explain the specific content of these conflicting worldviews: the place of reciprocal obligation in the conservative view, for example, or the commitment to gender defined as two essentially different types of human beings inhabiting different domains of activity. Nor did they help us understand how those holding morality to be fixed and transcendent, such as the members of Shawmut River, can take presumably unchanging moral absolutes and successfully apply them to the messy, ambiguous and continually changing circumstances of life.[2]

Seeing new-right activism not simply in terms of worldviews or ideas but in terms of lives organized in circles of cooperating kin helps explain why some people hold one worldview while others hold an opposing one—or why certain views make sense to some but not others. It also helps us understand both the larger framework and the particular elements of the conservative outlook in terms of a practical organization of life found widely among working-class people and those in small, family-based businesses, who, regardless of their religious backgrounds, tend to be more traditional, in certain ways, on issues of family and gender.

Indeed, this social base provides solid constituencies for conservative wings in all branches of American religious life, including Judaism, Catholicism, Methodism, Presbyterianism, Lutheranism, Episcopalianism and so on. In all these different religious traditions, each with its distinct theology, forms of worship and principles of polity and organization, conservatives can be found defending traditional gender roles and the authority of tradition in general. Conservative Episcopalians, for example, not only oppose same-sex unions, gender-inclusive language and the ordination of women and homosexuals but also prefer to address their priest as "father" and to use the old Book of Common Prayer from 1928. Popular conservatism cannot be seen, then, to spring from any particular religious ideas or traditions. It can be found, with its liberal counterpart, in virtually all of them. Even among the heirs of fundamentalist biblicism we find some evangelical Christians, especially in professional middle-class contexts, who come to affirm genuinely feminist critiques of traditional gender roles in the family.[3]

However, some religious traditions, such as the fundamentalist

Baptist one carried by Shawmut River, were so closely linked to this kind of pro-family conservatism that its congregations had become the backbone of the New Right's most insistent and popular wing. And ever since its emergence on the American scene at the beginning of the twentieth century, Protestant fundamentalism has been intimately connected with similar patterns of conservatism. What is it about the particular discourses of this religious tradition that makes it such a fitting carrier for conservative pro-family politics?

When Martin Luther coined the Reformation slogan "No creed but the Bible," authorities feared a wild profusion of Christian practices justified by passages of scripture that, according to Luther himself, could be strung together to prove even that beer is better than wine.[4] Yet these fears did not, by and large, materialize. Despite divergences here and there, such as Pentecostal snake handling and Mormon polygamy, fundamentalist communities in America have sustained surprisingly uniform readings of the Bible's potentially contradictory implications for daily life, including God's plan for the family. How is this so? What relation do fundamentalist discourses bear to tradition? And in what sense are they distinctly modern? My study of Shawmut River led to questions about the nature of Protestant fundamentalism itself.

In addition, much to the surprise of political commentators who had seen religion fading from importance in the modern world, fundamentalism exploded onto the world stage toward the end of the twentieth century, with the rise of militant movements among Muslims, Jews, Buddhists and Hindus. Though different in important ways from one another and from fundamentalist Protestantism in America, which first brought the term *fundamentalist* into being, these movements bore similarities to their namesake. They expressed militant opposition to modern secularism's assault on the traditional and the sacred, and used sacred texts to justify that opposition—even in Hinduism, where, in the absence of a single canonical scripture, Hindu fundamentalists elevated one text to central importance.[5] I wondered whether my experience of Protestant fundamentalism at Shawmut River held any lessons for understanding the growing importance of fundamentalism, in general, in the modern world. One key to approaching these questions, I believed, was recognizing fundamentalism's relationship to tradition, once certain misunderstandings about tradition—a surprisingly deceptive reality—were resolved.

. . .

MY EARLY OBSERVATIONS suggested that Shawmut River, like other fundamentalist churches in the independent Baptist tradition, was deeply involved in using Bible-based discourses to help its members deal with the ordinary problems of life—above all, helping them regulate, order and change family relationships, especially marriage. In my report to our seminar at Brown I suggested that members of Shawmut River found in scripture, among other things, support for traditional moralities of family life they already embraced. Now, after longer observation and experience, including Bible study at the Lavernes', I had a fuller picture of how fundamentalist discourse worked.

Within the medium of Shawmut River's vigorous oral tradition, I could better appreciate the gravitational force exerted by common culture to shape what biblical elements came into use and how they were understood. That included traditional divisions of labor incorporated into God's plan for the family and hostility toward what was seen as the special sin of homosexuality. It also included how basic theological realities were grasped: God, the Holy Spirit and Satan as concrete persons rather than immanent principles or forces; or the "disciple's" path as what a saved person owes Christ for his work on the cross; or how that "work" is seen as a necessary "payment" according to laws of the cosmos even God the Creator could not breach. Common culture also could be seen to shape what elements of scripture were left aside: greeting each other with a holy kiss, hair plaiting, polygamy and approved uses of wine or "strong drink."

By seeing how fundamentalist discourse meshed with vital oral traditions carried by family circles across generations and embodied in congregational life, I came to appreciate how moral absolutes drawn from scripture served in more flexible, adaptive and practical ways than we might otherwise imagine. This permitted not only sensible approaches to particular situations but also sensible adaptations to change over time, without altering the actual maxims or formulae used to order life.

Members brought these habits of moral thinking with them to Shawmut River. It was the nature of their lives organized in cooperating family circles that made them feel immediately at home in its down-home atmosphere, where the personal was readily publicized and members addressed one another as "Brother Dave" or "Aunt Margaret." They took readily to its ways of understanding what God expected of them, its ways of imagining God and his universe and the moral tools its Bible-based discourse provided their orally transmitted culture. In sum, there was a good fit between their habits of moral thought, cultivated in circles of relatives and family friends, on the one hand, and the theological and biblical discourses of this particular fundamentalist Baptist tradition, on the other. This is one way to understand fundamentalism's ready appeal and practical relevance to the kinds of people who find a home in churches like Shawmut River.

In addition, Shawmut River's all-encompassing round of activities and the family-like relationships of reciprocity it encouraged gave the congregation's own oral culture greater density, coherence and weight. Its close-knittedness lent Shawmut River the quality of village life, even among members spread out across a large urban-suburban area around Worcester crisscrossed by commuter-filled highways in late-twentieth-century America. The congregation's oral tradition provided a medium in which its Bible-based moralities worked in supple, flexible and adaptive ways. But why did members insist that these moral notions were absolute—that is, black and white and unchanging? And why were they so adamantly opposed to "situation ethics," which, on the face of it, did not seem to work all that differently?

To begin with, members of Shawmut River experienced the moral order around them as concrete and definite. Day in and day out they witnessed the confident assertion of collective standards over and against individual discretion, interest and will. The presence of such a moral order, for example, influenced Doug Laverne not to fire his younger brother when he abandoned work for the beach one summer day. Of course, Doug also knew what burdens that would place on other family members, such as his parents, with whom his brother still lived, and that other relatives would be looking at this situation in such terms. And he knew that just as he helped out his brother, so, too, other family members would help him out. This moral order also encouraged Dave and Sally Keener to care for Sally's grandmother and pledge never to see her put in a nursing home. And it is what led husbands and wives, more generally, to accept their respective duties according to a traditional division of labor seen as being embedded in God's plan for the family, while at the same time permitting sensible adaptations of these stereotyped roles in response to changing conditions, personal needs, and so on.

Members' lives worked this way, in part, because members sensed and acted on these moral standards as undiscretionary and unquestionable. If in one instance an aunt was supported in divorcing her husband, while in another a sister was pressed to try to make things work with hers, that did not give rise to doubts. In both instances, members had a sure sense that legitimate moral judgment had taken place. Embodied in the actions of a collectivity that knows and takes for granted much in common about the particularities of one another's lives, the "moral absolutes" at work here seemed present, tangible and standing above and beyond any individual's interests or desires.

To deny that these moralities are absolute and proclaim, instead, that all moral values are relative, changing and situation specific renders them something individuals should be free to decide for themselves. This opens the door to individual rationalization even wider than American individualism already permits and further weakens the authority of any group to enforce its moralities. A person's willingness to sacrifice self in relationships of reciprocity naturally lends itself to abuse, and members of Shawmut River were particularly vigilant about individuals' propensity to rationalize away obligations to others. It was part of their consciousness of the ever-present problem of sin, which they often summed up simply as "putting self before others." To consider that moral values are "relative" and that each person is free to do what he or she wants "as long as they don't hurt someone else" (conservatives' view of the "do-your-own-thing" mentality of the sixties) simply encouraged, in their eyes, greater rebellion, chaos and destruction.

But the situation-specific flexibility with which fundamentalists actually treat moral judgment bears a certain resemblance to "situation ethics," which they adamantly condemn. In fact, once after a long and heated discussion in our Bible-study group, Pastor Valenti actually conceded that situation ethics *was* justified—but "only God can do it," he added, in a critical qualification. The kind of situation ethics he and other conservatives abhorred is that which, according to one Christian ethics text from the 1960s, "extricates modern man from rigid, archaic rules . . . and declares that every man must decide what is right." That approach held moral judgment to be under individual, rather than collective or divine, control. Unlike Shawmut River, it presented morality as something individuals choose, rather than something they must accept.[6]

But why do fundamentalists insist that these moralities are timeless and unchanging? Members of Shawmut River were fond of citing Hebrews 13:8, that "God never changes. He's the same yesterday, today, and forever." His word never changes, they said, and the guidelines for living set forth in the Bible are eternal. This outlook reflects the traditionalism at work where life is ordered within an orally transmitted culture carried by family-based groups across generations.

Though traditionalists lend authority, by default as it were, to their elders and to what exists, they can, nevertheless, subject existing institutions to scorching critique as part of movements to reform them. But they always do so by claiming, for example, that America has departed from its *original* foundation as a Christian nation, that its citizens have drifted away from God's *original* "plan for the family" or that mainline churches have diverged from the *original* church set up by God himself, or from old-fashioned, "Gospel-preaching" churches of America's past. Traditionalism's characteristic mode of social criticism is restorationist. What is true and good can never be new. It must be discovered in the past and restored to its proper place. In fundamentalist Christianity this traditionalist mode of social criticism is manifest, above all, in its insistent appeals to practices in God's "original" church described in scripture. While liberal Christians, from the first fundamentalist-modernist controversy in the 1890s to the present, have stressed that the Gospel must be adapted to the new and changing conditions—freeing us from "archaic rules," as the situation-ethics text above asserts—fundamentalists insist that humankind must be brought back to God's unchanging standards.[7] Yet in this same process, fundamentalists, like all traditionalists, are often engaged in adapting traditional moralities to new circumstances, though in ways that are usually implicit and hidden from view.

This traditionalist posture toward a life undergoing continuous change is manifest in fundamentalist approaches to fashion, an inherently transitory reality in the modern world. When people see Pastor Valenti's long sideburns or his wide ties and broad lapels in the film we made of Shawmut River, they are reminded of 1970s fashion. But we shot our film in 1984. Being behind the times in these ways, however, was not a result of being inattentive or out of touch with current fashion. When I introduced the Valentis to a New York–based filmmaker who sported a mere wisp of a tail in the cut of his hair at the back of his neck (a style then in fashion in the hip art world), they immediately noted how "liberal" it made him look. Their own preference for dressing seventies-style in 1984 represented an effort to distance themselves from what was new and to look decidedly "old-fashioned." Yet this old-fashionedness, in which fundamentalists often revel, is always achieved in relation to the relentlessly changing landscape of fashion.[8]

To understand traditionalism, it is important to recognize that it is *not* a psychology or mind-set carried by individuals that orients them indiscriminately in all quarters of life from, say, marriage to marketing, or from parenting to electronics. Instead, it is a *collective* discourse, by which groups claim legitimacy for certain social institutions, practices or relationships. It is also important to recognize that tradition does not descend from the heavens, culture *ex machina*, to bind people to patterns of life from the past simply by its own force. Instead, its effectiveness depends on the actions of people over time, in concert, cooperation, conflict and struggle. Like any such collective activity, the discourse of tradition has a contingent, dynamic quality involving change, growth, adaptation and invention.

The word *tradition* first entered English usage, in fact, to mean the practice of handing over a doctrine, ordinance or custom "especially by word of mouth or by practice without writing." Tradition has its home, then, in an *orally* transmitted culture. It refers *not* to any actual continuities with past states of affairs but, instead, to a mode of transmitting customs over time. And in that process, without the fixity of the written word, a certain amount of slippage, change and adaptation is always taking place.[9]

Though change in tradition takes place, at times, in much-heralded reforms or restorations, it more often occurs gradually, in unnoticed ways, as newly minted practices quietly assume their place next to genuinely ancient ones. In time they all come together in an indistinguishable whole that a community values as "what we have always done *time out of mind*"—in that inimitable traditionalist expression. Actual change in tradition routinely disappears behind the veil of what the great sociologist Max Weber called the "eternal yesterday" of traditional authority.[10]

To say fundamentalists are *not* traditionalists, as some scholars have argued, because they combine modern or contemporary elements with genuinely old ones misconceives tradition by objectifying it as commitment to *x* number of genuinely old practices.[11] In this view, traditional village life could never change, which it obviously does—at times quite rapidly—yet without disturbing, in the least, members' continued practice of justifying all aspects of village life indiscriminately as what their ancestors have done "time out of mind." In the timeless realm of tradition, fundamentalist Baptists at Shawmut River combined elements from a variety of sources: from New Testament accounts of the second-century church, for example, to teachings about church polity from their Baptist Bible Fellowship forebears; and from nineteenth-century patterns of American family life to biblical passages expressed in the seventeenth-century language of the King James Bible. These various elements of tradition did not come into play as discrete entities, each with its historical specificity, but rather as a seamless, organic, timeless unity of what God originally intended his church and the human family to be.[12]

To DEFEND TRADITION in family life is no mean feat in modern-day America. Compared to other modern industrial nations, the United States is a country where individual freedom at the expense of collective obligation is more highly prized and given greater scope, where geographic mobility across territorial communities is greater, where higher education and scientific rationality have spread to a greater proportion of the population and where family-based communities capable of carrying tradition are most seriously eroded, especially among educated professionals. And it is for these reasons that such moral battles over the family—in which abortion, sex education and equal rights for women take on special meanings—are more pronounced in the United States than anywhere else. In place of tradition, rational schemes for ordering family life have proliferated in American life as nowhere else: therapeutic schemes, feminist, communalist, self-help and social-scientific ones, and so on.[13] In such an inhospitable environment, to defend social arrangements simply because they are what "we have always done" takes a degree of inventiveness. To achieve this feat, however, it is hard to imagine a more effective discourse than the one American fundamentalists have built with the Holy Bible.

To anchor tradition in a *book*, to begin with, satisfies the public's respect for science, which many see, above all, as book learning.[14] Doug Laverne and others, for example, were greatly impressed to find that they could *know* how to have eternal life—or how to have a strong marriage or discipline children—by finding answers in a *book*. For

Sharon Valenti the Bible provided a more satisfactory answer to "why" something was right or wrong than her mother's appeal to parental authority (see p. 110).

But the Bible is not just any book. As members of Shawmut River carried their Bibles to church, to Bible-study groups or to the home of an unsaved relative, they expressed their dedication to reasoning from a text that resonates like no other in American history. Without an established church, as in England or Europe, and with their strong tradition of individualism, Americans made the Reformation doctrine of "no creed but the Bible" a baseline source of authority for all sorts of religious movements and communities. Just as the Puritans took from scripture the "articles of covenant" for building their Bible Commonwealth in the New World, Enlightenment-inspired Unitarians challenged Puritan orthodoxy by championing the right of individuals to think for themselves by appealing solely to scripture. From religious movements on the American frontier giving rise to the Disciples of Christ, who rejected all theological language in favor of that drawn solely from the New Testament, to the public speech of Abraham Lincoln, studded with biblical references and drenched with the sounds and cadences of a book Lincoln deemed "God's best gift to man," the Bible has been, as historian Mark Noll put it, "woven into the warp and woof" of American popular culture as carrying the authority of the very word of God.[15]

The Bible inspires a reverence among ordinary Americans that finds expression in the public practice of swearing oaths on it, and in devotional practices such as one I occasionally found among conservatives I met in the 1980s (Catholic as well as Protestant) of recording births, deaths and other vital facts in a family Bible. Its supernatural power was expressed in a watchword heard regularly around Shawmut River, that God promises in Isaiah (55:11), "My word shall not return unto me void." Members took that to mean that whenever someone quoted scripture to a troubled workmate, opened the Bible at random to get guidance about what to do next or even left a tract with Bible verses in a phone booth—God would use all these acts to see that his word would have effect and consequence.[16]

If, then, any book could be said to gather to it and express the ultimate ends of a national American tradition, it would be the Bible. But the Bible serves conservatives' defense of traditional family life in more specific substantive ways as well. Members of Shawmut River found themselves more readily at home than I did, for example, in all the "family stories" they found in the Old Testament. They readily likened Abraham's conflicts with his nephew Lot, for instance, to the kinds of problems in family-based businesses they knew.

More important, fundamentalists get considerable mileage from the apostles' letters to the early church, because those congregations, not unlike their own, were made up of larger household groups, the "basic cell" of the early Christian movement, as historian Wayne Meeks describes them. Day-to-day cooperation in those households was governed by paternalist ties of dependence, norms of reciprocity and mechanisms of honor and shame—elements also part of the fabric of daily life for members of Shawmut River. On questions of parental or patriarchal authority, for instance, or on issues of sexual morality, including sex outside of marriage and homosexuality, fundamentalists have much more to gain from scripture than their liberal counterparts. In addition, the radical supernaturalism and the personified spirit world favored by members of Shawmut River make them much more at home with first-century Christians like Paul, who, as Meeks remarks, would explain changes in his travel plans by saying "Satan prevented me" as matter-of-factly as we moderns might say "I had a flat tire."[17]

But the Bible suits fundamentalists' defense of tradition not only in the *content* of its moral discourse but also in its very *form*. In the ancient world, moral discourse was also carried by the spoken word. It took the form of stories, parables and aphorisms, including Greek *gnomai* (maxims) and the fusion of story and saying in Greek *chreiai*, where a pointed saying is set within a brief story. An example is the story of Nicodemus coming to Jesus at night to ask how to know more about God, and Jesus replying, "Except a man be born again, he cannot see the kingdom of God." Generations before Jesus' teachings became incorporated into written texts eventually brought together in the Bible, they had a protracted life in the oral traditions of ancient peoples. One wonders, then, whether a book so deeply rooted in oral traditions of moral culture is likely to be understood more directly, in less mediated ways, by members of churches such as Shawmut River (or villagers around the world) than by postmodern intellectuals, who are apt to consider everything from the human body to food as "texts" to be "read."[18]

Yet, though fundamentalist discourse rests on the bed of oral tradition, it must also articulate and resonate effectively with the discourses of modern secular culture. And it is this two-sided articulation, I believe, that helps us better understand fundamentalists' deep ambivalence toward science and higher learning—their tendency both to claim the scientific nature of their enterprise yet to decry the vain foolishness of human knowledge.[19] At Shawmut River the Bible was handled in scholarly-like fashion, with "word studies" to define its terms as a specialized jargon, with the reduction of its theological teachings to a simple set of propositions, or "points"—such as "The Holy Spirit does four things in the newborn believer . . ."—and, above all, with a method of moving here and there throughout scripture to *prove* doctrines as rational propositions. As part of their Calvinist heritage, the independent Baptists at Shawmut River were thoroughgoing rationalists in their approach to faith (unlike some of their Pentecostal counterparts). We have seen how for many at Shawmut River conversion meant not a closing of the mind but its awakening, recalling Sally Keener filling notebooks from sermons and Bible studies after being saved and Doug Laverne and others learning to read.

Yet, at the same time, Pastor Valenti would rail against the "*phoolosophy* of the world" and insist that all we needed to understand the word of God was the Bible, a dictionary and a concordance. While taking scholarly or scholarly-like approaches to knowledge, fundamentalists also hold much of modern scholarship at arm's length. An enduring part of fundamentalist rhetoric has been directed against the foolishness and arrogance of educated elites over and against the common sense of ordinary people.[20]

Nevertheless, in its formative period at the beginning of the twentieth century, fundamentalism heartily embraced science, but following nineteenth-century Protestant thought, it favored science in the tradition of Francis Bacon's "common sense realism." That stressed the patient observation and classification of facts rather than the elaboration and testing of speculative hypotheses. Newtonian physics was the model of science fundamentalists held up, setting forth the cosmos as a timeless, law-governed order, in which God's design was manifest. Darwinian evolution, with its speculative hypotheses about chains of causation excluding God's creative acts, was dismissed as "science, so-called."[21]

However, this harmonious unity of fundamentalist Christianity and science in Baconian terms could not last, because fundamentalism as a popular movement rooted in tradition could not embrace certain ground rules of modern science as it came to define itself. One is that scientific propositions must always be seen as provisional and continually subject to revision or rejection based on appeals to evidence. Modern science has no place for eternal verities; it sees truth as an endless process of progressive realization. A corollary is that all scientific propositions must be framed in terms that can be confirmed or falsified by empirical observation of facts accessible to any person, regardless of faith, culture, etc. In this sense, science has no place for the actions of God knowable only through faith. These central canons of modern science, then, collide with both fundamentalists' supernaturalism and their view that God's word sets forth truths that are absolute and unchanging.[22]

For fundamentalists, "knowledge worthy of the name did not constantly change and evolve," Virginia Brereton writes in her history of the American Bible school, fundamentalism's main institution of higher learning, but was, rather, "a permanent treasure trove established once and for all by God, waiting to be rediscovered or merely acknowledged by those in every century who were serene and clear-eyed enough to discern it." For this reason, there was no advantage in consulting any literature beyond the Bible. Fundamentalists called their schools "Bible institutes" or "Bible colleges," which prided themselves on their sometimes exaggerated claim to teach *only* the Bible in their courses. It is the "best text on psychology," declared the catalogue of the Bible Institute of Los Angeles in 1920, and "sets forth man as he really is, and not as speculative philosophers imagine him to be."[23]

This does not mean fundamentalist thought or biblical interpretation does not change. In a stinging critique of what he sees as fundamentalists' "fossilized theology," a British Old Testament scholar concedes "a certain amount of change and shifting positions" *does* take place within fundamentalist thought. But change does not occur, he writes, "as a result of open criticism and a call for change, but rather as the result of a slow and secret process, the change being completed before anyone admits that it is needed, and the fact of change being concealed after it has taken place." That is, change takes place in a *traditionalist mode*, where it disappears from view behind the veil of tradition's eternal yesterday. One example is how fundamentalists' justification of racial segregation based on interpretations of Noah's cursing the descendants of Ham in Genesis (9:22–25) fell out

of favor and then quietly out of sight in the 1970s. These unconscious sleights of hand, as it were, succeed best where there is little
attention to documented historical record and where common culture
is transmitted predominantly by the spoken, as opposed to the written,
word.[24]

The Bible's treasure trove was a timeless realm offering explanations even for future events, such as Pastor Valenti's claim that the
Book of Daniel explains why Napoleon's empire came apart two millennia later, or claims that the Bible anticipates later discoveries of science. Each generation of fundamentalists has found in the Bible
correspondences, even if poetic, to established scientific findings of
their day. In the late nineteenth century, for example, a passage in Job,
"to assign to the wind its weight," was seen to anticipate discoveries
about the weight of air, and passages in Solomon, discoveries about the
body: "or ever the silver cord is loosed" was seen to refer to spinal mar-
row and "the wheel broken at the cistern" to the heart's circulation of
blood. As critics have pointed out, such interpretations did not restrict
fundamentalists to *literal* readings of the text.[25] For his part, Pastor
Valenti would cite Leviticus (17:11), "the life is in blood," to demonstrate the Bible's accuracy on scientific matters. Even if the heart stops,
he pointed out, we now know life can be sustained if an artificial pump
continues to circulate blood.

Like other contemporary fundamentalists, Pastor Valenti came to
believe quite passionately in the creation theory based on the occurrence of Noah's flood. That theory holds that the fossil and geological
evidence, when seen in light of the worldwide flood recounted in Genesis, reveals the earth to be much younger than believed (namely, not
older than ten thousand years) and that God created all earthly life in
six literal days. Earlier generations of biblical Christians tried to reconcile the Genesis account of creation with contemporary scientific findings by conceiving the Bible's days either as "ages" or as days with large
gaps of time in between. The new flood theory, propounded in 1961 by
a hydraulic engineer and an Old Testament scholar (both fundamentalists), took over "creation science" so completely in the 1970s and
1980s that many conservative Christians came to believe it represented
the traditional biblical view.[26]

As part and parcel of the modern world dominated by science and
its evident technological achievements, fundamentalists have consistently made use of scientific findings and have adopted some of sci-

ence's forms and methods. However, they cannot accept modern science's commitment to the provisional nature of truth or to schemes of causation that deny any place for the actions of God. If they enlist science to their enterprise, they do so in ways that preserve both traditionalist and supernaturalist outlooks—such as upholding Baconian and Newtonian approaches as "true science," concealing changes in theological propositions and treating geological and fossil evidence in ways that affirm God's miraculous acts of creation in their most striking forms. But nothing better illustrates how fundamentalists co-opt science, perhaps, than dispensationalism.

Dispensationalism is an elaborate intellectual scheme for interpreting scripture developed in early-nineteenth-century Ireland and England as part of efforts to comprehend what some evangelical Christians saw as the increasing apostasy of the Church of England. It went on, however, to achieve widespread popularity in the United States, especially with the publication in 1909 of the *Scofield Reference Bible*, judged by one historian to be "perhaps the most influential publication in millenarian and fundamentalist historiography." The work of Cyrus Ingersoll Scofield, a lawyer who, after his conversion, became an associate of the nineteenth-century evangelist Dwight L. Moody, the *Scofield Reference Bible* contained extensive annotations and cross-references to help readers "correctly divide the word of truth" according to seven dispensations, or periods defined by God's dealings with humankind.[27]

By distinguishing a "church age" from Christ's second coming, dispensationalism permitted believers to see the contemporary church as corrupt and apostate. Only the faithful remnant of true believers would be called to heaven in "the rapture" at the beginning of the end times. Dispensationalism also helped harmonize apparent contradictions in scripture by instructing readers to interpret passages differently according to which dispensation they addressed. And it was for this purpose that it was occasionally invoked at Shawmut River. Members used dispensationalism to explain away certain unacceptable practices found in scripture—such as polygamy in the Old Testament—and to dismiss Pentecostal claims of faith healing and speaking in tongues. These, they argued, had been intended for dispensations other than our own.

Insofar as this intricate and ingenious scheme of classification harmonized apparent inconsistencies in scripture by employing something like a historian's periodization, dispensationalism appeared scientific. Indeed, its creators contrasted it to earlier "unscientific" systems of biblical exegesis. And in certain ways it was modeled on forms of thought dominant in nineteenth-century Anglo-American culture, including Marxism, Darwinism and geological catastrophism. All these theories divided history into a chain of successive periods, each of which is brought to an end through conflict or struggle ushering in the next period in a grand scheme progressing toward fulfillment.[28]

But unlike the naturalistic explanations offered by Darwinism or Marxism, dispensationalism's periods were defined in terms of God's relationship to humankind, and its engine of change involved God's supernatural interventions in history, realities not observable to the ordinary, unbelieving eye. Natural or merely human causes, the substance of ordinary historical scholarship, assumed secondary importance. In addition, dispensationalists' claims that the Bible's prophetic passages would be fulfilled in literal detail provided ready-made explanations for events still unfolding in history. Everything from the Russian Revolution to the creation of the euro currency can be explained as God's work fulfilling prophecies set forth in scripture, eclipsing any efforts to explain them in merely human, naturalistic terms. In these ways, dispensationalism subsumes all events—past, present and future—under an interpretive scheme revealed once and for all in God's word given in scripture, making modern historical scholarship and naturalistic explanations of events, to that degree, irrelevant.[29]

FROM THIS VANTAGE POINT, fundamentalism can be seen as an effective means of defending timeless, divinely ordained tradition within a society increasingly dominated by scientific rationality, faith in evolution and progress and the belief that humankind is the author of its own destiny.[30] On the one hand, fundamentalist discourse takes root in the bed of oral tradition among members in local congregations, where it is used primarily to wrestle with the tough and tangled problems of life. On the other hand, it seeks plausibility and coherence for its truths in the language of modernity. It defends tradition in modern, scientific terms while, at the same time, undermining some of science's central claims. Wherever fundamentalism borrows from scientific discourse, or blends with it, it undercuts science's rejection of the supernatural and of absolute truth and insists that scientific knowledge conform, instead, to the timeless, eternal truths created by an infinitely wise God.

In these ways, fundamentalism is an integral part of the modern world. Rather than fading from view with the advance of the secular, scientific worldview, it is likely to enjoy a long life within it. For peoples struggling to maintain vital oral traditions at odds with modern secular society, it provides not only close-knit, villagelike congregations to support, repair and defend traditional family life but also a set of discourses that preserve tradition in terms that resonate effectively with the scientific ethos of modernity. Given how effective American fundamentalism's Bible-based discourse has been in defending tradition in even this most modern and individualistic of nations, it is not surprising that other traditionalist communities under similar pressures around the globe have used sacred texts from their own religions to create similar discourses. These other "fundamentalist" movements, and ones like them, are also apt to be with us for a long time to come.

PART THREE

14

To Film?

A lot of burrs under the saddle?

A S THE LONG WINTER digging into Bible study at the Lavernes' and collecting unemployment gave way to spring, troubles arose with my filmmaker-partner soon after we heard our project had been chosen for funding by the National Endowment for the Humanities. He had always assured me that since our film depended on the integrity of my relationship with the Shawmut River congregation, I would have editorial control over the production. But when other media professionals suggested I ask for a letter of agreement defining our roles in these terms, he balked at the idea. The more we talked about it, much to my dismay, the more it seemed to drive us apart. Having never made a film, I vainly struggled to imagine how various possible scenarios might affect my promise to the Valentis and others to portray their community in light of *my* understandings, not those of others.

Meanwhile, when I first discussed this issue with the National Endowment for the Humanities, an officer told me that its policy under these circumstances would be to let me, as project director, find another filmmaker to work with. But later she informed me that if I did so I would have to reapply for the grant and that there would be no guarantees that it would be accepted. The project I had hoped and strived for—and my only prospect for employment on the horizon—was at one moment in hand and, at the next, suddenly slipping away.

Bible Study
April 12

Toward the end of our meeting, I asked our leader, Fred, if I could make a prayer request.

"For the film?" he asked.

"Yes," I replied.

"In regards to what?" he asked, readying his pen to write it down. "Specifically in the endeavor with this individual?"

"The whole project," I replied, desiring, I guess, the most blanket coverage possible.

"Is it gettin' a lot of burrs under the saddle?" Fred asked.

"Yes," I replied in a voice heavy with worry.

"I imagine there would be," Doug Laverne offered consolingly as Fred jotted my request down on his prayer list. "Nothin' good ever comes easy."

"That's what the pastor said," I concurred. "He said, 'You know, this film thing came too easy. You have to watch things when they come easy; it often means the devil's in them.'"

"I tell you," Fred added thoughtfully, "you'd have a lot more success once you profess Christianity. I know it."

"That can't be my motive," I demurred. Fred, Doug and others around the table readily agreed.

Fred said "once you *profess* Christianity," not "once you *accept* Christ." These were two separate acts, and about this time I began hearing rumors around Shawmut River that I *was* saved but not *professing* it. My alleged reason, as I heard it from one source, was to protect the objectivity of my book. I heard this rumor from various quarters but, looking back over my notes, found the first trace of it in a conversation with Sharon's mother, Ada, in early March.

"I know you're a Christian, Jim," Ada said to me then, her eyes tearing. "I don't care what you say," she hastened to add before I could respond. "You've rounded out our church family. You've been a blessing to us." She meant it in a heartfelt way, and I took it as such. Her comment occurred three days after a surprising exchange with Pastor Valenti when he paid another visit to our Bible study group.

"I think I'm mad at you," he said abruptly, looking me straight in the eye. "Are you saved or not? No double-talk, now!" Those around the table quieted down. I was taken by surprise and wanted to choose my words carefully.

"I don't think so," I replied, knowing that in his eyes, if I ever had been saved as a child, I would still be saved now. I said that I had prayed as an adolescent, usually in times of need, but had never prayed for salvation.

"Things click too much with you," Frank then said, shaking his head with a puzzled look.

Fred interrupted. "I heard you pray a prayer!" he declared emphatically. "And you spoke to God!" I flashed on the prayer I had offered weeks before. I should have known it would not have gone unnoticed.

"You're sure you're not saved?" Frank then asked gently. "Either that or you're very close to it," he added with a friendly smile. "I was hopin' I'd get it outta you tonight."

Even though in response to Frank's pointed questions I denied ever having asked for salvation as a child or otherwise, the rumor that I might well be saved spread through the congregation. I was glad for it, because I realized it might lend needed legitimacy to the film project. Some would undoubtedly object to an unsaved person making a film about their congregation for national television. In fact, I wondered if such concerns had prompted these rumors to begin with. On the other hand, I worried about whether I had somehow conveyed a false impression about myself, especially by offering a serviceable prayer at Bible study that one evening. I was relieved, then, when months later I received a letter from Pastor Valenti signed "Brother in Christ?" with a question mark.

WHETHER IT WAS GOD trying to get my attention or Satan trying to pull a good thing down, negotiations with my film partner remained deadlocked. After agonizing deliberations, I decided not to go forward with the project without a letter of agreement. As my unemployment benefits ended and another academic year came to a close, I struggled to regroup and summon the energy to look for another filmmaker and sponsoring organization and go through the arduous process of re-applying for our grant.

But as I began these labors, I suddenly found myself in a surprising position. At a face-to-face meeting with a National Endowment official in Washington, D.C., I learned that, having committed funds to the project, the endowment *did* want to see it go forward. All that it required was that I recruit a filmmaker and nonprofit sponsoring organization it approved of. That still held risks, but it was not like applying for a grant anew.

Most surprising of all, this meant that I now was in a position to choose a filmmaker for a project already designated for funding. In a sense, I was now an employer, free to consider a range of possible candidates and to choose the one I wanted to work with most. I was also able to determine more judiciously the terms of our collaboration, something indispensable to a novice trying to incorporate his vision in a new and unfamiliar medium. To someone who had just seen his dream and livelihood suddenly disappear, this turn of events did, indeed, seem miraculous.

By midsummer I had recruited a nonprofit sponsoring organization in Five Colleges, Inc., the consortium to which Smith College belonged. It was a small, congenial and efficient operation and had a track record with NEH. And I signed on as coproducer and codirector Michael Camerini, a gifted filmmaker and cinematographer whose early documentaries on India had impressed me with their cross-cultural acumen. In addition, Michael seemed a good teacher for someone new to *cinéma-vérité* filmmaking. NEH informally expressed its approval for both choices, and we reapplied for the grant.[1]

That summer brought new developments at Shawmut River itself. Two families left over conflicts with Pastor Valenti—one, a very active extended family, included five adults. Each spring seemed to bring a new rash of conflicts, departures and financial crises, like the one involving Bill Tatum, the school principal, the year before. It was a pattern I began hearing members talk about. The Valentis attributed these annual spring crises to conflicts over the financial burdens the Christian Academy imposed on the small congregation. Pastor Valenti was apt to cut deals with members who had trouble paying the school's modest tuition—averaging $1,200 a year—and the school was less than rigorous about collecting unpaid bills. That spring he reported that 30 percent of teachers' salaries were now being paid from general church offerings.

While some members were unhappy about the financial burdens imposed by the Christian Academy, Frank and Sharon saw it as an important part of their mission to keep their children—and any children—out of the clutches of the public schools, which they saw as "the churches of secular humanism." Other members, I later learned, felt their children would have to learn to deal with "the world" sooner or later anyway, and that it did not make sense for a small congregation to support a high school as well as an elementary school.

At the annual Stewardship Banquet in June, Frank warned that in September the congregation would have to shoulder even greater financial burdens when the bond payments for the new gymnatorium would rise sharply from eighty to three hundred dollars a week. Despite these burdens looming on the horizon, Frank raised another issue not likely to alleviate concerns about finances: the issue of his own salary. Since the church's founding, he explained, he had not been paid a penny or even provided with housing. He lived off his veteran's disability, and his father had put up money for his family's home, a new colonial on a cul-de-sac in a nice section of Worcester. But, he now charged, "God will not honor the flock that does not support its pastor." He said he would put the matter into the hands of Phil Strong and Dave Keener. "Also," he added in conclusion, "we must start supporting missionaries if we are to get God's blessings."

"AMEN!" some exclaimed, so forcefully that it made the silence following the news of his impending salary all the more noticeable.

IN SEPTEMBER we received word from NEH that our resubmitted grant proposal had been approved and our project could now go forward. It was a presidential election year, and Phil Strong was running for a seat in the Massachusetts Senate, his first venture into politics. Ronald Reagan was running for his second term as president with George Bush, senior, as vice president. Their victory would consolidate what historians would later call the "Reagan Revolution" in national politics (and prepare ground for the Bush dynasty). We were eager to shoot events around election day in early November, since it was the critical role churches like Shawmut River played in conservative politics that made the church a fitting subject for national television.

Yet I had come to see that political action was actually a rare occurrence at Shawmut River. Pastor Valenti had recently urged members to attend a seminar at a nearby church given by the Christian Law Association, an organization dedicated to helping local fundamentalist churches fight legal battles over issues such as school accreditation, zoning, tax law and other ways they saw the state impinging on their God-given duties. But only one couple besides the Valentis showed up. And thin attendance was generally true of other fundamentalist churches represented at this event. Even Phil Strong's campaign for

local office stirred only limited interest among members of Shawmut
River. Looking back over the past year and a half, I realized that it was
only Pastor Valenti's occasional appearance on a television or radio talk
show that we could count on filming as an actual manifestation of the
church's political activism.

This was all the more remarkable since Shawmut River stood out
among the fundamentalist Baptist churches I visited as one of the more
political ones. Some pastors continued to uphold the traditional posture of a more stringent separation from the world that deemed all politics unspiritual. If Christ's coming was imminent and would come
before events ushering in his kingdom on Earth, were not human
efforts to reform the world in vain? These represented the unre-
formed—or as yet unawakened—ranks of fundamentalists and evangelicals to whom Pastor Valenti, like Jerry Falwell himself, continually
had to preach, "Religion and politics *do* mix."[2]

But deeper reasons for members' limited involvement in political
life were by now more understandable. Doug Laverne was one of the
few church members who did participate in Phil Strong's campaign for
office that fall, but that was a completely new experience for him. I
remember him telling me with self-deprecating amazement that he
could not remember ever even caring who won an election before. "I
never knew who was runnin' or nothin'," he said. Now he cared and
seemed to feel an expansive liberation standing at a polling place on
election day as we filmed him talking occasionally to fellow voters as
he stood holding a sign—PHIL STRONG FOR STATE SENATE.

Doug Laverne, like others at Shawmut River, had not been indif-
ferent to electoral politics because he was irresponsible or asocial. On
the contrary, Doug was gregarious, caring and a natural leader among
his peers. However, for him and others, it seemed their very absorp-
tion in the small but cohesive world of their family circles limited their
wide involvement in public life. Their family network provided them
with not only emotional and material security—Doug had obtained his
career in plastering from an uncle—but also a full round of social activities in birthdays, christenings, anniversaries, retirement parties and
funerals for a large number of active kin. Every weekend, it seemed,
there was some family event for Doug and Terry to attend. Apart from
church, few members of Shawmut River were involved in voluntary
associations of any kind—trade unions, PTAs, fraternal organizations
or bowling leagues. But that did not reflect social isolation or individualism, as some commentators might conclude, but rather their deeper,

more organic collectivism in the dense universe of a circle of relatives and family friends known in common.[3]

Related sources of members' limited involvement in public life were evident in one of the first events we filmed that fall, a party on election night at Phil and Jean Strongs'. In addition to church members, other relatives of the Strongs attended, as well as associates from Phil's business and from the campaign itself. Phil's own defeat in the race for State Senate did not disappoint Phil and Jean unduly. Local news commentators considered his strong showing as a Republican against a Democratic incumbent an impressive accomplishment for a first-time runner in Democratic Massachusetts. In the prayer Phil offered that evening to bring his campaign to a close, he affirmed, "We trust in *you*, Lord, not in politics or politicians."

The Strongs' party reminded me of other gatherings I attended where church members mixed informally with one another and with those outside their church fellowship. These were usually awkward, uncomfortable events. People drifted aimlessly about. Even though the crowd was, from a certain standpoint, quite homogeneous—from the same locality, speaking with the same accents and from similar class and educational backgrounds—most seemed uncomfortable engaging someone new in conversation.

Later in our production, when the film crew accompanied the Christian Academy's basketball team to away games, our production manager was astonished by the coach's inability to find his way around a strange town, though it was less than an hour's drive away. He did not seem able to read a map and felt uncomfortable asking strangers for directions.

These discomforts dealing with strangers or navigating new territory were the marks of the kind of close, family-based world in which most members had been immersed before coming to Shawmut River. It was a world in which the essentials of life were known in common by all those they knew, where people enjoyed the effortless comfort of taken-for-grantedness and the labor to make things explicit was unknown and unpracticed. In this context, people were generally not used to, or adept at, dealing with strangers, or simply giving directions to someone new. It was a world filled to the brim with "what everybody knows." In addition, for some, belonging to their own family-based groups and neighborhoods was undergirded by negative contrasts between "them" and "us" in ways that fostered a general, free-floating distrust of outsiders.[4]

These tendencies toward insularity also inhibited members' participation in wider public life, including politics and voluntary associations. And they threw into bold relief Shawmut River's remarkable
achievement in actually bringing such people together with strangers
in the first place. In this light, Pastor Valenti's exhortation to "make
yourself friendly and you will find friends," repeated like an incanta-
tion at the beginning of every Sunday-morning service, seemed much-
needed encouragement for what was for many an unnatural act.
Similarly, the ethnic jokes he frequently used to settle listeners down—
often poking fun at his own Italian background—can be seen as an
effort to relieve tensions among people rooted in circles of their own
kin, in different folk. Such humor was the way they normally negotiated these differences in other settings and organizations.[5] Attention
to such sources of tension was an abiding part of building a community
like Shawmut River.

On the other hand, built-in obstacles to relating to strangers were
hard for me to imagine, given how normal it was for me and my associates to meet and move among new acquaintances. The cocktail party
or reception, with its restless movement of contact and conversation,
all negotiated on a transient, voluntary basis among strangers, seemed
commonplace, if not emblematic of our world. But such a life was generally foreign to members of Shawmut River.

Watching Doug Laverne begin to shake free of those inhibitions
and feel, with a liberating sense of expanding horizons, the possibility
of affecting the world around him, I realized how revolutionary the
mobilization of conservative Christians into politics has been over the
past generation. Rather than representing a retreat into a closed, pro-
tected world, joining Shawmut River was for many an important step
outward, beyond the close world of their family circle and into the
wider world beyond.

Beginning with the Reagan years, for example, when Phil Strong
and Doug Laverne first became active in politics, and deepening and
broadening with Pat Robertson's campaign for the presidency in 1988,
the mobilization of conservative Christians into electoral politics
reached new heights in the election of 1994, which brought the first
Republican majority to the House of Representatives in forty-five
years. By that time, Phil Strong would be serving on the board of the
Massachusetts chapter of Robertson's Christian Coalition, and he and
his wife, Jean, and Doug Laverne would all contribute to its local and
national electoral successes.

Still, the obstacles to building broader ties across different family groups at Shawmut River turned out to be more formidable than I realized. I was surprised, for example, to hear Doug and Terry Laverne complain about the limits of church fellowship after being members for almost two years. Terry said there were some "snobs" at church who wouldn't even say hello. Yet our Bible-study group would discuss the marriage problems of some of the very people she spoke about. Although private matters could very easily become public knowledge at Shawmut River, that did not amount to building personal relations across stubborn family-based divisions in the congregation.

While the familiar and informal atmosphere of Shawmut River helped members feel immediately at home, that climate washed thinly over persistent cracks and fissures in the congregation. These would become more telling when divisive conflicts threatened church unity. I noticed, for example, that Sharon and her mother, Ada, had not attended Jean Strong's Joy Circle for church women when it had been meeting. "Oh, that's too far to drive," Ada explained to me, but it was not farther than some of her other daily trips.

IF MEMBERS OF SHAWMUT RIVER engaged so little in politics, that did not mean they had no political views or sensibilities or that they did not have a powerful impact on American politics.[6] But in our film, how were we to represent visually what made Shawmut River a Moral Majority church?

The main business of churches like Shawmut River, I had come to see from my secular standpoint, was to help members deal with basic problems in family and personal life by following guidelines found in scripture. Their politics and social criticism sprang quite naturally from such efforts and fastened on those elements in American life felt to undermine or tear at the kind of family lives they were continually struggling to repair and preserve. Their ideological leaders—such as Jerry Falwell, Phyllis Schlafly or Pat Robertson, on the national level, or the Valentis and Strongs, locally—helped members see connections many only dimly felt: for example, that sex education was spreading the destructive view that morality is *not* absolute and God given but changing, negotiable and a matter of individual choice, or that feminism not only was keeping women from becoming what God created them to be but also was "bringing them down to be walked on," as Sharon put it.

The strategy of our film, then, would be to follow stories that showed how Shawmut River helped members wrestle with problems of family life. One story might involve struggles over raising children, perhaps among rebellious teenagers, where discipline was most sorely tested. But high on our list of priorities was to show the congregation helping someone deal with problems in marriage. This was prominent in the life stories of Shawmut River's leaders and would certainly show up in the story we would tell of Frank and Sharon's getting saved, turning their troubled marriage into a firm partnership and founding their church. In addition, we hoped to portray someone's current struggles in marriage. While filming such personal matters would ordinarily be difficult, Shawmut River's public treatment of family issues made it more feasible.

While Pastor Valenti said he did most of his counseling from the pulpit, the one current marriage crisis he was handling was that involving Ben Kachudnis and his wife, Pam, with which I had become familiar in our Bible-study group at the Lavernes'. Pam had now returned from Florida with her boyfriend and was living with him in an old mill town about a half hour's drive from Worcester. One Sunday after morning worship, as I was standing in the church vestibule, I saw a dark look suddenly come over Ben's face as his eyes fixed on something outside the window. I looked up to see a rusty, beat-up American sedan on the far side of the church's parking lot. Seated in the passenger's seat was a woman with straight blond hair down her back, looking forward and away from us. It was my first glimpse of Pam. She and her boyfriend had come to pick up her three sons for a day's outing. The look that hardened in Ben's face was scary. It seemed to spread like a physical reaction throughout his whole body—a transfiguration. I feared what he might do and remembered his once joking about taking a .38 revolver with him to Florida to confront them.

Ben was still very much in the collective care of the congregation. He was one of the few regulars at men's prayer in Pastor Valenti's study before each worship service and was often around the church, finding support and encouragement from someone. Pastor Valenti had waived tuition for his three boys in exchange for Ben's doing some weekly cleaning around the church. The look on his face that morning made me hope the congregation would succeed in keeping him from cracking into a fit of rage and vengeance.

Meanwhile, Pastor Valenti had begun meeting with Pam at a neutral place, a Friendly's sandwich shop near her new home, to work on trying to get her back to church and back to her marriage. This seemed a doubtful undertaking, but members had seen the Lord save a number of other marriages felt to be hopelessly lost.

I had not yet met Pam but had come to know more about her from her aunt, Mary Shepperson, who taught in the Christian Academy's preschool and whose relatives, including Pam, had followed her to Worcester in chain migration from rural Maine. Some of them, including one of Pam's sisters and another aunt, also attended Shawmut River. And it was Pam's relatives' and children's continuing involvement in Shawmut River, I surmised, that persuaded her to allow Pastor Valenti to continue to be involved in her marriage difficulties.

Conflict in marriage would not only make for good drama in our film but also fit with our larger strategy of how to make any community of belief understandable to outsiders. That was, first, to show members grappling with problems any viewer could identify with and then to show them wrestling with those problems in the otherwise strange terms of their beliefs. In this fashion, the basic terms of their faith would become understood, like those of any language, by seeing them *used* in context. Two scholars I brought to the project, Karen Fields and the late Nancy Jay, both close friends and colleagues who had taught me much about the sociology of religion, helped impress this strategy on our creative team. By then that team included not only my codirector and cinematographer but also a film editor we had recruited to the project.[7]

To make Shawmut River comprehensible even to secular viewers, it would also be advantageous, I imagined, to tell the story of an outsider approaching the church as a potential convert. Besides the dramatic tension such a story might provide, an outsider would naturally provoke insiders to state and clarify in explicit terms beliefs they otherwise took for granted. Since most new converts coming to Shawmut River were drawn from members' own extended families, it would be instructive to follow the story of someone trying to lead a close relative to the Lord.

Conflict of any kind serves to develop drama and bring to light taken-for-granted moral standards defining community life. In this regard, Shawmut River's ongoing tensions with the local town government and its own recurring faction fights, splits and departures represented other possible stories we put on our "shopping list" of material we would try to film. This list was made up with an eye to how well certain stories might carry themes I had come to see were important about churches like Shawmut River.

As with all documentaries in *cinéma-vérité* style, where meaning is conveyed not through narration but through real-life scenes and stories told by participants to the camera, we could not know in advance what would happen in any potential story or what events we would succeed in filming. Our budget, which we would ultimately stretch to cover fifty-four shooting days, set the outer limits within which we had to work. We started with a prioritized shopping list, and we revised it as we went along.

15

Shooting

Just to give you that spiritual touch-up . . .

The Salem Inn
October 28

O N   T H E   E V E N I N G before our first day of shooting, we hosted a dinner for church leaders, their families and the film crew. We took a private room in a classy yet subdued New England country inn with big fireplaces, colonial relics and large menus written in long-hand. Besides the Valentis and their parents, I invited the Keeners and the Sandersons.

The crew included, in addition to my codirector, Michael Camerini, only a sound recordist and a production manager. None was a practicing Christian, though our sound recordist at the time had grown up in a Mennonite family, a fact Pastor Valenti noted from the pulpit when he praised how the Lord had put this production together. Like virtually everyone I met in the relatively small guild of high-end documentary filmmakers, all were well educated, cosmopolitan and liberal, if not left liberal, in political sensibility and outlook. Yet all would have to work closely with members of Shawmut River. Therefore, they had to be coached, and later supported, to quickly adapt to what they saw as a strange, at times discomforting and potentially hostile environment. They had all been chosen with these challenges in mind, and tonight's dinner was the culmination of our preparatory work.

I had already brought Michael to worship services, prayer meetings,

Bible study at the Lavernes', and classes, basketball games and meetings at the Christian Academy. We discussed the significance of these events, how they fit into stories we might tell and how to go about filming them. That included everything from lighting and electrical challenges to the difficulties of visually representing the collective nature of church life. Church members, in turn, had a chance to meet Michael and question us further about our purposes and methods. In this way we began building a partnership with church members around shared understandings of what we all would be trying to do together. While our challenge as a crew was to go about filming as unobtrusively as possible, their challenge would be to go about their normal activities as if we were not there. Doug Laverne, for one, seemed impressed and pleased that we aimed to tell our story through real-life scenes and what characters themselves said to camera. "I thought you'd just come in and take some pictures," he confessed, "and that would be it."

Our inaugural dinner had an air of excitement and anticipation about it, and in this heady climate an important question came up: Would there be any restrictions on what we might film? Some were concerned about the Christian Academy's practice of corporal punishment. "Corporal punishment is a necessary part of discipline," the school handbook insisted, citing, among other biblical sources, Proverbs 13:24 ("He that spareth the rod hateth his son . . .") and Proverbs 29:15 ("The rod and reproof give wisdom: but a child left to himself bringeth his mother shame").

Of related interest, one thing that had struck me at Shawmut River was how much physical affection members gave their children. I remember being struck when Sharon Valenti told me she and her fourteen-year-old daughter, Christie, still had a lot of fun together—for instance, wrestling. (I did not know any mothers who wrestled with their teenage daughters for fun.) I began to wonder whether expressing parental discipline *physically* was itself an important part of Shawmut River's affirmation of corporal punishment. In explaining why parents should use a paddle to spank children instead of their hand, Pastor Valenti reasoned this would separate spanking from "the hand that loves them."

But it was Jean Strong who first explained to me another logic for using a paddle. First, you have to go *get* the paddle, she pointed out. Young parents often let their frustrations build until they angrily lash out at a child, she said, yanking them by the arm or shaking them.

Having to go get a paddle makes them take time to calm down, to get into a different mode in which discipline is governed by deliberation and reason. In her view, the paddle—usually made of plywood—was part of lifting spanking out of the spontaneous torrent of life and making it a ceremonial, ritual occasion. Around spanking or any discipline, Shawmut River instructed parents to take time to carefully explain the reasons for punishment and to explain that God himself required they do it.

However sensible such practices might seem to someone like me, who as a child had been spanked occasionally, in ceremonial ways, by loving and exemplary parents, the question of whether we might film spanking for national television raised serious questions in a public climate that had grown up in the short space of a generation, that considered spanking child abuse. I remember how alarmed I had been, sitting in the apartment of Anne Sullivan, a single parent on welfare who attended Shawmut River, when a case worker from the state's Department of Social Services informed her that her children might be taken away and placed in foster care because she spanked them. A loving parent of two, Anne had been struggling with problems of discipline, which she attributed to a past family environment in which her children had regularly witnessed her being beaten by their father. She praised Shawmut River, above all, for helping give her "the authority" and "the confidence" to discipline her children and spoke of the Bible as "the best child-care manual going."

At the time of my visit, Anne was in the midst of struggling with her older child, a daughter of ten, about wearing makeup, panty hose and high heels, and staying out "all hours." One of her daughter's friends, an older girl, had told her about the local child-abuse hot line. "Parents can't hit children," she said, giving Anne's ten-year-old the hot line number and encouraging her to call. It had been her daughter's third call to the child-abuse hot line that had required this caseworker to investigate three instances of what had been recorded and become part of the official record as "child abuse."

I had been appalled by this clumsy and potentially tragic intervention by state agencies in family life. It was not the only incident of this kind I encountered during my field research at Shawmut River. Already uncomfortable with the impersonal and abstract world of bureaucracy, members of Shawmut River were apt to recount such events as frightening evidence of what was entailed in the growth of

Big Government solutions to the problems of life, especially family life. It bred in them a righteous indignation toward the state and the helping professions associated with it, whose interventions were governed by "new ideas" about child rearing as opposed to "old-fashioned" ones handed down to them from their parents.

However, there was a difference between parents spanking their own children and school officials doing it, and some members who stood by corporal punishment in the home, I later learned, had misgivings about it in Shawmut River's Christian Academy. Nevertheless, they accepted the school's policy of corporal punishment even in the face of potential threats from the state. They knew Christian schools that had been closed down simply because of their practice of spanking. That summer two Christian communities—one in South Carolina and one nearby in Vermont—had been raided by police because of reports of children's corporal punishment. Wild rumors about Shawmut River's own practices were heard around town. And some years later, inflated reports of corporal punishment in the Branch Davidian community in Waco, Texas, would become a key factor persuading Attorney General Janet Reno to approve federal authorities' fateful attack on that community, an event linked to the later bombing of a federal-government office building in Oklahoma City.[1]

When questions arose that evening about our filming spanking, Pastor Valenti dismissed the idea that there would be any restrictions on what we might film. "We have nothing to hide," he declared. Later he confided in me that what had finally convinced him to go forward with the film was a passage in the Bible where the apostle Peter exhorts believers to "be ready always to give an answer to every man that asketh you, a reason of the hope that is in you . . ." (I Peter 3:15).

But Sharon had strong misgivings about portraying spankings at their school. She remembered how disturbed she herself had felt when a visiting minister giving a "Family Life Seminar" had demonstrated how to spank a child correctly by using his son. Even though Sharon favored spanking as an effective and biblically sanctioned means of discipline, that experience had cautioned her about how dangerous representations of spanking could be.

For my part, I reassured church leaders that portraying spanking was neither a priority nor a special interest of ours. Furthermore, I cautioned, to portray anything likely to be viewed in distorted or sensationalist terms would require setting it carefully in its real-life context. That would require presenting spanking alongside the kinds of love and responsibility parents and teachers generally showed the children under their care. Still, I had to wonder whether any portrayal of spanking would not simply serve to fan the flames of condemnation and possibly lead to closing down the church's school.

This discussion raised for all of us a more general question with which we soon would have to wrestle: Would we ever be denied access to events we wanted to film? As Pastor Valenti left it, there would be no restrictions. But I knew there might be exceptions.

WHEN WE BEGAN FILMING that fall, Shawmut River's financial picture suddenly brightened. Church and school were running in the black, and Scott Sanderson praised God for miraculously putting his church in such surprisingly good shape for its debut on national television. The congregation's desire to put a good foot forward was understandable, but worried me. I was committed to making a true-to-life portrait of this community and felt the hard-nosed economic struggles and personal sacrifices involved in making such a venture work were important to show, especially because of the media's tendency to depict the new Christian right through frighteningly inflated images of the wealth, power and self-aggrandizement of television evangelists. I was relieved, then, when the church's desire to put forward good appearances was overwhelmed by the relentless march of needs, problems and crises occupying everyone in the forthcoming months.

Signs of continuing problems first surfaced at a Wednesday-evening service in January, several months into our shoot. Pastor Valenti called a "mini–business meeting" to follow worship. We were not filming, and I was present just to keep up with things. "Up until September," Frank announced gravely from the lectern to begin the meeting, "offerings had been averaging seventeen hundred dollars a week, and it looked like we'd be in the black for the first time and could pay the pastor, staff, etc., etc. But someone was not happy, because offerings dropped four hundred dollars the very week I started being paid." (In September the congregation had voted to start paying him a salary of two hundred dollars a week.)

"The church needs seventeen hundred dollars a week to make budget," Frank explained. "Week after week we are slipping deeper and deeper into debt."

In September the church's financial picture had looked surprisingly bright. Now crisis again loomed overhead, and discontent rumbled in the background. Frank may have been right to connect the sudden decline in giving with the first payments of his modest salary. When the congregation had voted on the issue, Frank had stepped outside the room to leave Phil Strong to preside. The vote had been taken with heads bowed. Though no one had cast a negative vote (I looked), some abstained, and afterward there were murmurings of discontent. But members were more likely to vote with their pocketbooks—or their feet—and weekly balloting by offering plate had once again brought the church to the brink.

Continuing to outline the gravity of the situation, Frank said that 20 percent of parents had not paid their tuition bills to the academy. In the past, 30 percent of teachers' salaries had to be paid from church offerings, he said. Now the figure was closer to 60 percent. Once again the school seemed to be an albatross around Shawmut River's neck.

Meanwhile, morale in the Christian Academy was deteriorating for other reasons as well. Several teachers, including Sharon, wanted to cut back to part-time work. In addition, Dan Keener and Judy Waters, who after a brief romance had recently married, said they felt the Lord leading them to move to Ohio to teach in a Christian school there. This was particularly hard news since Dan and Judy were mainstays of the school, and Judy, as an in-law of the Valentis, was one of Shawmut River's founding members and, by all accounts, one of the church's power elite. Now she was leaving both the church and, in some sense perhaps, the Valenti-Morse family circle.

Differences flared up over their decision to leave. "The Lord doesn't pull you away from responsibility," Sharon observed, "even if you're called. And he calls you not just through feelings, but makes things evident to you in other ways."

For her part, Judy was adamant that the Lord had made their call to Ohio "so clear" to her and Dan. "We already have a job and met so many nice people when we were out there," she told me. She criticized "some people" for "putting themselves in the place of the Holy Spirit and thinking they know what you should do."

The final item Frank raised at this delicate business meeting was the issue of finishing the new nursery. Since the classes of the academy had been moved into the gymnatorium, Frank had decided to put two of the portable classrooms together and refinish them as a nursery connected to the main church building by an enclosed hallway. It had seemed a modest project at first, and Frank's father had covered much of the cost of materials. But costs kept mounting, and each Sunday Frank appealed to the church men to come down on Saturdays to help finish it.

As the business meeting drew to a close, Phil reported that after years of witnessing to him, his older brother Sam had finally agreed to attend church sometime. "Please pray for him!" Phil exhorted.

Time is a key ingredient in *cinéma-vérité* filmmaking: time to build trust, get people used to the camera and follow stories as they unfold in real time. Of course, in any true-life story, decisive and revealing events will not always happen within a designated shooting period or when a camera crew is present. Whether you get enough material to portray anything significant about a given story or, better yet, show its dramatic development over time is something you cannot control. You make guesses and hope—and, if a believer in God's providence, pray.

At first, members took considerable interest in what we were doing—the lights we built in the gymnatorium, the dance the cameraman and sound recordist had to do not to disturb people's actions yet get the variety of shots needed to create a scene from an event and so on. But over time, with the camera crew moving about unobtrusively, members' awareness of our presence waned, and people began reporting their surprise at having forgotten the crew was even there. But submitting themselves to the camera in this way depended on more than time and technique. It rested, above all, on trust. The intensity of filming would see this trust grow, enabling us to film more and more intimate material over time.

We were shooting sixteen-millimeter film, which, with its lab and processing costs, is much more expensive than videotape. So in order to get people used to the camera, we spent days simply pretending to film—going through all the motions of shooting without expending a foot of film. But all the while we had to remain ready to "roll film" if something significant came up. This relentless vigilance and decision making made even pretending to film tiring. So, too, did our daily production schedule. It meant getting up before dawn to set up lights, rig and load camera and tape recorder, and get our heads together before the first events of the day. Then we had to stay well after the last events of the evening to break everything down, wrap cable, pack up the car, catch dinner and get to bed in order to start all over early the next morning. On days we were not filming, I was busy keeping tabs on potential stories and events, allaying whatever fears participants had about filming them and scheduling our shooting days based on best guesses about when significant events would occur. All the while, my codirector, Michael, and I had to keep an eye on budget and where the project was creatively. There was little time for note taking or reflection. On the other hand, filming ultimately produced thirty-five hours of footage of everyday life at Shawmut River and its school, which itself, along with transcripts, proved a great resource for research.

Also, I was surprised to find filming press me deeper into church life, into events where I otherwise had no place to stand as participant-observer. In the past, for example, I would have relied on people's accounts of what had happened at a personal counseling session, an evening visit to an unsaved relative or a women's prayer meeting. But now, if those events were to have a visible place in our portrait, I had to be there with camera crew on hand. At more intimate events, after initial greetings and settling down, I would drop back behind the camera—or sometimes even leave the room—inviting people to go on with their business as if we were not there. As a crew, we tried to move about in ways that preserved that illusion.

In addition, simply bringing three crew members to Shawmut River also changed my situation as a researcher. How should crew respond to questions about politics, about abortion or about a boyfriend they were living with? How should they handle questions about their salvation? If something needed to be coordinated or done, whom should they turn to in the congregation and how? What dress or demeanor would reassure and what disturb?

The biggest strain fell on our production manager, who often worked away from the rest of us, spending hours around the church office making phone calls and chatting with Sharon or whomever was around. Her exhaustion at managing conversation in this new world reminded me of my own first months of fieldwork. In general, it was eye-opening to watch crew members recapitulate some of my own experiences in becoming acclimated to Shawmut River. I watched them cringe, for example, at the church's prevailing musical style, which ranged from sentimental ballads about Jesus accompanied by banks of violins played through the sanctuary sound system to the punchy, martial sounds of old gospel hymns. Then, after a month or two, I would hear them whistling these same tunes as we packed up our gear.

More important, the crew brought new eyes, ears and sensibilities to the scene. This opened up new terrain for me, especially with Shawmut River's teenagers. But it also helped keep our fingers on the pulse of church life so we would not miss events we wanted to film. While we were shooting Dave Keener's senior-high English class, for example, our production manager would be up in the church office on the lookout for other film-worthy events: school discipline, someone arriving to see Pastor Valenti about a personal problem or just people horsing around in the office. Meanwhile, our sound recordist would overhear through her open microphone teenagers talking about an illicit party over the weekend.

"Shut up!" a boy sitting next to Christie Valenti hissed to her one day in class.

Christie grimaced into a broad smile and muttered, "When I tell my mother, she's gonna hand me a suitcase!" I suspected they were talking about a party at one boy's house last weekend that had gotten the teens in trouble. We had heard about it during one of several conversations we had shot with members of the girls' basketball team, driving to away games at other Christian schools in Massachusetts.

It was my codirector Michael Camerini's interest in portraying the teenagers that prompted me to get to know them better, and driving down the roadways, away from church, school and family, provided an occasion for greater candor on both our parts. On our first drive, Mary Shepperson's daughter Pattie was astounded to hear me say I liked Cindy Lauper and Tina Turner, who, at the time, when MTV was just coming into its own, both had popular songs out. "*Who* do you like?" Pattie asked me incredulously. "Are you *serious*? You like *them*?"

"So, tell me about the party?" Michael asked Pattie, sandwiched between her older sister, Paula, and two other teens in the backseat of our station wagon. As I drove, Michael was shooting from the front seat while our sound recordist, lying flat on her stomach out of sight in the back of the station wagon, monitored sound taken from a microphone taped to the car ceiling.

Pattie Shepperson was struggling to put on mascara as our car jounced down a country road. She had a flat, oval face with small eyes, a button nose and thinly drawn eyebrows. She was an irrepressible cutup, something of an independent spirit and leader among her peers. "You don't tell Pattie what to do," Christie Valenti observed. On one drive I remember Pattie describing to us one incident in her struggles with her mother, Mary.

"She's a pyro," Pattie said cryptically, trying to suppress a laugh. "She burns things."

"An incurable pyromaniac," her older sister, Paula, affirmed, grinning.

"I had four Van Halen tapes," Pattie recalled about one of her heavy-metal rock-and-roll favorites. "My mom found them in my drawer and she burned them all on me." I imagined mild-mannered Mary Shepperson grimacing matter-of-factly as she dropped Pattie's cassettes into the family's wood stove. She had once done the same with a pair of Pattie's jeans she thought were too tight.

The teens involved in last weekend's party had been given a stern talking to at school (spanking was considered inappropriate beyond a certain age). Pattie, Paula and others in the car were reluctant to speak about what had gone on that evening. "We'll get in big trouble," Pattie said, laughing with the others, "called exiled, kicked outta school!"

Someone had brought "a bunch of booze," they finally said, and everybody—well, almost everybody—had gotten drunk.

I suspected they were exaggerating for our benefit, though their accounts of the antics of several drunken partiers were totally convincing. Later we filmed one of their parties, held on a Friday evening at the home of a high-school senior whose mother worked nights. Retreating to a bedroom to load film magazines and confer, we came across a bottle of wine tucked under the bed. There were more than twenty young people present, all but one or two students from the Christian Academy, and no one seemed drunk.

The teenagers had spent that evening mostly talking—mostly girls with girls and boys with boys—catching up on gossip and listening to rock music. Several of the boys pulled out instruments—electric keyboard, guitar and bass—and jammed a little. All this seemed quite tame compared with what teenagers might have been up to in the 1980s—or even what my peers and I had done in the 1960s.

Shawmut River's youth, like teenagers elsewhere, sought to test the bounds their parents set. "If they tell us smoking will hurt you," Pattie once said, laughing and giving a shrug of her shoulders, "you know, we could go up in smoke!" But if teenagers are bound to rebel against whatever limits their parents set, I wondered what difference it made how loosely, tightly or wisely those limits were drawn. Quite recently mainstream journalists covering Christian rock concerts have been struck by how tame such events seem. "Hell, no one here even smokes," remarked a *Newsweek* reporter. "And groupies? Out of the question. In fact, some band members even bring their wives."[2]

Though expressing the independent-mindedness of youth, Shawmut River's teenagers, nevertheless, shared many of their parents' values. They saw abortion and homosexuality as anathema and were apt to criticize their parents mostly for not practicing what they preached—for example, a teacher's telling a white lie to extract a confession from them or parents condemning smoking, but then being so desperate for a cigarette after a long church service that they would rush off to their cars to smoke. On one of our drives, Pattie criticized the adults for sometimes presenting their own views as God's. "They'll harp on *their* views," she said irritatedly, "and then at the end say, 'Well, I suppose if it's God's will,' just to give you that spiritual touch-up, you know?" she said, pursing her lips to mimic the adults. "Show how *good* they are, how *godly* they are, how many Bible verses they know—they'll quote a verse or two." She smirked. "It's not what you want to hear."

The teens, like young people elsewhere, were concerned with issues of integrity. They themselves knew firsthand how to apply "spiritual touch-ups" to life, to use Pattie's choice phrase. Her older sister, Paula, for instance, said she had found herself "playacting" when she was ten and their parents had just gotten saved and started bringing them to a fundamentalist church. "I saw how everybody else acted," Paula explained, "and in order to fit in, you gotta act that way, too." When she finally did accept Christ into her heart, she said, everyone was shocked. "It was like 'You mean, you *weren't* saved? . . . You acted it so *well!*'"

When I asked Paula why she had finally stopped just pretending to be saved, she replied, "I guess the Holy Spirit touched me and said, 'You've been acting . . . and you're not gonna go to heaven if you keep it up.'"

That teens in a Christian school could *look* pious was evident in a television news profile at the time of a Christian academy nearby. Typical of slash-and-burn TV journalism involving no more than one day of shooting, the program portrayed that school's teenagers as tightly disciplined automatons carefully toeing the line of their parents' beliefs, though I later learned that the pastor of this same church had struggled with his own teenage son's drug use.

Shawmut River's teenagers represented a classic problem faced by any religious community or sect defined by adult conversion and voluntary membership: How do you bring the faith to the next generation, which grows up having it forced on them and taking it for granted? Among children in fundamentalist churches, born-again experiences pass through particular age groups like the measles. "I got saved when I was four, I think," Christie Valenti told us. "I know that God died for me, he died on the cross, and I'm going to heaven and the whole bit," she continued rapid-fire, "but I wasn't old enough to where I could appreciate it as much as somebody who was older can really appreciate it. Whereas if I was unsaved, drank, was addicted to drugs and the whole thing, it would be a real experience for me. But it wasn't." She once said that sometimes she wished she could "just go out for a week and have unsaved parents" to see what it was like.

Still, many might have said along with Christie that they believed Jesus died on the cross for them and "the whole bit," or that they prayed regularly, as Christie did, "like when I'm getting dressed," she said. "God hears and sees everything you do," she noted thoughtfully, "so no matter where you go or what you do, God's always listening to you. And it's amazing how he can hear everybody at the same time!" Christie had evidently given some thought to this and other theological matters, and I wondered how she and the other young people of Shawmut River would respond to problems besetting them as adults. Would they draw on their faith to grasp and deal with the problems that came their way?

In certain ways, I could see how Shawmut River's teenagers were learning how to live within the kind of close-knit, family-based universe they inhabited. "The youth group's more our family," Pattie said. (Indeed, for some, it included actual siblings, cousins and old family friends.)

"We stick up for each other and stuff," another member of the girls' basketball team chimed in.

"Yeah, take the blame or stand up for one another," Pattie affirmed. "We're pretty much a family. Some people consider it a gang, but not really."

"Having a family is good to whereas you can help each other," Christie pointed out about the church's youth group, "but I think sometimes when everybody knows everything, when you get too close, it becomes a problem. Different cliques get together and they start talking about this group because this group doesn't like so-and-so. It gets started, and by the time it's finished, it's just been exploded so much that it's almost impossible to get the truth." Not surprisingly, Shawmut River's teenagers were learning to negotiate a world like that of their parents.

16

Marriage

He did not create a bowling ball . . .

I F YOU HAVE YOUR BIBLES, open them up to Ephesians," Pastor Valenti said from the pulpit to launch the first in his two-part series of messages on marriage. The sound of fluttering pages filled the gymnatorium sanctuary. This was the second set of Sunday worship services we filmed. Frank began by assuring his flock that "the Bible guarantees a beautiful, warmhearted relationship for every man and woman who are married on the face of the earth. In fact, God's guarantees in marriage are *so vital* and *so critical* and *so applicable* that you don't even have to be saved to have this kind of love for your wife or husband. It's *yours!* It's yours for the building!" Yet, he went on, "too many Christians have a louse instead of a spouse for a husband." By and large, it was men—"the armpit of humanity," he called them—who "could solve ninety percent of the problems in their marriages. I know that when I have problems in my own relationship with my wife," he confessed, "it's immediately corrected by me taking account of what I'm doing and how I'm doing it, and who I'm doing it for. Somewhere along the line, I've just left my wife out of things. You see, we as men have our own lives. . . . We like to do things *away* from our wives."

He turned to address the women in the congregation with Ephesians 5:21: "'Wives, submit yourselves unto your own husband as unto the Lord'—okay, ladies, this morning we're going to nail you; next Sunday we're going to nail your husbands. I promise revenge."

"The key phrase is *your own husband*," he continued. "Ladies, that phrase is telling us *personal possession*. That husband belongs to you! Whether you realize it or not, he's yours to make, or yours to break!" He went on to assure them that "you *can* understand your husband" (just as he assured the men the following week, "You *can* figure women out") and, like "a ball of clay," you can make of your spouse something beautiful or something ugly. Turning back to Genesis, he reminded the men that God made for Adam in the garden "a lady." "He did not create a bowling ball," he continued in rhythmic cadence:

> He did not create a fishing rod.
> He did not create a Garcia lightweight spinning reel.
> He did not create an automobile.
> He didn't create Bondo to fix it with.
> He didn't create problems. He created—
> yes, gentlemen, like it, lump it,
> do what you will with it,
> please digest it in any fashion you will—
> he created [he paused and dropped his jaw] *your wife*.

The crowd roared its approval.

FRANK VALENTI'S PREACHING on marriage must be understood in context of the kind of marriages and families his congregation generally knew and took for granted. They were marriages in which a wife might turn to her mother, or another women relative (or close friend), to share the daily burdens and joys of child care, while her husband's life revolved around work and leisure spent with men outside the home—like Frank's own pattern as a young husband, hanging out with guys at the garage and hunting or fishing with his cousin on weekends. "We like to do things away from our wives," Frank admitted matter-of-factly to the men in his flock this morning. Yet against those tendencies, he preached that God did not create for Adam a bowling ball, fishing gear or anything else that typically might preoccupy men outside the home.

In the kind of marriage his flock generally knew, two spheres of activity separated by gender gave rise to two distinct social worlds in which different sensibilities and habits of thought naturally prevailed. They cultivated two different kinds of human beings. "Frank's affections were at the garage," Sharon had said of the early years of their marriage, "and mine were with the children." Between such different beings, communication and trust, let alone intimacy, were not easy. In this context, the claim that "you *can* understand your husband" or "you *can* figure women out," as Frank exhorted this morning, was not self-evident. Rather, it cut against the grain of long-standing habits among both women and men. And the idea that, in submitting to your spouse, you would be able to influence him or her so fully as to create something beautiful represented a radical proposition.

Before they were saved, many at Shawmut River had entered marriage with a dim, distrustful view of the opposite sex, an attitude that could easily turn exploitative or oppositional. As one church woman described the rule of thumb she had adopted in relating to her husband at the start of their marriage: "Once you got one, see what you can get from him." Indeed, relations between the sexes planted so firmly in separate worlds bristled with tensions and frictions, even of a visceral kind. I remember Pastor Valenti and one deacon once concurring that neither could tolerate a woman barber touching him to cut his hair. They shuddered to think of it. Tensions between the sexes were often released in humor, sometimes as part of solidifying same-sex solidarities. "Women! Go figure!" was the kind of thing men at Shawmut River might utter in jest to hold their wives' claims at a distance. Or notice Frank this morning promising church women "revenge" when he would "nail" their husbands the next week.[1]

Given the limited common ground between women and men and their tendencies toward hostility and distrust, it is remarkable that anyone would choose to marry someone of the opposite sex to begin with, were it not for an overriding heterosexuality and the compulsion to have children, a family, and to achieve adulthood in socially approved ways. Otherwise, I wondered, might it not be easier to imagine achieving mutual understanding in same-sex relationships? Perhaps this added steam, I thought, to the emphatic rejection of homosexuality in this social world.[2]

When members of Shawmut River *did* marry, they often did so abruptly. Fred Webber proposed to his wife the day after he first met her, and Phil and Jean Strong decided to marry on their second date. Pregnancy was not infrequently a precipitating factor propelling a couple into marriage and parenthood all at once, as with Doug and Terry Laverne.

In marriages of this kind, with limited communication and common ground, sex itself was not readily seen as an important vehicle for emotional intimacy (as opposed to something done simply for pleasure). Pastor Valenti reasoned from scripture that sex was given by God essentially to build faith. But, as folk wisdom had it in this milieu, whatever sexual spark might be present in courtship should not be expected to continue very long into marriage. To awaken people's expectation that sexual pleasure should be an expected part of marriage—or of life in general—was seen to be dangerously misleading, distracting people from what were felt to be the real foundations of marriage in self-sacrificing love as duty, rather than romantic love or sexual passion. "Love is not feelings," Pastor Valenti never tired of hammering home from the pulpit. It is instead, he preached, the willingness and commitment "to keep on keeping on," emphasizing the perseverance required to fulfill the duties of one's "station in life." From this vantage point, even the term *sexuality* could be resented for unduly elevating sex's importance in life, as one outburst during one of my early interviews with right-to-life activists showed.[3]

Such conservatives have an instinctive feel for the sociological truth expressed by Max Weber that sexual passion is an inherently unstable element upon which to base social organization.[4] In this regard, matter-of-fact discourses on sexual pleasure or sexual identity found in high-school sex-education curricula, the prominence of sexual situations in television programs and rock and roll's preoccupation with romantic love were all seen as part of demonic attacks on the real foundations of family life and marriage.

In condemning rock and roll, adults at Shawmut River were apt to mention with alarm direct references to Satan in certain lyrics and shun any music, as Scott Sanderson put it, that makes you feel you want to move your hips. However, the example Pastor Valenti most often used in his criticisms of rock music was Sonny and Cher's version of "I Got You Babe." What is the problem with a mellow song like this, I asked myself, with no driving beat and no references to Satan?

"I got you babe, I got you babe," Frank would mimic the song's lyrics from the pulpit in a whiny voice laced with sarcasm. "We don't need this, we don't need that . . . ," he sneered, "I got you babe." What he objected to simply was the song's elevation of that one romantic relationship at the expense of all others in a family—children, parents, grandparents, siblings.[5]

The kind of marriage Pastor Valenti's preaching assumed struck me with particular force while I was talking with Mary Shepperson, the woman from Maine, whose teenage daughters we filmed and whose niece, Pam, was married to Ben Kachudnis. "We weren't talkin'," Mary told me about her marriage before she and her husband were saved. "Well, we don't talk a great deal," she explained, "but we weren't talkin' hardly at all then. He would go to work, and then go to the barroom and come home late at night, so there's no need for talkin'."

"See," she said, squinting intently, "you can turn people off being in the same room with them; you can pretend they don't exist, so that's what I did. He stopped smoking two weeks before I realized that he stopped—that's how much attention I was paying to him!" She laughed and added matter-of-factly, "That's awful!"

Mary had hoped her marriage would change faster than it did. But after getting saved and "getting into the word" for some years, her husband had backslid and, by the time we met, was only rarely attending Shawmut River. Mary described how much she had thought and prayed about her decision to work full-time in the church's nursery. She and her husband had had problems years before with their oldest daughter when Mary had taken a factory job, and now their three younger girls were going through adolescence. But since they all attended the church's school, working at the nursery would permit Mary closer contact with them than her factory job had. "We talked it over before I took the job," Mary said, "and he was in agreement with me. And last week he says, 'I think we made a mistake.'" She paused and furrowed her brow in intense reflection. "That's the first time he's ever called it a joint agreement, so I think there's been progress there. You know," she added, pointing to the crux of the matter, "we made a step forward, because I wouldn't make a decision like that without asking him." In the past she would have.

For Mary and others at Shawmut River, progress in marriage meant asking a husband to participate in a decision as well as his seeing it as "a joint agreement." It meant, as Frank preached from Ephesians this morning, "submitting yourselves one to another in the fear of God" (5:21). Frank went on in that sermon to quote the next verse from Ephesians: "Wives, submit yourselves unto your own husbands, as unto the Lord."

"God does not ask you to do stupid things," he hastened to point out, reminding them that God's plan for the family required husbands to love their wives "even as Christ also loved the church, and gave himself for it" (Ephesians 5:25).

"This means, men," he said, "you're going to have to stop being selfish with yourselves, okay?"

Shifting ground, Frank had his flock turn with him to I Corinthians 7:5, which exhorts husbands and wives not to "defraud" each other and to come together so that Satan not tempt them. "See that little word there, *Satan*?" he asked, pausing. "Most people don't understand something. Your marriage is under attack by the wiles of the devil right now." He went on to hit out against various demonic attacks on marriage, including alcoholism, which is "a manifestation of selfishness" and the "single greatest cause of divorce"; superheroes on television, which promote individualism; and even *Little House on the Prairie*, which, he said, "even makes family life look antiquated!"

"The devil's main thrust in this world today," he said, gathering steam, "is to get ahold of the people in high places with the power that God has endowed to them, so he can develop a philosophy that is sexually motivated. And I submit to your scrutiny this morning these simple truths: ABC, CBS and whatever major networks you're looking at today, their main thrust is to destroy the home. *Three's Company*—trash! Its main thrust is to destroy your home, your husband and your wife. Everything that comes out of the philosophy of this world is designed to neutralize the influence that you have in your husbands' lives, ladies. The NOW, National Organization for Women—'Hey, ladies, you know what you ought to do? You ought to stand up, become a man—I mean a woman! You ought to go to work! Don't let anybody push you around!'

"Yea, hath God said, ladies, when we come to the simple realization that God created you for your husband, and that he is your possession, and that you are to make of him a spiritual giant, your life will take on meaning. It will take on zing. . . . Do you realize that if the men who called themselves Christians were to follow the simple procedures found in Ephesians, chapter five—being controlled by the spirit of God—that we would wipe out the women's liberation movement overnight?"

PASTOR VALENTI'S VIEW that women's liberation could be wiped out overnight by Christian men fulfilling their scriptural role as husbands—a view taken up by the Promise Keepers movement a decade later—might be dismissed simply as men's wishful thinking or their drive to dominate if it were not a view shared by the women in his congregation. When I asked Jean Strong, for example, why some women were feminists, she replied simply, "Weak men."

Sharon Valenti confessed that the same question had always puzzled her, "unless it could be," she theorized, "that they're after something else . . . like communism." On another occasion, she imagined it was perhaps homosexuality that feminists were "really pushing," and other church women expressed this same view. Otherwise, they had difficulty understanding feminism's rationale and its straightforward appeal to women like them.

At the same time, it is tempting to see the basic thrust of Frank's preaching on marriage as feminist, insofar as it required husbands to focus more on family responsibilities and aimed to increase communication and effective partnership in marriage. Indeed, as mentioned before, some writers have seen these themes on submission in marriage as evidence of feminism's widespread influence on Christian fundamentalism or as evidence of their actual feminist orientation.[6]

Such interpretations are difficult to reconcile with Sharon Valenti's view that feminism is "diametrically opposed" to Christianity and "an insult to my intelligence." Or with Sally Keener's affirmations that, as a woman, you should "stay home and take care of your house and your kids and your family" and that "feminists make women a bunch of neurotics"—views not uncommon at Shawmut River or among conservative women I met. More important, it would be hard to explain why progress in fundamentalist marriages proceeds not by *denying* traditional gender roles but by *affirming* them, not by exhorting women to greater *independence* but by encouraging greater *dependence on*—or *interdependence with*—their husbands.

These paradoxes can be resolved by imagining them in the context of the kinds of families that members of Shawmut River lived in and took for granted. So, too, can conservative women's at times puzzling views of feminism. Given the hostility and distance from feminism that Shawmut River's women expressed, I was initially puzzled, for instance, when Sharon mentioned during our first interview that before she was saved she was "more of a women's libber." (Though on another occasion she doubted whether feminism as a movement had even been around at the time [see p. 92]). I was even more surprised to hear this same self-assessment from Mary Shepperson and Sally Keener.

"What do you mean?" I asked Sharon.

"You know, listen to him and do what I want," she replied, blinking at me nonplussed. "Listen to him, do what I want" was not a description of being feminist that I might have heard from my own feminist friends and colleagues, yet it turned out to be what Jean, Sally Keener and others had in mind by having once been "women's libbers." But it made perfect sense in the kind of families that members of Shawmut River took for granted, where feminism's call for women's greater independence would simply underwrite the traditional bifurcation of men's and women's worlds they already lived within. As Sally Keener described the early years of her marriage to Dave, "I just did what I wanted when I wanted. I ran all the household money and the budget. I would never consider asking Dave to do anything! Good heavens!" In this context, the feminist call for independence would have meant excluding Dave further from the affairs of family life. It meant, as Sally put it, to be "totally domineering" or, as Sharon saw it, simply to "do what I want."

Furthermore, to continue along that path stood to short-circuit any effort to involve husbands in domestic affairs, to bring them to see family decisions, as Mary Shepperson struggled to do, as matters of "joint agreement." Progress in marriage, from this standpoint, involved encouraging wives *not* toward greater *independence* but toward greater *inter*dependence with their husbands. Within the kind of marriages women of Shawmut River knew, feminist independence seemed fruitless, if not regressive. It served to legitimize men's unbridled detachment from family responsibilities and promised no end to the relentless conflict and chaos in marriages bridging men's and women's wildly separate worlds. No wonder they had trouble understanding modern feminism and tended to dismiss it as simply being "totally domineering" or a "communist plot."[7]

But even if fundamentalist teachings on submission helped focus men on domestic responsibilities, would they not ultimately condemn women to their husbands' domination? To be sure, members of Shawmut River were more apt to stress the *mutual* nature of submission and, following Genesis, to point out that Eve was made from Adam's rib "not to be walked on but to be by his side." And like Jean Strong, they would caution that the entire viability of God's "chain of command" set forth in scripture depended on a husband's demonstrating Christ-like self-sacrifice toward his family.

Nevertheless, the lines of authority were clearly drawn, and, if push came to shove on any family decision, all agreed a husband should have the final say. Yet on the face of it, the women of Shawmut River did not seem dominated by their husbands in any respect. On the contrary, women like Sharon Valenti, Jean Strong and Sally Keener seemed very much on top of things in their homes and families. Furthermore, they felt their biblical approach to marriage—especially, but not only, when their husbands shared it—represented a marked improvement in their condition as women.[8] And their thinking about these matters did not seem naive, unrealistic or untested. Both Sharon and Jean had gone through periods of angry, if not hateful, conflict with their husbands, bringing their marriages to the brink of destruction. In the crucible of such experiences, it is reasonable to assume, they learned much about how best to defend their interests. Why, then, did they embrace fundamentalist teachings on submission, which gave their husbands final say over them?

As noted earlier, in the kind of family found at Shawmut River, the roles of housewife and mother did not isolate women socially, as the feminist critique of the family supposed. Instead, these roles involved women in ties of day-to-day cooperation and mutual dependence with women relatives. This family-based circle generated a lively collective discourse within a group stretching beyond husband and wife, a discourse that could exercise considerable influence over day-to-day struggles for power and authority within any marriage. And since knitting together wider family ties was traditionally seen as women's business, such collective discourse rested more in women's than men's hands. However much God's plan for the family at Shawmut River encouraged men to play a responsible part in family life, it never abolished different roles for men and women. They remained like "fractions with different denominators," as Jean Strong put it, requiring Christ as the common denominator to unite them.

With the help and support of other women relatives to rely on, women at Shawmut River exercised a certain factual control over the continuous flow of the varied and densely connected things that make up domestic life. In family life, power resides less in commanding than in the doing of things—things that are so interconnected with one another that their consequences are difficult to resist or undo. And it is in this context that men's headship in the family must be understood.[9] To explore its workings, I presented members I interviewed with a hypothetical situation where a husband exercised his prerogative of "final say" to decide something everyone would consider wrong and against the interests of his wife and children. What if he decided, I suggested, to spend scarce household money on something for his sports car rather than on a washing machine his family needed?[10]

Sharon was most circumspect in responding. "I know the Bible says a man who doesn't provide for his family is worse than an infidel," she replied, "but it doesn't say what to do with him." She said she would turn the matter over to Frank, who was called of God and accountable to him. But she was concerned Frank might advise the woman simply to sit back and wait until her husband "fell flat on his face."

"'Fell flat on his face'?" I asked incredulously.

"That would be my question," Sharon admitted, "unless she went out there and tripped him," she added, laughing. But others commenting on this hypothetical situation quite readily imagined concrete ways for her to do just that. Not to have his shirts ready for an important business meeting, Sharon's stepfather, Tom Morse, suggested, or finish them stiff and wrinkled. Not to stock the house with things he needed or, in cleaning up, to misplace things he needed were tactics others imagined. Rather than counseling a wife's submission, members suggested indirect ways to achieve her legitimate interests by working within her traditionally designated domain of household responsibilities. In employing such tactics, she could depend on material and moral support from the women in her family circle and, perhaps, her own husband's relative distance from those realities.

Jean Strong, who as head of the church nursery was most involved in teaching younger women what submission meant, described its virtues in this way. "What's really great," she explained, "and is all rolled into the submission thing is the man has got to love the wife as Christ loved the church and gave his life for it. Christ never came back and browbeat us. He never screamed and yelled and hollered or humiliated or tormented. He always thought of us first, all right? It's very easy to be submissive when your husband thinks of you first, and it's very easy for a wife to build up a man who acts that way." But, she allowed, a lot of Christian men did not know how to lead in this way. "And it takes a lot for that woman to let go of the reins and literally force him to be the leader, and then support the decisions he makes."[11]

It is difficult for an outsider to see, let alone understand, struggles for power in any marriage, in the dense thicket of circumstances that is the stuff of domestic conflict. My research was not so intimate that I could observe these processes up close, but I was able to get a basic feel for certain marriages, including the Valentis', Strongs', Keeners', Sandersons' and Lavernes'. In all these, it would be preposterous to imagine husbands dominating their wives. If anything, I had the impression that greater factual control of all the dense, interconnected things making up domestic life—and, therefore, subliminal authority—rested in women's hands.[12]

It was more likely that I would be able to observe such struggles for power in the wider church community, where the same patriarchal model of authority prevailed. But even in those struggles, power would be difficult to trace, since in conflicts I had already witnessed—around the departure of Bill Tatum, for instance—the decisive mode of struggle was by defining through talk how situations and people were collectively perceived.

I also knew that although Sharon Valenti held no office at Shawmut River, she exercised considerable influence and was routinely counted by members as part of the church's power elite. I had scheduled a second interview with her when we began shooting. In part, I wanted to clear the air of any misgivings she might have about the film. I was seeking both her support and her suggestions. I also wanted to talk with her about women's power and influence in the church, including her own.

November 18
The Valentis' Home

Soon after we began filming, Sharon and I sat down to talk in their front living room while their dog, Freckles, slept under the polished wood coffee table where my tape recorder sat. Frank was in the family room at the back of the house meeting with Andy Church, Shawmut River's one dedicated politician. A bachelor in his thirties who still lived with his mother, Andy pursued politics with impulsive enthusiasm and was head of the Massachusetts chapter of an independent conservative political action committee.

Sharon and I began by discussing a project she had envisioned to educate women on political issues. "I don't think the equal rights amendment speaks for the majority," she said of that feminist-sponsored legislation at the time. But many women, like herself, she said, had been misled into believing it meant simply equal pay for equal work, which she, too, favored. Few knew, she said with alarm, that it approved of homosexuality. She also resented the message she felt it put out that women who saw themselves first and foremost as housewives and mothers were "stupid"—that "all you can do is stay home and clean the house." (The view that feminism devalues housewives and mothers was expressed by other women at Shawmut River.)

I remarked that this was ironic since feminists made a point of saying housework should be recognized and valued as work, something expressed for a while in the "wages-for-housework" campaign in the 1970s.

"I think it's more than housework," Sharon objected. "Proverbs thirty-one talks about the virtuous woman who owns real estate, who goes out and gets supplies for her family, who comes home and cooks—she even waits on servants. I mean, she was a woman of *class*, and my goodness, by that description it seems the man is a namby-pamby. So you're not limited within the confines of your house," she observed. (Later in our conversation, Sharon credited teaching her first ladies' Bible-study group at Shawmut River with making her feel better about her abilities and herself.)

We were then interrupted for a moment as Frank saw Andy Church to the front door. Making his way out, Andy told Sharon that he wanted to get "Christian women involved in the lecture circuit."

"You can really argue with those feminists! Tell 'em you've been liberated for years!" he chortled enthusiastically. "Tell them you wear the pants in the family!" He threw his head back and laughed heartily.

When we returned to our conversation, Sharon said she hated the kind of confrontations you had to face in public debate but recognized she was a "scrapper" when backed into a corner. "My gift is being in the background," she observed. "I probably belong back in the Dark Ages," she said with some embarrassment, "but I'd much prefer men running the nation and the church." Yet she admitted she could exercise strong influence over Frank—not as a person who would "gab" or "carry tales," she said by way of qualification, but "mainly over biblical issues—how we might see things." For someone who saw the Bible as the ultimate source of all moral standards, this was no small matter. It had been clear all along that Frank gave considerable weight to Sharon's views. In fact, given her situation, Sharon was concerned the congregation might think she had too much influence in church affairs. For example, she told me, she would not want them to know that she wrote many of Frank's letters (after he had given her the gist of what to write). Suddenly all the letters I had received with Frank's signature appeared in a new light.

"I wouldn't want the congregation to think I have any pull or sway," Sharon continued, "yet I do, so it's a very awkward position. Like I said, I can tell Frank something and put fear into him over something I might see, whether it's real or not." *Whether it's real or not*, when I thought about it later, seemed a remarkable distinction to observe.

To provoke Sharon's reflections on women's power and influence at Shawmut River, I read to her, as I sometimes did to church women I interviewed, portions of an article on fundamentalism that appeared at the time in the academic journal *Feminist Studies*. "This article spotlights the fundamentalist devaluation of women," the author began, "and the degree to which church women remain closeted—that is, locked into the narrow and inflexible confines of a male-defined belief system."[13]

Sharon immediately objected to the writer's inference that, as she put it, "where the men say it, we believe it. I'm not answerable just to Frank," she insisted. "I'm answerable to God." Moreover, she felt Christianity elevated women rather than devalued them. "When we had Christian principles in our country—even fifty years ago—it was nothing to see men who would watch their tongues around women. They wouldn't think to swear. They would open doors for women, lift packages for women, open car doors for women—treat them like they were special. Now, with the ERA movement in, you see—'Women, do your own thing! [she mimicked men exhorting women on] Hey, you're no different than we are.' . . . Now their mouths are worse than the men's!"

When conservative women assert that feminism threatens women's position in society, they often put forward examples like this, of men complying with forms of etiquette marking traditional gender differences—opening the door for a woman, for instance, or not swearing in front of women as men regularly did among themselves. Such examples lift up the fact that traditional gender roles require certain behaviors on the part of men to fulfill their male status and, simultaneously, mark women's. Some of those behaviors, especially those prompted by perceived injuries or threats to male honor, could become quite aggressive, muscular and even violent on occasion.

I asked Sharon's opinion of another passage in this article. "It is important to note," it read, "that the mind and voice of evangelicalism remain male. Only men make definitive pronouncements on every-thing that matters."[14]

Sharon agreed. "I don't think it really is a woman's nature to be out there proclaiming," she explained. "I think most wives enjoy having their husbands speak for them." But, she insisted, this did not mean women were stifled. Indeed, she felt she had to be careful, "because I know I can be such an influence on Frank, and I don't think I'm any-thing unusual—I think most wives can."

I pointed out that making pronouncements, or proclaiming, did not amount to making decisions. "And before a decision is made," I observed, "there are many things that happen to lead someone to real-ize this is right for this church—all those conversations . . ."

"She's seeing the surface," Sharon interrupted. "She's not seeing the underground movement and workings of the church."

I told Sharon it would be great for our film to get a glimpse of the church's "underground movement and workings," as she put it—and asked her to be on the lookout for stories that might do just that.

17

Ben and Pam

Hatred will consume you like a fire.

T HE FILM CREW AND I drove to the home of Ben's wife, Pam, whose marriage conflicts we hoped to portray. When I first told Pam by phone that we were interested in filming an interview with her, she was adamantly opposed. Then we met face-to-face at an away game of the Christian Academy's basketball team, where she had come to watch her two older sons play. We were filming the game, and afterward I introduced myself and she warmed up as we discussed the education her boys were getting at the academy. When I phoned her several days later, I was relieved when she agreed to the interview.

Pam was aware of the fervent prayers for her marriage being offered up by the congregation at the time, a community that included her aunt, sister, cousin and nieces, as well as her sons. Even her boss at the family bakery where she worked happened to hear from a friend that Ben went up to the altar at every service to pray for their marriage. "He cries for you!" Pam reported hearing. "He's got the whole parish praying for you!" Pam may also have heard from relatives about the prayer her eight-year-old son had offered during prayer-request time at one Sunday-evening service we filmed. "I pray for my mother," he said, standing up in front of a hushed congregation, his small voice breaking in sobs, "that she comes home."

As we pulled up in front of the three-story wood-frame walk-up where Pam lived with her boyfriend, Mitch, huge mounds of freshly plowed snow from a storm the day before were melting in the late-morning sun. We found a spot to unload the equipment, and Michael and I walked to the door. Pam greeted us and invited us in.

"I'll come in," I said, "while Michael gets the crew and equipment."

"What equipment?" Pam said suddenly with alarm.

"The camera, some lights, everything," I replied, somewhat puzzled.

"I didn't think you were bringing cameras," she said. "I'm not gonna do that. I thought we were just going to talk."

Had we really had a misunderstanding, or was Pam just having second thoughts? Michael and I looked at each other, wondering what to do. "Well, as long as we're here," I suggested, "and we have nothing else scheduled this morning, why don't we bring the equipment in and we can just talk. We'll set up, but if you don't want us to film anything, we won't."

Pam agreed. Michael went to organize the equipment, and I followed Pam into the living room, which, though hastily furnished with threadbare furniture, had a cozy feel. I met Mitch, a medium-set man of few words. He sat next to Pam on the living room couch and held her hand as we talked.

People enmeshed in painful, conflict-ridden situations often have a strong impulse to tell their stories, if for no other reason than to justify themselves, or simply for the comfort of a sympathetic ear. I knew parts of Pam's story from Ben and her aunt, Mary Shepperson. Before meeting Ben, she had had her first two sons with two different men, one of whom she had married. The other had spent some time in jail. "She was having a very bad time in her life," Mary Shepperson said in her understated way, "a very bad time."

As we began talking that morning, it soon became evident that if the story of Pam's conflicts with Ben and the church were to be told, she wanted her side represented, and she agreed to filming our conversation.

"When Frank and I talk," Pam said in anguish to the camera, "it's always how wonderful Ben is, how wrong I am . . . and that if God is in this relationship at all, he'll take care of it. I said, 'Frank, you don't listen. I don't want to move back in with Ben!'"

"That's it," she recalled Frank saying. "You've got the big *I* in your vocabulary." ("And he had to draw it on a napkin," Pam said, tongue in cheek.) "All you're thinking about is yourself. You're not thinking about the three children."

"I don't think that's true," Pam now declared, wincing in pain.

She also disputed Frank's belief that Ben had changed. "Does that mean he's not puttin' Mikey's head through the wall?" she snapped, speaking of an incident with her teenage son. "I would like him to try to put Mikey's head through the wall now," she said with a sneer, "because from what I've understood, Mikey's doing weights now and will put him into the ground. I'd love to see it—God help me, but I would!"

Whatever reservations Pam had about Ben's parenting, they had not kept her from letting her sons return with him from Florida. "If they wanted to go see their father," her boyfriend Mitch explained, sitting next to her on the couch, "we had no bones about it. I mean, I could've thrown him down the stairs, punched his face in," he added matter-of-factly, "which wouldn't have accomplished anything. They had their own free will . . . and you know, you can't hold kids and keep them unhappy." He shrugged his shoulders.

"It wasn't good," Pam admitted. "Maybe they were better off with Ben" she said, her face twisting in anguish. "It hurt, but they wanted to, so they went."

Pam put forth a number of grievances: not only the time Ben had blown up at Mikey, grabbing him by the throat and putting him up against the wall, but also his jealous rages against her. Once, Pam said, when she came home after going out for a beer with her sister, Ben walked into the house demanding to know where she had been. "I says, 'It's none of your damn business,'" Pam recalled, and they fell into an argument, "screaming and yelling."

"He shoved me so hard I fell back into the room on the tail of my spine, and they believe it was fractured."

Ben had told me that this was the time when he suspected Pam of having an affair with Mitch. "She was trying to push past me, and I pushed back," he said, "and she tripped backing up over the threshold of the door."

"He never hit me," Pam continued, recalling the one other "accident" with Ben she felt worth mentioning, "but he shook me so hard I had to wear a neck brace." Later, she proudly recalled once kicking Ben "ass over teakettle" across a room.

Mitch and Pam also criticized Pastor Valenti's handling of the situation. Mitch felt Frank was inconsistent in condemning his and Pam's "living in sin," as Mitch put it, while overlooking Pam and Ben having done the same thing for years before they married. "I don't see it in the Testament being that way," he said.

Both felt that Frank wrongly projected his own and others' experiences onto Pam's. But most of all, Pam was unhappy that Frank was not letting her come down to the church to pick up her sons if she continued to bring Mitch along. "I won't go down there without Mitch," she explained, "because I'm afraid of Ben; I wouldn't put anything past him." Having witnessed Ben's reaction to their presence in the church parking lot once, I could appreciate her fears. But his reaction also meant that Pam's coming to church with Mitch was not a prudent thing to do in the first place, and I could appreciate some of Pastor Valenti's reasons for stopping it. But, Pam said, "Ben took it a step further, and I'm not allowed to see the kids, period! I don't know whether that was on his own, or if Frank helped him."

I was not sure at the time either. Much later I learned from Frank, and had confirmed, that Mitch had been rough and unkind toward Pam's boys in Florida. That probably had much to do with Pam's decision to let the boys return to Worcester with Ben in the first place. The boys were afraid of Mitch, I learned, and that was one reason Frank did not want them to go with Pam when Mitch came along. At the same time, Frank admitted he was "preaching to Pam through her kids." Not letting the kids go with her when Mitch was around amounted to "a big flashing neon sign," he said, pushing his hand forward and backward and opening his fingers in the pulsing rhythm of a flashing neon sign, constantly telling Pam, "You're living in sin . . . You're living in sin . . . You're living in sin."

Despite their criticisms of Pastor Valenti, Pam and Mitch showed they accepted certain moral standards he applied to their situation. Mitch criticized Frank for not applying "the Testament's" stand against sex outside marriage consistently. For her part, Pam said her sons were being taught in the Christian Academy that "living in sin is bad— which, okay, it is," she said, flinching slightly. "I don't have any other choice," she went on to explain. "Even if I wanted to live alone—which I do not—I couldn't afford it. I already told Frank, and I've already told Ben," she said, her voice gaining strength, "if Mitch walked out the door today, I'm not saying that I wouldn't be sad, and I'm not saying that it wouldn't be hard, but I would rather *die* than go back to Ben!"

"What are your hopes for the future?" I asked.

"Like I told the lawyer," Pam said calmly, "I want the divorce and I want at least partial custody of the kids. I am ninety-five percent happy," she continued. "If I can get the kids back even part-time, I'd be happy a hundred percent. But I am ninety-five percent happy, probably—no, not probably, positively!—for the first time in this damn blessed life!"

We hoped that after this interview Pam would let us film her regular meeting with Pastor Valenti at a Friendly's restaurant four days later. Though she objected to Frank's involvement in her life—"I didn't tell them how to run their church," she said, "why are they trying to tell me how to run my life?"—she still felt obliged to continue meeting with him. Her children and relatives were still part of the church family Frank pastored.

PASTOR VALENTI IMAGINED this might be his last meeting with Pam unless he saw some sign of progress. He hoped Pam might eventually come back to Ben, a hope that sprang not only from his belief that God "hates divorce" and "honors love" but also from his diagnosis of Pam's situation and the changes he saw in Ben. Though he viewed Ben's behavior toward Pam in their marriage as "dictatorial and abrasive," he felt Pam's leaving him was "the best thing that ever happened to him." By totally humiliating and humbling him, Frank felt, Pam's departure had unleashed changes that had made Ben "ten times the man now that he was then."

"I don't make out Ben to be a perfect individual," he said, "but I don't know of anybody—though he has his days when he doesn't have peace—who's got a better handle on life, who's going through what he's going through. I mean, he's got three kids. One of them is a teenager, one's about to become a teenager and the other one is only seven years old. And he's a single man and he's working. I'm sorry, but there aren't many men who bring home the low-income salary that he brings home and can cope with three kids at the same time." I had to agree, having watched Ben come home after a hard day's work in a heat-treating plant, where the fumes from its chemical baths seared his throat and lungs all day long, and cheerfully go about caring for his three boys. "But he's in church, isn't he?" Frank added. "And he loves it, doesn't he? And he loves doin' what's right. And he's got a sense of security for the future." All this augured well, Frank thought, and in the end, he believed, love for his children would pull Ben through.

But Frank's hope also sprang from his assessment of Pam's situation. "She doesn't know it," he said, but "she's not repulsive toward Ben; she's repulsive toward men, *period*—any men. But at the same time, she finds her security in men. Underneath that facade," he reasoned, "there's a woman who's worried about her future—totally insecure. This guy," Frank said of her boyfriend, Mitch, "he drinks, he smokes, he's not working. He's mooching off her, they're living in sin. She did that with Ben. She did that with the guy before that, and the guy before that. When this guy crushes and crumbles," he concluded, "and Ben keeps his testimony, she'll come back."

Above all, Frank believed that regardless of the circumstances, God could make it happen. He worried only that by the time it did happen, Ben, like many other spouses he had seen, might have "hardened his heart" and not be willing to come back. "So I work on Ben all the time," he explained. "When he's not in prayer meeting in my office, I fuss with him. I say, 'Hey, you and I and Bruce Ginder are the only ones praying in this church. If you don't show up, God's not going to show up!'"

Friendly's Restaurant
January 29

The restaurant manager finally gave us permission to film Frank and Pam's meeting, provided it took place in a section of the restaurant closed for business that morning. Pam arrived soon after Frank.

"Is all this stuff going to bother you?" Frank asked, gesturing to the camera crew, as he and Pam slid into opposite sides of a booth.

"I'm getting used to them," Pam replied coolly. She was dressed in blue jeans and a velour shirt, Frank in a sport coat and tie.

"Are you? They're kinda ornery folks, you know," he said lightheartedly, winking at all of us around.

"They're not ornery to me," Pam said flatly, raising her chin.

"No, I was only teasin' . . . How're you doin'?"

"Pretty good," Pam replied, returning to their conversation as if we were not around.

From the booth next to theirs our sound recordist was extending a microphone over Frank and Pam on a boom pole as Michael moved back and forth to shoot each as he or she spoke or listened. Our production manager sat at the end of one of the neighboring booths to give the impression of other patrons being present in this otherwise empty section of the restaurant. Meanwhile, I sat across the room listening to the conversation and occasionally consulting with Michael in whispers as the clanging and clatter of dishes from the kitchen echoed in the background.

After small talk about Pam's job, she and Frank ordered coffee and juice, and Frank opened their meeting with prayer. Frank told Pam that the reason he kept calling her, wanting to get her marriage with Ben, "if at all possible, back on the right track," was not for Ben, for her or even for the children, but because he really believed "*God* wants it."

"You once accepted Christ," he reminded Pam. "God is not going to let you alone." Since she was living in adultery, he said, "every bit of strength that you've got is going to be zapped and tapped by the Lord. God could really make your life miserable," he warned. "Now, I'm not saying that it hasn't been, but, Pam, all the things that have happened in the past have left emotional scars. But the one thing that you have to understand is that keeping on going in that same pattern is not going to work."

"It's *not* the same pattern," Pam interjected. "How do you see it as the same pattern?"

Frank explained that though he had heard it only secondhand, "Mitch's wife has many of the same complaints about Mitch as you do about Ben." He reminded her that at an earlier meeting, when he had asked Mitch whether he could guarantee he would "never beat Pam" or "never pick on the kids again," Mitch had answered that he could not. "Pam, if you fail three times, what makes you think you're going to succeed the fourth?"

Pam looked sullen and said nothing. "Let me show you something," Frank said, opening up his Bible to II Corinthians, chapter 5. "I hope this will help you understand. It says, 'Therefore, if any man be in Christ, he is a new creature'—and that word *creature* there is a created thing—'All things will pass away or are being passed away and behold, all things are becoming as new.'

"Mitch is not saved," he continued. "Mitch does not know Christ as his personal savior. The chances of him changing, Pam, from what he was with his wife to something you would like him to become—it's not going to happen." After the "excitement" and "relief" of "getting away" is gone, he said, "you're going to settle down into a normal routine of life, and Mitch is going to get just as bored with you as he did with his wife. And you're gonna get just as bored with him as you did with Ben."

Pam stared at Frank impassively, slowly chewing her gum, as he described how his own marriage to Sharon had been saved by their "getting closer to the Lord." Ben has "come a long way since the last time you guys were together," he assured her, from not being much of a parent to being "better than most." He warned that in choosing Mitch, she would just be "marrying more problems. . . . Stop, put the brakes on," he said emphatically. "You've got something with Ben!"

"I don't have anything with Ben!" Pam suddenly erupted, leaning forward and shaking her head.

"What I'm telling you, Pam," Frank replied with conviction, "is that Ben has changed. You've got something to work with." He paused as Pam resumed chewing her gum. "You do yourself a favor, okay? Call Mitch's wife."

"I've talked to Mitch's wife," Pam said, swallowing her words slightly.

"About him?"

"No, not about him," she replied with less conviction.

"Don't you think it's time to?"

"No."

"You mean you want to go into this relationship blind? You don't want to know what you've got?" Pam shook her head.

"You don't know what you've got?" Frank asked incredulously.

"I *know* what I've got," Pam retorted, leaning forward to take the offensive. "I've got a warm human being that cares about me, that would love to have the kids back with us. . . ."

"Lemme ask you a question. Does he drink?"

"Yes," Pam replied with weakening conviction.

"You don't have a warm, loving human being," Frank said, "because if he drinks, it's only a matter of time before a chemical brain will beat you up." Pam drew a deep breath of impatience and fixed her gaze at some point on the table. She rocked slightly back and forth as if marking the time she had to listen. "If he drinks," Frank continued, "it's just a matter of time before that chemical brain will beat up Mikey, if Mikey comes back . . ."

"Well, Ben didn't drink and he put Mikey's head through the wall a few times," Pam countered, "but that's okay?"

"No, I didn't say that was okay. Who says that's okay? Did I condone that?"

"No," Pam replied curtly.

"What I'm trying to tell you is, Ben's changing and Ben's different."

"Oh, Ben doesn't grab him by the throat anymore?"

"No, not to my knowledge," Frank replied with some exasperation. "I've seen Ben deal with Mikey. He's not perfect by any stretch of the imagination. But Pam, Ben is different.

"But Ben is not the issue," Frank continued, taking another tack. "Do you understand? What I'm asking you today, first of all, is to consider your future. What I'd like you to do is break up with Mitch and get back into a Bible-believing, fundamental church. There's one right here. You don't even have to come to our church. Get back into fellowship with the Lord. Let him do for you things you cannot do for yourself, and then just keep making it a matter of prayer."

Frank opened his Bible again, this time to chapter 13 of I Corinthians, and read the famous passage on love in which God promises, as Frank pointed out, that "love never fails."

"You're not in a love relationship with Mitch," he remonstrated. "A physical relationship, a companion-type relationship, that is not love. Anything out of wedlock is not love.

"If Mitch loved you," Frank reasoned, "he wouldn't compromise you. He wouldn't dirty your reputation. He'd say, 'Hey, let's do this right.' Do you really think what he's doing *wrong* is going to end up *right*? Do you really think God blesses *that kind* of relationship? What else can I do to *convince* you, Pam? Can't you use your head? Think clear. If the man's compromising you, does he love you, or is he taking advantage of you?"

Their conversation circled back on itself, touching on the same points again and again, and then turned suddenly to a deeper level of Pam's experience. Frank was speaking about the great qualities he had seen in Pam when she had taught in their school and then observed, "With all you've gone through in your life, you haven't committed suicide yet. I don't know if you've attempted it or not," he added, dropping his eyes.

"I came close a few times," Pam replied flatly.

Without inquiring into the circumstances, which I now realized he already knew, Frank leaned forward to follow up on this point: "That's the thing that I'm going to tell you, Pam!" he pleaded. "Those things are *not* going to go away!"

"But they have," she said, raising her chin.

"But they're going to come back."

"I don't think so," Pam said with less confidence.

"Think about it."

"I have."

"What if the same things occur with Mitch as they have with Ben?"

"Then I go by myself," Pam said with resignation, raising her eyebrows and reaching over to the ashtray to flick an ash from her cigarette.

After saying this was the last time he would meet with her, Frank finished his juice and left. Pam lit another cigarette. Her body shuddered. "What makes me maddest," she told us to camera, "is that the things he says, he doesn't *know!* He just believes he knows because of the Bible. I could leave Mitch at any time," she offered. "I could leave him today—and I won't . . . All my life I've been through—like he said—three different guys, which is fine. They all left me, *fine!*" she said bitterly. "You don't want me? *Fine!* . . . I want to get rid of a *jerk*, and I got to stay with him for the kids. It just doesn't seem right."

"What do you think you're going to do next?" I asked.

"I'm going to go see my lawyer," she said softly, getting up to leave. "See you guys later."

On her way out, Pam and Frank passed each other at the front door of the restaurant, and Frank took this opportunity to say one more thing. "Don't hate Ben," he advised gently. "Hate will eat you up. Ben is no less a victim of his childhood than you are." And with that, Pam walked out into the bitter January cold. Only much later did I learn some of what Pastor Valenti was reminding Pam of here about Ben's childhood: that his stepfather had routinely beat him and his mother and threatened to kill them all if she left.

Shawmut River Baptist Church
January 29, 3:00 p.m.

"The evil men do lives after them," one teenage boy read aloud from *Macbeth* in Dave Keener's senior-high English class. We were filming the class while we waited for Ben to arrive at church. He would come directly from work to do his usual cleaning chores and, knowing the pastor had met with Pam that morning, would go straight to Frank's office to find out what had happened. We had lit the office and were waiting for Ben's arrival.

"It's going to be tough telling him," Frank had said with a sigh that morning right after his meeting with Pam. "She made his life miserable; he made hers miserable. Now they're both suffering the consequences. He's done his best to make it work. It isn't that his love for her failed; she's just refusing it. Love hasn't failed. It will pull him up, pull him out.

"She's got all of these arguments inside of why she hates Ben and why she can't do this and why she can't do that. She was very quick to point out how Ben grabbed Mikey by the throat, but the thing she neglected to say, that I didn't bring up, was that Mitch did the same thing when they were in Florida.

"There's always the possibility," Frank had gone on to theorize, "that once we let go, we just make it a matter of prayer and stop talking about it, that the Lord will have something to do in her life. It'll keep cropping up. God will use it. It'll be a horrible life. She'll not be happy. You can do a sequel to this thing in five years," he wagered, "and she'll be right in the same place."

When Ben arrived that afternoon, we said hello and followed him upstairs to the foyer outside Frank's office, where Frank greeted him—someone was in his office—and the two fell into conversation. But we had lit the office, not the foyer! Fortunately, the winter afternoon light fell gently on Ben and Frank from a window they stood near as Frank began to explain what had happened that morning.

"Basically she hates you very, very much," Frank said shaking his head. "It's a defense mechanism she's built up because she just wants to get out of that life."

"Get out of what life?" Ben asked through the rhythmic chewing of his gum.

"Whatever life she had with you at the time when she left. She just wants to leave that whole mess behind." Ben's hands were on his hips, and he shifted his weight tensely from one foot to the other as he listened. A glazed look came over his eyes as the truth sank in. "So my recommendation is just push on with your life," Frank concluded.

"What did you tell her?" Ben asked, bristling with anger.

"The advice I gave her was (A) break up with Mitch, and (B) go to a Bible-preaching church, so you can think clearly."

"Yeah, she really bought that, didn't she?" Ben sneered.

"No, not at all," Frank said gently but firmly, "but that's the advice I gave her. The thing of it is, Ben, not to get bitter or angry; there's nothing you can do about it. Just go on with your life."

"Frank, I'm going to tell you something, okay?" Ben said, pointing his finger at Frank for emphasis. "I'm angrier now than I've ever been! Okay? You know why I'm angry? I'm angry now, okay, not only because of me, okay, but there's three kids downstairs that need their mother, okay, and nothing's been done about it. Absolutely nothing!"

"There isn't anything we can do about it," Frank replied matter-of-factly. "You can only talk and just pray that she does something. Let's just give the Lord an opportunity to finish whatever work she's started in her heart."

"Frank, she hasn't done anything in her heart!" Ben exploded. "You can see that!"

"Well, let me say this. God had to harden Pharaoh's heart before he could get Pharaoh to let his people go. Let's just wait and see what happens. She hasn't learned her lesson; she isn't going to learn her lesson. I made it pretty clear it was just one stupid move after another."

"Well, I'll tell you one thing, okay? I've just about had it with her stupid moves!" Ben said spitefully. "She's left me in the same boat, Frank! And she's having a gay old time laughing about it, and she's left me right in the same boat! I've got to be alone. I've got to raise the kids alone. I've got to work like a dog, okay, to raise the kids. Hey," he said, throwing his hands up in disgust, "to her it's a piece of cake! She don't care!"

"So take the responsibility that God's given you," Frank said calmly, "and take the help that he gives you to do it."

"Fine, I'm going to do that, but I'd like to have maybe a little help somewhere along the line, and I've got a wife thirty miles away that's not giving me any help."

"And you're not going to get any help."

"Well, something's got to be done," Ben said angrily.

"All right, think about it and pray about it and give me a suggestion and I'll let you know if it's possible or feasible to get any kind of support to help you with the kids . . ."

"Oh no," Ben interrupted in disgust. "I don't even want nothin' from her. I don't want her even breathin' in this direction!"

"I wish you could've said that with a little less hate in your face," Frank said, casting his eyes down. "My personal feeling is, at this stage, I'm glad God hasn't brought Pam back to you, because with that kind of reaction to hatred God did not conquer the world. You know what I'm saying? And that's just an area that you're going to have to work on. Because Christ mastered the world by . . . when they spit in his face, he blessed them.

"If you think the devil's going to loosen up his hold without some kind of fight, you're crazy. We've done what we can do. We've done *everything* we can do. . . . So now, let's just not get aggravated, let's not get cutesy pie, don't get angry. It isn't going to do you a bit of good to get angry. All it's going to do is cause your blood pressure to go up."

"How long?" Ben asked in hollow agony. "How long?"

"You don't have to wait any longer, as far as I'm concerned."

"I don't have to wait any longer for what?" Ben asked, now wondering what Frank had learned today of Pam's plans.

"Just wait until she gets a divorce," Frank continued.

"Wait?" Ben interrupted, shocked by what he had just heard.

"No, she'll get one," Frank said, rubbing his thumb across his lip and casting a worried look at Ben. "I think she's already got a lawyer. Just let her go ahead and get the divorce, contest the divorce. Then, when she does leave, the Bible says you're not in bondage in any way."

Realizing now that Pam was divorcing him, Ben exploded. "Let me tell you one thing, Frank, okay? She's going to pay for this, okay, by my hands or somebody else's. The four of us haven't suffered like we've suffered for nothing, okay?"

"Well, Ben, I don't see as you've been suffering, other than emotional strain and drain."

"Well, I'll tell you something," Ben said, jabbing his finger into the air again. "I'd rather have somebody punch me in the mouth every day than wake up every morning feelin' the way I do!"

"I agree," Frank readily conceded. "I would, too."

"And I'm sure the kids would rather have that, too . . . I'd rather have somebody beat on me all day with a whip, 'cause *that* I can get over." Ben looked out the window. He wiped tears away from under his glasses. Meanwhile, Ben's teenage son, Mikey, had come to the foyer doorway wearing his basketball uniform.

Frank glanced his way and asked, "What's up, Mike?"

"I was just lookin' for Dad," Mikey said.

"He'll be down in a minute," Frank said. Mikey headed back down to the basketball game now getting under way in the gymnatorium.

Frank turned back to Ben and urged him to calm down and make up his mind that "it's completely and totally in the Lord's hands. There isn't anything we can do about it. If she goes for a divorce, God is not going to bless her. God will definitely bless you if you get your attitude and keep your attitude in the right position. He's already blessed you . . ."

"I know that," Ben said, nodding his head in affirmation.

"Just let her get the divorce, get married to Mitch . . . and if that's the way God wants it, then let's not worry about it. Let's let *him* do it."

"I'll tell you something, okay?" Ben said bitterly. "I would stake my life on it, that that's *not* the way God wants it . . . okay?"

"Well," Frank interjected, "put the word down there like this, then: 'the way God will permit it.'"

" 'Til the day I die, okay, I will *never* allow her to see the kids if she marries him, *never!*"

"Well, there you don't have that privilege."

"Yes, I do. I most certainly do! I'll tell you what. When she's supposed to come down, I'll take the kids out! I'll force them to go out!"

"Well, now you're talkin' like an idiot again," Frank said soberly.

"Frank, I just can't handle this thing anymore," Ben said shaking his head, looking out the window and fighting back tears. "I just can't handle this anymore."

"All right," Frank offered, joining him in a long look out the window. "What's Philippians 4:13 say? . . . 'I can do *all* things through Christ.' So it's not a question of whether you *can* or not. Yes, you *can*. It's a question of whether you *will* or not. So don't say, 'I *can't* handle this anymore,' say, 'I *won't* handle it.' So at least you're thinkin' square.

"Remember this one thing," Frank said in closing. "If she does hate you, hating her is not going to help matters at all. I'll tell you," he said, shaking his head woefully, "hatred will consume you like a fire. It will make you miserable with yourself and your kids. It'll destroy you. You know, love never fails; hatred always falls short. Right now it's just a mental adjustment you're going to have to make, you know? It really is. Come over to the house for supper tonight after the game, all right?"

"All right."

"God bless you, brother. Hang in there. Don't let it eat you up. Go down there and cheer for me, will you?"

THE CHEERS from the basketball game rang in the background as we sat with Ben downstairs in the pews of the old sanctuary. "I've been waiting for God to do something to straighten this matter out," Ben explained to camera with clear resolve. "I think he has, but he hasn't straightened it out the way *I* think it should be straightened out. See, and what *I* think matters to me, because I've got to live with me, see?" He pointed his finger at his chest, cocked his head quizzically and continued. "I've got to go to bed with me every night. I've got to wake up with me every morning." He gave his head a weary, knowing nod. "I've even got to think about Pam with me."

"So what are you going to do now about that?" I asked.

"I'm gonna fight very hard against me. Because one Ben is going to want to take a gun and shoot her. And the other Ben's going to say, 'No, it ain't right. . . .' I know that Ben will win out," he added, "but see, that's the thing, just having that other one in there causes me pain and frustration. And something that causes me pain and frustration, it's definitely going to affect my kids, right? And when my kids look at me," he said in anguish, "they look at my face and they know why I'm frustrated, they know why I'm angry, they know why I act the way I do. And I can see it reflect back at me. It's like a mirror looking at a mirror when I look at them, see? And I don't even know why it's happening. I don't even understand it, Jim. I don't even understand it.

"When I get to heaven," Ben continued, "I will look at God and I will say, 'God, you tell me what good it did!'" He jabbed into the air again to punctuate his phrases. "I think I have a *right* to know what good it did. I have a *right* to know what good it did in my life, I have a *right* to know what good it did in the boys' lives, and I have a *right* to know what good it did in her life. I have a *right* to know, and I want to know."

18

The Wisdom to Manage

Allow the Holy Spirit to work in your life now!

Tₕₑᵣₑ ᵥₐₛ ₛₒₘₑₜₕᵢₙg sad and reassuring about the way the old-home crowd sang out one of its favorite hymns to open this evening's worship in the close quarters of the old sanctuary in the bakery building.

> *Mercy there was great and grace was free,*
> *Pardon there was multiplied to me,*
> *There my burdened soul found liberty,*
>   *At Cal-va-ry!*

It was three weeks after Pastor Valenti's meetings with Pam and Ben, and the film crew had returned for what would be our next-to-last shoot. These stints, ranging from three to ten days, had become progressively longer and more intense, now that we had focused on what stories we were following. In these last two shoots we filmed interviews with principal characters to get their accounts of events already filmed or stories we were following, as well as their reflections on major themes we wanted to address.

At the close of the opening hymn, Frank asked, "Are there any testimonies or prayer requests?" Ben raised his hand and came forward. Just before the service Dan Keener had told Ben that he and his new wife, Judy, had decided to give Judy's old car to Mikey, Ben's teenage son. When they told Mikey this, he had gone off beaming.

"This church may not have much money," Ben said from the podium, "and we may not have the most beautiful church, but the love that this church shows, it's just . . . it's gotta be godly. My son Mikey told me that he never realized how much he was loved," Ben said haltingly, fighting back tears, "and it's because of the people in the church . . . It's because of the brotherly love that we found through Jesus Christ. And I just want to thank God for it all."

"*Amen!*" rose up from the flock.

"Anybody else got a testimony they'd like to give?" Frank asked, surveying the crowd.

From his customary seat in the front row, Phil Strong raised his hand and reminded Frank that they were supposed to discuss "finances and things like that." He meant issues that had come up several days before at the men's Saturday-morning prayer breakfast. Frank himself had not been present that morning. He had been home with a severe earache, an occasional affliction stemming from his war wounds. But his father-in-law, Tom Morse, had been there, in addition to Doug Laverne, Scott Sanderson and Phil Strong. When the men had gotten down on their knees to pray in Frank's study, Phil had prayed that God give him "the wisdom that's necessary to be a manager of a house of yours" and the ability to "discern the spirits and understand the motivations of people" and to allocate church responsibilities to those "mature enough to handle them."

This was the first time I had heard public prayer for what Frank and Sharon both acknowledged privately to be Frank's weakest suit: the ability—or wisdom, as Phil put it—to manage. The church's financial situation was getting worse, and fresh grievances over Pastor Valenti's nursery project had surfaced at that very meeting. Doug Laverne and others reported having heard rumblings of discontent: If the pastor could launch this or that new project on his own whim, there was no limit to the financial burdens he might impose.

Phil had suggested raising the nursery issue for discussion with the entire congregation after Sunday worship the very next day and trying, as he put it, to turn a "mistake" into an "asset" by "marketing the nursery as a day-care center."

"This *has* to happen," Tom Morse had agreed, but he defended Frank's decision to build the nursery in the first place.

On the next day, however, at Sunday worship, Frank nixed the idea of discussing the nursery question. "There are too many visitors on Sunday," he explained. (Later he told me legal issues regarding town occupancy permits made him wary of an open discussion of the nursery project.) "We'll do it on Wednesday," he offered. But now, at Wednesday-evening worship, when Phil reminded him of that plan, Frank reneged. "There's no need to belabor that thing, Phil," he insisted. "As of right now," he explained to the congregation, "we're about nine thousand dollars in debt, and you know, folks, the people in the church are just goin' to have to dig into their pockets. I don't know where else the money is going to come from. You know, God is not going to drop it out of heaven. It's up to his people."

Phil began to say something, but Frank interrupted. "I don't want any of that other stuff coming out," he said firmly. "It's irrelevant, as far as I'm concerned. Well, let me just put it mildly," Frank continued. "Some folks seem to think that the great giving in the church dropped off when people thought I took on another project with the nursery, you know."

"I don't think it was intentional," Phil interjected, "but back in people's minds . . ."

"Whatever it was," Frank said dismissively, "the nursery is done and it's in beautiful shape."

"Amen," a small chorus affirmed from parts of the sanctuary.

"If we're going to grow, we're going to have to have the nursery," Frank declared, "and I think the important thing is that folks need to smarten up."

In the midst of tensions over finances and the nursery project, Frank floated another proposal not designed to allay misgivings. The church's buildings were situated on fifty acres of land. Frank now proposed using church resources, particularly the skilled labor of its many builders, to construct several houses on that land. These would be for staff, including his own family. And since his father-in-law was on the verge of retiring, Frank suggested privately that Tom Morse might find some service in the church and that he and Ada might eventually live in one of those homes.

The following week Frank called a finance meeting at the home of another church member. Those invited were men who because of seniority, faithfulness or financial acumen were felt to hold church finances in trust. I was not present, but when the film crew returned the following Saturday to begin our final week of shooting, the fallout was still hot.

Men's Prayer Breakfast
March 2

As men gathered over coffee and donuts for their weekly prayer breakfast in Pastor Valenti's study, Phil remarked that he had been pleased to see "no patronization" at the finance meeting—that is, no subservience to the pastor.

"I was *not* pleased to see there was no patronization," Frank snapped. "It's good to get problems out," he admitted, "but the way they came out was the most unspiritual thing I've ever seen in my life!"

"If you don't find out what is on their minds," Phil remonstrated, "when you do find out, it's going to be too late."

"I said," Frank jumped in, "and I quote, 'I was glad to see it come out'—in a sense, but the way it came out was *so unspiritual* that it was most appalling to me."

Despite Frank's and Phil's different attitudes toward what had transpired at the finance meeting, all agreed on certain things. One member had raised the question of what would happen with church property if the congregation dissolved, and this touched off a larger discussion. In addition, some troublesome facts about the church's financial situation had surfaced, including some long-overdue oil bills.

"Those things are all reasons why I want to involve a lot more men in the finances," Frank explained to the others. "I've tried to bring the men in on three different occasions in the past year and a half, and the men, until now, haven't wanted to get involved. And one of the beauties of the meeting is that, heretofore, I've been criticized for having the church running in the red from time to time—all right? It's going to be interesting to see how the men of the church take a seventeen-hundred-dollar-a-week budget and run it on twelve hundred dollars. Then I'm gonna stand back and say, 'Hey, fellas, you're not doing so good!'" He rocked back in his chair and chuckled. "Then I'll take the finances back."

"Let me say this," Phil pressed. "I don't think that is going to be the case, and I'll tell you why . . ."

"Because the offering is gonna come back up to seventeen hundred dollars," Frank answered knowingly, in telling recognition of offering-plate democracy.

Phil's eyes twinkled. "You knew that, huh?"

"Absolutely," Frank replied.

Tom Morse then turned to his son-in-law. "I hope, Pastor, that your placing the responsibility for finances on the men is not to teach us a lesson that we can't learn any better than you can, but rather to free you up."

As discussion continued, Frank proposed that a "covenant" be written up for church membership. It would clearly state what would happen if the church dissolved. After all bills were paid, Frank proposed putting into writing, "all the money goes to another church of like faith."

"I never understood that," Doug Laverne admitted. "I always wondered about that, even when I first became a member. After a while, I didn't care . . . But lots of times my father would say, 'You tell me what happens if that church breaks up! *You* tell me where the money is going to go!'"

"Good!" Phil exclaimed. "Now you can tell him."

"I don't think you have a lot of faith," Frank then said disapprovingly to Doug.

Phil looked intently and kindly at Frank. "You didn't really care for that aspect, did you?" Phil observed. "There is one thing I *do* want to say, okay? I'm praying for you, that you don't take it personally."

"Oh, I have," Frank insisted, shaking his head woefully.

"I *know* you have!" Phil implored. "Don't take it in the flesh. Get outta the *flesh* and get in the *spirit!*"

"Taking it *personally*," Frank objected, "does not necessarily mean I'm taking it in the flesh. Very few people have recognized that a man does not work for six years for nothing, put in five to eight thousand dollars of his own cash, bleed his family dry, build and take and push and work . . . Show me something I haven't worked on in this building!"

"Who are you looking to recognize?" Phil asked with a glint in his eye.

"No, no, no, no!" Frank objected. "Hang on! I'm not lookin' for recognition at all. What I'm simply saying is, for anybody to imagine that a man would pour that kind of effort into an organization and then look forward to it collapsing so that he can collect two hundred thousand dollars is nuts. He's nuts!"

The discussion continued. Frank insisted that he was not looking for credit and had not taken the questions Doug Laverne and others had raised as an insult. Rather, he said, "the Bible talks about a wounded spirit, and I've got one."

"Well, let me say something," Phil said pointedly. "Because people turn around and do not appreciate it, do you turn around and stop doing it?"

"No," Frank replied. "I said I was hurt."

"But I listen to you, and I see bitterness coming out . . ."

"No, you saw a wounded spirit."

"And what I've seen come out," Phil continued, "your saying, 'From now on these people will not blankety-blank, blank, blank, blank, blank . . . from this man.'"

"Don't make it sound like I'm swearin', Phil," Frank said wryly, gesturing to the camera crew, who were filming all this, and recognizing that their discussion might show up on national television. Everybody laughed.

Frank did not show the same defensiveness or anger during the interview we shot with him at his home two days later. Conflicts in the congregation and his sense of betrayal were still present. That week he had learned that some teachers had met privately at someone's home to discuss the church crisis, instead of attending the revival service being held that night at church (and every night that week). But at home in his favorite armchair, he found equanimity in assessing the situation when I asked him what lessons he had learned from his first experience pastoring a church.

"If I've failed anywhere in the ministry," he replied, "it's been no communication. You know, I don't paint enough word pictures of what's inside me for people who are working under me. Therefore, it's a guessing game, and they have to guess whether I'm pleased or not, and that's wrong.

"Now," he continued, "why haven't I communicated to these people before that if the church comes to a demise, the thing is sold, the bills are paid and the balance is designated to go to another church of like faith? I just found out at the last business meeting that eight or nine guys were just curious, and have been for two or three years. It just so happens one of them was bold enough to ask. And I said to myself, 'Lord, why? Why don't they trust me?'

"Communication," he said in answer to his own question. "You know why my wife trusts me? Because I communicate with her. If people in the church don't trust me, it's because I fail to communicate. I'm a great communicator from the pulpit . . . maybe—some people say I am—some say, you know, mezza-mezza." He shrugged his shoulders. "But I have to learn how to communicate the total ministry to the people in the pew, so that when I make a decision, they trust me. If that's my failure—and it is—it's a bad one. I've got to clean it up. And when I get that thing squared away, we're going to fly!"

As our shooting drew to a close, developments suddenly took place in another story we hoped to follow: Phil and Jean Strong's efforts to see Phil's older brother Sam get saved. Sam proved to be a beguiling character. A ruggedly handsome man, six foot five and two hundred fifty pounds, Sam was a jack-of-all-trades who was working at the time as a cook in a school cafeteria. He had apparently seen a lot of trouble in life. He told me that his first wife had been an alcoholic and after they divorced she had made it difficult for him to see their three sons. He had remarried, to a teacher nine years his junior, and with her encouragement had eventually won custody of his sons. Together they had had another boy, now eleven. But it was problems coming to a head in this, Sam's second marriage, that Phil and Jean felt were finally "softening his heart toward the Lord."

Sam's wife, Brenda, attributed the problems in their marriage to Sam's drinking, but Sam saw it differently. He said that she always felt he "didn't make enough money to support the household," and that they argued all the time, if not about money, then about something else. "And for thirteen years," he said, "I can remember getting out of work on a Sunday afternoon and not wanting to come home, because I knew I was coming home to just some more fighting. So I'd stop at my brother-in-law's, have a few beers and then finally come home, usually feeling pretty good. Then it became a habit."

Sam said Brenda had become "uninterested" in their marriage and that he had become increasingly jealous and had begun checking up on her. "Things got so bad," he said, "she wanted me to see a psychiatrist." One evening, while looking for her after a road race she had run, he had found her in a restaurant with fellow runners: a couple and another man. That night he had taken an overdose of the antidepressants his psychiatrist had prescribed, along with a good deal of alcohol. "I guess they pumped me out," Sam said with a laugh. "But I never cared whether I lived from day to day. It didn't make any difference whether I lived or died."

Phil and Jean saw these events as the Holy Spirit's work, drawing Sam "through a knothole backwards," as Phil put it. Though Sam once told them he would never come to Shawmut River, he had recently started attending and felt that had started a mysterious process of change in his life. "I found there was a change in my house," he said in wonderment. "I had to go back. And the next week things changed more. *I* changed more! And I don't think we've had five weeks of getting along this well since we got married. And now it's really changing, and it makes you believe *more*."

Reflecting on the inner dynamics of these changes, Sam noticed himself thinking about God on the way to work. "I drive to work thinking, 'Well, God, am I going to make it today? Am I going to be good today? Am I going to behave today?' And it's funny, it's strange, to go through every day now trying to please *him!*" In this heady climate, Sam found himself occasionally moved to tears during worship at Shawmut River and once, during the invitation, felt "pins and needles" going through him and thought, "Maybe Christ will appear!"

Wanting to take advantage of this ripe moment in his brother's life, Phil decided to visit Sam at home one Tuesday evening. Tuesday evenings were set aside in the church's weekly calendar for "visitation." Usually this meant going out to evangelize the unsaved, but it was also done to woo a prospective member or discuss a problem with an existing one.

Phil decided to bring his nephew Tommy along, since it was Tommy's testimony about the miraculous turnaround in his own marriage that had first prompted Sam to look into what being "born again" was all about. Now, after praying together at Phil's house as dark settled on the Worcester plateau, Phil and Tommy set out for Sam's home, an eighteenth-century saltbox nestled into a hillside fifteen minutes away.

Meanwhile, the film crew and I were at Sam's home setting up lights. After expressing some misgivings, Sam agreed to our filming their meeting. As we chatted further with him and with his wife,

Brenda, and their eleven-year-old son, they all seemed comfortable with the idea.

When Phil and Tommy arrived, Sam pulled chairs into a circle in a sitting area separated from their kitchen by a wood stove. The film crew stepped back into the shadows to begin filming the event. Brenda, who seemed interested in the whole process, decided to join in, and early on Phil raised a question to draw her into the conversation.

"How do I judge whether I'm right or you're right?" Phil asked, "because my right and wrong might be entirely different than your right and wrong, okay? So it's not common sense anymore, is it?" he pointed out, in recognition of the nature of a pluralist society. As Christians, he said, we look to "a common denominator," God's word in the Bible, to "find out what God wants us to do." The sleeves of his tan polyester shirt were rolled up, and he held a thick Bible in one of his callused hands, an index finger stuck inside to hold his place. He opened to James 1:13–15 and read:

> Let no man say when he is tempted, I am tempted of God, for God cannot be tempted with evil, neither tempteth He any man.

"In other words," Phil interjected, "God doesn't go around tempting you with evil. He doesn't have some slinky-looking lady with no clothes on come walk in before you." He continued reading:

> But every man is tempted, when he is drawn away of his own lust, and enticed. Then, when lust hath conceived, it bringeth forth sin.

If a man looks twice at this "scantily clothed" woman, Phil explained, and then goes up to talk with her, he begins sinning.

"But Phil," Brenda said in consternation, "you say 'scantily clothed.' Now, my whole lifestyle is in running shorts. You can't be more scantily clothed than that. So if I'm enticing people, that means I'm sinning?"

"If you find out that it *does* cause men to lust after you," Phil replied, "even married men, do you think you should be dressed that way?"

"By me running in clothes that are comfortable to run in?" Brenda asked, shaking her head in disbelief. "I mean, how would I ever know? I'm so *into* what I'm doing."

"I don't really know the answer," Phil said. "All I know is what God's word says: If you find yourself in a situation that you are tempting somebody, then you're supposed to know enough to stop, even though it becomes an uncomfortable thing to you . . . This is where thinking about others instead of yourself comes in. This is what God's all about!"

In this indirect way Phil touched upon the jealousy aroused in Sam by Brenda's relationships with fellow runners. However indirect, the reference was not lost on those present or on Jean Strong, who heard about the conversation later. "Her outlook," Jean said of Brenda, "is as long as I'm not doing what's wrong, what do I care how you take it? So if I go and sit down and start talking to some strange guy, even though I run with him, how does my husband take it? You know, that was causing a problem."

Phil and Jean saw Brenda's attitude as a prime example of the humanism undermining moral order in American society. "What pleases *me* is important," Jean explained, "regardless of what it does to *you*." They likened it to Sam's drinking.

"Drinking affects him, not anybody else," Phil observed. "That's his attitude. This is the biggest thing, I think, in society today. People don't realize that they can't be selfish, but they gotta think about others in every action they do. That's what God expects us to do." Such thinking had informed Phil and Jean's efforts to tackle problems in their own marriage years before.

Now this Tuesday evening at Sam and Brenda's, conversation turned to how people could be freed from the bondage of sin. Phil recounted what Jesus said to the Pharisee Nicodemus when he asked Jesus what it meant to be "born again."

"The physical things of the flesh are born of flesh," Phil said, paraphrasing Jesus' reply in John 3:5–6. "The things of the spirit have to be born of the spirit."

"Adam and Eve were brought into this world," Phil elaborated, "with a body, a soul and a spirit." But when they ate of the fruit, "the spirit, or the communication with God, was severed, because they disobeyed God," and since the Fall, "every child is born with a body and soul, and they're already on their way to hell."

This touched off a lengthy discussion about how old a child had to be to sin knowingly, until Sam, impatient with such theorizing, blurted out, "Is it a sudden thing? All of a sudden I'm born again?"

"No," Phil answered gently, as Sam, sitting upright against the back of his chair, eyed his brother carefully. "It comes about with a prayer," Phil explained. "It comes about with a humbling attitude toward God, when we don't rebel against God, but we realize that God is a holy God, and that God loved us enough to turn around and have Christ, who has no sin, come in and put himself up as substitute for our sins, to take in the death of the cross and the humiliation of having his clothes ripped off him. And having him whipped until you couldn't even tell that he was flesh or if he was a carcass of an animal!

"When you realize that Christ was willing to do that for you," Phil continued, "and that God gave you a way out, that you don't have to face God at the white throne of judgment and have God say: 'Samuel Strong, you did a lot of good things in your life, but you continued to go and break my will. Why? If I'm a holy and righteous God, I can't allow that to happen. But I provided a way through my son, that if you would have accepted it, I could let you go, because I won't punish you twice. The punishment was made once by Christ, and so you're free, you're saved, you're born again of the spirit of my son, Jesus Christ.'"

"I feel like you're preaching to me," Sam complained, stretching out his arms in frustration, "rather than telling me your feelings and how you became born again. . . . If you're born again, can you still sin?"

"Yes," Phil answered, "but if you turn around and commit sin, then you're crucifying Christ afresh."

As an example, their nephew Tommy confessed that the other night at the checkout counter in the supermarket he had noticed that the cashier had undercharged him thirty-three cents. "I really couldn't care less about the thirty-three cents," Tommy said, "but the point is, I had a chance to say something and I kept my mouth shut."

"You knew it was wrong?" his uncle Sam asked. "It went through your mind that 'I'm doing the wrong thing; I'm actually stealing!'"

"That's right," Tommy acknowledged. "I stole thirty-three cents from Big D, and I made a mistake."

"Thirty-three miserable cents, and you could slap God in the face?" Sam asked his nephew in wonderment. "For thirty-three cents? And this is the guy that you've been born again with?"

"Are you judging him?" Phil asked.

"No!" Sam said, pulling back and pressing his big hands on his chest. "I'm trying to find out what born again is! See, my life isn't great. I don't feel my life is great, see? And I really would like to know how to make my life great . . . I feel your life is pretty great," he said looking at his brother and leaning forward to reenact a conversation between them:

"I've said, you know, 'Gee, Phil, how're things going?'

"Great!'

"Why, Phil?'

"The man upstairs.'" Sam pointed his index finger upward.

"Amen," Phil affirmed.

"And I say to myself, 'Boy, what am I doing wrong?'"

"All you have to do, Sam," Tommy interjected, "and it'll change your life for good and you'll never regret it—you have to say, 'God, I humble myself before you. The good works that I do for you are nothing. The only thing that's going to get me to heaven and give me this new life is the blood of Christ.'"

"And you think it's that easy?" Sam asked, staring at him.

"It *is*!" Tommy exclaimed. "It's *exactly* that easy!"

Sam sat back in his chair. He explained to them that he had been going to church for the last month or so and each time the minister had invited those who wanted to be saved to come forward. "Do you think *I* could go up there?" he asked incredulously.

"You don't have to do a thing!" Phil jumped in.

"All you have to do is ask!" Tommy urged.

Sam gasped, pressed his hands to his chest again and exclaimed, "I would have to be a helluva lot more than I am right now!"

"See, God accepts you the way you are," Phil declared. "God doesn't wait for you to change . . . He'll do it for you." He recalled Tommy's taking thirty-three cents from the grocery store and pointed out that Tommy was forgiven.

"I don't feel that way, though," Sam confessed, more somber now, "because I think it's just too easy to say, you know, 'I'm going to be forgiven' . . . I don't feel that I could just kneel and turn all my sins over to Christ." (This seemed to be the sticking point for Sam, one that, I realized much later, continued to haunt him for years to come.)

Moments later, Phil asked his brother to pray with him.

"What do you mean, 'Pray with me?'" Sam asked, as he looked for a match he had dropped on the floor after lighting a cigarette.

"Pray with me," Phil repeated. "Accept Jesus Christ now!"

"I *do* accept Jesus Christ," Sam objected.

"No," Phil interrupted, "I mean kneel down with us right here in the middle of your floor right here and tell *God* that. . . . And don't be embarrassed about the people standing around us," he said about the film crew hovering in the background. "That's not important. The one you've got to talk to is *God*. *That's* who's important. Do it right now with us right here on the floor! I'll kneel down with you; Tommy will kneel down with you, and we'll pray together. Allow the Holy Spirit to work in your life *now*, Sammy!"

Phil had slipped onto his knees in front of Sam. "Put your cigarette aside," he asked gently, "and kneel down with us—please?"

"Sure," Sam said, his face contorting in anguish, "and tomorrow I'll be smoking . . ."

"It doesn't make any difference," Phil assured him. "Kneel down with us right now, Sammy."

"No," Sam groaned as he broke into sobs.

"Come on, brother," Phil said tenderly. "If you want, they can turn the camera off right now." Sam was sobbing now, supporting his head with one hand, his elbow propped up on the table behind him.

"Hey, brother," Phil said, going across the floor on his knees to him. "I love you, brother," he said, embracing Sam as Sam remained motionless and continued crying. "It's important," Phil said in earnest. "It really is."

TWELVE DAYS AFTER Phil's visit to Sam's house, we were filming our last Sunday worship at Shawmut River to pick up elements of the service—people singing and walking forward to pray, and an a cappella anthem by Sue Sanderson. She sang the traditional folk song "There's Not a Friend but the Lowly Jesus" in her clear, breathy voice with no other accompaniment than the discreet tapping of her foot. Later we would splice these elements together with pieces of sermon from other services to build various worship segments as if all its parts were from the same occasion. Also, at this last meeting with the entire congregation, we planned to shoot still photographs of all the church families present to have some visual representation of the extended families making up the congregation. Everyone had turned out wearing their nicest clothes, and that, along with the sense that we were completing our filming, may have contributed to the unusually charged atmosphere I and others felt that morning.

At the end of the service, Michael, my codirector and cinematographer, was kneeling on the dais panning slowly across the faces of people singing the familiar hymn of invitation:

> *Just as I am, without one plea,*
> *But that Thy blood was shed for me.*

Behind us, Pastor Valenti floated his usual entreaties over the crowd: "Have you seen Christ here? Are you scared? . . . If Christ calls you, won't you come?" I was crouching next to Michael on the dais, watching the crowd as his shot came to rest on Ben and Pam's youngest son returning to his pew from praying up front at the rail. Just then, out of the corner of my eye, I caught a glimpse of someone moving. Sam was stepping out into the aisle and coming forward.

"Sam's coming forward!" I quickly whispered to Michael, who whip-panned across the crowd to catch Sam emerging from the pews. Sam walked forward, his large frame tight with anguish, tears streaming down his face, and knelt down at the rail to pray.

Pastor Valenti made his way down the steps and put his arm around Sam's shoulders. "Do you mind if I pray with you, Sam?" he asked. "Our great God and Father in heaven," he prayed softly, "we ask, Lord, that you touch Brother Sam. We thank you for him, Father. Hear his prayer. We ask it in Jesus' name." He patted Sam reassuringly on the back and rose to return to the pulpit. Sam remained kneeling, his head bowed, his body shaking lightly with sobs. When he finally stood up to return to his seat, Phil walked forward to embrace him. Phil tried to speak with him, but Sam pulled away and returned to his pew, taking his place next to his wife and son, who took hold of his father's arm and looked up questioningly at his tearstained face.

Sam did not say the "sinner's prayer" or "accept Christ" that morning, but he had taken a remarkable step. "Do you think *I* could go up there?" he had asked Phil and his nephew less than two weeks before. For Phil, Jean and others at Shawmut River, this remarkable turn of events was a result of the Holy Spirit's work.

My own experiences at Shawmut River during this five-month

shooting period held their own lessons about how such a close-knit congregation might contribute to what members saw as the Holy Spirit's work in changing people. Filming had intensified my involvement in the daily life of the congregation, requiring me to be there days on end, not only while filming but also between shoots, when I had to keep abreast of developments and prepare the ground for subsequent filming. And in the midst of this more continuous involvement in church life, I noticed that I had completely stopped swearing. This was not just around Shawmut River but in all quarters of life, even on occasions when it seemed called for.

"Habits are hard to break" is a truism that bears acknowledging—whether it is smoking, swearing or reacting to a spouse or child in a particular tone of voice. And when members of Shawmut River gave evidence of the dramatic and miraculous changes brought about by the Holy Spirit in their lives after getting saved, it was often changes in deeply rooted habits they pointed to as the most telling kind of evidence—like Sharon giving up smoking or Frank, swearing and Percodan. This was significant because the "sin problems" members suffered from most—ranging from defensive and vengeful reactions to a spouse to addictions of various kinds—were often matters of habit. And now even I, though unsaved, found my fuller involvement in this church community had helped uproot at least one deeply ingrained habit.

In addition, one afternoon toward the end of our filming I found myself in Harvard University's Widener Library doing some research between shooting days. Winter was waning, but a heavy snow had fallen the night before and was quickly melting under the strong March sun. I had just lost a pair of gloves and hoped I might get through the season without buying new ones. Hurrying out Widener Library's back door, I noticed a pair of men's gloves left at a pay phone. I could use them, I thought, to clean the snow off my car for my drive back to Northampton that night. In any case, someone else would soon pick them up, I reasoned, and with that, I took them.

But driving west that night toward home, I was struck by feelings of shame and guilt about the whole matter, something I was not prone to do. After all, I now thought, despite my rush, I could have turned the gloves in to the Lost and Found, where their owner might have found them. I noticed, too, that my shame sprang, above all, from thinking about what my friends at Shawmut River might think about this act and my self-serving rationalizations for it. Shawmut River had become for me, I realized, a moral community whose influence extended beyond its own small compass to my general orientation to the wider world around me—a "reference group," as some sociologists would put it. These might seem like petty examples, like Phil's nephew's stealing thirty-three cents from the supermarket. But if this was true for me—a researcher only peripherally involved in this congregation— how much more would it affect those whose larger lives were encompassed by churches of this kind?

PART FOUR

19

"They've slandered my character!"

AFTER FILMING, we broke for a couple of months before settling into our editor's studio in Cambridge, Massachusetts, that summer to begin editing a ninety-minute film from the thirty-five hours we had shot. The entire process, with breaks for fund-raising and reflection, would take the better part of two years. And though my co-director, Michael Camerini, liked to joke that even a chimpanzee could cut a film from footage as rich as ours, our editor, Adrienne Miesmer, seasoned in *cinéma-vérité* work, confessed it was the hardest film she had ever cut—mainly because of the difficulties of launching, sustaining and interweaving several different stories, all with the help of only minimal narration.

From the outset we felt that public-television viewers would most strongly identify with an outsider approaching Shawmut River—someone like Sam. The question "What will Sam do?," we felt, would pull many viewers through the film. Meanwhile, soon after we began editing, Sam accepted the Lord, was baptized and became a regular member of Shawmut River, while he and his wife moved toward divorce.

In addition, we had the story of Ben and Pam's marriage. It had also ended in divorce, and I was surprised to learn that the court had awarded Ben custody of the three boys. Other stories we began assembling from our footage included the challenges posed by the church's teenagers and by conflicts within the congregation. All these stories we imagined folding into the initial one of Frank and Sharon's getting saved, restoring their marriage and building the church.

We recognized we had more stories than one film could bear. Deciding what to cut was often painful, yet the temptation to include too much was clearly an occupational hazard of documentary filmmaking. Rich and telling scenes had to fall to the cutting-room floor—say, of Pastor Valenti appearing on a television show to debate opponents from an organization called Fundamentalists Anonymous and from Norman Lear's People for the American Way. So, too, did the entire story of church conflicts. It was complicated and involved many elements, including objections to the nursery project, the departure of successive principals and Pastor Valenti's proposal to build houses on church land. And apart from interviews, we had few scenes to tell it, though two of them—one men's prayer breakfast and a remarkably candid conversation between Frank and Sharon late at home one night—made wonderful and telling scenes.

By the following fall, the political turmoil at Shawmut River had subsided, but in its wake, several families had left. They included one of Phil Strong's sisters and her husband, who had for some time objected to Pastor Valenti's hard line against charismatic Christians, and the whole Keener clan. Dan Keener and Judy Waters, now married, had left for Ohio, and differences between the Valentis and Dave Keener had led to his leaving his teaching job at the Christian Academy.

During this period my visits to Shawmut River dropped off (and some of my swearing, I noticed, reappeared). The following March, after ten months' editing, I phoned the Valentis to invite them to our studio in Cambridge to view some of the sequences we had assembled. I had not spoken with them since attending Sunday worship the previous November. On that occasion, I noticed that Sharon's mother, Ada, stood up during testimony time to thank God for the Strongs, the Lavernes and Mary Shepperson, "that dear lady who never has guile on her lips." Her comment suggested that there were those who *did* have guile on their lips. By now I had learned how to read the signs and suspected old conflicts had resurfaced.

Two weeks earlier I had been surprised when Frank announced during worship that he was taking thirty days off from the pastorate. He thanked the Strongs publicly for offering Sharon and him plane tickets to Florida to get away and relax but said he had to decline. Instead, I heard later that he and Sharon were driving Christie to Lynchburg, Virginia, where she would finish high school at Jerry Falwell's Christian academy while living with Sharon's younger sister, who had married and settled there. This, too, surprised me.

Now when I phoned the Valentis to see about their coming to our Cambridge studio, Sharon asked if Christie could come along. "I thought she was in Lynchburg," I said with surprise.

"Well, she had a look," Sharon said, "and decided it wasn't for her." She paused and then added, a bit confused to recognize that I was not aware of some important developments: "You knew Christie was pregnant, didn't you?"

"No," I replied, dumbfounded.

The father was Jeff, Sharon went on to explain, the star of the Christian Academy's basketball team the previous year and a figure all the younger students had looked up to. "It wasn't because we weren't strict enough," Sharon said in defense of her and Frank's parenting. "We didn't even let her date!"

Once the news had broken, I later learned, Christie had felt it would be a "bad testimony" to be around the other teens and had decided to go to Lynchburg to attend Falwell's "Save-a-Baby" school, a much-publicized ministry for young women with unwanted pregnancies. But she and her parents were disappointed to find the school filled, as Sharon put it, "with girls whose own parents wouldn't even support them." The atmosphere, they felt, was sad and demoralizing. In addition, they were not pleased that the school's principal encouraged Christie and others to put their babies up for adoption. So Christie had come home.

As I drove out to Worcester the following Sunday, I wondered what consequences Christie's pregnancy might have for both the Valentis and Shawmut River. At morning worship everything seemed calm and normal. Jeff, the expected baby's father, was there. Since graduating from the Christian Academy last spring, he had been unloading trucks at a warehouse and not attending church. At the close of the service, he walked toward the door, his head bowed and his eyes raised just enough to navigate the knots of people in the vestibule. As he came near Pastor Valenti, Frank looked at him cautiously and said, "Good to have you out, Jeff." Jeff smiled sheepishly and continued toward the door.

The Valentis invited me for Sunday dinner, and I was pleased when Frank suggested Christie drive with me to pick up pizza and grinders at our regular spot. It was a cold, bright March day, just warming up in

the midday sun, and Christie seemed in good spirits, her usual effer-
vescent self. True to character, she was keen to know, above all, how I
had learned the news. "Who told you?" she asked with relish. Once
that was out of the way, I asked what she was going to do. "I think I'll
finish school and get married *after* I have the baby," she said with
determination, "but I'm not sure yet."

"People say you'll be missing your youth," Christie continued,
laughing. "I never had any. I didn't like hanging out with other teens
and wasn't free to date or do anything anyway." She shrugged her
shoulders. "Besides, I like little kids a lot, you know. I'm looking forward to it." All that was true. Christie had become increasingly aloof
from the church's teenagers, and she had always taken pleasure in helping out in the church nursery alongside adult women like Jean Strong.
Now she felt she shared even less with her fellow teenagers. Mornings
she now attended classes at the Christian Academy, and afternoons she
studied upstairs in the church office in the company of Sharon and
other women staff.

"My mother's my best friend now," she declared with enthusiasm.

"I guess I see her as a woman now," Sharon told me later, "and not
as my little girl."

I asked Christie if this Sunday was the first time Jeff had been to
church. "How did you know?" she shot back.

"Well," I explained, "someone said, 'Nice to have you out,' so I
assumed . . ."

"Yeah, my dad said that," she said chuckling, tickled by his gesture.
Later I learned that Frank and Sharon had been watching carefully to
see if Jeff would start coming back to church to "face his sin," as they
put it. They saw that as an important gauge of his condition and,
therefore, of the advisability of Christie's marrying him.

"How did your mom and dad react to the news?" I asked.

"They were shocked," Christie said, "but got over it. Things are
fine now."

As the afternoon unfolded, I was relieved to find the same loving
spirit between Christie and her parents that I had always seen. But they
had been through an extraordinarily painful ordeal. "All I could do was
cry," Sharon told me months later. "I'd wake up every day and cry. I'd
go to school and cry."

"You have to have strength," I offered lamely.

"Well, *you* don't have it," Sharon insisted, correcting me. "God *gives* it to you." This was a theological statement I had no reason to dispute.

"If Sharon hadn't known the Lord," her mother, Ada, confided in me, "I really thought she would have taken her life." And it had been to help support Sharon through this ordeal that Frank was taking a month off from the ministry, as I had heard him announce from the pulpit.

By now Sharon had come to terms with the situation. She summed it up by saying, "We're all going to sin; but when you *do* sin, you don't run from your sin; you face it. You do the responsible thing." The responsible thing, in Sharon and Frank's eyes, was for Christie and Jeff to keep the baby and stay in church. Abortion was never mentioned as a conceivable option. Some church members, Sharon said, felt they should just throw Jeff in jail. Others felt he should not be allowed in church. "But we feel that's the best place for him," Sharon declared. "It's a hospital for sinners, right? We're all sick, and we need to be restored."

Christie told me her pregnancy had prompted her father to offer to resign as pastor, but then he had changed his mind. "It all shouldn't come back on him," she insisted, "because it wasn't anything he did or knew about." She knew all too well what some church members might make of a father's responsibility for his daughter's actions. It was an important facet of what was entailed by fathers' being seen as heads of household, that is, accountable for what family members did.[1]

I already knew that Christie's pregnancy might become an explosive issue in the congregation, given the conflicts probably still smoldering beneath the surface of community life. That Sunday morning, in fact, when I asked Scott about someone who had apparently left Shawmut River, he took me aside. "How much do you know about Pastor's taking a month off?" he asked in a hushed voice. I said I knew only that Christie was pregnant. "Well," he said with raised eyebrows, "the Keeners called to warn us that the phone tree's been active." He reported that one former member, who had left the church in an angry dispute with the pastor, had recently phoned and Sue answered.

"I heard someone there's *expecting* . . . ," the caller said in a provocatively knowing way.

"Yes . . . yes . . . ," Sue replied, hemming and hawing, until she finally rescued herself by saying, "we're *expecting* a big turnout for the cantata." But, Scott noted, the speaker came back to the question like a magnet to steel. The scandal had already been seized upon by Pastor Valenti's enemies outside the church. It remained to be seen what would come of it from within.

I was always impressed with how much this shadow community hovered in the background of church life. In succeeding months I would hear about Christie's pregnancy from several former church members scattered around Worcester and beyond. Talk spread more widely into other conservative circles. One member heard from a conservative Catholic priest that Pastor Valenti had been fired. Frank himself heard a rumor that one town official had canceled a "perk test" for church land because "the pastor's daughter's pregnant, the school's closed and he's been fired." That was enough to convince Sharon that "everybody knows," and when she had gone to pick up a prescription at a local drugstore, she had lowered her head and mumbled her name, she admitted with a laugh.

The Sunday following my conversation with Christie, Phil and Jean Strong were not in church. Jeff and Christie were sitting in a back pew, their legs entwined. They seemed to feel themselves a legitimate couple now, untroubled by shame or guilt. Later that week, when the Valentis came to Cambridge to view our edited material, I mentioned to Christie that I had noticed Jeff in church again. She beamed brightly and said in her usual rapid-fire delivery, "He's been coming Sunday morning, Sunday evening and Wednesdays. The only thing I haven't been able to get him out for is Sunday school! He has trouble getting up!" she added, laughing with delight. She told me that the following Saturday she and Jeff would be married. The ceremony would be done in low-key fashion at home with Frank presiding. She and her new husband would begin married life living with Frank and Sharon, occupying her bedroom along with an assortment of stuffed animals and dolls accumulated over a happy childhood. The atmosphere around the impending birth was cheerful and hopeful. It seemed at that point that the Valentis had turned an unwanted pregnancy into a wanted one.

A month had passed when I called the Valentis to let them know we had received a grant from the Corporation for Public Broadcasting to finish our film for national broadcast. Frank and Sharon had been pleased with the segments they saw when they visited our studio. Their reactions were gratifying, particularly Frank's comment on our intercutting his and Sharon's accounts of their marriage into a single sequence. "I never knew you could make art out of a life," he had observed.

After congratulating me on our grant, Frank asked, "Do you have some time to listen to something?"

"Sure," I replied.

"I don't know how much you've heard already . . . ," he began.

"Well, nothing."

"You knew I resigned, didn't you?"

"No, only that you had offered," I confessed.

"They've slandered my character!" he then exclaimed abruptly, saying that "they" had told outrageous things to Blaine Titus and George Howell, two leading fundamentalist pastors in the area.

"Who did?" I asked.

"Well, Phil and Doug pulled a power play," Frank replied, after realizing I needed filling in. On Easter Sunday, he explained, he had resigned and announced a "Pulpit Committee" to find a replacement for him. To that committee he had appointed three local fundamentalist pastors, but only one member of Shawmut River, in an observer capacity. "Scripturally only pastors can pick a pastor," Frank explained, citing Titus, Timothy and Acts.

Sharon concurred when I spoke with her later. "I certainly would want to go to a doctor who had been tested by other doctors," she reasoned by analogy, "so I think it was very biblical, very solid reasoning." Above all, Frank said that he wanted to make sure that after eight years of hard work, he did not "leave this place in the hands of a stinking, rotten liberal."

Phil was irate, Frank said, because he was not on the committee, and consequently had "pulled" eighty members out of the church. Phil had slandered him, Frank said, "snuck the land thing in," and so on.

In addition, Frank said that he had had "to fire Scott on the spot for gossiping, backbiting and splitting the church." Summing up all these developments, Frank said, "Satan got into Phil's household through his wife, and she turned Doug against us through Terry."

The church was splitting. It was hard to grasp the fact that things had finally come to this, a full year after conflicts over the nursery and other issues had burned hot in the congregation. Two days later I reached Scott by phone to hear his account. He recalled times during the past year when Frank spoke of leaving, including his resigning when news of Christie's pregnancy broke. He reported that Frank had gone so far as to gather the teachers together to announce his resignation and then retracted it. But, Scott observed, that had planted a powerful seed in people's minds.

According to Scott, on a Tuesday in mid-March, the weekly night for visitation, a group of men went to talk with Frank in his office. They included Phil, Doug Laverne, Scott and several others. They had met at Doug Laverne's the night before and turned to scripture to see how Pastor Valenti measured up to biblical standards for pastoring. The following night they went to Frank and, referring to passages in Timothy and Titus, suggested he resign. When I asked Scott what passages had been decisive, he replied that it had been the part that says, "He who cannot keep order in his own household cannot order the household of God" (referring to I Timothy 3:4–5). The reference could not have been calculated to calm matters down. Scott said Frank reacted angrily and fired him on the spot.

By the following Saturday passions had cooled. Gathering the same group of men together, Frank and Sharon said they had prayed about it and decided that Scott would *not* have to leave because Frank would instead. "They were in tears, and we were all hugging," Scott recalled.

In the week that followed, a number of meetings were called and then canceled. Then suddenly, at Easter-morning worship, representatives of the Baptist Bible Fellowship appeared in the pulpit and read a resignation letter from Pastor Valenti to a surprised congregation. The letter established the Pulpit Committee to find a new pastor, Scott said, and called for the resignation of all staff pending his arrival.

In the meantime, the Valentis were attending Temple Baptist Church nearby in Connecticut. Frank had appointed its pastor, the Reverend Brian Lovitt, as interim pastor of Shawmut River and member of the Pulpit Committee. Lovitt told Scott that he and his family had to move out of their church house as soon as possible. Reverend Lovitt's motto, the dissidents now joked, was "Lovitt or leave it."

The following Monday was bedlam at Shawmut River, according to Scott. Many members were confused about what was happening to their church and their school. Several teachers quit, and the coach and youth minister told Sharon, "You've got a mutiny on your hands!" Scott said that Frank had arrived, an argument had erupted and Frank had fired him again. He recalled going to his office to pack up things accumulated over seven years of service. Tom Morse had been sent to watch over him, Scott said indignantly, and accused him of stealing tapes. That Monday was the last time Scott and Sue saw the Valentis.

The Valentis had different versions of these events, but all agreed that a solid majority of Shawmut River's membership had left. Some were now meeting at Phil and Jean's home on Wednesday evenings for Bible study. One group, Frank and Sharon recalled, had gone to a Falwell-related church not far away and voted Frank out, elected Scott interim pastor and were now tithing to him. Fellow dissidents had helped the Sandersons move out of the church house, and Scott and Sue had landed the very first apartment they called about. It turned out to be right near Phil and Jean's home. "It was almost like the Lord had it planned," Scott mused.

There seemed to be no going back. The next Wednesday I went to Bible study at the Strongs' home and found a group of about twenty adults busily establishing temporary quarters for their church and school. Two teachers were painting a room in the Strongs' basement to use as a classroom. Since Scott was in Lynchburg, Virginia, attending a pastors' conference, a new teacher led the adults in Bible study. He chose Ephesians 6:10–14, in which Paul exhorts the Ephesians to put on "the whole armor of God" to enable them "to stand against the wiles of the Devil" and "against spiritual wickedness in high places."

"We need to wear the breastplate of righteousness against Satan working even in our church," he declared. "We can't just use physical things, because the forces of evil aren't visible, though their effects are."

In the discussion that followed, Doug Laverne suggested keeping in mind a verse warning against speaking "guile" or "evil." The conflicts in the air seemed to weigh particularly heavily on him, partly because of his pacific nature but also, I suspected, because of his relationship with Pastor Valenti, who had led him to the Lord. In fact, Frank had visited the Lavernes at home the Friday before and told me that Doug had promised him then that he would not leave the church.

This evening at the Strongs', Doug took issue with the view that Frank's actions had been "unscriptural." Nevertheless, he objected to the way Frank had acted. Frank hadn't told them about his resignation beforehand and had appointed a Pulpit Committee without consulting them. Laypeople should have *some* input, Doug and others felt. They took issue with Frank's appointment of only one church member to the Pulpit Committee—moreover, someone who they felt was "too young a Christian" and had too little experience in church. During most of the Bible study, Jean and Terry Laverne talked alone together in the kitchen.

In conversation afterward some reviewed the long list of families who had left Shawmut River over the years, often out of conflicts with

Pastor Valenti. Someone repeated the story of one pastor who, in an effort to mediate between Frank and a family who had left, had said he had not believed Frank. One of Phil's relatives spoke about an "extremism"—or "neofundamentalism"—in Frank that led him "to reject even good Christians because they were charismatic." Several fell into a discussion about what authority "elders" and "pastors" should have. They opened up their Bibles here and there for guidance, but their judgments remained inconclusive.

IT WAS DIFFICULT attending the secessionist Bible study at the Strongs' while continuing to see the Valentis and those loyal to them. I found myself caught between two warring parties, having relations of trust and affection for those on both sides. It was a painful, yet illuminating, time, especially for what it revealed about how a fundamentalist pastor's authority—in principle absolute and unquestionable—could suddenly unravel. In time, further inquiry into these events would shed light on what forces had brought this about.

Though Pastor Valenti might have held on to a small rump of his congregation, he was now opposed by a majority who judged him *not* to be God's man for them. To hold on to the church he and his family had founded and struggled to build would have caused Frank's family economic hardship. Even his disability pension—a cushion most fundamentalist pastors did not enjoy—would not begin to cover the church's debts and operating costs. At the same time, Frank's long-standing desire to continue his education gave him further reason to consider leaving.

Pastor Valenti's changed political situation had come about largely through talk, and the war raging around me was essentially a war of accounts, reports and stories. It was hard to find an event that was not disputed. About the group who had come to ask him to resign, Frank said Phil and Doug had "faked him" into thinking the group had come for Tuesday visitation and then shut the door behind them. Doug, on the other hand, said they had "gently" said "it might be a good idea" for him to carry out the resignation he had already announced, and "he blew up." A supporter of the Valentis told me it had become a "roast-the-pastor" meeting and had been "terrible." Frank said Doug had later confessed to him, "I knew it was wrong the moment I walked through the office door."

Speaking of past events, Scott said he and others had once reported to the pastor that Jeff had had his hand on Christie's leg in school and Frank had not done anything about it. The Valentis said they had grounded Christie for two months because of the incident and complained that Scott had spread this "lie" to a senior fundamentalist pastor in the area.

Such stories tended to characterize opponents as essentially untrustworthy. They lied, reversed themselves, engaged in deception and so on. A supporter of the Valentis, for example, pointed out the hypocrisy she saw in one dissident's coming up and hugging her. "I love you," he had said. "I really do."

"He never did that before!" she said indignantly. "And I said to him, 'Is this because you feel guilty?'"

In fact, guilt engendered by turning against those you once treated as family seemed a major force driving members to diabolize one another in their accounts of one another's actions. In Scott and Sue's early years at Shawmut River, for example, Tom and Ada Morse had taken them under their wing as "parents" and as "grandparents" to their daughter. Now Tom stood over Scott as he packed up his things in the church office to make sure he did not steal anything.

Listening to stories that so demonized others made it hard to continue normal, trusting relations with them. I felt myself running the risk of being taken as a partisan simply by hearing and comprehending such wildly opposed accounts. If the subjects of these stories were so deceitful or untrustworthy, according to my conversation partner's account, how could I continue having fellowship with them? My status as an outside observer made it easier for me to sustain relationships with both parties under conditions of escalating distrust. But others could hardly resist the enormous pressures thrusting them into one camp or the other. And it was usually members' deeper, long-standing ties with certain partisans that determined which side they identified with. Because she was not tied in a strong way to either the Valentis or Strongs, Mary Shepperson was one of the few who resisted being incorporated into either camp. Otherwise, in this way, a war of accounts developed inexorably into a split like a log split by wedges driven deeper and deeper into it.

This war of accounts was also important in each side's struggle to establish its legitimacy more widely among fundamentalist Baptist pastors in the area, some of whom got involved in trying to settle this conflict. Because Shawmut River, like other independent churches, was not part of a larger church body whose authority could be drawn upon to settle disputes, the congregation turned in customary fashion, following biblical precepts, to pastors of similar churches in the area to help mediate. And neighboring pastors took on this responsibility even if it was not convenient or pleasant to do so.

When he first learned Christie was pregnant, Frank sought advice from a veteran pastor in the area. Should he resign because of Christie's sin? Frank and Sharon reported this pastor sharing with them his own ordeal with his teenage son's drug use. There were limits on how much you could control your own children, he counseled the Valentis, and that in itself should not require Frank to resign. Later, Frank appointed this pastor to the Pulpit Committee and, once the split occurred, solicited his support as part of a Fact-Finding Committee in bringing church discipline against dissidents.

For their part, opponents shared with this same pastor, much to Frank and Sharon's distress, the story of Frank's failure to respond to reports of Christie and Jeff's displays of affection. That pastor told them, dissidents reported, that he recognized some of the problems they saw in Frank Valenti's ministry. They also took their case to another pastor, who paid a visit to Frank, they said, to suggest he resign.

Even though the opinions of these pastors would not carry the force of law (in church or state), they carried the force of custom, underpinned by the biblical injunction fundamentalist Baptists held not to take fellow believers to court but, instead, to follow procedures recommended in scripture. How these outside pastors were influenced to see things, then, would shape the outcome of a struggle in which everything was up for grabs: followers, buildings, land.

20

"Everybody could see it."

THE PULPIT COMMITTEE acted swiftly, and in late April a candidate to succeed Pastor Valenti was scheduled to come preach—on a Thursday evening, so as not to conflict with Wednesday services at other churches some dissidents were now attending. Given dissidents' objections to not being represented on the Pulpit Committee, it was unclear whether they would come to hear its candidate. Though the congregation, according to Sharon, "had the final opportunity to say whether they wanted this pastor or not," the mechanism by which that would happen remained unclear.

I drove out to Worcester that Thursday and, since the Valentis themselves felt it inappropriate to attend, I stopped by their home beforehand to visit. Tom and Ada were there and angry about the opposition's using Christie's pregnancy to press for Frank's resignation. "They cite First Timothy," Ada snapped. "They never mention Christie, but that's what they mean."

"One of those men has two daughters," Tom Morse added, "and I was tempted to say, 'Buddy, you better build a moat around your house!'"

Behind opponents' use of the Christie issue, however, Frank and Sharon felt the crux of the matter was that dissidents did not accept the principle of a pastor-run church, which the Valentis, following Baptist Bible Fellowship principles, saw as essential to the fundamentalism they practiced. On those terms, they said, Scott and Sue had not been fundamentalists for the past seven years. They pointed out that it was only when Frank had announced the formation of a Pulpit Committee with limited advisory representation for church members that the dissidents had left.[1]

"It all boils down to that," Sharon said. "The fundamentalist view is that the pastor is the ultimate authority in the church—not necessarily that he makes every decision without any kind of counsel, but when the ultimate decision comes down, the pastor is the one who makes it." She likened it to a husband's having the final say in a marriage. For lay members to oversee a pastor's selection, she felt, meant "putting themselves above the pastor—kind of like the wife making the decisions, reversing roles, which doesn't work." She recalled Phil telling Frank several years before, "If you start another ministry, we'll leave." The nursery project had been the most recent of those, and "the Christie issue," Sharon felt, was "the first concrete thing they could point to in order to get Frank to resign."

The candidate for Shawmut River's pastorate who was preaching this evening had come from Indianapolis. The Reverend Peter Davis was a soft-spoken man in his forties, pleasantly plump, with a rosy glow in his cheeks and a strong head of wavy black hair. A senior member of the Pulpit Committee had found him through his Baptist Bible Fellowship network. Davis had graduated from Baptist Bible College, the BBF's flagship school in Springfield, Missouri (and Falwell's alma mater). For thirteen years he had served the same Indianapolis church in which he had been saved, beginning as youth minister and working his way up to senior pastor. A good crowd had gathered from both camps this evening to hear him preach.

"How many of you had a fight today?" Reverend Davis began, taking his departure from I Corinthians 1:10, which urges church members to "all speak the same thing, and that there be no divisions among you; but that ye be perfectly joined together in the same mind and in the same judgment." This was a tall order given the hostilities seething around him, and I had to admire Davis's gumption in addressing the issue head-on. Reminding us with the bodily metaphor so often used at Shawmut River, Davis asked, "What if cells of your hand said, 'We don't want to be hand cells anymore'?" He also reminded us it was natural to love the person who led you to the Lord or discipled you, touching tender bonds now rent by the split.

Reverend Davis succeeded this evening in appealing to Shawmut River's hostile factions and in establishing his gentle, pastoral manner, along with his fundamentalist credentials. When asked about Jerry

Falwell during the question-and-answer session, he criticized Falwell's tendency toward compromise, citing Falwell's decision to drop "Baptist" from what was now called simply Liberty University.

Two days after Davis's promising appearance, conflicts set off by the split continued their relentless course. Members of the Fact-Finding Committee appointed by Frank summoned the Sandersons, Strongs and other leaders of the split to meet with them in the presence of the Valentis. The committee forbade dissidents from running an alternative church and school at the Strongs'. In addition, Sue said that she, Scott and two other teachers had had to write letters of confession and read them aloud to the congregation at a Wednesday-evening service. In their letters they had had to acknowledge their role in leading people against the pastor and to promise not to work within a fifty-mile radius. Scott was defrocked and his ordination papers taken from him.

"It was like looking into a slaughterhouse and seeing the blood of all the other lambs," Scott recalled Jean Strong saying of this "inquisition."

"They called me and told me I had to come in," Jean remembered. "I said, 'No, I don't have to. If you want to stage a catfight, you can go sell tickets someplace else!'" After Jean refused to appear, others like the Lavernes followed suit. In retrospect, Jean felt the pastors on the Fact-Finding Committee, even though they expressed reservations about Frank's leadership, ended up closing ranks in defense of the pastorate. For their part, the Valentis felt vindicated because the committee had found the charges against them to be unsubstantiated.

Given the bitter conflicts and instabilities at loose, it seemed miraculous that within a month Reverend Davis had succeeded Frank Valenti as Shawmut River's second pastor and that most of the dissidents, including the Strongs and Lavernes, had returned. Frank and Sharon were pleased to leave their church in Reverend Davis's hands and glad that most of the congregation had returned. Thanks to the Lord, Sharon said, "it worked out really perfect." She and Frank planned to move to Florida, where Frank would enroll in a master's program in Christian education at a Christian college. Christie and Jeff would go with them and, in time, get their own place nearby.

As the Valentis prepared to leave for Florida, I went out to Worcester in late August to see Christie's newborn baby girl and have one last conversation with Sharon and Frank. Sharon confessed to feeling apprehensive about moving so far away. About missing her parents and Frank's family, she said she was "just praying that we'll be adopted when we go down to Florida.

"When you become a born-again Christian," she said, "you're a babe, and each stage is a new phase of life and it's a challenge, and it's something to look forward to: 'What's God going to teach me this time? What am I going to learn? How am I going to grow closer to God? How am I going to see God provide this time?' So we're not going down there *without* family," she observed. "There's family down there—we just haven't met them yet."

Sharon and Frank both felt the ordeals they had just gone through provided the necessary experience for knowing how to handle church problems in the future. But, Frank confessed, "We were totally un-prepared for what was about to take place when we left college. How can anyone prepare for something like this?" he said, scrunching his shoulders up with a look of incredulity. "We left college thinking that everybody who worked in a church—though they had their problems—always pulled together, that everybody always wanted the same things: to see people saved and the church grow. And then all of a sudden you find out that Christians are human beings; they sin like everybody else!"

"I think we have the experience," Sharon said of their present situa-tion. While Frank was "top-notch" in theology, she felt "he lacked administrative skills, and you need that. You just need to be able to know who to hire, when to hire and how to deal with people. The school of education that we've had here has been more valuable than any school could possibly be. And I wouldn't have traded it for the world."

About the leaders of the split, Sharon said, "Those people are still the family of God, and I still love every one of them. I don't hate any-one, and I hope it's a growing time in their life. You know," she contin-ued, using a familiar aphorism, "problems can make you bitter or better, and hopefully, you know, they've made us better Christians."

Whatever else might be said about Frank and Sharon's leadership at Shawmut River, it had to be recognized that this had been their first experience running a church—and not simply a church but also a school covering kindergarten through twelfth grade. They had launched these institutions in their late twenties while raising three children and felt the experience had taught them some important lessons. One they emphasized was, as Sharon put it, that "purity is more important than growth." Both felt, in retrospect, that they had been too interested in growth rather than in making sure members accepted certain guidelines essential to fundamentalism as they understood it, like the principle of a pastor-run church and their stand against charismatic Christianity. Yet they realized that when they first started the church, they themselves had not been clear about those things.

Despite their positive outlook on past events, leaving Shawmut River was painful. Years later, Frank still remembered his last day in the office, propping his elbows on his desk and looking out the window onto the large playing field where the church's youth played softball on summer evenings. He found himself picturing in his mind's eye the work it had taken to make the field that way—like the forty or fifty boulders they had had to excavate, some the size of his car. He remembered Mary Shepperson's husband taking out a permit for dynamite to break the larger ones into pieces small enough to remove by truck. Images flooded his mind of all the work his family and others had done to build Shawmut River. Not just the physical work, he said, like putting up the rafters in the new gymnatorium or putting in the septic system, for which they had dug four trenches two hundred feet long—but also the spiritual work. "That took some *really* heavy lifting," he recalled. "And," he observed, "a little piece of you dies when you leave something like that."

"It was like our baby," Sharon said, likening their experience of the split to the story of King Solomon faced with two women claiming the same baby. When Solomon proposed dividing the baby in two, the true mother revealed herself by renouncing her claim so that the child might live. Sharon felt that she and Frank had done the same to save their church.

"But I just praise God for the pastor there," Sharon said of Reverend Davis, "because he's a real peach. He's got a pastor's heart. He just loves people, and he's the man that that church needed. And I think everybody's accepted it, even Frank's dad."

While Frank's parents, Joe and Marie, happily settled "under" Reverend Davis's preaching, Tom and Ada could not. "What church can please," Ada said sadly, "when you gave your life's blood to it—all I could see was hours of painting and scrubbing—and no one cares." She sized up the church's current situation in this way: "What Phil says is law; Pete Davis is a puppet."

The Strongs and Lavernes embraced Reverend Davis's pastorate. While some granted that Davis was not as dynamic a preacher as Frank Valenti, they praised Davis, above all, for having a "pastor's heart"— that is, a gentle, compassionate spirit. In this way, Shawmut River quietly underwent the most decisive transition in its short eight-year life: from being a pioneer church led by its founding pastor to a settled congregation hiring a new pastor, who now had to adapt to existing constellations of power and influence. With this new leadership configuration, Shawmut River began again to grow and change.

AT THE TIME OF THE SPLIT, in the heat of conflict, with the temperature of moral indignation rising, I had not pushed my inquiry into its sources as vigorously as I might have. To question people's stories too thoroughly would risk identifying myself as a disbeliever in their accounts and, hence, an enemy. In any case, I was too busy at the time editing our film to do much more. It was three years later, then, in 1989, when I first began drafting chapters on these events, that I revisited these conflicts in a series of conversations over the telephone with some of those centrally involved. I called from my office in New York City, where I was then living and producing documentary films.

Though passions had subsided, I was impressed by how painful events surrounding the split still were. "It's like a death in the family," Sharon told me over the phone from Florida. "We try not to talk about it."

"We tried to erase it from our memory," Scott said when I reached him in a small town in Massachusetts near the Rhode Island border, where he was serving as music minister in an independent Baptist church.

"There are scars," Sue observed. "We still talk about it," she admitted. "We try not to."

Even ten years after the split, pain still hovered around memories of it. And over time, as historical memory faded, people's claims for legitimacy had been refined. While the Valentis claimed the split all "boiled down" to dissidents not accepting a pastor-run church, the dissidents themselves expressed their support, in principle, for this fundamentalist Baptist teaching, while noting various qualifications or limitations. Scott pointed out that when the group of men first went to Frank to suggest he resign, they began by saying, "We do not have the right to ask you to resign." And Sue, when asked how her current pastor viewed the matter of church authority, replied, "The pastor has authority, yes, but not absolute authority. We're talkin' the pope here!"

Putting the matter most sharply, Jean Strong said, "No one challenges the fact that the pastor has absolute authority. But," she added, in a critical qualification, "the pastor's authority is absolute only when that pastor's in line with God. You would be an absolute fool to follow a man who was not following God and not living up to Timothy and Titus.

"I'm sorry," she recalled telling the Fact-Finding Committee, "but that's what they did down in Guyana" (referring to Jim Jones's People's Temple, whose members committed mass suicide in the jungles of Guyana in 1978). Summing it up, Jean now affirmed simply that Frank "wasn't God's man anymore, and everybody could see it."

But how were members to judge whether a pastor was "God's man" or not? If Frank Valenti had been accepted as God's man during the early years of his ministry, how had some arrived at the conclusion that he no longer was? And if scripture provided the ultimate guide, how could members arrive at interpretations contrary to those of their pastor, who, in principle, was their final arbiter on matters of biblical interpretation?[2]

The biblically based criticisms of Frank Valenti's pastorate that Jean mentioned derived from passages in Titus and I Timothy, in which Paul writes that bishops must be "blameless, the husband of one wife, vigilant, sober, of good behavior, given to hospitality, apt to teach; Not given to wine, no striker, not greedy of filthy lucre; but patient, not a brawler, not covetous; One that ruleth well his own house, having his children in subjection with all gravity (For if a man know not how to rule his own house, how shall he take care of the church of God?); Not a novice, lest being lifted up with pride he fall into the condemnation of the devil" (I Timothy 3:2–6).

Now, three years after the events, the requirement of "having his children in subjection" assumed secondary importance to dissidents and was seen only as a "symptom" of deeper problems. Some of those problems attached to phrases requiring that a bishop not be a "striker" or "brawler," and "not a novice" who might be "lifted up with pride." Scott, for one, felt "the pride thing" had controlled Frank's response to personal conflicts. For Phil Strong, on the other hand, who had run a number of businesses, Frank's problems stemmed from his weaknesses as a manager, largely because of his lack of experience, his being "a novice" (I Timothy 3:6).

On other counts, dissidents now spoke of Christie's pregnancy as a result of Frank's putting "his ministry over his family," as Jean put it, and that his children, especially Christie, "were really rebellious about that." (Though putting ministry, or church, above family was often mentioned around Shawmut River as being a cardinal wrong, I never heard any scripture cited to support it. And in all the commentary on Christie's pregnancy over the years, it is worth noting, no one ever mentioned the potential relevance of sex education, which had been resolutely opposed in the very founding of Shawmut River's school.)

As evidence of the Valenti children's rebelliousness, several dissidents now pointed to a "whole teenage conspiracy thing" surrounding Christie's pregnancy. Some said, for example, that the teenagers had known about Christie and Jeff's trysts before Frank and Sharon did. Knowing how protective and loyal Shawmut River's teenagers were toward one another, this was neither surprising nor remarkable. Some claimed the teenagers had even known about Christie's pregnancy before her parents. But around these assertions historical memory seemed unreliable.

One deacon, for example, told me with alarm that he had first heard Christie was pregnant from the teenagers. Yet his wife distinctly remembered him phoning her from a deacons' meeting at the Valentis' home to report the startling news just told them by the pastor. This suggested how judgments crystallized in common opinion might even alter individual memory of past events.

There were also disagreements about whether Frank had fired Scott and others when his resignation letter was read from the pulpit on Easter Sunday, or later. My limited effort to determine the timing of any of these past events was thwarted by the complete absence of any documented record related to them. Even a copy of Frank's resignation letter—one of the few written documents pertaining to these events—could not be found in church records.

In any case, now, three years later, a more decisive reason for judging Frank not to be "God's man" anymore had emerged. "The problem wasn't Christie," the deacon quoted above now insisted. "It started with the preaching, when he stepped out of the word of God." This was the first time, but not the last, I heard this judgment, so decisive in undoing the apparently unassailable logic of a fundamentalist pastor's legitimacy.

It appeared that this view had not become established among dissidents without dissent or struggle. Even now, Sue Sanderson remarked that she, for one, did not believe Frank's departure "had anything at all to do with what he said in the pulpit." And when I asked Phil Strong whether he felt Frank had no longer been preaching God's word, he replied, "Yes, but it was Jean who first noticed it. We actually had some fights about it."

When I reached Jean later by phone, she explained how she had come to realize Frank's preaching was "off the wall" and "way out of whack." She said it was she who first noticed it, paradoxically enough, because she heard *less* of Frank's preaching than others did. Working in the nursery on Sunday mornings and Wednesday evenings, she heard his messages only on Sunday evenings. "When you sit under preaching for a long period of time," Jean explained, "and it starts to go slowly, you don't see it. But all of a sudden you walk in and say, 'Phil, that didn't line up.' So we took the preaching tape home," she recalled. "I said, 'Here are four or five commentaries, check it out,' and Phil started checking it out. Then he would start saying, 'Hey, you're right. This is off the wall. This isn't what it's saying at all.' Then others started taking a closer look and not taking things at face value. Then *they* started saying, 'This isn't right. He's not on target anymore. He's straying.'"

"Do you remember any specific example of that?" I asked.

After some struggle to recall a concrete instance, Jean mentioned a message about Jesus washing the disciples' feet. Frank "totally took it away from Christ being a servant," she said. "He was going off on some tangent with it" (not unlikely, given fundamentalists' ways of preaching from scripture). "That example stands out in my mind, because Phil and I had such a big blowout about it. At first he started to argue with me," she explained, qualifying her earlier remark that Phil had readily seen her point on his own. "Then he started lookin'."

So, too, did others. One dissident, for example, who had grown up in a German Lutheran family and fondly remembered learning to sip beer on his grandfather's knee, now faulted Pastor Valenti for claiming that scripture totally prohibited drinking alcohol. "The Bible says deacons should not drink *much* wine," he said authoritatively. "It doesn't say *none*."

In our first phone conversation, Jean had said, "It was just that Frank wasn't God's man anymore, and everybody could see it." Now, in this second conversation, she provided a rare glimpse into the process by which that had come to pass. Her apparently pivotal role in the process was not missed by the Valentis or Morses. At the time of the split, Frank had summed it up by saying, "Satan got into Phil's household through his wife, and she turned Doug against us through Terry." Apart from Satan's role, Frank's interpretation suggested a pattern of influence that I, too, could now see.

Jean Strong's role in these events seemed significant also because the split had taken place along the fault line of the Strongs' own network of family and friends, over and against that of the Valentis'. The Strong clan, along with those who gathered regularly for Sunday dinner at Phil and Jean's, those employed in their company and those young women, like Terry Laverne, whom Jean routinely took under her wing, all coalesced into the dissident bloc. The smaller Valenti-Morse clan, plus Frank and Sharon's childhood friends and the church secretary, all remained loyalists.

For her part, Sharon felt she now understood, with the benefit of hindsight, how certain conflicts between her and Jean had influenced the split. Seven months before the split, Sharon had hired a young woman to replace her as kindergarten teacher so that she could devote herself full-time to managing the school. "Jean didn't like that decision," Sharon recalled, "and it was a battle over power."

As Jean saw it, "They had replaced Sharon in kindergarten with an eighteen-year-old girl who had just graduated from high school, never taught, never did anything, wasn't from this church. Nobody knew her, and I wanted to know more about her."

"If they want to control the school," Sharon recalled saying to Frank about Phil and Jean, "they can have it." Frank called the Strongs and told them to come over to straighten the problem out.

Jean said she felt they were being "called on the carpet for questioning." It was about this time that Sharon discovered Christie was pregnant. Within a week Frank announced he and Sharon were taking a month off from the ministry. In retrospect, Sharon believed that Jean saw Frank's leave of absence as a reaction to the kindergarten teacher conflict. Out of sympathy, the Strongs had offered the Valentis a trip to Florida to relax.

"Had I known she was hurting," Sharon now realized about Jean, "I would have gone to her. But like I said, nobody came into the picture. I couldn't get out of bed! . . . I guess I was so consumed with my own thoughts."

Two months before the split, Pastor Valenti, always vigilant in scanning the sea of public opinion, told Phil that he had noticed that he and Jean didn't seem happy with his ministry. If they weren't, he said, he wouldn't object if they left.

For her part, Jean saw in Frank, at the time, a man mistrusting everyone around him—"a man in stress," she said, "ready to have a breakdown." Into this volatile situation, brimming with layers of unresolved conflict and eroding trust, the news of Christie's pregnancy dropped with uncanny timing.

2 I

"The neck that turns the head"

T HERE IS SOME IRONY, if not surprise, in the fact that it was a woman, Jean Strong, who played a critical role in bringing members to believe Pastor Valenti had "strayed" from God's word, a decisive event in the life of a community reserving positions of authority in church as well as family for men. But this and other evidences of women's power are not surprising to anyone familiar with such churches—or for that matter, with many African-American congregations, among others, sharing a similar makeup: where positions of formal authority are reserved, according to a patriarchal model, for men, while organizational strength is built through family ties sustained, by and large, by women. These realities are surprising only for those who are at some remove from such churches and who take at face value the image of male control they insistently project.

But even for those familiar with fundamentalist churches, the fact of women's power is not easy to hold in view. Members of Shawmut River who at one moment named certain women among the church's power elite might in the very next breath say that men "make all the decisions." Such contradictions were often handled gingerly and with generous doses of humor. "The man's the head," Sharon once quipped about men's headship in church and family. "The woman's the neck that turns the head."

However witty, Sharon's imagery expresses something true, I believe, about the nature of women's power in churches like Shawmut River, as well as in the kind of families making it up. For the power Jean and Sharon exercised did not reside in any officially recognized authority to make decisions. Instead, it rested in their merely factual capacity to shape decisions and political events indirectly, by defining how basic elements determining them were perceived in common by others—by bringing about what "everybody sees," as Jean put it about Frank Valenti's not being God's man anymore. However familiar, such powers are not easy to notice and even harder to document. They represent "the underground movement" and "workings" of church life, as Sharon once described them. Not only are they indirect and behind the scenes, but they also take place gradually and ineffably through countless instances of day-to-day talk among those familiar with one another and with the persons and situations involved. And that talk can be done as much unconsciously as it is intentionally (if not more so). Yet all the while it weaves among community members a common grid of "what everybody sees" and "what everybody knows." And it is through that grid, especially where it becomes taken for granted, that all reasons and judgments affecting decision making become decisively altered—"the neck that turns the head," perhaps, as Sharon put it.[1]

To understand how such opinion-setting talk is so readily wielded by women in communities like Shawmut River, it is helpful to begin by recognizing that it was along lines of family-based networks that daily talk spun the tough, resilient fabric of common belief. Contrary views of Pastor Valenti's leadership were elaborated along different family-based networks. And maintaining those relationships, which involved mutual aid and domestic reciprocities, was done, by and large, by women. Women's prominence in the reciprocities making up extended-family life is manifest in the tendency among American families—outside the propertied upper class at least—to be more involved with a wife's relatives than a husband's. But even when more involved with a husband's family—as in Jean Strong's case, where her mother's illness weakened ties to her own family—these relationships were still primarily women's doing. Witness Jean's impressive efforts to build a network of support among Phil's family and younger church women.[2]

Within each family, then, as husband and wife face each other, collective meanings and the weight they naturally carry over and against individual opinion are more apt to be arrived at through women's relationships than men's. In the Valenti household, this could be seen in the greater presence of Sharon's parents than of Frank's, and in the weight Ada Morse's views carried. The presence of Sharon's parents as allies and supporters, I believe, contributed to her ability, as she put it, to "put fear" into Frank about something, "whether it's real or not," even with as strong-minded a person as Frank. It was Ada who introduced Sharon to fundamentalist Christianity, and Ada and Tom who, after Frank was saved and preparing for the ministry, marveled at his progress and supported him at every step in becoming a "true gentleman" or "man of God," according to *their* standards of what that meant.[3]

Sharon, like anyone else, was more apt to take note of women's powers when they impinged on her. She complained about them, for example, when she saw them undermining deacons' meetings just prior to the church split. "The women wouldn't come," she recalled, "but they might as well have been there, because their husbands were mouthing what they felt. You would see guys coming in there confused—'Now, how am I supposed to think on this thing?'" She squinted and gave the look of a deacon straining to find something at the back of his brain. "And their wives would be at home: chip, chip, chip, chip . . . ," Sharon said, expressing metaphorically the relentless work of carving out authoritative opinion in talk. "I was aware of what was happening behind the scenes with the women," Sharon continued, "and I said to the guys, 'I wish your wives would come and voice their opinions, and maybe things could be straightened out.' Women have power to do good and women have power to do bad," Sharon concluded, "and they have more power than you think—because they have a lot of control of their husbands. You can get your husband riled up, and you can calm him right down."

While in this situation men were expected to express opinions *individually* as deacons and heads of households, women were fashioning them *collectively*. And by considering such differences in patriarchal gender roles in family and church, we can begin to appreciate some of the different mechanisms and powers men and women have available to them to shape events in congregations like Shawmut River. Take gossip, for example, which we have seen is much feared and preached against, often quite strenuously, in fundamentalist churches (see chapter 7). While gossip can be recognized, among other things, for its role in forming and nurturing ties of intimacy and community life and in enforcing a community's moral standards, it is most feared for its capacity to affect reputations. And it is by tarnishing or destroying *some* reputations, while it builds others, that gossip is continually knitting together the common bonds of community life and enforcing its moral standards.

Reputations themselves, however, are mysterious things. As the collective identity a person carries in a community, reputation does not consist simply of the sum of what all members might think about a person *individually*. Instead, reputation must emerge as something members assume to be *commonly* known about someone. It must rise to the level of the *collective*. And it is gossip's qualities as a specific kind of talk, I believe, that give it the capacity to do just that. For gossip involves a speaker positing tacitly what *we* know about persons— that is, *collectively*—rather than what he or she thinks about them *individually*.

To say to friends, for example, "I don't think he disciplines his children well. What do you think?" does not carry the authentic ring of gossip—or its power. It expresses disapproval as the speaker's individual opinion, permitting and even inviting it to be questioned, challenged or discussed as such. However, to say, instead, "Did you see how he yelled at those kids? [and, as listeners nod their heads affirmatively] What a father!" has something of gossip's authentic feel. Here disapproval remains implicit, insinuated as something "all present can (and must) see." Even to know what is actually meant by this utterance, we might notice, requires taking into account those *common* judgments it presumes. Otherwise, how would we know that "What a father!" was meant negatively rather than positively? (Perhaps those kids really needed yelling at.) The judgment implied is provided, in part, by the group participating in the talk itself and preserving its easy and unrestrained character, one of the defining features of gossip. And it is by achieving such a *collective* voice that gossip has the capacity to affect reputations—to bring about "what everybody sees," as Jean Strong put it about Frank Valenti's no longer being God's man for Shawmut River.[4]

However, to achieve this collective voice, gossip must distance itself from the voice of individual authority and individual accountability. But patriarchal authority, whether in father or in pastor, requires the posture and voice of *individual* accountability. Furthermore, as heads of households, men are, as individuals, continually vulnerable to questions of honor, forcing them into defensive and aggressive postures and efforts to save face and to be and appear strong. This contributes to men's recognized adversarial style in conversation, such as their testy banter with one another. But competitive banter among male egos is poles apart from—and even inconsistent with— rapport-presuming and rapport-building talk like gossip, in which the voice of individual authority is submerged in a collective one.[5]

While men at Shawmut River made public declarations and engaged in aggressive actions (coming to Pastor Valenti's office to suggest he resign or standing over Scott as he packed up his belongings), women remained in the background, elaborating day in and day out the ground of common belief. In such a context, men become practiced at confrontation—whether they like it or not—while women become accustomed to acting indirectly, behind the scenes. Remember Sharon pointing out, about women's power over their husbands, that they can "rile them up" or "calm them right down."

In the traditional regime of gender, then, women's place in the family—where families involve broader ties of mutual aid among relatives—and the posture of individual strength and accountability required of men as household heads give women certain advantages in elaborating common belief in ordinary talk. Removed from positions of formal authority, women thereby enjoy certain indirect means to shape an oral tradition through the continual stream of day-to-day moral judgments carried largely in talk. And it is at least partly for this reason, perhaps, that women are seen in settings like Shawmut River to be the principal carriers of morality. And when we consider the specific moral judgments involved in conflicts at Shawmut River over these years—buying soda instead of other foods, getting too close to teenage girls when you talk to them or a teenage girl's pregnancy as a sign of her rebellion—we might recognize, in the traditional view, the authority of women's as opposed to men's particular expertise.[6]

In fact, many of the collectively held assumptions through which members of Shawmut River read the Bible—especially its implications for family life—would be seen by the traditionally minded as things women, rather than men, could rightly judge. These included what submission in marriage means, the meaning of Eve's having been made from Adam's rib, what it means for a husband to provide adequately for his family and so on. More decisively, it includes what these and other standards mean when applied concretely to specific situations guided, as we have seen, by what members know in common about them—and what they establish in talk about them.

From this vantage point, we can better understand why members of fundamentalist congregations—and especially women—endorse a model of authority giving their pastors (almost always male) seemingly absolute and unchallengeable authority over them, not unlike a king's or village chief's. A pastor, or course, has his own special authority to say what the Bible means for his flock, and we should not forget how considerable his powers may be. But like the king's or village chief's, his authority rests on divine sanction—in this case, on his followers seeing him as "God's man" for their congregation. However true and knowable this might be, it depends on human interpretation and human perception, which are subject to change for all kinds of reasons. Though the rapid dissolution of a pastor's authority, like Frank Valenti's, is not an everyday occurrence, it reveals in one brief instant how *every* pastor's authority depends on the beliefs and perceptions of his congregation. Furthermore, those common beliefs affect members' participation and financial support—manifest in offering-plate democracy—which are materially decisive, especially for independent, stand-alone churches like Shawmut River. In this context, a pastor's authority is absolute only in theory. In practice, it can be swiftly undone.

This is not to say tyrannical abuses of power do not occur in fundamentalist churches (or fundamentalist homes). They do, but they are not the rule, as many outsiders assume, taking at face value the formal model of a pastor's (or father's) absolute authority. In fact, there are powerful countervailing forces surrounding any pastor in an independent fundamentalist congregation where he has no larger organization to back him up. And, I would suggest, abuses of power and political bullying may not occur any more frequently in fundamentalist churches than in mainline ones run along formally democratic lines—or, for that matter, in quite progressive academic departments or political collectives proudly adhering to forms of egalitarian democracy.

From this perspective, it is also easier to understand why women, who generally make up a majority in fundamentalist churches, accept a model of governance that excludes them from positions of formal authority. And why they, on occasion, vigorously defend such traditional gender arrangements in the face of feminist criticism. For the powers they have at their fingertips, and customarily rely on to protect their interests in both church and family, depend on traditional oppositions that cast men as individually accountable heads of households by the same stroke they cast women as nurturing caregivers. In this context, women's power resides in an exclusive sphere of women's responsibilities, relationships and talk created *in and through*—not despite—traditional gender roles in the family. And it is precisely the traditional boundaries defining men's and women's spheres that women themselves might invoke, if necessary, to defend their powers in this domain. At one teachers' meeting at Shawmut River, for instance, I remember the principal chiding a woman teacher for counseling another mother about parenting problems that were seen to have moral and spiritual dimensions. It should be the pastor or principal who handled such matters, he asserted.

"I'm speaking to her as a woman!" the teacher snapped impatiently. Pastor Valenti and the principal momentarily cast uneasy glances at each other, not knowing what to do next. Nothing more was said and the teacher's argument carried the day.

Given their vested interest in these gender-defined domains, we might better appreciate conservative women's complaints about the loss of seemingly trivial gender-marking observances, such as men opening doors for women, watching their language in front of them and so on. These are the kinds of day-to-day ritual acts that make the invisible boundaries defining gender undeniably real. Moreover, to reject traditional gender roles in the family, as the women of Shawmut River saw feminists doing, can be seen to threaten, or even dismantle, women's discourse organized in and through those roles. In this way we might better understand conservative women's charging feminism with "bringing women down to be walked on" and their pointing to seemingly inconsequential things such as men no longer opening the door for women as threatening their very security and well-being as women. "I see Christian women as very much in control," Sharon told us in an interview, "and feminist women being very much out of control."

On the other hand, for those urban professional women not enjoying the collective support of a circle of women relatives around them, there is little to lose in jettisoning traditional roles in the family. To be a housewife and mother stands to isolate them in the home, and they are apt to find identity-forming relationships with other women not through family ties but, rather, through reading groups, voluntary organizations or, for my feminist friends and colleagues in the 1960s and 1970s, women's consciousness-raising groups. And it was through the latter that feminist women, struggling to make "the personal political" as they put it at the time, rebuilt, in a certain sense, a woman-controlled moral discourse on family and personal life.[7]

This does not mean to say that women in churches like Shawmut

River typically enjoy *more* power than men. Men's power to make authoritative decisions individually as pastors or heads of household can be substantial, and actual balances of power in any particular community (or family) are always unique and fluctuate over time. Nor does it mean that women experience no strains from traditional gender roles in family and church, or that specific abuses of power against individual women do not occur. Abuses do occur—though from my observations at Shawmut River, they can be as much, if not more, the result of judgments arising in the women's community itself. That was true in the case of one single woman on welfare who was given a hard time by opinion makers at Shawmut River. And it was partly true of Ben's wife, Pam, whose actions were not approved of by church women knowing some of the particulars of her situation.[8]

We could go on to explore some of the characteristic limits, constraints and contradictions such indirect forms of power involve. Sharon's complaint about the paralysis and lack of accountability they created at deacons' meetings in times of conflict points to one kind of weakness. As she was shrewd to point out, "Women have power to do good, and women have power to do bad." With those powers, she felt, comes women's responsibility for what they do with them. But such considerations would not alter what is important here: that is, whatever their scope and limitations, these are the *kinds* of power women rely on in communities like Shawmut River organized around family-based networks.[9]

Furthermore, members of Shawmut River had brought these patterns of relationships, and their characteristic mechanisms and powers, with them to Shawmut River. They felt immediately at home in a community that addressed its own as "Granny Gund" or "Aunt Margaret," recognizing them, in one totalizing formula, not only as *women* carrying the essential qualities of gender but also as *elders* holding authority and as *family* compelling obligation. Shawmut River strengthened those kinds of relationships and extended their reach and effectiveness by helping members create new ones involving similar affections and expectations.

Without bearing in mind this pattern of family-based relationships, with its traditional, gender-segregated character grounded in assumptions about women's and men's essential differences, we will not understand the dynamics of power in communities like Shawmut River, "the underground movement" and "workings" of church life, as Sharon described them. And by the same token, we will not be able to understand conservative women's felt interests in traditional gender roles in the family and their hostility to—and even incomprehension of—feminists' rejection of those roles.[10]

These observations about informal powers supported by women's place in traditional family life pertain also to other institutions or communities organized in and through extended-family ties—African-American or Hispanic-American congregations, for instance, or family-run businesses, upper-class communities or fundamentalist colleges and universities. We smile at the quaint charm of news from Bob Jones University, for example, that Bob Jones III has now succeeded his father, Bob Jones, Jr., as the third Bob Jones to preside over that fundamentalist school since its founding in 1927. Or Oral Roberts, Jr., succeeding his father at Oral Roberts University. This is not how university presidents are chosen at Yale or Iowa State. Yet we scarcely begin to imagine what these facts mean for how such institutions are governed—where family life, instead of being separated from institutional life, as all our modern assumptions presume, provides the loom on which the warp and woof of institutional life have been woven now for more than three generations. What role do women play in the family politics inevitably involved in governing such institutions or in governing the kind of church communities from which they spring?[11]

Similar forms of power are also available to women in family-based upper-class communities. For instance, a summer community neighboring one in which I grew up in New York State's Catskill Mountains had kept much of its upper-class character since its founding in the late nineteenth century. It was centered on several extended families whose interrelationships were marked by common family names given as middle and even first names—relationships that cohered, in part, around interests in significant family fortunes. It was not a community in which feminist enthusiasms prospered in the 1960s and 1970s. On the contrary, its members, women and men, seemed to relish quite stereotyped gender roles in which men golfed together, while women, always turned out in decidedly feminine ways, organized parties, benefits and other community events. Within this world of strongly marked spheres of women's and men's activities, women exercised significant power and influence over the basic flow of community life.

Such similarities between upper-class life and congregations like Shawmut River are a source of common values and politics these otherwise divergent groups share around issues of family, gender and tradition. They make it possible for a woman like Phyllis Schlafly, who, after growing up in the home of a struggling inventor, married into the cohesive upper class of St. Louis, Missouri, in the 1950s, to articulate a vision of family, gender and social order attuned to the needs and realities of people like those at Shawmut River. The same might be said of the conservative talk-show host Rush Limbaugh, who got his start in radio during high school at a station partly owned by his father, the most prominent attorney (and himself the son of a notable attorney) in Cape Girardeau, Missouri (population: 34,000), where Rush stayed on to attend college locally. Or the Christian Coalition's founder, Pat Robertson, who, as the son of a U.S. senator, spent his youth in the 1940s and '50s in the family's hometown of Lexington, Virginia (population: 6,800), where he, like Limbaugh and Jerry Falwell, attended college locally while living at home.[12]

It is such shared experiences in communities cohering around ties to family and place that underwrite powerful conservative alliances across class, linking upper-class interests with popular, mass-based support among the kinds of working-class and small-business people who come to churches like Shawmut River. Those alliances rest on common commitments to family obligations and the traditional gender roles in which they are cast. Such commitments are also a source of this conservatism's appeal to new immigrant groups such as those making up the United States' rapidly growing Latino population. These alliances across lines of class and ethnicity have been decisive in fueling the Republican Party's resurgence on the national scene, making it possible for it to wrest control of the New South from the Democratic Party and to take control of the House of Representatives for the first time in forty-five years.[13]

While these conservative alliances can be relatively firm around issues of family and gender, which furnish their greatest common currency and, therefore, voter power, they suffer from inherent strains and weaknesses. They may well diverge, for example, on issues of economic policy, social welfare or military interventions abroad. The fact that Frank Norris, the virulent anticommunist forebear of Shawmut River's fundamentalism, initially supported President Roosevelt's New Deal during the Depression reveals some of the spaces these differences open up. I also remember once listening to Frank and Sharon Valenti wrestling with the question of whether capitalism was truly part of the social order prescribed by God. They agreed that if God was for capitalism, it must be the kind of capitalism represented by a conservative couple they knew who owned and operated a small manufacturing plant next to their rural-suburban home. God did not have in mind, Frank and Sharon reckoned, corporate capitalism, which they judged to be impersonal, bureaucratic and liberal.[14]

But in any case, in terms of sheer numerical strength and voter power, it is small, often family-based business that gives popular political strength to conservative enthusiasms for free enterprise over and against government regulation. While small businesses like Phil and Jean Strongs' insulation company chafe under the paperwork required by growing government regulation, large corporations with permanent legal departments handle it more easily. And if there is one discovery made by historians of government regulation of business life, it is that from its very beginnings in the Progressive Era, regulation was spearheaded by large corporations themselves, who used it to make their own business environment more stable and predictable and to preserve their established place within it.[15]

Why new-right women insistently affirm traditional gender roles was one of the questions I originally set out to answer when I embarked on my field research. Events at Shawmut River showed that the traditional framework of gender embraced by fundamentalists as God's eternal plan for the family did provide mechanisms women used to pursue and defend their interests.

These powers were available to women in the kinds of families I found among other conservatives I met: in right-to-life groups in the Connecticut River Valley; in the Fourniers' Holy Family Academy; and in Parents for Traditional Values fighting sex education in Athol, Massachusetts. All lived or came of age within clusters of kin, even if sometimes small, in which these same powers rested on traditional gender roles, which carved out a sphere of women's activity just as they designated men head of household. Some were from working-class families. Others were in small businesses—from construction to private medical practice—all of which rooted them in particular localities. And a few grew up within the upper-class circles of a provincial city. Where the clusters of kin they lived among were small or weak, I could appreciate how the formation of larger family-based organizations championing traditional values—such as a fundamentalist Baptist church, an Orthodox Jewish synagogue or a homeschool collective—could strengthen family-based relationships among women and the powers such relationships held.

Shawmut River not only incorporated existing family ties but also gave kinship metaphors pride of place in its symbolic order. It helped its members create new, family-like ties of mutual dependence. And, underpinning all these relationships, its Bible-based moral discourse meshed effectively in form and substance with vital oral traditions elaborated across generations, while defending tradition in ways that appealed to the literate, scientific ethos of the day. It gave absolute sanction and meaning to a pattern of life they saw to be ordained by God. There could be nothing more valuable or desirable to the believer—no professional success and recognition, no living the good life of fine foods, pleasant vacations and educational experiences, no personal growth or self-understanding, no enjoyment of the paraphernalia or substance of power or prestige as displayed in the mass media—than living according to God's eternal plan for the family. That meant, above all else, the willingness to sacrifice self to meet obligations to others.

Within Shawmut River's vigorous oral tradition regulating life in church and home, women played key roles by virtue of their traditional place in families and family-based networks. My inquiry into the sources of the split at Shawmut River provided a glimpse of women's powers in such contexts and helped make sense of their commitment to traditional gender arrangements in the family. It brought that research project to a close.[16]

OUR FILM, *Born Again: Life in a Fundamentalist Baptist Church*, was to be televised on PBS, as a national prime-time special, in September 1987. It would go on to win significant awards and be broadcast in Britain, continental Europe and elsewhere around the world. As we put the finishing touches on it in New York City, I moved to San Diego, California, to be a visiting lecturer in sociology and ethnographic film at the San Diego campus of the University of California.

During this period, screening rough cuts and then our completed film with various audiences provided a fresh stream of lessons about how churches like Shawmut River were perceived. At a weeklong film festival in New York City, for instance, I hopped into a taxi to go to a festival event downtown with a newfound colleague from Munich. As an outsider to American politics, she confided in me with amused delight that "a lot of people have been talking about your film" and wanted to know, above all, "whether you are *for* born-again Christians or *against* them." Normally in film circles, a documentary that treats a matter of public controversy without betraying an evaluative standpoint would simply be praised as such, as some colleagues indeed did. But for others, this evenhandedness toward fundamentalists was cause for alarm and, in this case, talk behind the filmmaker's back. And this reaction came from people who in the next breath would castigate fundamentalists, above all, for insisting that the world be viewed in black-and-white terms. Experiences like this have taught me in what ways fundamentalism might be seen as an Achilles' heel of American liberalism, a point at which its ideals of tolerance often collapse.[17]

Conservatives themselves tend to see such intolerance as evidence of liberals' essential hypocrisy and bad faith. I am apt to see it, instead—in many cases, at least—as part of a pattern of misperception and misunderstanding that is as habitual as it is widespread in the liberal intelligentsia. One of the most frequent misunderstandings occurred at a screening of *Born Again* in a Presbyterian church in Albany, New York. "I respect *their* beliefs," one well-intentioned woman offered about members of Shawmut River portrayed in the film, "but I don't see them respecting *mine*." Such observations are often given as grounds for denying fundamentalists the same tolerance and civility accorded others.

But what she and other liberally minded people often do not realize is that rather than respecting fundamentalists' views, they are denying them by insisting that religious beliefs or ethical standards be seen as personal, private matters we must all tolerate in one another—that moral standards are relative, not absolute. Recall Sharon Valenti saying she could always pick out a secular humanist because he would soon say something that showed he did not believe in absolutes. In Sharon's observation, secular humanists did not proclaim these beliefs but, rather, took them for granted in what they said and did. "Their only absolute," as Frank Valenti once aptly remarked, "is that there are no absolutes."

I went on to point out to these Presbyterians that Shawmut River's commitment to absolutes was in keeping with the binding character they saw in the family obligations through which their world was organized. To see moral standards as personal and relative, on the other hand, widened the scope of individual autonomy and freedom in ways that denied and threatened to undermine lives that depended upon seeing family obligations as nondiscretionary—not as something individuals can choose or not choose, but as absolutes they have to accept. This commitment to absolutes, I said, does not preclude change, flexibility or the ability to deal with ambiguity on a practical level, which I found amply demonstrated at Shawmut River.

I cannot begin to count how many times I have had exchanges like this, in which an unwittingly prejudicial judgment is made even in the course of a well-intended, if not sympathetic, comment on conservative opponents. Such naively prejudicial remarks rankle and infuriate conservatives, who remain vigilantly on guard for them—at times, perhaps, like anyone facing routine prejudice, even too vigilantly on guard.

"What do you mean, you're not pushing a philosophy?" Sharon exploded in the interview we filmed with her, when I suggested that some people would criticize her for imposing her views on others. "You know, true, you're *unbiased*," she said, catching her breath. "You're unbiased for the homosexual movement, you're unbiased for women's rights, you're unbiased for any kind of immorality. That's right. You're very—what you'd call 'open-minded,'" she said, holding her fingers up in quotation marks of irony, "except for the Christian principles. There *is* a philosophy being pushed!" she declared.

The experience of being judged *intolerant* by someone who denies your own values while implicitly imposing her own is just one among many sources of resentment that routinely undermine trust and civility in even the most well-intentioned efforts at dialogue between conservatives and liberals. It feeds the righteous indignation that pundits like Rush Limbaugh tap to heap scorn on liberals. But, we should note, conservatives' anger at being judged intolerant betrays the value they recognize in *genuine* tolerance—that is, one not presuming liberal, secular, morally relativist assumptions, and where their distinct views are at least recognized.

Though our film *Born Again* received universally positive reviews, certain responses disappointed and concerned me. One tendency I noticed among some journalists and academics was to see the story of Sam Strong and others to be essentially about people suffering from "social isolation," as one put it, and trying to find some therapy-like handles on life. To see Sam as socially isolated—despite the film's depiction of his brother's continual efforts to see him saved and still photos placing both brothers in the church's "largest family," made up of fourteen adults plus children—seemed further evidence of how stubbornly urbane intellectuals could project their assumptions about family realities onto others.[18]

Another response to *Born Again* that grieved me came from a fellow sociologist reviewing it for a major journal in our profession, even though I appreciated much he had to say. Though praising our film, he judged its subjects not to be articulate—to suffer from what he called "symbolic impoverishment" and "inner poverty." It outraged me that a colleague could judge as inarticulate and symbolically impoverished a person like Frank Valenti, who described a hospital emergency room as a "body shop" and shrapnel tearing into him in Vietnam as "a wind of lead," or Jean Strong, who spoke of men and women as "fractions with different denominators"—and on top of that, to do so in such jargon-clogged prose with which he went on to describe Shawmut River's members as "an emotionally restrained but socially casual, moralizing faction located somewhere toward the center of American society in the lower-middle and upper-working class. . . ." (Now who is symbolically impoverished here?)[19]

But this reviewer was simply reflecting misperceptions found more widely in academia. Looking back on my own experience, I remember what unlikely events first alerted me to Frank Valenti's remarkable intelligence: for example, his instructions on my golf swing the summer after we first met—in a sport he had just taken up—or his sizing up the human tragedies in a hospital emergency room one afternoon. Why hadn't his intelligence been crystal clear to me right away?

Shawmut River's metaphoric narrative and deeply implicit ways of grasping social life are worlds apart from those prevailing in academia, which give pride of place to knowledge cast in explicit generalizations constructed with abstract categories. Expressed in terms that make the identity of speaker and hearer seem irrelevant, academic discourse is more at home in the written, rather than spoken, word, where its meanings are presented so that anyone, even a stranger removed in time and place, can presumably understand them. Anyone who spends time in educated circles becomes accustomed to this form—this idiom—of knowledge. But it is wrong and practically misleading to mistake it for intelligence, articulateness or symbolic riches *in general*. This is an error deeply embedded in American intellectual culture, manifest in everything from intelligence testing to social theories judging moral or theological thought *not* taking the form of abstract, general principles to represent a lower stage of human development.[20] Such assumptions are deeply rooted in the Western intelligentsia's perceptual framework and do grave disservice to the vast majority of humankind from Worcester to Accra, who live villagelike lives in city or countryside and know and communicate things, by and large, in different ways. "We speak of the 'inarticulate masses,'" I remember my teacher and mentor, the sociologist Egon Bittner, once saying to us students with a bemused sparkle in his eyes as he held his fingers up in quotation marks of irony around that phrase commonly heard among progressive scholars at the time. "They're not inarticulate," he observed. "We just don't know how to communicate with them."

2 2

"But what about you?"

R EACTIONS TO OUR FILM *Born Again* held other telling surprises, some with personal consequences for me and, I would
later learn, the Valentis. When I first showed my parents some sequences
we had edited, including scenes of a group praying in Pastor Valenti's
study, I was shocked when my mother exclaimed with a laugh, "They
pray just like the church I grew up in! You know, 'We just thank you,
Jesus' or 'We just praise your holy name.'" She beamed to recall it.

It was in her hometown of Bethlehem, Pennsylvania, a city of sixty
thousand, where she had been born into a pious Pennsylvania Dutch
family of German, Dutch and Scottish extraction. Her church, the
Emmanuel United Evangelical Congregational Church, was part
of the Atlantic Conference of the Evangelical Church, a German-
founded sect, some of whose congregations later joined the Evangelical United Brethren, which eventually merged with Methodism. (Her
own congregation was too conservative for either of those associations
and remained independent.) Revisiting the neighborhood of her childhood several years later, I learned that her grandmother, aunts and
cousins had all attended the same church located in the densely settled
streets of brick town houses where they all lived in close proximity to
one another. It was enough of an ethnic community that when my
mother, as a teenager, moved to a new town, her peers made fun of her
German accent and forms of speech.

But my mother's conservative evangelical heritage was not sustained by the life she went on to lead, beginning with her own family's
move to Sayre, Pennsylvania, a railroad town of some five thousand,
where the family settled into the local Methodist church and she met
my father. The small-town Methodism of the Sayre church, however,

was not too far removed from her own family's tradition. During those Depression years, for example, its youth group, with my father as president, hosted an appearance by Billy Sunday's former musical partner, Homer Rodeheaver. My father, with strong roots in farm families around Sayre, was traditionally minded about family and gender (though in time he became a firm supporter of women's liberation). But as the son of a railroad worker victimized for trade union organizing during the Depression, he and most of his family remained lifelong New Deal Democrats.

After World War Two, when I was born, our small family moved from place to place, first, for my father's college and graduate education and, later, for the various churches my parents served, adding two daughters and another son along the way. During the tumultuous sixties and seventies, my parents lived in divinity schools, first at Union Theological Seminary in New York City and then at Drew University, where my mother participated in a feminist women's group. Later, as the wife of a Methodist bishop in charge of that denomination's missions around the globe, she traveled the world, visiting local churches from Zimbabwe to China. Through these experiences, my mother had taken on an expansive liberalism—and feminism—which made me forget what I had dimly known growing up: My mother had conservative evangelical roots.

My mother's revelations shed light on my own impulse to better understand this kind of conservatism in American life. It was rooted, I now understood, in unconscious sympathies taking shape in my own family caught up in the crucible of change in postwar America. My mother's mother—dear "Nana" to us children and one of the kindest, most sensible people I have ever known—retained much of her biblical conservatism. She was one of those people, for example, who continued to give Richard Nixon the benefit of the doubt when he claimed, after the Watergate tapes had been released showing his complicity in those crimes, that *only he* knew what he meant by what he said on those tapes. Now my mother reported attending annual conferences of the United Methodist Church where she walked past knots of members of Good News (that denomination's conservative group), who prayed, she noted, just like members of Shawmut River. Yet many of those conservatives probably now saw her and my father as part of the problems plaguing their denomination. What would she and my father think of our film?

The Valentis' response to *Born Again* carried its own surprises. I sent them a videocassette of the finished film in Florida. When they had not called back after several days, I began to worry. Finally Frank phoned. "It was like culture shock," he began. It was not at all what they had expected. Despite what we had communicated about the stories we were following, they had still expected a film covering all their ministries—choir, school, home Bible studies, Easter Cantata, etc.— almost in home-movie fashion. And though they saw the story of Sam's getting saved as triumphant, they regretted the prominence played by the story of Ben and Pam's failed marriage. It was not one of the numerous success stories they could point to of God's saving a marriage by spouses following his guidelines in scripture.

Furthermore, Frank regretted, as did I, that it was not clear from the film why he had refused to let Pam see her children at church (see above, p. 263). On this and other counts, the Valentis worried that their church might be viewed as a "cult"—that is, a church that exercised coercive power over its members. They were, therefore, much relieved to see the film show Frank *asking*, rather than ordering, Pam to leave her boyfriend and to attend *any* Bible-believing church, not necessarily theirs. And they were pleased to see that while Pam criticized Frank for not praying before one of their meetings, the film showed him praying before the one we filmed.

I was impressed by how carefully the Valentis and Sharon's parents had watched the film. In the end, Frank said, they appreciated the approach we had taken, instead of the survey of ministries they had expected. "The film showed three or four families whose lives had been changed by Christ," he said, "trying to help others find the same solution to their problems. Christ was at the center, not our ministries, and that was the right decision."

For her part, Sharon said she had winced at some of the language Frank used in counseling, telling Ben at one moment, for example, that he was "talkin' like an idiot." She had worried all along that their church "might come across as Hicksville," as she put it. But, she admitted, "I got into the stories and was pleased, all in all, with Frank's counseling."

Soon thereafter we took the film to Worcester to show it, first privately, to our main characters, and then to the congregation as a whole. Pam watched it over her ironing. She seemed satisfied with our portrayal of her story but, when Ben appeared on-screen, stopped everything to rail against him. Ben reacted similarly. Looking back on the whole experience, Ben said he had "gained strength" from church and from God but was disappointed with the outcome of his marriage. "The only thing I know for sure," he said, "is that I have to love my children as much as I can, love my family as much as I can—and my friends—and give people respect. That's the only thing that's concrete to me now."

When Sam saw *Born Again*, he looked up after the closing credits and grinned. "You know," he said, "I felt like I died when the film ended."

When we screened the film for the whole congregation, they reacted with gusto, laughing, crying and clapping enthusiastically at the end. It was gratifying to feel them transported by the stories. Afterward I found Sam talking with Ben in the back of the sanctuary. They had never met before but were in the midst of conversation. Sam was telling Ben that, given the changes he had gone through, if he ever experienced such pain again, it would not be as hard to survive. In the midst of our three-way conversation, Sam then turned to me and repeated his recurring question: "But what about you? What's it mean for you?" I said I would have to wait until this project was behind me.

MONTHS LATER, the week before *Born Again*'s national broadcast, I was in New York City, serving as a Visiting Scholar at Trinity Church, an Episcopal church on Wall Street in downtown Manhattan, where I occupied an apartment over the residence of a group of Episcopal nuns. PBS flew Pastor Valenti up from Florida to tape a segment of *Sonya Live*, a CNN talk show. The night before, Frank and I attended Sunday-evening services at a fundamentalist Baptist church in the South Bronx, whose pastor, a Greek-American trained at Liberty Baptist College, had given Frank a place to stay. I was surprised to find such a multiracial congregation in a Moral Majority church, and afterward, at a bustling Greek diner whose owner greeted our host like family, Frank marveled at how the Lord had brought together such different kinds of people to serve his kingdom.

The next morning at CNN's studios in midtown Manhattan, the woman attending to us in the makeup room introduced herself discreetly as a Christian and prayed for us as she sent us out onto the set. Sonya, the talk-show host, speaking to us on a monitor from Los

Angeles, asked Pastor Valenti pointedly what his church taught its children about how they should relate to people who were not born-again Christians. Frank replied that "they need to reach out to them and that they need to love them. . . . Although we're commanded to change people, we are also commanded to tolerate them." Afterward we met my codirector, Michael Camerini, for lunch at an Italian restaurant nearby, and in the prayer Frank offered to bless our food he thanked the Lord for "bringing together such opposed philosophies to make this film."

The Sunday before I left New York to return home to San Diego, I decided to attend one worship service at Trinity Church, in part as a gesture of gratitude for the warm hospitality parishioners had shown me. That week I had learned by phone that a woman I was involved with in San Diego had decided to end our relationship, having realized she did not want to be tied down with commitments just when her career was taking off. I was brokenhearted. Trinity's celebration of the Eucharist, with a train of robed celebrants bearing a cross, flags and incense, parading up and down the aisles of its magnificent sanctuary, was as foreign to me as anything at Shawmut River. Yet as we sang a familiar Protestant hymn to accompany this joyous parade, I was over-whelmed by feelings of reassurance amid my pain and sadness and I broke into tears. A trembling union of alienation and reconciliation came over me. I regained my composure, but that chorus of feelings stayed with me the rest of that day, like the reassuring sound of the surf on some nearby beach.

When I returned to San Diego that week, I found a letter awaiting me from the Reverend Alan Collister, pastor of the Community Church of San Diego. He had seen *Born Again* on television and wrote simply to thank me for my "good work" and for "the somewhat un-usual sensitivity and respect with which you treated one of our sister congregations." He described himself and his wife as Berkeley grads who wanted to bring "the tools Berkeley offered into the church," believing that "here is where the real, essential things are taking place." (At Berkeley he had studied engineering.)

"The church here," he said of San Diego, "is practically invisible except to people we touch individually. We meet in a YMCA, for example, while scores of similar churches here in town are meeting in schools. My father, and his, were ministers in mainline denominations. But the truth is, the message they preached has much more in common with what we preach in our little churches than it does with the message of the Methodist or Presbyterian churches they served. The visible churches have changed," he concluded, "but the believing church has continued on, sometimes in new clothing."

Collister's letter was a breath of fresh air, unlike some disappointing responses our film received from members of the conservative evangelical establishment. Though admitting they found *Born Again* engaging, true to life and unbiased, some were nevertheless unenthusiastic. They wished a better version of Christianity had been put forward to the public. They usually had in mind a more polished, sophisticated one—like their own.

I was grateful, then, for Reverend Collister's letter, and in the weeks that followed, I called him, curious to see what his and the "scores of other little churches" meeting in YMCAs and schools across San Diego County were like. We met for lunch at Denny's in La Jolla, and in the parking lot afterward he asked me, in his gentle, unassuming way, whether he might pray with me. My years at Shawmut River had accustomed me to pause anywhere in the highways and byways of life to pray aloud, and on this occasion I welcomed it.

And as the weeks and months unfolded, I found myself turning more and more to God. The process was not smooth. It was racked by recurring doubts at times so severe that I once cried out to God for a sign that he really existed, that he was there. I was not disappointed. I realized I was a believing person again and began what would become, over the next decade and beyond, the slow, halting process of learning how to relate to God.

April 12, 1988
La Jolla, California

My parents flew across the country from Pennsylvania to spend Easter weekend with me. The night before Easter Sunday we attended a communion service at a large United Methodist Church my father knew, and the next morning we went to worship at Reverend Collister's Community Church of San Diego, which I had begun attending. About a hundred and twenty members gathered each Sunday at a YMCA building for worship. The church kept offices in a small commercial building not far away.

Community Church was more liberal than Shawmut River in many respects. Its music was organized by a gifted young composer of contemporary classical music with a Ph.D. from the University of California-San Diego's well-regarded program in modern music. But it was decidedly conservative on family issues and could be called "conservative evangelical." It was made up largely of families who had moved to San Diego from other parts of the country (except, among others, a Mexican-American San Diegan married to an Anglo woman). Some were from traditional backgrounds in the Midwest, the South and elsewhere, including one family from the Isle of Wight off England's coast. Several of its other families were made up of Asian women married to white Americans, and another family was a Nigerian married to a white American.

At the end of a long, pleasant weekend together, my parents and I were having a bite to eat in the snug kitchen of my apartment in La Jolla before I drove them to the airport. Thinking about *Born Again*'s portrayal of Shawmut River, my mother said simply, "I'm glad you didn't make fun of them. It would have been easy to do," she said, perhaps remembering similar prejudices she encountered in life, "and you didn't."

Then my father, in his characteristic ministerial manner, sought to sum up our weekend in so many words. "Your mother and I have had a wonderful time this weekend with all the things we've done," he said, eyeing me kindly and recalling some of our outings. "But I can't tell you what a moving experience it was for me to take communion with you the other night. I can't remember the last time we did that." Tears welled up in his eyes, and he was choked with emotion. My mother eyed us both without saying a word.

It was an emotional moment and took me totally by surprise. Afterward I realized that over the past twenty years my parents had spared me from ever feeling there was anything wanting or unfulfilled in our relationship, anything that could separate me from their unconditional love. When I eventually had a child of my own, I realized that this is the kind of love parents can have for a child. Like faith in God, perhaps, it is impossible to understand without experiencing it.

A close friend and colleague, an African-American woman, once warned me that the academy would never forgive me for admitting that my experience at Shawmut River had led to my becoming a Christian. Even though the breakthrough to faith came after my time at

Shawmut River—first in Trinity Church's almost regal setting on Wall Street and then in Reverend Collister's plain nondenominational church meeting in a YMCA where I was baptized in the swimming pool out back—it was, above all, my years at Shawmut River that had awakened my senses to God's presence and had encouraged me, and given me ways, to relate to God. The years I spent with its members sharing our problems and needs as we put them to God in prayer, hearing daily reminders of God's work in one another's lives and experiencing the congregation's care and support in Christ's name, as I faced my own difficulties in life, had prepared the crucial groundwork. But on second thought, my colleague reasoned, the academy might not judge me so harshly, because my conversion *did*, after all, represent a return to my parents' heritage and my childhood faith. And if it had not?

The summer following my parents' visit, I hosted a screening of *Born Again* at the annual meeting of the American Sociological Association. It happened to be scheduled at the same time, I noticed, as a meeting of the Christian Sociological Association, a group I had never heard of. Out of curiosity and desire to promote our film, I left the screening once the projector was running and made my way to the hotel room where its meeting had begun.

I found thirty or so sociologists, young and old, women and men, sitting in a circle sharing "war stories" about how and when colleagues had learned they were Christians and the variety of reactions they had encountered. The reactions they reported were often disapproving, even hostile. As the meeting broke up, one bright young Korean-American woman told me reassuringly, yet in a hushed, discreet way, that she even knew a well-regarded professor at an Ivy League institution who was "a believer."[1]

My own peculiar path to Christian faith, however, is not without sociological import, for the sociological framework I used to understand the conservatism of members of Shawmut River (as well as other new-right activists from a variety of religious backgrounds) enabled me to appreciate the truths of their faith apart from their traditionalism or conservatism, neither of which I felt compelled to accept. My sociological perspective was also critical in keeping me from dismissing their experiences as totally removed from my own. It kept me from seeing in their words and deeds a hopeless illogic, for example, or an incapacity to deal with change or ambiguity—in short, as less human than I or my friends and associates. Instead, it helped me see and appreciate in them all these human qualities in fresh and, at times, impressive abundance.

My sociological framework had also met other practical tests persuading me of its usefulness and, hence, validity. In helping me see coherence and integrity where others saw illogic and hypocrisy, it was essential in winning the trust of Shawmut River's leaders for an extraordinarily intimate documentary about their congregation for national public television. For even though Sharon had confessed she "never knew" where I stood on things, she had decided to go forward with the film anyway because, she felt, "somehow I think you understand."

"But where *do* you stand on these things?" readers may well ask, as did Sharon and Frank when I saw them recently. Soon after finishing *Born Again*, I developed a film project that, if funded, would have told the story of bringing a group of fundamentalists and right-to-lifers together with a group of feminists and progressives for three days of sailing and conversation on board a schooner off the coast of New England. "Will there be enough life jackets?" a lesbian-feminist colleague recruited to the project asked half jokingly. Others from both camps expressed similar fears about being at sea with their enemies. The project's strategy was to organize their experience together— especially through conversations orchestrated to reveal common human experiences against the background of their quite different lives—in order to make evident to them and viewers alike that their enemies saw things differently because they started with different *assumptions* about life and had different assumptions about life because they, in fact, had different *lives*.[2]

Sharon, too, was uncomfortable with the prospect of being in close proximity to those who disagreed so sharply with her. But after thinking about it, she agreed to participate because, as she concluded, "understanding doesn't mean accepting, does it?"

It doesn't, I agreed. But if you do come to understand, as I did, that your opponents' views make sense and have a validity in lives that work quite differently from your own, that understanding gives you a new political standpoint. For one thing, you cannot then dismiss their claims as irrelevant or inhumane. You cannot see, for example, their opposition to state welfare as a reflection of their mean-spiritedness or incapacity to give. Or their insistence on moral absolutes as a consequence of their fear of change, or of their incapacity to deal with it. And you cannot see their ideas about authority in church and family as "oppressive to women" in all circumstances. For the women at Shaw-mut River found their fundamentalist Christianity "liberating" and saw contemporary feminism as potentially debilitating.[3]

For my part, seeing the conservative pro-family movement as an effort to defend a life lived through family obligations within a family circle by creating supportive conditions for it in the wider culture, I cannot ally myself with political efforts that would deny the interests of my conservative friends or exclude them from a place at the table of public life. It would be not only unjust but also imprudent, given how widespread their way of life, with its traditionalist outlook, is in America, and what positive human values it sustains.

When my mother recently attended her high-school reunion in Pennsylvania for the first time in many years, she was astonished by how many of her classmates still lived in the same area, within easy reach of their families. I know other friends and colleagues who have experienced similar surprises. However stereotyped or idealized some images of traditional family life might be in the hands of conservative ideologists, the forms of family life they seek to defend are not bygone realities, a figment of either a sinisterly manipulative or self-deluded imagination. Nor do they exist solely in the realm of worldviews, values or common culture. Instead, they are embodied in the concrete, practical organization of daily life. The fact that recent surveys show that 45 percent of all American preschool children are regularly cared for by grandparents or other relatives when their parents are working or otherwise unavailable (compared to only 30 percent in all preschool, kindergarten and day-care facilities combined) attests to the enduring significance of ties of reciprocal obligation among kin in contemporary America.[4]

That we in the liberal intelligentsia are so unaware of the extent of such patterns is one reason we are so surprised when fundamentalist Christianity suddenly reappears in public life, when political initiatives we see as sensible and right-minded are soundly defeated by our fellow voters or when we discover that so many of our high-school class still live near home. In general, we have little awareness of how limited our kind of living is. But for every Cambridge, Ann Arbor or Berkeley, there are dozens of Woburns, Toledos and Oxnards. (And that is not even considering the South.) And even in our favored haunts, we can be easily surprised when traditionalists vote down even mildly progressive measures.

My own town of Northampton, Massachusetts, is a case in point. A county seat and college town of just under thirty thousand in close proximity to other colleges and the University of Massachusetts, it has experienced a large influx of affluent (and not so affluent) professional people over the past twenty-five years and became nationally known for its large lesbian community. Yet in 1995 supporters of a modest same-sex partnership ordinance for the municipality were stunned when their measure was repealed at the polls. Everyone *they* knew and talked to supported it. Much opposition came from longer-term residents, who continued to live within the orbit of family-based networks, like a dental assistant I spoke with while having work done on my teeth. When she remarked offhandedly that she enjoyed still living with her parents right next to the homes of her brother's and sister's families on the same street, I mentioned I was writing a book about the differences between that kind of life and the lives of the professional people moving to Northampton who did not live in daily contact with their relatives.

"I see that as a selfish life," she said curtly and without a moment's hesitation. When I contacted her months later to ask what she had felt about the same-sex ordinance, she said she felt tolerance, even affection, for some gay couples she knew and worked with, but she did not think they should be treated as married couples. "A man/woman— that's a marriage," she said simply.

I also recall a conversation I recently fell into by chance with a bright high-school student who pumps gas for me. "I wish I could move to a town where there aren't so many freaks around," he said quite spontaneously, referring to Northampton. He told me his ancestors had come here from Poland and settled, as many did in the late nineteenth century, but somewhere along the way they had become Congregationalists. "Newcomers took over our church," he said of the first Congregational church downtown. "Now it's just a political organization, a center for feminist activism," he said, shaking his head. "You can't hear the Bible preached there anymore." His family now attends another Congregational church nearby, which is affiliated not with the mainline United Church of Christ but with the more loosely knit and conservative National Association of Congregational Christian Churches, headquartered in Oak Creek, Wisconsin.

Furthermore, when I look back over events in the past twenty years, I think it can be said that the conservatism I encountered at

Shawmut River in the mid-1980s has made significant contributions to American life as a whole, however one might evaluate them. For some of the ideas the Valentis and others hammered at in the mid-1980s, which appeared radical and extremist at the time, have since then become respectable preoccupations in mainstream discussion. To cite just a few examples: *Harper's*, a long-standing journal of mainstream liberalism, convened a group of scholars in 1990 to discuss whether our nation needed a "Bill of Duties" to counter ways in which our "expansive talk of individual rights" might be undermining "our notions of obligation and community"; the educational establishment dusted off old-fashioned notions such as "character" and "virtue" as vital things to be taught from kindergarten through college; a liberal Democratic president, Bill Clinton, recast his campaign in terms of family values and then presided over dismantling the federal welfare state; and mainstream social commentators showed a newfound willingness to face more squarely the deleterious effects of divorce on children, as the *New York Times* declared that "the idea of working at marriage is now in vogue." Even the recently identified "southernization of America" and the meteoric rise of country music as a mainstream—even *urban*—phenomenon can be seen as manifestations of a broad-based turn in our culture toward values at the heart of the popular foundations of new-right conservatism.[5]

And as the new Christian right moved into the mainstream of American politics, helping the Republican Party capture control of the House of Representatives for the first time in forty-five years, coalition building came to replace the rougher-edged radicalism of its first generation. Placing a premium on greater respectability, tact and a willingness to compromise, it ushered in a new style of leadership, replacing Jerry Falwell, with his bold claims to represent the "Moral Majority" (versus an implied immoral minority), with Pat Robertson, Ralph Reed and their Christian Coalition. Jerry Falwell even retired from politics. This shift was also manifest, at the grassroots level, among members of Shawmut River. While Frank and Sharon Valenti, radical thinkers holding fast to hard-edged principles, dropped out of politics altogether, Phil Strong, the pragmatic businessman and one-time candidate for public office, became an active board member of the Christian Coalition's Massachusetts chapter. "It's a mixture type of thing," Phil explained about working with charismatic Christians, drawing on the distinction between chemical compounds and mixtures to explain that you can keep your identity as a true fundamentalist while working with Pentecostals.

That new-right concerns have filtered into mainstream American life, becoming part and parcel of how Americans perceive and address problems they face, suggests the relevance of this kind of conservatism to the American people, its capacity to address and meet their needs. If it did not, how could it have been such a recurring feature of American politics over the past century, cresting in pendulum-like swings from the "gay nineties" and the emergence of fundamentalist Christianity at the end of the nineteenth century to the roaring twenties, setting off conflicts over divorce, the "flapper" and teaching evolution, and down to the upheavals of the 1960s, bringing forth conservative reaction in figures from George Wallace to Pat Robertson?

Fundamentalism and the New Right, along with feminism and the New Left, are part of a distinctly American pattern of conflict. While many foreigners look upon our national debates over abortion, sex education and the like with bemused wonderment, as if gazing at the bizarre rites of an aboriginal tribe, we Americans—at least white Americans—often feel them bone deep, setting off in us a panoply of all-too-familiar reflex reactions.

Seeing new-right conservatism as an effort to demand that Americans stiffen their resolve to meet family and family-like obligations even at the expense of individual freedom helps us understand why this has been a distinctly American pattern of conflict and an integral part of American culture. With the restless mobility of a people who originally left home for a new life, and acted out this leaving again and again as westward-moving pioneers in a new land, no other advanced industrial nation has loosened more greatly the ties binding individuals to communities of place or kin. American life has thereby provided, perhaps, the greatest scope for individual freedom of any nation on Earth. That freedom has been carried furthest, perhaps, by salaried professionals, who move from place to place for training and specialized employment and whose salaries afford them the kind of financial security permitting them, at least in good times, to live autonomously, free from ties of reciprocity and mutual dependence. And it has been the urban middle class that gave rise to the "New Woman" in the 1890s and the "flapper" of the 1920s, who took up office employment and made their way as single women in the metropolises of the new industrial order. And in later generations, it was the salaried middle class that became the principal carrier of the New Left and the women's liberation movement of the 1960s and 1970s, whose collective ideals imagined individuals, rather than families, as the starting point for their efforts to organize for social change.[6]

Americans most embroiled in conflicts between conservatism and liberalism are often stalked by the specter of their opponents completely taking over: for liberals, the lockstep uniformity of a theocratic state; for conservatives, the Brave New World of Big Government. But it never comes to pass. These nightmares of enemy domination generally serve to galvanize the commitments of partisans. So, too, does summoning up heinous acts of the enemy—bombing abortion clinics or killing doctors known for performing abortions. But these acts, like the violence of the Weathermen on the New Left in the sixties, are the work of a small number of individuals on the fringe and are, in my experience, deplored by the vast majority of supporters, however much they might be reluctant to add to the chorus of condemnation such acts provoke against their cause.

Contrary to the views of sociologist James Hunter, published more than a decade ago, I believe neither side will win, or can win, the so-called culture wars.[7] Each side depends too intimately on its enemies for its thought, sensibility and practice—for its very identity. What would long hair and beads have meant in the sixties, for example, without the order of gender of the fifties with its models of Ike and Mamie Eisenhower? What sense would fundamentalist uses of scripture to "prove" God's plan for the family make without the proliferation of scientific rationalizations of family and gender embodied, say, in psychology, feminism or sociology? Or how would the voluntariness of fundamentalist congregations work, enabling members to pick up and leave when they choose, without commitments to individual freedom and dignity deeply rooted in American culture? Neither side is interested in abolishing human freedoms. The struggle between them has to do with how much such a radical degree of individual freedom, in world-historic terms, is to be reconciled with community life based on ties of a binding nature underwritten by tradition. And the focal point of these conflicts has been the institution of the family. Even the fact that Second Wave Feminism in the 1960s and 1970s defined itself in terms of its challenge to gender roles in the family, not simply in the marketplace or public life, correctly targeted the point of greatest conflict and resistance.

Rather than becoming increasingly polarized until one dominates the other, I suspect that one side will grow in power and influence, as conservatives have since the mid-1970s, spreading their influence more deeply and widely throughout the body politic, until the American public, tired of hearing the same songs—and perhaps needing them less—will readily turn its ear again to songs composed in the key of individual freedom. Like a seesaw, the weight of our culture will swing yet again one way, then the other, from renewed visions of individual freedom to a restored sense of obligations that bind. Only when threatened from without, as we have been recently with the specter of international terrorism, do we suddenly sense and pay attention to the considerable common ground we share.

A more realistic danger, I believe, lies in the way these morally charged conflicts can paralyze our nation's efforts to grapple with the pressing problems we face: the need to reform education, health care and welfare; to protect the earth; to limit crime and create a firmer basis of civic order; to avoid the perils and realize the promise of an increasingly multicultural society fueled by unprecedented immigration and to help create new forms of peace in a rapidly changing world prone to explosive conflicts based on primordial loyalties to tribe, ethnicity and religion. It becomes impossible to address any of these problems in straightforward, pragmatic ways when these issues inevitably churn up such radically opposed and mutually hostile value commitments. The moral indignation each side feels on seeing its opponents ready to tear down everything they themselves see as good and just supports an unending chain of vindictive acts and resentments, ripping apart attempts at cooperation, compromise and even communication.

Moreover, the preoccupation of many Americans with tallying up what "we" or "they" get, often figured in symbolic rather than practical terms, or with bringing down public figures solely because of what they represent on this moral battleground, stands to undermine creative, sensible, practical approaches to all the pressing problems we face as a nation, internationally as well as domestically. There is too much at stake, and Americans have too prominent a role in world affairs—for better or worse—to have our hands tied politically in these ways, especially when we might otherwise understand, as suggested here, the meaningfulness, if not good sense, of our opponents' views.[8]

Our collective paralysis, of course, is most powerful and intransigent around issues directly colored by these moral conflicts. Efforts to educate youth about AIDS, for example, are routinely undermined by bitter conflicts about what values are embedded in sex education curricula designed for schools.[9] Or, to take another example, many conservatives, as outdoor enthusiasts (like Frank Valenti) have a natural interest in preserving the environment. But when ecological initiatives are tied to the creation of new federal bureaucracies that, as a sign of their authority, create walkways, signs and fences, as well as a host of regulations, extending bureaucratic civilization into nature, or when these initiatives betray a moral bias, say, against hunting, they alienate much potential support among conservatives. Nevertheless, on environmental issues it is not hard to imagine how compromise might be achieved by appealing to higher common goals.

"Compromise," I can almost hear my liberal colleagues exhale hotly. "*They* are incapable of compromise! They see everything in black and white!" Timeless absolutes, of course, permit no compromise—in principle. (Neither do the abstract principles defining radical groups, we might add.) But in practice, communities like Shawmut River permit a supple flexibility providing scope for tolerance, adjustment and actual change—and, hence, de facto compromise. But the form such compromises take, and the art of politics they require, differ in communities governed by oral tradition from ones governed by formal democracy, impersonal bureaucracy and the written word.

Consider abortion, for example, the issue most used as a litmus test of commitments to one side or another in this family of disputes. It presents itself from both sides as admitting no compromise. Yet I met right-to-lifers whose family members, or they themselves, had had abortions yet had not thereby been marked or condemned by pro-life activists as murderers. At the same time, most pro-choice activists argue that abortion must not be taken lightly but, instead, be weighed against countervailing wrongs: an unwanted child, a child with a birth defect, a threat to a mother's life, etc. Why weigh it against anything if it is just a naked right and does not amount to taking a life?

In one of the most insightful studies of the abortion controversy, sociologist Kristin Luker pointed out that one of the first movements to establish abortion as a woman's right arose in California, where safe, hospital-based abortions were already practically available to any woman who wanted one (and could afford it). It had to be approved, however, by a hospital committee, which, except where it would endanger the woman, granted the operation pro forma. Abortion was available, then, but not as a publicly heralded individual right, and a movement arose to make it one.[10]

Even on this issue, then, writ in morally absolute terms, there seems to be space for compromise. But it would have to be artfully pursued, bearing in mind not only the discourse of legislative and legal bureaucracy, but also the discourse and politics of tradition. Compromise would also have to be negotiated across the treacherous terrain of potential miscommunication and misperception in which innocent and well-intended remarks could easily be taken as demeaning attacks or deceptive ploys.

It is beyond the scope of this book to set forth how in this or that area of moral controversy we might fashion workable compromises by imagining potentially productive approaches and ways to wisely avoid the pitfalls they hold. Or how we might simply address more effectively a host of issues we face, including international ones, without being held hostage to such morally divisive conflicts. Rather than setting forth potential answers to these and other practical questions, I hope this book will provide readers with at least some fresh angles of vision to address the political impasse of moral conflict in which we find ourselves. I hope it might help some discover new ways of opening up discussion, as well as new capacities to listen more patiently, carefully, intelligently—even generously—to our opponents, and in our various efforts and experiments find ways to move forward.

My years with members of Shawmut River, and the friendship and colleagueship we have enjoyed, have demonstrated to me the possibilities of finding common ground on which to build and resolve even the most intractable problems. When not defending themselves against those whose words and deeds repudiate and demean them, even if unintentionally, members of Shawmut River showed themselves consistently to be responsible, caring, tolerant people, responsive to human need. Even in the face of daunting crisis and change, they showed themselves able to grow and mature. I have been enriched immeasurably by my time with them, in addition to the spiritual awakening it brought. They taught me much, I now see, about the patience involved in parenting, about the care with which human quarrels need to be addressed, and about the value, goodness, joy and fun of simply passing time together. When I was with them most while shooting our film, their influence as a moral community penetrated even to my most habitual actions and influenced me permanently for the better.

In addition, my time with them helped me better understand my own life and the lives of friends and colleagues in the professional middle class—our ways of grasping life and the kinds of blinders it sometimes imposes as we look upon others. In documentary-film projects in varied settings, from African-American, Latino and African communities, on the one hand, to the largely white upper-class trustees of an elite southern university, on the other, those understandings helped me enter into those worlds more fully and relate to characters in them more effectively.[11]

And if at times in their own relationships members of Shawmut River showed a capacity for impatience, pride, self-justifying distortions of truth and perhaps even hate, how were they any different in this regard from other human communities I have known, such as academic departments, new-left collectives and mainline churches? To be sure, these unenviable qualities, most strongly felt in events surrounding Shawmut River's split, assumed their own distinct forms. In a close-knit, independent congregation where members treat one another like family, open conflict was seen as personal betrayal, indirect ways of handling differences were preferred and shaping legitimacy through talk was a crucial means of struggle. These kinds of struggles leading to splits and splinter groups are not unique to Shawmut River but are endemic in these kinds of churches. It is also worth noting that these painful conflicts were part of a political process that saw Shawmut River through a difficult and awkward transition from an energetic founding pastor and his family to a new regime, all without the assistance of any higher organizational authority to adjudicate. And through all those bitter conflicts none of those centrally involved was destroyed. Instead, as time would tell, all went on to grow, change and prosper.

In any event, members of Shawmut River would have no trouble accepting their own human failings—theoretically, at least—for they represent a central Christian teaching they firmly avow: that we carry God's gifts in "earthen vessels," irremediably flawed, fragile and weak; that as human beings we cannot escape the lifelong tendency to do wrong—even to fail those we love most, let alone our enemies—the lifelong struggle, as they would put it, between the spirit and the flesh.

Epilogue

I REMEMBER MY FIRST VISIT to the Valentis' home on the Florida panhandle, where they have lived for the past fifteen years. It was the summer after *Born Again* was broadcast nationally on PBS, in 1987, and was the first of a half-dozen face-to-face visits and innumerable telephone conversations we have had since then. Their home was situated on a lake in a new suburban development. It was spacious and well appointed, and behind it, overlooking the lake, they had put in a pool and patio bordered by flowers and a picket fence. Frank took pride in the craftsmanship he put into these and other home improvements. He liked building and had time on his hands. I had been surprised to hear he had recently dropped out of the doctoral program in Christian education at a local Bible college after finishing only his master's degree. Only several years later did I learn why, when it came up quite by accident.

"I wasn't going to tell you this," Frank said, "but I will. You can put it in your book if you like." When *Born Again* aired, he explained, someone at his college taped it and showed it privately to a group of faculty and staff. They took offense, he said, at how some of Shawmut River's teenagers came across: their passing notes in class, perhaps, and the fresh insubordination they showed in one classroom scene. This was not what a Christian school should look like, they felt. And from then on, Frank and Sharon reported, the school made them feel unwelcome. Even though Frank was carrying a 3.25 average, he felt he had to withdraw.

I was shocked and saddened that our film had caused the Valentis harm—even persecution—in this way and that it had deprived Frank of this opportunity to advance his education. And it impressed me that

Frank and Sharon had kept this fact from me for so long simply to spare my feelings. In any case, Frank now insisted, he and Sharon stood firmly behind *Born Again*'s portrayal of their Christian Academy. "The more I see of Christian schools," he said, "the more I see the same kind of struggles with teenagers." He and Sharon happily reported the many fundamentalist pastors and heads of Christian schools who had come up to them and said they saw themselves and their own struggles in *Born Again*. On the other hand, Frank noted, "most fundamentalists with TV ministries, colleges or fiefdoms don't want to be associated with ordinary churches with only one or two hundred members. They disapprove of the film because they don't want to be associated with low-class, hicklike people. And ours was that way."

Since Frank was no longer in school, Sharon had taken a job in an office while he stayed home and played "Mr. Mom," as they adroitly put it—a linguistic invention that affirmed in one neat amalgam two traditional gender-role references, "Mr." and "mom," while dispelling any tensions this radical role reversal might provoke. Frank cooked and cleaned, they explained. "The cupboards have a new order," Sharon said ruefully. Each day Frank prepared "dinner" for Sharon and took it to her at the office so they could spend her half-hour lunch break together.

Frank's duties sometimes involved taking care of Christie's young daughter. Christie and Jeff had an apartment nearby. After having a second child, however, they parted ways and were divorced. "They were just too young," Sharon concluded. Jeff continued to be a good father, she said, taking the children every other weekend, and the Valentis maintained good relations with him.

Meanwhile, Christie moved forward in life with the kind of energy and verve she always had. Even as a single parent with two young children, she was able, with her parents' and grandparents' help, to finish both her high-school equivalency diploma and a training program to become a police officer. It was this decision to attend police school, Christie told me, that had been the last straw for Jeff. He was against it, and they separated and divorced. No one, it seemed, insisted that Christie simply obey her husband's wishes in this regard.

"You've reached Valenti Enterprises," an answering machine replied when I phoned Frank and Sharon's office to make plans to visit them. Christie returned my call. She told me she was now working full-time at the family's business office. Four years before, she had married a fellow police officer and had a little baby boy, her third child. Now in her second marriage, with two teenage girls and a young son, she was just thirty. Sharon, now a grandmother of six, was still in her forties. (Opportunities for strong family ties across generations are much improved by having children earlier rather than later in life.)

I told Christie I had recently gone through the legal technicalities of my own divorce after being married for nine years and having a son who was now eight. "Join the club," she said sympathetically. "I guess that's happening to everybody these days. It seems like people are going in such different directions, husband and wife both working, changing in different directions. It makes it hard to stay together."

Over the past fifteen years Frank and Sharon had started several businesses. The first was a community newspaper carrying comics and classifieds, and the second, a copy and print shop. Sharon's parents, Ada and Tom, had moved to Florida from Lynchburg, Virginia, where they had relocated after Shawmut River's split to be near Sharon's younger sister and her family. They had begun helping out in Valenti Enterprises.

Sharon, in particular, enjoyed her involvement with the wider public their business ventures provided. She said she was surprised to find that people in "the world"—that is, the unsaved—were a lot nicer than she had expected.

"You won't believe it," she told me once by phone, in 1991, "and perhaps Frank won't either, but he's mellowed out a lot."

"That's *not* a compliment," Frank offered warily on the other phone.

"Yes, it *is* a compliment," Sharon insisted, "in some respects—not in beliefs, convictions or theology," she added, to assuage any bad feelings he might have about his status as a fighting fundamentalist being thrown into doubt.

"Well," Frank explained, knowing what she had in mind, "it's not important to me anymore for other people to believe what I believe.

It's just important that they listen to me and try to understand it, and they can do what they want with it after that."

In retrospect, Frank and Sharon both felt they had tried too hard to make members of their flock think as they did. It had been the first church they led, having started it when they were still in their twenties. Frank realized he would now counsel young pastors to "be dogmatic in your own personal life and be dogmatic in the pulpit, but, please, let people be people. Let them live, and let the Lord bring them to the place you are." (I did not ask what he would counsel if the Lord brought them to someplace different.)

"So," I asked, "what other conclusions have you come to?"

"That the world's on its way to hell on a one-way ticket and there ain't no savin' it," Frank retorted half jokingly. This mellowing had not altered the Valentis' political outlook. It had distressed Sharon unduly to see "liberal-feminist sixties people," such as Bill and Hillary Clinton, running the country. Both judged the United States to be more than ever a "pagan nation." Though Sharon felt she was now more flexible—"See, I'm wearing shorts," she noted—she thought Rush Limbaugh had become too liberal and too full of himself. And she and Frank now judged their mentor, Jerry Falwell, as "nothing but a washed-up Southern Baptist," as Frank put it.

I had watched Falwell's trajectory from a distance over these years: his withdrawal from active politicking, his dissolution of Moral Majority, Inc., his joining the Southern Baptist Convention and his seeking greater legitimacy for his college by dropping "Baptist" from its name and calling it "Liberty University."

"Students go to classes now in blue jeans and high heels," Sharon noted with disapproval. She told me gravely that Falwell had even recently hosted a group of homosexuals at his church.

With time on his hands, Frank had begun tinkering, and it was his inventions, surprisingly enough, that contributed most to Valenti Enterprises over these years. It started in a grandiose way with his inventing a new way to propel helicopters, one that did not require the complicated transmissions that make helicopters so heavy and treacherous to fly. After painstaking efforts over several years, he found out how to patent his "vortex helicopter," recruited business partners and even went so far as to sit down with a number of prospective financiers willing to consider spending hundreds of millions of dollars to develop such a product. He was even flown to Thailand to meet with potential investors, his first trip outside the United States since military service in Vietnam. In the end, no one proved willing to undertake the necessarily long, expensive and risky process to develop such a machine. Frank and Sharon came away with nothing but a greater knowledge of patents and of the inherently conservative nature of capital investment.

One evening, however, in the midst of this frustrating process, Frank's mother-in-law, Ada, who was at the Valentis' home sewing curtains for their new print shop, found her work suddenly halted. The circular blade she was using to cut fabric had broken. "Now, Frankie," she said, teasing him gently, "why don't you invent something *useful*, like something to sharpen these blades. Once they get dull," she complained, "I have to throw them away."

Frank went down to his shop in the basement and in a few hours came back with a prototype sharpener. With the lessons learned from the helicopter project, he patented it, arranged for its manufacture and began selling it through ads in sewing magazines. A year later, when we met for lunch in Florida where I was screening a documentary at a conference, the family was celebrating their first $15,000 day in sales. Over a five-year period, this small product netted the Valentis and Morses $1 million.

After his blade sharpener, Frank invented and developed a number of other products, including a device that enables a single person to hitch a heavy trailer onto a car in a single try, a humidor for coffee and a tool for quilt makers that makes complicated folds for quilt joints in one easy and continuous motion. The last was one among a half-dozen inventions for sewing and quilt making inspired by his mother-in-law. "I think we might have hit it big on this one," Frank reported. It had taken them several years and $200,000 to develop the product, using funds from the blade sharpener. He and Sharon were flying to Buffalo, New York, to give demonstrations at a convention for quilt makers. Just recently, Frank's helicopter design was taken up for development by the aeronautics department of a major state university.

Whatever the outcome of their increasingly promising ventures, Frank and Sharon felt confident that the matter was "in the Lord's hands."

"He knows," Frank explained, "that we are not in it for the money. Don't get me wrong," he hastened to add, "I'm not against cell phones or Cadillacs." (He was driving one.) "But our end goal is to create a fund to help Christian schools." One way he and Sharon aimed to help was to provide funds to schools that felt they could not afford to expel "problem students." They had in mind the kind of student who had sometimes come to Shawmut River's academy, a teenager expelled from public schools for behavioral problems who had nowhere else to go. They also planned to supplement teachers' salaries to attract the most talented teachers to Christian schools.

On my most recent visit to the Valentis in Florida, family members gathered to pay their respects. Sharon's sister, Kathy, drove their parents, Tom and Ada, to the Valentis from where they all now lived, an hour's drive away. Ada was still active in the sewing notions side of Valenti Enterprises. Her son-in-law, Kathy's husband, was enjoying success in the Christian music industry, which was growing and changing rapidly. Christian musicians now enjoyed crossovers into mainstream music, Kathy reported enthusiastically, and were even allowed to do songs about love.

As we settled down for a barbecue on the pool patio, two of Frank and Sharon's children, Christie and Ted, checked in by cell phone to communicate their whereabouts and arrival times. They played on the same softball team and had a game that evening, so Christie's husband would be bringing Christie's two teenage daughters over. Their own two-year-old son was coming with Auntie Carol (Judy Keener's daughter) and her two boys. Now divorced, Carol had moved to be close to the Valentis, whom she praised as "my family." She worked with Christie in the company office and, with Christie's encouragement and help, had gone back to college.

Ted, the Valentis' youngest child, was also involved in the family business and also in the process of getting a divorce. Sharon had become the main caregiver for his three-year-old daughter, who called her "Mama" and cried when taken from her. Sharon had spent that afternoon with her granddaughter on her lap downloading Bible stories from the Internet and reading them to her.

Watching this swirl of domestic improvisations, all facilitated by a constant stream of cell-phone communications—everyone had one—I realized the Valentis were coping with some of the same kinds of social and logistical problems of divorce and blended-family living that I and many others now faced. But the close proximity of family members gave the Valentis more people to cover child-care responsibilities than I had available to me with my eight-year-old son. Though Sharon had anticipated meeting new "family in the Lord" when they first moved to Florida, most of their time now seemed to be taken up with *actual* family, which had reassembled around them.

The next day, after eighteen holes of golf, Sharon and I were talking around their pool, and our conversation turned to the relationship of Christian faith to higher learning, a subject that had always concerned her. Shadrak, Mishak and Abednego, she pointed out, had been thrown into the fiery furnace for refusing to kowtow to the scholarly community of their day. And Solomon was "a sociologist of sorts," she said, and concluded, "All is vanity."

"It was not through higher learning that people come to God," Sharon pointed out. "In the Gospel of Luke Jesus says, 'Whosoever shall not receive the kingdom of God as a little child shall in no wise enter therein'" (18:17). That is, she said, coming to faith as a little child meant *without* higher education.

If she and Frank ever made big money with their products, Sharon said that the one project she would like to fund would be to study how colleges and universities promote liberalism and secularism in American life. What worried her most about this book, she said, was whether, from a scholarly standpoint, I might deny the faith we now shared in conversation. Though she conceded that my sociological perspective might help outsiders better understand fundamentalist Christianity, she wished that I had portrayed some of the intellectuals found in the fundamentalist camp and worried that readers might be left with the impression that all educated people—the so-called intelligent ones, she said with some irony—were liberal. She wanted readers to know about people such as David Bergman, she said, an electronics systems engineer educated at the University of California, who, since retiring as a top technical engineer in advanced missile development for the air force and navy, had developed an electromagnetic theory of matter that, in his view, is scientifically superior to quantum theory with its assumption of randomness and uncertainty imposed by nature. By contrast, Bergman's "common sense science," he writes, "is based on order in nature imposed by God, who not only created all things but also controls and sustains the universe."[1]

Despite Frank Valenti's dreams of contributing to Christian education in philanthropic ways, he yearned to be back in ministry. He found it much more satisfying than his business activities and hoped God had not finished using him yet. But as he and Sharon made the rounds of fundamentalist churches in Florida, they encountered obstacles. "I'm too fundamental for the Southern Baptists down here," he once concluded, "and too independent for the fundamentalists with big operations." To be fundamentalist Baptists in Massachusetts, where that tradition stood outside the prevailing culture, required the leaders of Shawmut River to be more self-conscious about their beliefs, to think them through and express them in more explicit ways. In Florida and elsewhere in the South, where Baptist fundamentalism is mainstream and conventional, it may become, over generations, a hollow shell encrusted with apathy and hypocrisy.

But the Valentis' involvement in a new church had also been inhibited by painful memories of the split at Shawmut River. Now, however, fifteen years later, the feelings of hurt and indignation seem to have receded and I have noticed more charitable, evenhanded views of opponents. "We were all young," Sue Sanderson now confessed, reflecting a view expressed by most of those centrally involved. Only recently did she feel she had come to appreciate, from experiences in her present congregation, how difficult it must have been for the Valentis to be told to leave a church they had sacrificed so much to build. She now felt ashamed of some of her and other dissidents' actions during the split, that they had not always been governed by the kind of humility following Christ requires. But subsequent events had also taught her that "we have the wherewithal," through God's forgiveness and the Holy Spirit within us, "to overcome these things."

For her part, Sharon drew on scripture to come to peace with having such unseemly events recounted in this book. "I don't imagine King David or Paul, if they were given a choice," Sharon now reckoned, "would ever have agreed to have their stories told in the Bible." She had in mind David's adultery with Bathsheba or his son Absalom's turning against him, or Paul's overseeing the persecution and killing of Christians. In this context, she felt, changing the names of the book's central characters made sense. "We're not proud of all that's happened," she said, but, like the stories of David and Paul, "it's a good lesson to show—that humanity is frail."

Looking back on church conflicts, Terry Laverne found it helpful to remember that "we're not fighting *each other*—the Bible says we're fighting powers and principalities." She was referring to the role of Satan and his minions in getting the faithful to not see things as God sees them, reflecting the advantages of indirectness such spiritual conceptions afford those who must deal with conflicts close-up in families or family-based communities.

"We were all part of a family," Jean Strong said, recalling Shawmut River at the time of the split. She pointed out that Frank's parents regularly took their youngest daughter out to Sunday dinner and out shopping on her birthday, and that she called them Grandpa and Grandma. "Like a family," Jean observed about their conflicts, "you get through these things; it just takes time." Those who left the church, Jean said, "still have very loving feelings toward Frank and Sharon." She and Phil had recently even invested in one of Frank's inventions.

Jean also shared with me a letter of reference Frank had written for Phil several years before. In it Frank absolved Phil of any responsibility for "starting trouble" at Shawmut River and commended him as "an asset to any ministry."

"Sometimes we did not see eye to eye," Frank's letter continued (and I imagined Sharon's hand in it), "but as I reflect back upon scriptures, this is not so unusual. For Paul oft times disagreed with many of God's elect. Unfortunately," it concluded, "we can never take sinful humanity out of the picture so long as we are in this old flesh."

Jean was now able to affirm that Frank Valenti had been good and necessary for Shawmut River because "it takes a forceful person to plant a church." Managing one was another matter, however, and by this time, Shawmut River had gone through five pastors. Under Frank's immediate successor, Shawmut River recovered from the split and flourished for a decade. This pleased the Valentis, who recognized how often churches decline after their founders leave. During these years the Strongs and Lavernes remained pillars of the church. Dan and Judy Keener, who had a child of their own, returned to teach at the academy, and Dan eventually became principal.

Shawmut River took out a second mortgage to finish the gymnatorium as a sanctuary. It now had a carpeted floor, new pews and an enclosed sound room in a back balcony. Its newly plastered walls were lined with framed drawings depicting Christian missions in various parts of the world.

Frank pointed out, however, that these improvements had sacrificed the athletic uses of the gymnatorium and, therefore, the children's interests. "We did everything for the kids," he said of their ministry. And in time, Shawmut River's school languished as conflicts continued to plague its management. First, the high-school grades were dropped. Then, within a year after Frank's successor left, Shawmut River's Christian Academy closed for good.

Under its next pastor, the church foundered. "He ran it into the ground," Joe Valenti said bluntly. According to Jean, he had little compassion and was not a people person. As more and more of the "main tithers" and "core people" left, like the Lavernes and the Strongs, this pastor was forced to take an outside job working at construction. Another followed, and then another. When I once attended Sunday worship during this period of instability, I hardly knew a soul present.

But this exodus of past members of Shawmut River did not mean a fall from faith or wholesale backsliding among them. All those I have spoken with in recent years, except Ben and Pam and Sam Strong, have gone on to other fundamentalist churches. The record of the teenagers and children I got to know at Shawmut River is not as strong but still impressive. Of the twenty who are now adults, two-thirds are actively continuing the faith, most through involvement in fundamentalist congregations but several through Bible studies at home.

Meanwhile, Scott and Sue Sanderson continue to serve the same church they moved to right after the split, near Providence, Rhode Island. (Aunt Margaret followed them there.) It had been founded by a fellow graduate of Liberty Baptist College, who copastored the church with his father-in-law. Several years ago, according to Scott and Sue, their congregation was rocked by two scandals. The first saw the son-in-law removed from the pastorate. The second, which involved one member in the process of a divorce deciding to marry another, saw almost half the congregation leave. The church managed to keep Scott on salary, but that year parishioners could not do their annual Christmas musical at the local mall, dressed up, as they always had been, in old-fashioned Dickens costumes. "We lost our alto section," Scott reported dryly.

"We went through hard times," Sue recalled about that period. Weekly worship, she said, "was formulaic, like going through the motions. But God worked it out, and we are now very much one body." When the new pastor—in fact, another son-in-law of the elder pastor—arrived to lead their reunified congregation, the church was hard-pressed financially to keep Scott on staff. In addition, the new pastor held tighter standards for music and judged the syncopation on some of the background sound tracks the Sandersons used as having a "rock beat" and, hence, being unacceptable. Nevertheless, the church leadership worked out compromises on these issues, and Scott stayed on as music minister. Then, as a result of a personal issue arising in his counseling ministry, Scott and Sue decided it was best he resign. Through one church member, Scott got a job handling the phone lines at a local Home Depot and, on his day off, worked testing sand at another member's sandpit.

Sue was grateful for Scott's willingness to work at two jobs so that she could homeschool their two children. To manage, she said, they "did with less," something the Sandersons were practiced at. Sue found homeschooling both effective and fulfilling. She found good courses on-line, she said, from Bob Jones University, and was pleased with the special opportunities homeschooling afforded her children—such as her daughter's participation in a first-rate local choral society. One day after Rush Limbaugh's radio program, which she listened to regularly, Sue heard a local talk-show host praise stay-at-home moms and called him immediately to register her heartfelt thanks for his comments.

Over the past fifteen years I have also kept in touch with Phil and Jean Strong. After leaving Shawmut River, the Strongs settled into Lincoln Square Baptist Church in Worcester, which, since its founding in the late nineteenth century, has continued to be a fundamentalist church. After having been part of the General Regular Baptist Convention for years, it had recently become independent. In its sanctuary, done in the amphitheater style popular among turn-of-the-century evangelists, Dwight L. Moody's name is enshrined in one of the stained-glass windows.

"It's a board-run church," Jean explained, "not a pastor- or deacon-run one." Both she and Phil served on the executive board. "For practical reasons it works well," Jean observed, comparing it to Shawmut River, where a new pastor could simply "do what he wanted without any easy way to get rid of him." Shawmut River's latest pastor, she reported disapprovingly, was now using the "*New* King James Version" and had what she saw as a rock band playing from the dais at Sunday-morning worship. (The Valentis agreed with Jean's criticisms, and it saddened them that the church they had founded had eventually "gone liberal.")

When Phil and Jean first arrived at Lincoln Square Baptist Church, it was down to only eighteen members. Now, they said, attendance was running between eighty and a hundred each Sunday. The church had bought a home for abused and unwed pregnant women and was on the verge of consecrating a new Christian school. Phil and Jean enjoyed being part of the leadership team seeing a small church grow. When I once attended worship with them, their role in that growth was evident. They had brought several families with them from Shawmut River, including two immigrant ones from the West African nation of Liberia. After worship that morning, another African, a bookkeeper from Cameroon, came up to greet us and told the story of Phil befriending him in a public park not long after he had first arrived in the United States. "I was thinking about Jesus," the young man recalled, when he suddenly saw Phil in front of him. Phil approached him, and he and his family ended up visiting Lincoln Square. Phil found him some work with Doug Laverne, and now he and Phil joked about Phil's being his "spiritual father."

That same Sunday, a young professional couple from Puerto Rico also came up to chat with the Strongs after the service. They, too, had recently immigrated and, though raised Pentecostal, had found through the Strongs a church home at Lincoln Square. As Phil and Jean had been accustomed to do at Shawmut River, they invited this couple and others to join us for an impromptu dinner at their home. Jean hurried off to get things started.

More than any other members of Shawmut River, Phil and Jean have remained committed political activists. Though Phil never ran again for public office, he served for many years on the board of directors of Pat Robertson's Christian Coalition for Massachusetts. More recently, after a period of prayer and fasting, Phil had felt called to become a "political evangelist." He and Jean planned to sell their insulation business, buy a camper and travel around the country preaching to Christians to get involved in politics. They envisioned setting up a database and using e-mail to maintain contacts with fellow believers they met on the road. Above all, Phil wanted "to make churches aware of the devil's work" in American society. "The Bible tells us we are to fight powers and principalities," he explained. "As humanists get into office, they want to prevent absolutes from being recognized and God from having any influence." He felt that a prime example of this, and the most pressing issue of the time, was the homosexual movement. In Massachusetts, he said, it was pushing homosexuality and promiscuous sex through the "Safe Schools" program, which told students, according to him, first that sex was "for you to decide," and second, that "we'll show you how to do it safely."

"God's provided a lot of things for the ministry," Jean noted, "a camper, and then a better camper with a regular closet. Meanwhile, we prayed for a buyer for the company," she said, and in answer to their prayers, a prospective buyer came knocking on Phil's office door. When they sold it in 1998, the deal was worth more than a million dollars.

But other wrinkles emerged in their plans. Phil was now retired and around the house all the time, wreaking havoc with Jean's domestic order. "He doesn't *have* a sense of order!" Jean exclaimed when we discussed the situation once by phone. "He thinks he still has a secretary. He opens the mail and leaves everything on the table!" Plans for their ministry evolved accordingly. Instead of driving around the country in a camper together, they imagined Phil working the New England region so he could take day trips or one-night stay-overs on his own. Then they decided to relocate entirely to South Carolina, to join their two oldest daughters and three grandchildren, who now lived there within the orbit of Bob Jones University.

Phil and Jean remained in touch with Phil's brother Sam and were troubled by what they saw as his continued decline. Not long after the church split, Sam left Shawmut River. He once told me by phone that it "disgusted" him that Pastor Valenti had been dismissed from the church "because his teenage daughter got pregnant . . . I couldn't believe it," he said, "and that's one of the reasons I left."

Sam moved back to Florida, where two of his three sons settled near him. I remember him calling me once out of the blue. He appeared to have been drinking and told me he had heard an evangelist on TV say you needed to ask God to forgive each and every sin you had committed. He said he had begun to write all his sins down, but they seemed so overwhelming that he had given up on the idea that God would forgive them all. That still seemed to be the sticking point for Sam; he did not feel his sins were forgiven.

While Sam's faith in his salvation had perhaps not taken hold, others experienced new breakthroughs. I remember hearing first from Jean Strong that Terry Laverne had accepted the Lord. Terry admitted, Jean explained, what others, including myself, had sensed all along: that all those years in our Bible-study group and beyond, she had only professed conversion but "had not accepted Christ into her heart," as Jean put it.

"Before I was saved," Terry now explained to me by phone, "I was *trying* to love him. Now that I *know* him, I just love him and want to serve him—not how *I* want to," she added, "but how *he* wants me to."

Though she had taken longer than her husband to come to Christ, she now seemed firmly planted in her faith.

Terry and Doug had gone through a very tough time with a downturn in Doug's plastering business. "They almost lost everything," Jean said, and were faced with eviction notices, the IRS trying to repossess vehicles and so on. And they were fighting a lot. When Doug would do work around the church, Jean said, "Terry had a fit." Now Terry remarked to me how surprised she was to find herself down at their church painting walls. They were now members of Heritage Baptist, the same church Dave and Sally Keener had attended when first saved and where I had witnessed Doug and Terry's baptism years before.

Two church members I had no contact with over these years were Ben and Pam, the couple whose broken marriage provided one of the stories for our film. And it was, perhaps, the extremity of that crossroads in their lives that left me always wondering what had happened to them. I did not even know if I would be able to find them and was relieved when I found a listing for Ben in the Worcester telephone directory and later that day heard his familiar raspy voice returning my call.

"It's good to hear your voice," he told me.

"It's good to hear yours," I replied, but I had to confess that I had heard it many times in the intervening years, on film and videotape. In fact, I reported to him that one professor of theology had recently told me that, having seen *Born Again* now more than thirty times for courses he taught, some of the most satisfying lines he had memorized were those Ben uttered—for instance, what he said on camera after Pastor Valenti told him his marriage was ending. "When I get to heaven," Ben had said, jabbing his finger at the camera, "I'm gonna put my fist up in the face of God and say, 'You tell me what good it did!'" Now, fifteen years later, I asked Ben what good he thought his breakup with Pam had accomplished.

"I've gotten to be so much stronger," Ben answered without hesitation. "My relationship with the boys is so much better. When you're with someone," he explained, "you depend on them—you ask them, 'Should I do this? Should I do that?' Since I've been on my own, I've made all the decisions myself. It was hard at times, but right now I'm a very confident person."

Moments later, however, he admitted he did not know what he would have done without his mother. He and the boys lived with her soon after the divorce. Later they moved into an apartment just a block away from her, where Ben still lived, on the first floor of a three-story walk-up owned by his brother. "He gives it to me at a good price," Ben explained. "The core infrastructure of our family is still there." His mother was still living, he said. "Yeah, she's still kicking. She says she won't let go," he chuckled, "until I find a wife to take care of me!"

Ben told me the three boys were fine. Their youngest son, now twenty, had moved out of Ben's apartment only months before to live with his girlfriend.

"And what happened to Pam?" I asked.

"She married that guy," Ben said of Pam's boyfriend back then, "and divorced him—and three or four others after that!" (The latter proved untrue.)

I was surprised to hear from Ben that Pam was still living nearby and was working at a McDonald's. He promised to get her phone number for me. I was also surprised when Ben told me he could now sit in a room and talk peaceably with Pam. I wondered how that had come about.

As promised, Ben called me with Pam's number at work, a McDonald's that, it turned out, she managed. We arranged to meet during her afternoon break the following day, and later that same evening I planned to visit Ben at his home in Worcester.

I almost didn't recognize Pam with her short gray hair cut in that pert Dorothy Hamill style Sue Sanderson decried as de rigueur for New England matrons. She was neatly dressed in her McDonald's uniform: a light blue striped blouse tucked snugly into navy blue pants with a dark patterned scarf hanging loosely around the collar. She remained watchful of business around her as we talked at one of the tables where she had some financial record-keeping forms laid out in front of her. Every now and then, when the line of midafternoon customers grew too long, she would excuse herself, jump up and help dispatch them with cheerful expeditiousness.

Pam had come to McDonald's seven years before, she explained, after developing carpal tunnel syndrome in both hands at a garment factory where she had done piecework. On the basis of a little management experience she had once had at a radar detector factory, she had entered McDonald's management track, where she had risen quickly through the ranks.

"I like the work," she said. She seemed to enjoy the varied challenges of managing—such as knowing which electrician to use for this or that kind of work and, her greatest passion, how to move the people under her upward through the organization, always improving and motivated to do their best. She had to watch costs and profit margins carefully and proudly reported that in her first six months as manager, her own McDonald's rose in profitability among its parent company's eighty restaurants, from thirty-seventh to sixth.

Other things Pam had to report were not as bright or cheerful. She said the divorce proceedings that gave Ben custody of the three boys had been unfair. Her decision to give the boys back to Ben in Florida, she noted, had weighed heavily in court. Pam had been given visitation rights on Tuesdays and Saturdays. She remembered crying for two months straight, she said, because she missed them so.

At that time, Pam was still with her old boyfriend, Mitch, but after seven or eight years together, they parted ways. "His mother died of alcoholism," Pam explained, and she hoped her death would lead him to cut down on his own drinking. Instead, she said, it grew worse, and they were living largely on her paycheck. He finally committed himself to a drying-out program. But three or four months after completing it, Pam recalled him turning to her one day and saying, "I don't like you anymore; you've changed."

"I haven't changed," Pam countered. "You're just sober." She said she packed up and left that very day.

Pam was more involved with her sons over these years than her limited visiting rights suggested, partly because her family and Ben's were "so intertwined," as she put it. Her cousin was married to Ben's younger brother, who owned the apartment building Ben and the boys lived in. And her cousin's mother (Pam's aunt and Mary Shepperson's sister) lived in the apartment directly above Ben. Meanwhile, one of Pam's sisters, who had once lived with Ben and Pam, had become their youngest son's confidante. When he was ten and began questioning his parents' divorce, Pam encouraged him to talk with her sister to confirm what she herself had told him. "When I needed some space," she remembered telling him, "Dad didn't give me an inch." Her face contorted in pain just to recall those times and looked exactly as it had fifteen years before. "Ifs, ifs, ifs!" she exclaimed, as tears welled up in her eyes at our table in McDonald's. "We couldn't have made it work," she said, finally regaining her composure as she lay hold of old reasons, "because of his relationship with his mother."

When Ben opened his apartment door later that evening, I was surprised at how the years had worn on him. He had put on weight, and the puffiness of his face made its lines and wrinkles more pronounced. Ben's days now, as he described them, were quite predictable. Six years ago several strokes had left him debilitated, and since then, he had not worked. He often spent his afternoons playing golf. Ben kept all the doors of the extra rooms in his apartment shut to save on heat. Behind one he showed me his youngest son's room, vacated just months before. Nothing seemed touched since then.

As we sat around his kitchen table, Ben told me how it had come about that he had made peace with Pam. It was when their youngest son was ten, he recalled, and suddenly refused to go to school. He gave no reasons, had no complaints, and the more Ben questioned him about it, the more puzzling his son's actions became. It was at this same time, I remembered Pam saying, that their son had become preoccupied with why his parents had divorced. This was two years after the divorce itself, and, from Ben's account, he and Pam were still fighting bitterly. Ben recalled Pam once standing in the street outside their apartment and hurling a torrent of abuse at him for all the neighborhood to hear. And he remembered returning it word for word.

But one evening Ben found himself staying up late into the night, pondering his son's strange behavior. He finally realized his son was blaming himself for their continual fights. Ben resolved to put an end to them. "You're crazy to harbor ill feelings toward her 'cause she left you," he remembered telling himself. "She just had problems. Everybody has problems," he observed. "Hers just got in the way of our relationship."

WHEN I NOW TALK BY PHONE with my friends from Shawmut River, I do so from my study, which looks out from the second floor of my house on a quiet street in Northampton, Massachusetts, where I first began my field research among new-right activists in 1983. The three-year process of making *Born Again* introduced me to the art of *cinéma-vérité* filmmaking and brought me into contact with some of the best practitioners of the various crafts involved. It also brought me into contact with two foundations, and with their support I was able to mount a number of documentary projects, all of which developed my production skills.

I discovered in *cinéma-vérité* filmmaking a fruitful way to apply my sociological training, and one that I found more satisfying personally than the solitary pursuits of scholarship. I enjoyed the teamwork and people work it required: forming relationships with subjects as partners, working with crew members to understand the social worlds we set out to portray and working with editors to make those worlds vivid and understandable to those outside them. I also noticed that documentary filmmaking drew on, and resurrected, artistic sides of me that had withered within the prevailing ethos of higher education. Music, the painterly eye, drama and the spoken word—all these and more came to bear on crafting moving picture and sound to tell socially significant stories. In the process I also discovered I had a gift for winning people's trust to share their stories, however painful they might be.

"You are a compassionate person," Sharon Valenti told me recently. I came to see it as something inherited from my father, who had, as Sharon and Frank might have put it, "a pastor's heart."

"Your mom and dad must be pretty happy with the way things worked out," Frank said.

"They are," I said. "I talk with them a lot about my projects, especially when they have to do with the church, and we now share the events of our lives as fellow believers." When my father retired as the United Methodist bishop of western Pennsylvania, I was surprised to read in the article covering it in the Pittsburgh newspaper that he was known for his rare ability to speak to both sides of the liberal/conservative divide in that denomination.

Since I have become more involved personally in the Christian church, I have inevitably become concerned with the destructiveness caused by these conflicts. The acrimony and hate they inspire assume special significance for those whose faith is perhaps unique in calling on followers to love even their enemies.

Partly because of my former wife's background, I started attending Episcopal churches, first in New York City and then in Massachusetts. Near the end of our stay in New York, I screened a series of my documentaries in our parish in lower Manhattan and was interested, and at moments saddened, by my fellow Episcopalians' responses to the persons and events in *Born Again*.

It did not surprise me when most of these Manhattanites objected to what they saw as Pastor Valenti's imposing his own values on Pam and others. These were urbane, largely professional people used to moving about in the anonymity of the city life as free, autonomous individuals. But I was taken aback by one lawyer's perception of Baptists going forward to the altar in response to the invitation as "sheer exhibitionism." I wondered out loud how fundamentalist Baptists—or any Baptists—might view Episcopalians' customary practice of parading in colorful vestments behind flags and crosses to celebrate the Eucharist. What rubbed him wrong, it seemed, was the way in which an individual's inner experience was not kept *private* but, rather, so readily made *public*.

One fellow parishioner said he did not see in *Born Again* any trace of *his* Christian faith. A young gay priest allowed that, if he closed his eyes, he could hear "some truths" of the faith taught at his seminary but was troubled by the "absence of learning" the film's characters showed.

"They've perverted it," one woman snapped, unwilling to grant members of Shawmut River any claim to a common Christian heritage. Yet for me, it was from members of Shawmut River that I came to understand many of the basic elements of liturgy we Episcopalians routinely recite each Sunday, such as the opening prayer, which calls on God to "cleanse the thoughts of our hearts by the inspiration of your Holy Spirit, that we may perfectly love you and worthily magnify your holy Name."[2]

"Asking us to tolerate them," another fellow Episcopalian declared, "is like tolerating the Nazis."

On the other hand, others confessed to being "challenged by the film," as one man put it, because he was "impressed by the Christian principles" of its central characters. It provoked another to remember the time he had spent, before moving to New York, in a Church of the Nazarene (the conservative tradition in which Sharon's mother had been raised). "I needed it, and it was very comforting," he confessed. "Part of me misses it and yearns for it." (His urbane Episcopal congregation was evidently not meeting all the same needs his Nazarene one had.)

One aspect of these seemingly intractable divisions in the church was manifest in a talk given not long ago at Trinity Church, on Wall Street in downtown New York, by the writer Frederick Buechner, as

popular as any among liberal, learned Christians, like those Episcopalians in my audience. "To say God acts in our lives," Buechner said,
"does not mean that he makes events happen to us, which move us in
odd directions like chessmen on a chessboard. Instead, as I see it,
events happen on their own steam as random as rain." For instance,
Buechner continued, he did not believe the crucifixion had been
"caused" by a loving God. Instead, he argued, "it was a combination of
Roman colonial policy and Jewish religious zeal that caused it."

Post-Enlightenment science requires its practitioners to address a
domain of events seen to be independent of God's actions. And so it is
with Buechner's explanation of the crucifixion, as well as the sociological interpretations set forth in this book. But what justifies making
such assumptions a priori about all of life's events? Don't such assumptions project the mission of post-Enlightenment thought to *all of life*,
rather than just scientific pursuits? And in Buechner's case, why rule
out the possibility that God caused the crucifixion *in and through*, say,
Roman policy, Jewish zeal or the tangle of relationships feeding Judas's
hurt, envy and ambition?[3]

There is often an arbitrariness and irrationality—an assumption
beyond reason—in the limits many intellectuals place on the actions of
God. And this dilution of the supernatural in everyday life is radically
at odds with the supernaturalism at the heart of the worldview and personal experience, not only of fundamentalist and evangelical Christians in the United States but also of masses of ordinary people around
the globe who believe every event is, in some way or other, "meant to
be."[4] Perhaps the post-Enlightenment worldview suits the habits of
thought of modern, urbane, atomized individuals facing a world of
abstract forces, whose effects must be duly calculated, rather than
those of villagers enmeshed in a web of interrelated persons, whose
collective and often subliminal effects and influences must be grasped
as what life is all about. In any case, whatever advantages these post-
Enlightenment assumptions may hold for developing the scientific
imagination, if taken too globally and naively, they can separate intellectuals, including academically trained clergy, from the vast majority
of peoples around the world, whose sense of the transcendent and of
God's actions in life (and those of Satan and other spiritual beings) is
more pervasive, encompassing and ultimately more mysterious than
those assumptions allow.

Any events can be subjected, after the fact, to causal explanation by which we try to give them sense and meaning: how, for example, a young sixties scholar like myself, in the process of research on conservative activists poles apart from him politically, would return to faith through an encounter with a fundamentalist church. The aphorism "An apple does not fall far from the tree" provides one handy explanation in a traditionalist idiom. In its place we could also erect a matrix of sociological generalizations about class, intergenerational mobility and change in social context and worldview. However, to also see in these events the actions of God does not deny any or all such other causes we may attribute to them. It does add something else, though, that can be affirmed only by faith.

For my part, when I think of how, through a tortuous series of ups and downs, I found new and fulfilling work, tapping talents I had lost touch with, and in the course of these events, found a childhood faith revived, reuniting me with my parents around the ultimate things of life, I am moved to say, above all perhaps, simply, "Thank you."

NOTES

Prologue

1. This documentary film, *Born Again: Life in a Fundamentalist Baptist Church*, appeared on PBS in 1987 and is distributed by James Ault Productions, P.O. Box 493, Northampton, MA 01063, and at (www.jamesault.com).

Part One

1 / Meeting

1. For distinctions among various constituencies making up the New Right during this period, see Klatch, *Women of the New Right*. In this study I was interested in understanding the mass of "social conservatives," in Klatch's terms, who were animated largely by family-related issues, rather than "laissez-faire" ones, who espoused a radical free-market, libertarian ideology. In this context, Richard Hofstadter's overall impressions of the makeup of America's "extreme right" in the 1960s are also relevant. Apart from an affluent group of conservatives, Hofstadter noted a "large lower middle-class, somewhat less educated and less charmed than the first group by old-fashioned economic liberalism but even more fearful of communism, which it perceives rather abstractly." See Hofstadter, *The Paranoid Style*, p. 72.

2. The term *fundamentalist* was first coined by a Baptist journalist in 1920 to describe those conservative Protestants then involved in militant movements both inside and outside North American denominations to defend what they saw as certain "fundamentals of the faith." In their view those fundamentals included the virgin birth, the second coming of Christ and, most important, an inerrant Bible—realities embodying the supernatural—which they saw being rejected by contemporaries who adopted modern liberal theologies and historical approaches to scripture, and who carried new notions about gender, sexuality and family life that challenged traditional ones.

Part of fundamentalists' militance was expressed in their willingness to separate themselves from what they perceived as apostate parts of the church. Though many fundamentalists remained in their established denominations, others "came out" and formed loose networks of independent congregations and denomination-like associations often governed as the personal fiefdoms of charismatic leaders. From the

Great Depression into the postwar period, these fundamentalists created a vast infrastructure of churches, schools, Bible institutes, seminaries and other parachurch organizations.

During World War Two and its aftermath, a movement emerged from fundamentalism to temper its radical separatism and engage more effectively with social currents of the day, including modern intellectual life. This movement came to be called "neo-evangelicalism" and, in time, simply "evangelicalism," laying claim to a term used to describe general currents of eighteenth- and nineteenth-century American Protestantism that emphasized personal conversion, revival and winning the unconverted to Christ. For accounts of fundamentalism and evangelicalism, see Marsden, *Fundamentalism and American Culture;* Bendroth, *Fundamentalism and Gender,* pp. 3–5; Carpenter, *Revive Us Again;* and Christian Smith, *American Evangelicalism,* chap. 1.

3. For the emergence of feminist groups within the evangelical movement, see Margaret Bendroth, *Fundamentalism and Gender,* pp. 120ff., and Sally Gallagher, *Evangelical Identity,* p. 44ff. The emergence of biblical feminists and the diversity and malleability of conservative Christians' views of gender have led some scholars to conclude that evangelical teachings on family and gender cannot be explained solely by their religious ideas—for example, biblical literalism. See Gallagher, *Evangelical Identity,* p. 82, or Bartkowski, *Remaking the Godly Marriage,* pp. 163–64. James Hunter demonstrates the emergence of more liberal attitudes especially among more educated and affluent evangelicals in his *American Evangelicalism,* especially pp. 100–1 and pp. 111ff.

4. For how this question was posed, existing answers addressed and a framework for understanding advanced, see James Ault, Jr., *Class Differences in Family Structure.* Inspired by Elizabeth Bott's classic, *Family and Social Network,* its starting point was the recognition, widely shared among central figures in the women's liberation movement of the 1960s and 1970s, that the movement's distinguishing feature, and what gave it its cutting edge, was its call to transform gender roles in family and personal life. As one of its chroniclers put it, it was the "critique of family and personal life" that Second Wave Feminism "made the very cornerstone of its existence." Evans, *Personal Politics,* pp. 217–18. (See also Ault, *Class Differences,* ch. 1 and fn. 1.) Quite recently one veteran feminist from that period wrote in the left-wing journal *The Monthly Review,* "Contemporary feminism emerged out of the rebellion of young middle-class women against domesticity, and their demand for careers outside the home." Epstein, "What Happened to the Women's Movement?" p. 12. Even where leftist, egalitarian and revolutionary ideas were present, for example in the urban ethnic communities of radical Jewish immigrants, modern feminism, with its critique of the family, had not arisen. See Trimberger, "Women in the Old and New Left."

5. See Carter, *The Politics of Rage.* Summing up George Wallace's role in the transformation of American politics, Carter wrote in 1995, "The genius of George Wallace lay in his ability to link traditional conservatism to an earthy language that voiced powerful cultural beliefs and symbols with a much broader appeal to millions of Americans: the sanctity of the traditional family, the centrality of overt religious beliefs, the importance of hard work and self-restraint, the celebration of the autonomy of the local community" (p. 12).

6. *Excursus on method:* Some might consider a story in which a researcher's own background comes into play a *subjective* rather than an *objective,* and properly sociological, account. Yet the things of the social or cultural world are not merely *objective,* because their very existence depends on the common assumptions, beliefs and values of conscious *subjects* living together in human communities of various kinds. Social realities exist, then, *between* subjects. They are *inter*subjective realities, to use a term

drawn from phenomenology, a school of thought that influenced my own sociology. To know them depends on the knower's own capacity to understand—or enter into—such collective meanings—a capacity gained, to begin with, through his or her own formation in particular cultures. For this orientation to social thought, see, especially, Alfred Schutz, *The Phenomenology of the Social World*, and his *Collected Papers*, and Harold Garfinkel, *Studies in Ethnomethodology*.

Does it matter, then, if the person striving to know something about this fundamentalist church is a secular Jew or an African-American raised in the church, a sixties activist or a midwestern Republican burgher, a West African Muslim or, looking ahead, a late-twenty-first-century fundamentalist? I think so—even if they all were sociologists. Each would approach understanding what this community means by "spirit" and "flesh," to take just one example, from different starting points and along different paths. More decisively, perhaps, they might have in mind different things by more matter-of-fact terms like *family* or *sexuality*. From these diverse starting points, they would inevitably raise different questions and pursue different truths, guided by the empirical bedrock of elementary facts that each would conceive and, more important, simply *perceive* in different ways. This is what Max Weber meant by his puzzling and often misunderstood doctrine that *all* knowledge of social reality is necessarily related to the values of the knower. The idea that sociology attains universal and purely objective knowledge of any social reality, unaffected by the knower's own standpoints and shared uniformly by all, regardless of time, place and cultural formation, is a fantastic idea that has crippled and trivialized sociological practice in our age. It takes its toll, above all, but not only, in survey research, in which apparently identical answers to questions about, say, "family," "sexuality" or "spirituality," from different and culturally diverse individuals, are added up as if they meant the same thing.

Later, in chapter 6, I will draw on my own life experience, and those of friends and colleagues, to construct an "ideal type," in Max Weber's terms, to contrast with another ideal type formed from observing family patterns at Shawmut River Baptist Church and among other conservatives I met. I will use these contrasting types to interpret a number of things in American life, including conflicts between conservatives and liberals over issues of family and gender. For Weber's views on sociological method, see Weber, *Max Weber on the Methodology*.

7. Sandeen, *The Roots of Fundamentalism*, p. ix. For another prediction of fundamentalism's demise after the Scopes trial, see the *Christian Century*'s description of fundamentalism in 1926 as "an event now passed." Carpenter, *Revive Us Again*, p. 13.

2 / Frank and Sharon

1. Though part of the Pentecostal movement, the Church of the Nazarene disavowed speaking in tongues and, early on, dropped "Pentecostal" from its name. See the entry by John Brasher in the *Encyclopedia of Religion in the South*, edited by Samuel S. Hill, pp. 164–66.

2. Parts of this are paraphrased from Proverbs 5:18–19. All Bible quotations are from the King James Version, the standard translation used at Shawmut River Baptist Church, even though Liberty Baptist graduates were not taught this was the only, or best, translation of the original texts.

3. For the prominence of Bible-based discourse on family life in fundamentalist and other conservative Christian settings, see Ammerman, *Bible Believers;* Stacey, *Brave New Families;* Manning, *God Gave Us the Right;* Pevey et al., "Male God Imagery";

Bartkowski, *Remaking*; Gallagher, *Evangelical Identity*; Ingersoll, "'Traditional Family Values' in American Protestant Fundamentalism"; and Brasher, *Godly Women*.

4. Armstrong, *The Battle for God*, p. 275.

5. Falwell, *Strength for the Journey*, p. 311.

6. For J. Frank Norris's place in southern fundamentalism and the South's limited role in fundamentalism's first wave, see Carpenter, *Revive Us Again*, p. 49, and Hankins, *God's Rascal*, p. 5. One biographer called Norris "the religious Joseph McCarthy of his generation." Russell, *Voices of American Fundamentalism*, p. 45.

7. For these assessments of the Baptist Bible Fellowship, see Liebman, "Mobilizing the Moral Majority," pp. 61–66.

3 / The Shawmut River Baptist Church

1. Falwell, *Strength*, p. 182.

2. For a discussion of fundamentalism's relationship to tradition in family life, see chapter 13.

3. For the separatist impulse in fundamentalism, see Carpenter, *Revive Us Again*, pp. 43ff. Pastor Valenti's own diagnosis of this tendency to split, stemming from the fact that older members start missing the "close-knit stuff" they enjoyed when their congregation was smaller, bears some resemblance to tendencies toward fission in African villages. See Turner, *Schism and Continuity*, chap. 6, especially pp. 174–78.

4 / The Old-Home Crowd

1. For more on dispensationalism, see chap. 13.

2. Figures from Dudley and Roozen, *Faith Communities Today*. For Southern Baptist figures, see Web site: www.FACT.hartsem.edu. I am grateful to Scott Thumma of Hartford Seminary for helping locate these data.

3. This new wave of historians included Sandeen, *Roots of Fundamentalism*; Marsden, *Fundamentalism and American Culture*; and Timothy Weber, *Living in the Shadow of the Second Coming*. One of the most satisfying historical studies of fundamentalism appeared more recently. See Carpenter, *Revive Us Again*.

4. Quotation from Marsden, *Fundamentalism*, p. 43. On Princeton theology, see pp. 109ff.

5. Marsden, *Fundamentalism*, passim, and Sandeen, *Roots of Fundamentalism*. On the invention of the term *fundamentalist*, see Marsden, p. 107.

6. See Carpenter, *Revive Us Again*. Meanwhile, a parallel pattern of discovery has taken place in the history of political conservatism associated with fundamentalism. Just as a new wave of historians discovered fundamentalism's deeper roots in American religious culture, others unearthed the deeper roots of popular conservatism that resurfaced with the New Right in the 1970s. They pushed back its origins—first, to George Wallace's incendiary campaigns for the presidency, especially in 1968, which shocked political commentators with its powerful appeal to masses of blue-collar workers in the North and Midwest—and then back even further to supporters coalescing around Barry Goldwater's bid for the presidency in 1964. See especially Carter, *The Politics of Rage*, and, more recently, Rick Perlstein, *Before the Storm*.

7. See Nelkin, *The Creation Controversy*, p. 33, and Numbers, *Darwinism Comes to America*, p. 85. Numbers writes that the Scopes trial has been "grotesquely misunderstood" (p. 76).

8. For the idealist approach to the study of fundamentalism, see Sandeen, *Roots of Fundamentalism*, and Marsden, *Fundamentalism*. For Marsden's recognition of the importance of small Bible-study groups in the development of fundamentalists' grasp of scripture, see Marsden, *Fundamentalism*, pp. 61–62. On the distinction between popular and scholarly fundamentalism, see Stevick, *Beyond Fundamentalism*, p. 57.

Carpenter notes the lack of studies of local fundamentalist congregations and reminds us that fundamentalism was a popular phenomenon based, above all, in local churches. Carpenter, *Revive Us Again*, pp. 58, 61. More recently a number of studies have appeared based on firsthand observation of conservative Protestant congregations, but they have tended to be charismatic, evangelical and more drawn from middle- and upper-middle-class constituents. See Manning, *God Gave Us the Right;* Pevey et al., "Male God Imagery"; Bartkowski, *Remaking;* Ingersoll, "'Traditional Family Values' in American Protestant Fundamentalism"; and Griffith, *God's Daughters.*

In her study of the charismatic interdenominational women's fellowship, *Women Aglow*, Griffith, though describing it as part of the "small-group movement" in American life and recognizing that the "most intense religious experiences" take place in "domestic settings" (pp. 20 and 72), does not bring readers into those elementary cells of the organization she studied or into the relationships making them up.

Two insightful analyses of fundamentalist discourse, Susan Harding's *The Book of Jerry Falwell* and Kathleen Boone's *The Bible Tells Them So*, get good mileage from the notion that the meaning of any discourse or text depends on its apprehension and use by an "interpretive community" (Boone, pp. 19ff.), who, as Harding puts it, are "co-producers" of that discourse, yet neither brings us into the realities and relationships making up that interpretive community so decisive in defining contemporary fundamentalism: the local church. Nancy Ammerman's *Bible Believers* still remains the best study of a fundamentalist Baptist congregation. See also Peshkin, *God's Choice*, and Covington, *Salvation on Sand Mountain*. Brenda Brasher's *Godly Women* treats one charismatic congregation with blue-collar members and is discussed further in chap. 21, note 9 below.

9. Marsden writes: "The phenomenon that I have defined as 'fundamentalism' was overwhelmingly American in the sense that almost nowhere else did this type of Protestant response to modernity have such a conspicuous and pervasive role both in the churches and in the national culture." Marsden, "Fundamentalism as an American Phenomenon," p. 216. Marsden poses, but does not resolve, to my mind, the relative absence of fundamentalist mobilization in Britain, despite the presence of ideas central to its development.

10. For the view that feminism and the alleged breakdown of the family were not important in First Wave fundamentalism, see Marsden, *Fundamentalism*, p. 228. This view was overturned by the pioneering work of historian Betty A. DeBerg in her *Ungodly Women*. For DeBerg's critique of approaches to fundamentalism that focus on theological and religious ideas, see pp. 1ff. For Marsden's missing the presence of gender issues in fundamentalism's first wave, see DeBerg, pp. 152–53. For First Wave fundamentalists' focus on divorce, see p. 38, and on "the New Woman," pp. 27–28, 117, 124, 133. Another distortion this idealist approach to fundamentalist history involved was the bias it carried toward more intellectually oriented Protestant traditions, paying far greater attention to Presbyterians, for example, than Methodists. For this critique, see Donald W. Dayton, "The Search for the Historical." Impressions of the prominence of Norris and his lieutenants in fundamentalist discourse on the family were drawn from DeBerg. For the assessment of John Rice's *The Home*, see Carpenter, *Revive Us Again*, p. 269, note 13.

11. Marsden, *Fundamentalism*, p. 7, identifies fundamentalists' ambivalence toward intellect as one of the three paradoxes he explores to interpret the movement as a whole.

12. "If the biblical primitivism of the Mennonites echoed the Gospels," writes historian Joel Carpenter, "and the pentecostals lived out the Acts of the Apostles, fundamentalists identified with the Epistles. The apostles' admonitions to the hard-pressed young churches living in a pagan world resonated powerfully with fundamentalists' experience and temperament." Carpenter, *Revive Us Again*, p. 69.

13. For a liberal interpretation of this passage from Paul, see Peter Gomes, *The Good Book*, pp. 155ff. Reverend Gomes, preacher at Harvard University's Memorial Church and Professor of Christian Morals at Harvard College, argues that in Romans Paul was not talking about homosexuality as he understood it then or as we understand it now. He was talking about the fallen nature of humankind. And in this context, Gomes writes, Paul was speaking of homosexual acts among heterosexual people, including pederasty and male prostitution. "All Paul knew of homosexuality was the debauched pagan expression of it. He cannot be condemned for that ignorance, but neither would his ignorance be an excuse for our own" (p. 158). To correct our own ignorance, Gomes goes on to suggest that homosexuality was considered wrong in the ancient world because it wasn't linked with procreation and suggests we go beyond this kind of thinking by responding positively to the questions posed recently by an Anglican moral philosopher: "Are there sound reasons for revising the traditional account of what the wrongness of homosexuality consists in? Is the idea that physical intimacy between men or between women can only be unnatural an idea that the best available understanding of the relevant facts will no longer support?"

"In other words," Gomes concludes, "are we able to advance beyond the moral hypothesis of Saint Augustine and Saint Thomas Aquinas that the sole natural function of sex is procreation?" (p. 171)

5 / Phil and Jean

1. The one exception I found to this pattern of antifeminism among the women of Shawmut River was a college-educated woman who had fled an abusive marriage in a nearby city and ended up finding help in the congregation. See the story of Anne Sullivan in chapter 6. Unbeknownst to others at Shawmut River, Anne worked part-time at a shelter for battered women alongside feminist colleagues. She tended to dismiss antifeminist statements by Pastor Valenti and others as incorrect and irrelevant. She apparently hid her job at the shelter so well that at one point she was run down in talk around Shawmut River for, paradoxically enough, *not* working when her children were now all in school. She shouldn't be relying on public welfare, some felt.

For interpretations of conservative Christian women as de facto feminist or postfeminist, see Stacey and Gerard, "We Are Not Doormats," and Stacey, *Brave New Families*. More recently, Gallagher, *Evangelical Identity*, p. 84, has argued that "evangelical family life reflects the pragmatic egalitarianism of biblical feminists while retaining the symbolic hierarchy of gender-essentialist evangelicals." For Brasher's account of women's power and orientations to feminism in two charismatic congregations (one with considerable blue-collar membership), see chap. 21, note 9.

On the model of marriage presented in God's plan for the family, two early accounts of gender in conservative Christian communities, those of Stacey and Gerard, "We Are Not Doormats," and Rose, "Women Warriors," provide refreshingly realistic perspectives on the substantively positive effects of conservative Christian gender ideology on the lives of women members. Many of their observations about how its doctrines of male "headship" and wifely, or mutual, "submission" actually work coincide with my own observations at Shawmut River, even though neither study was set in as conservative, fundamentalist or working-class a congregation as Shawmut River.

Rose's study was in an independent charismatic church near Ithaca, New York, in the shadow of Cornell University, it seems. Its members ranged from farmers to professors and included graduates of "an Ivy League university." Stacey's study grew out of a personal relationship formed with a feminist woman reared in a progressive political family in southern California, who after divorce and a period of raising children as a single parent managed an antipoverty agency in Silicon Valley. Stacey, *Brave New Families*, pp. 28ff. and 47ff. Stacey was dismayed when her acquaintance converted to an independent nondenominational charismatic ministry. It had been started by a woman and organized communal households among its members. Thus began Stacey's explorations of "evangelical gender ideology."

The other subject whose family network Stacey studied was selected through personal contacts. The woman had once been an assembly worker in a Silicon Valley electronic plant and then had taken feminist courses in a community college women's reentry program and had a history of involvement in community and feminist activism (p. 29).

On the basis of such selective evidence (and the existence of a relatively small number of evangelical feminist groups), Stacey judged evangelical Christians to be "postfeminist"—by which she meant they have simultaneously incorporated, revised and depoliticized some of the central goals of Second Wave Feminism (Stacey and Gerard, "We Are Not Doormats," p. 99). For a recent critique of this assessment, see Gallagher, *Evangelical Identity*, p. 77.

2. Phyllis Schlafly's antifeminist manifesto, *The Power of the Christian Woman*, had been published just a few years before my interview with Sharon Valenti.

3. Epstein, "What Happened to the Women's Movement?," p. 12. For accounts of how and why various groups of women in American life disapprove of feminism for fostering too much individualism, see Epstein, pp. 10–12, and, more generally, Fox-Genovese, *Feminism Is Not the Story of My Life*, and Klatch, *Women of the New Right*, p. 127.

Recent studies of conservative Christian women, written largely by feminist-minded scholars, have taken heart in pointing out their support for certain feminist-sponsored initiatives in public life (such as legislation against marital rape), in recognizing certain advantageous trade-offs the doctrine of marital submission provides and in exploring the surprising compatibilities between conservative Christianity and feminism. They have read these to mean that conservative Christian women are "mistakenly construed as antifeminist," "say yes to feminist values" or are as feminist as they are antifeminist. See, respectively, Griffith, *God's Daughters*, p. 12; Manning, *God Gave Us the Right*, part II, pp. 85ff.; and Brasher, *Godly Women*, pp. 160ff. and 176ff. These commentators have more difficulty making sense of their subjects' expressed opposition to feminism: for instance, their saying "no to the feminist movement," their seeing it as "hostile to their moral and spiritual values," as a source of "disorder" and "chaos" in family and society or their acceptance of ideas and practices that "abet male dominance" and contribute to their own "disempowerment." See, respectively, Manning, *God Gave Us*, part III; Gallagher, *Evangelical Identity*, pp. 148 and 166; and Brasher, *Godly Women*, p. 112. The relation of these and other studies to this one on Shawmut River is clouded by the fact that none is on the kind of fundamentalist congregation it represents. They are generally on more middle-class congregations. For further discussion see chaps. 16 and 21 (especially note 9).

4. Recent studies of conservative Christian communities have pointed out the prevalence of young families involved in raising children. See, for example, Brasher, *Godly Women*, pp. 127ff.

5. For views of fundamentalism as a movement on the part of men to control women, see Betty DeBerg's otherwise pathbreaking historical recovery of fundamentalism's original concerns with issues of gender and family (DeBerg, *Ungodly Women*), and on contemporary fundamentalism, see Karen Brown, "The Fundamentalist Control of Women," p. 177.

It is interesting to note that two diametrically opposed views on fundamentalism's relation to feminism focus on two different sets of actors. The view of fundamentalism as de facto feminist or postfeminist focuses on its women, never asking whether, for that reason, its principal leaders or spokespeople—that is, fundamentalist men—should not, therefore, also be considered feminist. On the other hand, views of fundamentalism as efforts to control women focus on its male members and have little or nothing to say about the majority of fundamentalists who are women. For some who do mention them, fundamentalist women can be characterized as helpless victims caught in false consciousness or in destructive psychodynamics, in which their activism is seen, according to one author, to be "based on self-loathing, fear, and humiliation." See Dworkin, *Right-Wing Women*, p. 35. For an effort to keep both sets of actors in view, women and men, see Bartkowski, *Remaking*. In much of the recent literature on issues of gender in conservative Christianity, these divergent perspectives have yet to be satisfactorily resolved. For further discussion, see chaps. 16 and 21.

6 / Reckoning

1. See, for example, the text the Athol group objected to in their public schools: Sasse, *Person to Person*, pp. 72ff. Made up of a small circle of like-minded people, Parents for Traditional Values provided one of the most moving events I witnessed during this phase of research: an open meeting of the Athol School Board to hear testimony regarding sex education for its schools. I especially remember the extemporaneous speech given by a tall, big-boned Mormon woman, the mother of three and a member of the group, who took issue with the classic bag-of-flour exercise done in her daughter's human-development course. It required students to carry a sack of flour around with them everywhere they went for a week or so, to impress upon them the relentless burdens of child care. She criticized what she saw as its one-sided, negative depiction of parenting. "I never walked the floor from three o'clock one morning until three the next, until I couldn't put one foot in front of the other, for my sack of flour," she pointed out with steady resolve, and drew to a conclusion with a litany of such examples: "I never worried myself sick because my sack of flour was two hours late coming home from school, or burst with pride when my sack of flour took her first steps, or had my sack of flour hug me and say 'I love you.'" When she sat down there was an awkward silence as some board officials seemed to squirm in their seats. Even I, who had not yet experienced the emotional power of parenting a child, could appreciate her point.

2. An important distinction to make in assessing the effects of education or occupation on kin-based networks is the difference between being a self-employed profes-

sional, tied in various ways to a given locality, and a salaried professional, apt to move to take advantage of particular career opportunities within specialized markets covering larger geographic areas. For further clarification, see Ault, *Class Differences*, chap. 3, pp. 8off.

3. "The poorer you are, the more likely you are to pay back," say the poor African-Americans whose patterns of reciprocal obligation are described in Carol Stack's pioneering ethnography, *All Our Kin*, p. 43, which influenced my thinking on relationships of reciprocity in kin-based networks.

4. For the prevalence of selfishness as a cardinal wrong in fundamentalist Baptist churches, see Ammerman, *Bible Believers*, p. 89. These findings agree with Judith Stacey's, that the nondenominational charismatic congregation she studied offered members "flexible resources for reconstituting gender and kinship relations." Stacey, *Brave New Families*, p. 139. It also echoes Joel Carpenter's observation that earlier generations of fundamentalists "seemed to be trying to recreate the religious culture of earlier small-town America . . ." Carpenter, *Revive Us Again*, p. 10.

5. For an account of conflicts arising from similar perceptions of welfare policies to deal with the urban poor in industrial capitalism's first great metropolis, London, see Jones, *Outcast London*, chap. 13, "The Deformation of the Gift," especially pp. 251–53.

6. For an example of such a statement by a conservative that is perceived by a social analyst as "unrealistic" and as an example of a "projective" and "essentially pathological" politics, see Hofstadter, "The Pseudo-Conservative Revolt—1955," pp. 65 and 77, and Hofstadter, "Pseudo-Conservativism Revisited: A Postscript—1962," pp. 83 and 85, both in Bell, ed., *The Radical Right*. This initial perception of right-wing politics as fundamentally irrational led to a prevalent tendency among scholars to explain them by identifying possible causes of that irrationality: for instance, status anxiety, the rootlessness of American life, rapid social change, etc. Why such forces as "status anxiety" or "rootlessness" did not equally derail the rationality of progressive academics like themselves, as subject as any (if not more so) to forces of rootlessness or status anxiety, was not something these scholars ever addressed. See, for example, Hofstadter, "The Pseudo-Conservative Revolt—1955," and Lipset, "The Sources of the 'Radical Right,'" in Bell, ed., *The Radical Right*. The status politics tradition of interpretation, in my view, is better seen as an effort to influence culture, rather than as efforts on the part of the psychologically distressed to solidify their own identity. A good example of that approach is Joseph Gusfield's study of the temperance movement, *Symbolic Crusade*. For Hofstadter's misgivings about his initial "status politics" approach, see Hofstadter, *The Paranoid Style*, pp. 86ff.

7. The logic of this conservative sensibility is not so compelling, however, as to prevent those holding it from responding to pressing social needs. Frank Norris, for example, Shawmut River's populist conservative forebear, even supported President Franklin Delano Roosevelt's New Deal in its early years, before his political alliances with businessmen persuaded him to oppose it. See Hankins, *God's Rascal*, pp. 95ff. Members of Shawmut River did not advocate scrapping all welfare without assuring that needs would be met, instead, by churches and individuals.

8. Brown, "The Fundamentalist Control," p. 177.

9. That opposition to abortion rights is best seen as symbolic and rhetorical action—for what it means rather than does—is evident in the actual tolerance among right-to-life activists I met toward those among them who had had abortions. (They are not treated as murderers.) And it is evident in the best sociological account of the abortion controversy, by Kristin Luker, who came to see it as a struggle about how motherhood is to be seen: as a matter of choice versus what life and womanhood are all

about. Luker, *Abortion and the Politics of Motherhood.* On the issue of capital punishment, I believe conservative thinking is more colored by the ethic of reciprocity seen in traditionalist terms: that is, a life for a life.

10. For a fuller account of factors facilitating and impeding the reception of modern feminism in different types of family structure associated with class, see Ault, *Class Differences.*

11. These different standards of privacy came into view for my mother in a working-class Methodist congregation she and my father served in the 1950s. At the congregation's annual Christmas party, church women presented her with an apron and then came up, one after the other and in view of all, to pin varying amounts of money on it as their Christmas present to our family. My mother was mortified.

12. As in Max Weber's classic conception, ideal types are not meant to describe any class of phenomena but, rather, are concepts created as tools to say things about them. The contrasts I draw between patterns of family life observed among members of Shawmut River and new-right activists, on the one hand, and those common among my friends and colleagues, on the other, are intended as ideal types in Weber's terms. Weber, *Max Weber on the Methodology.*

13. There can be considerable differences between the social determinants of the mass base of any social movement, on the one hand, and that of its leaders and spokespeople, on the other. For example, Karl Marx, in his *Eighteenth Brumaire of Louis Bonaparte,* his most supple work of political analysis, notices how different and idiosyncratic the backgrounds might be of those who become leaders of any class-based movement. Writing about the spokesmen for a movement representing, in his view, the petty bourgeoisie, he writes: "What makes them representatives of the petty bourgeoisie is the fact that in their minds they do not go beyond the limits which the latter do not go beyond in life." Marx, *The Eighteenth Brumaire,* p. 44. Here I am suggesting there can be particular life experiences that help leaders become more explicitly conscious of what followers more dimly feel.

14. This hypothesis fits scattered evidence of various kinds, including early journalistic accounts of new-right activism in the late 1970s: Andrew Kopkind's "America's New Right," which portrays it in small towns overrun by metropolitan suburban expansion, and Stephen Arons, "Book Burning." William Kornblum, *Blue-Collar Community,* pp. 149ff., shows new-right strength among those who have moved out of close-knit, ethnic, working-class neighborhoods to areas of second settlement. Studying fundamentalist/modernist splits in a variety of congregations in the United States and Canada at the beginning of the twentieth century, Walter Ellis found, for example, in one town of nine thousand inhabitants, that the fundamentalist movement was carried by new migrants to the town, many from rural backgrounds, who came to this small industrial town to join the laboring classes in a period of agricultural depression. See Ellis, "Social and Religious Factors," summarized in Carpenter, *Revive Us Again,* pp. 9–10. Margaret Bendroth, studying membership cards of the fundamentalist Tremont Temple in Boston from the late nineteenth into the twentieth century, is coming up with results similar to Ellis'. Personal communication.

In addition, Nancy Ammerman's careful study of parties involved in conflicts between conservatives and liberals in the Southern Baptist Convention in the 1980s has evidence that seems to support arguments advanced here about the social bases of conservatism and liberalism on relevant issues. Ammerman finds, for example, that three-quarters of the fundamentalist laity were originally from blue-collar or farming homes, while "the world of the moderates was almost exclusively a white-collar and professional world." Ammerman, *Baptist Battles,* pp. 133 and 129. However, those who spent all their lives on farms or in small towns were less likely to be involved on either side of the conflict (pp. 147–48 and 154–55).

15. Personal communication from M. Jean Heriot. See also her then-unpublished paper, Heriot, "Perspectives on the Southern Baptist Convention." Her point corresponds to Nancy Ammerman's findings in *Baptist Battles* reported in note 14, especially pp. 154–55. In similar ways, I have the impression that for many African-Americans and immigrants firmly situated in extended-family life, battles over the Equal Rights Amendment, abortion or sex education sometimes appear like the psychodrama of a strange tribe. What feminism did arise among African-American women took quite different forms than the white, middle-class movement. Calling themselves "womanist," they did not subject traditional gender roles in the family, or the family itself, to such stinging critiques as did the white feminist movement.

16. Personal communication from Margaret Bendroth from her research, among other things, in Tremont Temple's membership files. At the beginning of the twentieth century, Professor Bendroth notes, Tremont was known as "the Stranger's Sabbath Home" and, informally, as "the Canadian church." Her findings are being incorporated into a book on fundamentalism in Boston during this period.

17. For descriptions of Norris' ministries in Forth Worth and Detroit, see Hankins, *God's Rascal*, pp. 13 and 90ff. When I recently phoned Norris's old congregation in Detroit, the woman I was connected to as the keeper of its history told me she remembered first coming there in 1948 as a new migrant to the city from a rural farming community in northern Michigan. "It was such a friendly church," she recalled. "Most people were from the South. They made you feel so welcome, would have you home for dinner—that type of a southern tradition." Recently the church, now boasting five to six thousand members, moved to a suburban location and changed its name from Temple Baptist to the Northridge Church, she said, to stimulate growth in its new setting and in an era when so many people are unchurched.

18. FitzGerald, *Cities on a Hill*, p. 137. "They are," FitzGerald continues, "clerical workers, technicians, and small businessmen, and skilled and semiskilled workers in the new factories," a description that fits the makeup of Shawmut River, too.

19. For the southernization of America, see Carter citing John Egerton in Carter, *The Politics of Rage*, p. 14.

20. See H. Richard Niebuhr, "Fundamentalism," p. 527. Here we might note the prominence of rural migrants to cities in fundamentalism's social makeup (see note 14, above) and Joel Carpenter's observation that "fundamentalists seemed to be trying to recreate the religious culture of earlier small-town America." Carpenter, *Revive Us Again*, p. 10. In this context, in contemporary Boston, as folk wisdom among fundamentalist Baptist preachers has it, it is much easier to plant churches *outside* Route 128, Boston's ring highway, than it is *inside* it. Shawmut River had its own migrants from rural and more traditional communities, including Mary Shepperson's extended family from backcountry Maine.

21. This paper was revised and published. See Ault, "Family and Fundamentalism."

22. LaHaye, *The Battle for the Family*, p. 18.

23. For Billy Sunday, see McLoughlin, *Billy Sunday Was His Real Name*. When I once asked Pastor Valenti why he emphasized men's place in the church, he said it was because it was much easier to attract and win women to the faith and to church life. Evidence from other conservative Christian congregations suggests that women more often become members first and, then, if possible, bring their husbands along. For this tendency in two charismatic congregations, see Brasher, *Godly Women*, p. 111.

24. Details of domestic life were not something the men of Shawmut River felt comfortable talking about in realistic ways among themselves. In her early and insightful study of women in a charismatic church in upstate New York, Susan Rose notes, without any evidence or explanation, that in talk between husbands and wives leading to joint decisions about domestic matters, "women often dominate the conversation." Rose, "Women Warriors," p. 257. Whether this is not a predictable and socially structured reality rooted in traditional gender roles in the family is not something Rose explores in this context.

25. Ault, "Family and Fundamentalism," p. 34. For further discussion of these issues, see chapter 21.

26. Such discomforts were evident in responses to my doctoral dissertation in the early 1980s. At that time, for example, I remember being introduced to Robin Morgan, editor of *Sisterhood Is Powerful!*, an early and influential feminist reader, and being urged to tell her about my dissertation. When I said that in it I had tried to explain why sixties feminism had found greater support among middle-class rather than working-class or Third World women, Morgan replied dismissively, "Well if that ever was the case, it certainly isn't anymore." This discomfort can still be found in the, at times, strained attempts among feminist scholars to characterize fundamentalist and conservative women as feminist, and the difficulties they then have in making sense of the patriarchal or pointedly antifeminist views they enunciate. See chap. 21, note 9.

27. Robert Putnam, *Bowling Alone*, Appendix 1, pp. 415ff. For further evidence bearing on faulty assumptions underpinning Putnam's standards of measurement, see chap. 14, p. 227. Fortunately, this kind of mismeasurement does not undo the relevance of Putnam's central findings about the decline in Americans' civic engagement, which seems an important trend to address in American public life. But it does distort specific conclusions and diagnoses he makes from his data. For example, Putnam attributes North Carolina's much lower measures of educational success compared with Connecticut's to differences in the two states' "social connectedness," measured largely in terms of associational life. For North Carolinians to improve their educational performance, Putnam argues, they should *not* do things like lower classroom size but, instead, say, "double their frequency of club meeting attendance" or "triple the number of nonprofit organizations per thousand inhabitants" (p. 301). Yet are North Carolinians, as southerners known for stronger ties to kin and place, less "socially connected" than the people of Connecticut, known for its large affluent suburban populations? Perhaps clubs and organizations are the prevailing form of social connection for Connecticut's suburbanites, while a good portion of North Carolinians (including, indeed, its large African-American population) are too involved in their families to be interested in "club life"? Furthermore, perhaps their different levels of educational achievement have more to do with other facts—for example, with how differently these two patterns of life engage with prevailing forms of education and of educational testing. For more on that possible line of reasoning, see chap. 12 below.

28. Family life's taken-for-grantedness registers in the shock we experience when we first encounter families quite different from our own. I remember as a child, for instance, my utter surprise at first experiencing the Italian-American household of a boyhood friend, with its palpably different sights, smells and sounds—loud talk, for example, face-to-face, with strong gesticulations. For a recent example of sociologists' criticizing the sociology of the family as a field limited unduly to the "middle-class" family, see Gerstel et al., *Families at Work*, Introduction. The same pattern of misperception among scholars may also account for that recurring feature in urban sociology, where researchers repeatedly posit the disappearance of primary groups in city life,

only to be surprised later on to discover their remarkable persistence, often among working-class or poorer residents. For one example of a social policy discussion where helping relations among kin should have been considered but were not, see Suzanne Woolsey's criticisms of early debates over day care. Woolsey, "Pied Piper Politics."

29. For shared parenting among poor African-Americans, see Stack, *All Our Kin*. Columbia University's School of Journalism awarded a Peabody to *CBS Reports: The Vanishing Family* (CBS News, 1986), produced and directed by Ruth C. Streeter with Bill Moyers as executive editor. The case of Clarinda Henderson, who became pregnant at fifteen, is the first one to appear in the program. Though her grandmother on her mother's side was also mentioned as a presence in Clarinda's life, she was not pictured along with her daughter, granddaughter and great-granddaughter as part of the kin network involved in raising the family's children. For other examples of such misjudgments, see below, chap. 13, p. 317; chap. 21, pp. 462–64 and note 9; and chap. 22, p. 479.

In popular culture, on the other hand, the presence of kin in family life is registered, appropriately enough, in one of the top all-time hits in American television. With an astounding run of twenty years, Norman Lear's *All in the Family*, featured the outspokenly right-wing, yet utterly human, Archie Bunker, his wife, Edith, and their daughter, Gloria, and son-in-law, Mike, aka "Meathead," who lived under the same roof with them, as Meathead studied, of all things, sociology.

In addition, in much of the recent literature on gender in conservative Christianity there is little sense that different kinds of family life might be something worth looking at or that people's families of origin are important in understanding their attitudes toward gender. For further discussion, see chap. 21, note 9.

Part Two

7 / Spring

1. Ignorance of key organizations or figures involved in public controversies over the politics of the family does not mean people do not have political leanings or sensibilities in these matters—dispositions that end up directing, among other things, their voting. Even in the midst of the most heated battles of the 1980s such ignorance could be found among people committed to conservative enthusiasms at the time. Sally Keener, for example, with her firm critiques of the welfare state and of feminism, was tickled to think that journalists "would call us 'pro-lifers' and 'the new right' and we've never heard the term. We're just living the life we think God wants us to." Evidence of such ignorance has wrongly been taken to mean by some researchers that the "culture wars" were a media myth. See Smith, Gallagher, et al., "The Myth of Culture Wars," pp. 180ff. In their article dismissing the "culture wars," Smith and Gallagher do not bring to bear the results of their own survey research among evangelical Christians published elsewhere. Those data, which were gathered in the mid-1990s, when these controversies were already more muted, reveal evangelicals' preoccupations with, among other things, a perceived "breakdown of the family," with feminism seen, by the majority, as "hostile to their moral and spiritual values," with moral relativism and secular humanism as major problems in American life, with resentments toward liberally biased news reporting on abortion, homosexuality and free sex, etc. (For views of feminism and chaos resulting from a decline in men's headship in the family, see

Gallagher, *Evangelical Identity*, pp. 148 and 166ff. For the salience of other issues, see Smith, *American Evangelicalism*, pp. 129–42.)

2. See Numbers, *Darwinism Comes to America*, pp. 5–6.

3. Years later, Bill Tatum insisted that he had never opposed Frank as pastor of Shawmut River and never spoken badly of his ministry, a claim that rang true to at least one other person close to the scene at the time.

4. I cannot now locate this reference, but for a sense of the relatively transitory character of consciousness-raising groups, see Carden, *The New Feminist Movement*, p. 72, and Cassell, *A Group Called Women*, pp. 37–38.

5. For a further discussion of gossip at Shawmut River, see chapter 21.

6. Ammerman, *Bible Believers*, pp. 123–26.

8 / Fall

1. Carpenter, "Contending for the Faith," p. 107.

2. For further discussion of why members of Shawmut River did not feel compelled to resolve such logical inconsistencies, as part of exploring the nature of their moral discourse as an *oral tradition*, see chapters 12 and 13. Scholars have a tendency, I believe, to see one doctrinal stand or another as more difficult to overcome than they actually are for fundamentalists—or that for fundamentalists to take on a view contrary to one they hold means a wholesale departure from the latter. See, for example, Boone, *The Bible Tells Them So*, p. 57. Logical consistency is less pressing in an oral tradition than a text-based one.

3. For conversion to fundamentalist Christianity as taking on a new language, see Harding, *The Book of Jerry Falwell*, chap. 1.

4. More personal styles of giving were prominent in the one working-class Methodist congregation my parents served where, at its annual Christmas party, church women presented my mother with an apron on which individuals then pinned various amounts of money. The benevolent work of fundamentalist congregations tends to be done personally and not handed over to specialized agencies. It is often linked with evangelism and invitations to join their community, for example, in Shawmut River's bus ministry. In its early historical development, fundamentalists were involved in benevolence among the urban poor though they objected to "social gospel" ministries conceived in broad programmatic terms to be carried out by impersonal, bureaucratic organizations.

5. Stevick, *Beyond Fundamentalism*, p. 57.

10 / Bible Study

1. In a world dense with face-to-face talk where one is rarely alone, thinking could quite understandably take the form of talking to oneself, and Pastor Valenti had rightly judged Doug as a particularly thoughtful person and, therefore, as someone who might talk to himself a lot.

2. It is perhaps popular conservatives' grounding in oral culture that leads them to champion the "phonics" approach to teaching reading with such a moral fervor. It is also reflected, naturally enough, in weak spelling.

3. See Harry Stout, "Word and Order in Colonial New England," in Hatch and Noll, eds., *The Bible in America*, pp. 23ff.

11 / Prayer Life

1. See, for example, Elaine Pagels, *Beyond Belief: The Secret Gospel of Thomas.*

2. This relation to biblical stories, making them part of shared lived experiences, is similar to that described for the Christianity of African-American slaves. See Raboteau, *Slave Religion*, p. 250.

3. For fundamentalists' stress on the supernatural, see, for example, Marsden, "Fundamentalism as an American Phenomenon," p. 215. See also Torrey, ed., *The Fundamentals*, including articles originally published in 1917. See chap. 1, pp. 14 and 18, and, for Genesis, p. 103.

4. Hague, "At-One-Ment by Propitiation," in George M. Marsden, ed., *The Fundamentals*, vol. 11, p. 29. *The Fundamentals* were booklets published together and widely distributed. For more on this important publication in the history of fundamentalism, see Carpenter, *Revive Us Again*, p. 7.

5. The idea of substitution is inherent in the view of reciprocity as a system developed by the French social theorist Marcel Mauss in his classic study, *The Gift.* In Mauss's analysis, gifts or services to others are always restoring imbalances created by other gifts at different points in the system. "What goes 'round, comes 'round" does not refer to one gift in the concrete but, according to Mauss, to the spirit of that gift moving throughout a system of giving-and-receiving relationships. For an illuminating discussion of conservative Catholics' treatment of the Eucharist as a sacrifice, see Nancy Jay, *Throughout Your Generations*, p. 112. For the modern view of the world as "separate individuals, joined in temporary, voluntary association," see ibid., p. 150.

In his scholarly treatment of atonement, which he relates to the modern concept of alienation, Dillistone finds it impossible to apply past understandings of atonement as substitutionary payment from, say, Hebrew or Roman law, because, he concludes, "no strictly penal theory of atonement can be expected to carry conviction in the world of the twentieth century." In his discussion Dillistone does not consider the continued force of reciprocity in the lives of many sharing that century with him and their close resonance with those presumably archaic legal categories. Dillistone, *The Christian Understanding of Atonement*, chap. 5, especially p. 214.

6. Franklin Johnson, "The Atonement," in *The Fundamentals*, vol. 6, chap. 4, p. 61. To say this understanding of Christ's passion as substitutionary atonement leads to "passivity" in religious life, as Marcus Borg argues, depends on ripping this doctrine out of the cultural context within which it emerges and has its meaning. Borg, *Meeting Jesus Again*, p. 130. Members of Shawmut River would hardly be considered *passive* in their faith, nor do they see Christ's work on the cross as the end of their spiritual journey, as Borg sees it. Instead, presuming this cultural context, they feel obliged to pay him back with their lives. The activism they pursue, of course—including fulfilling self-sacrificial duties to others, spreading his good news, supporting his church or fighting to see their nation turn back to God—does not go in directions Borg sees as *real* activism: that is, to "challenge the culture," as he puts it, or, we might go on to imagine, to promote programs for human welfare or social reform relying on impersonal bureaucratic means of the state or church. One step in the development of liberal theology in its struggle with fundamentalism was the claim that God's inspiration was not verbal or propositional, but rather *conceptual*—that is, imagined more abstractly. Timothy Weber, "The Two-Edged Sword: The Fundamentalist Use of the Bible," in *The Bible in America*, ed. Nathan O. Hatch and Mark A. Noll, p. 107.

7. In my description of the culture of Shawmut River's members, some may recognize my debt to Richard Hoggart's exemplary portrait of English working-class culture in his classic *The Uses of Literacy*, especially where he describes working-class life as "the 'dense and concrete life,' a life whose main stress is on the intimate, the sensory, the detailed, and the personal" (p. 88). The first of the series of Harry Potter books by J. K. Rowling was *Harry Potter and the Sorcerer's Stone.*

8. This characterization of the post-Enlightenment worldview is taken from an interview I conducted with Dr. Andrew Walls, professor emeritus and founder of the Center for the Study of Christianity in the Non-Western World at the University of Edinburgh, which we filmed at Yale Divinity School in July 2001 for a documentary film project on African Christianity.

9. For a liberal clergyman's rejection of the idea of substitutionary atonement, see Spong, *Rescuing the Bible*, p. 69.

12 / Biblical Morality

1. In this connection, it is interesting to consider differences in moral outlook found by sociologist Kristin Luker in her study of right-to-life and pro-choice supporters. According to Luker, unlike her pro-life activists, who saw morality as an "eternally valid," "inflexible" and "unambiguous set of rules," her pro-choice activists saw morality "as the application of a few general ethical principles to a vast array of cases" and "often find themselves debating moral dilemmas with themselves." Luker, *Abortion and the Politics of Motherhood*, pp. 174 and 184–85. Similarly, the sociologist James Davison Hunter finds the culture wars to be "rooted in different systems of moral understanding," which he describes and terms, respectively, *orthodox* and *progressive.* Hunter, *Culture Wars*, pp. 42 ff.

2. I have in mind here Lawrence Kohlberg's conception of "universal stages of moral development," in which he characterizes as more "rational," "mature" and "adequate" moral orientations where decisions of conscience are made "in accord with self-chosen ethical principles," which are "abstract" and "universal principles of justice." Kohlberg, *The Philosophy of Moral Development*, especially essay 1, "Indoctrination Versus Relativity in Value Education," p. 19, and "From *Is* to *Ought*: How to Commit the Naturalistic Fallacy and Get Away with It in the Study of Moral Development," pp. 105 and 147–68. See also James Fowler's similar conception of "faith development" in stages, in which the "mythic-literal" stage, found initially in children and relying on "stories, rules, and implicit values of the family's community of meanings," is eventually superseded by an "individuative-reflective faith," where there must be "a critical choosing of one's beliefs, values, and commitments, which come to be taken as a systemic unity," and "matters of more explicit commitment." See, for example, Fowler, *Becoming Adult, Becoming Christian*, pp. 52–62. To my mind, these approaches miss the point that while individually chosen, abstract and explicit forms of faith and morality might be suitable for urban middle-class situations in modern industrial society, they are less suitable for villagelike communities all over the globe in which the vitality and coherence of an oral tradition make more implicit and collectively assumed forms, and more concrete, narrative ones, work better. Young people growing up in such settings can be seen learning progressively how to orient themselves in such a world. For Shawmut River Baptist Church's teenagers, see chap. 15, pp. 344–45.

3. Even at the level of the Bible school, as one historian of that key fundamentalist

institution has shown, education itself tended to be equated with evangelizing. See Brereton, *Training God's Army*, p. 159.

4. Ibid., p. 96.

5. But curiously enough, "Don't count your chickens before they hatch," which I heard two church members marvel about being in scripture, turns out not to be in the Bible. Rather, it is to be traced to an Aesop's fable. See Flexner and Flexner, *Wise Words*, pp. 42–43. Apparently the difficulty keeping straight which sayings are actually in the Bible and which are not is a familiar one in fundamentalist circles, as a charming book of humor addressed to born-again Christians shows. Tongue in cheek, it puts to readers the test of picking out genuine Bible quotes from a list of sayings, including: "An eye for an eye . . ." [Matthew 5:38]; "There is no new thing under the sun" [Ecclesiastes 1:9]; "A watched pot never boileth" [sounds like the King James Version, but it isn't there]; and "Let it be" [spiritual truth from Paul McCartney]; etc. Klein et al., *Growing Up Born Again*, p. 37.

6. As this book nears completion, a vigorous movement is under way among fundamentalist Baptists to insist upon the King James Version as the only authoritative one for true Christians, even if fundamentalist seminaries, like Falwell's, teach that it is not the best available translation.

7. Problems of logistical consistency become more troublesome for fundamentalist scholars than for local congregations, recalling Stevick's observation, quoted above, that what is true about fundamentalist scholars is not likely to be true of popular fundamentalists, and vice versa. Stevick, *Beyond Fundamentalism*, p. 57. For example, after detailing some of the absurdities fundamentalist scholars arrive at in trying to reconcile the inerrancy of the Old Testament over and against contrary teachings from Jesus, James Barr quite sensibly recognizes: "Here again, as in so many things [*sic*], it is probable that the living religious instinct of fundamentalists is to see things differently from their scholarly apologists." Barr, *Fundamentalism*, p. 82. For similar observations about the nature of moral teachings in Greek poetry drawn from an oral tradition, including their tolerance of inconsistencies and contradictions, see Havelock, *Preface to Plato*, pp. 185ff.

8. In this vein, it has been noted that conservatives often have difficulty discussing the rationale for pastoral counseling decisions they make. Personal communication, Jane Garrett, who, in addition to being this book's editor, is an Episcopal priest.

Much scholarly discussion of Bible-based teachings about gender roles in the family among fundamentalists, I believe, is weakened by not bearing in mind these aspects of their normal context of use in close-knit congregations and the family circles making them up. Scholarly commentators treat writings in Christian self-help literature (which are rarely mentioned by subjects) or biblical sayings expressed by subjects as general rules, without seeing how they are used in real-life contexts. From a typical scholarly standpoint, divergent views are seen as so many inconsistencies and contradictions, rather than as a multifaceted, commonsensical approach to creating a "godly family" over the infinite particularities of concrete contexts.

9. For biblical prohibitions of divorce, see Matthew 5:32, Mark 10:2–12 and Genesis 2:23–24. For instructions on how to divorce properly, see Deuteronomy 24:1–2.

10. Phil Strong's proposal to turn social welfare over to local churches occurred fifteen years before this idea became embodied in legislation permitting the federal government to fund social services through "faith-based" communities. Phil described his proposal in straightforward ways without discussing problems that might arise from requiring citizens to be associated with particular religious communities, from

problems of scale and geographic mobility within and across states or from the massive amount of documentation and record keeping that would be involved.

11. In moments of ideological dispute, this awareness of a culturally conditioned common sense at work might appear more explicitly, as when, for example, the contributor to *The Fundamentals* on atonement appealed to what "any man with sense today" understands, or at the time of the famed Scopes trial, when Williams Jennings Bryan appealed to "the common people" to provide "the final and efficient corrective power" on the truth of evolution or creation. Dyson Hague, "At-One-Ment by Propitiation," in *The Fundamentals*, ed. George M. Marsden, vol. 9, chap. 2, p. 29. For Bryan, see Numbers, *The Creationists*, p. 44. For other fundamentalist appeals to "common sense," see Marsden, *Fundamentalism*, pp. 61 and 111.

13 / Fundamentalism and Tradition

1. For an exploration of modern feminism's affinities to individualism, see Fox-Genovese, *"Feminism Is Not the Story of My Life."* For another assessment of feminism's adopting middle-class individualism, see Epstein, "What Happened to the Women's Movement?," pp. 10–12.

2. For efforts to explain "pro-family" conservatism in terms of worldview or elements of moral culture, see, for example, Luker, *Abortion and the Politics of Motherhood*, and Hunter, *Culture Wars*. Such approaches leave us with conflicting worldviews descending on the body politic out of the blue, culture *ex machina*, as my friend and colleague Nancy Jay used to say, with little rhyme or reason why they are found among some people—or groups of people—rather than others.

One of the conclusions of recent writings on conservative Christians' attitudes and practices surrounding gender and family life is that elements of culture, in and of themselves, cannot account for observed differences. As Bartkowski puts it pointedly, *contra* Hunter, "The culture wars thesis does not explain how a shared evangelical commitment to biblical inerrancy (an orthodox form of moral authority) can produce such radically divergent gender and family discourses among conservative luminaries." Bartkowski, *Remaking*, pp. 163–64. Compare also Gallagher's point that the idea of biblical inerrancy isn't what makes evangelical Christians accept men's headship in family and church. See her *Evangelical Identity*, pp. 79–82.

Other scholars have tried to ground these conflicting worldviews in other dimensions of social reality. Brigitte and Peter Berger, in *The War over the Family*, conceive of liberal support coming from the New Class, or "knowledge class," but explain it mainly in terms of the knowledge class's vested interest in the expansion of the welfare state and the educational/therapeutic industry, not in terms of how their lives and families are organized. This conception affords us no way to explain, or make better sense of, the ensemble of interests and enthusiasms associated with either the "professional camp" or the "neotraditionalist" camp the authors identify—for example, the professional camp's tendency to see the individual as the unit of society. Nor does it enable us to understand those members of the helping professions—for instance, the nurses or self-employed doctors rooted in particular localities—who are staunch conservatives. On the other hand, *descriptively* speaking, much of the Bergers' account, including their recognition of alliances between the old upper-class and working-class groups around traditionalist enthusiasms regarding family and gender, fits the analysis put forward here. (For a similar application of "new class theory" to explain the emergence of "humanistic moralism" in family matters among educated and affluent evangelical Christians, see Hunter, *American Evangelicalism*, pp. 107ff.)

Another approach to accounting for differences between conservatives and liberals in this realm of conflict has been the opposition between "locals" and "cosmopolitans" originally conceived by the sociologist Robert Merton and further elaborated by Alvin Gouldner. This starts from the observation that some people in a community have an orientation to local concerns, others to more cosmopolitan ones. One particularly instructive example of this approach is an unpublished doctoral dissertation on fundamentalist-modernist conflicts in early-twentieth-century America. See Ellis, *Social and Religious Factors*. Ellis's findings, which are unique in trying to provide sociologically relevant data on opposed parties in the conflicts, do much to corroborate the argument advanced here. (See chap. 6, note 14.) But the opposition between local and cosmopolitan *orientations* simply posits people with these different orientations without trying to explain why different people in the same settings would have these different orientations to begin with. Neither does it help us understand the particular commitments of either group to issues of gender and family, which have provided so much of the substance of the conflicts in question.

3. For the emergence among evangelicals of biblical feminists, see Gallagher, *Evangelical Identity*, pp. 44ff. Recent studies of evangelical Christians have pointed to weaknesses in the "culture wars" thesis of sociologist James Hunter by asking whether "culture" itself is a source of conflicts between conservatives and liberals. They point to the existence of biblical feminists and a wider range of views among the carriers of conservative Christian culture than Hunter's model of polarizing cultures would suggest. Smith et al., "The Myth of Culture Wars," and Bartkowski, *Remaking*, pp. 163–64. By grounding contrary politics of the family in different patterns of organizing family and personal life, the account offered here allows us to conceive of change in the carriers of particular religious traditions and among whom, and under what circumstances, we would expect liberalization to occur. It also does not presume the kind of polarization Hunter predicts. See chap. 22.

4. Martin Luther, *Works*, vol. 6, p. 301, cited by Hatch in Hatch and Noll, eds., *The Bible in America*, p. 61.

5. Hinduism has a more expansive, open-ended corpus of sacred writings. See Gold, "Organized Hinduism," pp. 542ff.

6. This characterization comes from the cover material for a book by Joseph Fletcher, *Situation Ethics*. Fletcher was then, in 1966, Professor of Social Ethics at Episcopal Theological School in Cambridge, Massachusetts.

7. Marsden, *Fundamentalism*, p. 25.

8. Fundamentalists are fond of naming their new radio or television programs things like *The Old-Time Gospel Show* or *The Old-Fashioned Revival Hour*. In his historical account of fundamentalism in the 1930s, Joel Carpenter describes the fundamentalist flagship school at the time, Wheaton College, in Wheaton, Illinois, as "revelling" in its old-fashionedness. Carpenter, *Revive Us Again*, p. 63.

9. For this definition of *tradition*, see the *Oxford English Dictionary*. This conception of traditional legitimation comes from Max Weber's classic conception of it as one type of legitimation. See his *Economy and Society*, vol. 1, chap. 3, "The Types of Legitimate Domination," pp. 212ff. My friend and colleague the late Nancy Jay used the expression "culture *ex machina*" to characterize certain facile sociological arguments attributing any social fact to culture. Jay, *Throughout Your Generations*.

10. Weber uses this phrase, taken from Schiller (*Das ewig Gestrige*) in "Politics as a Vocation," p. 78.

11. For the argument that fundamentalists cannot be considered traditionalists, see the editors of a multivolume study of fundamentalism: Marty and Appleby, "Conclusion: An Interim Report on a Hypothetical Family," pp. 825–27. Marty and

Appleby's point that fundamentalists are a new movement that is part and parcel of the modern world is well taken, but that does not preclude the practice, logic and primacy of traditional legitimation, particularly in the realm of family and personal life. Marty and Appleby introduce this volume by saying that fundamentalists "begin as traditionalists" but then "fight back with great innovative power." (Do they then immediately become nontraditionalists?) Marty and Appleby, "The Fundamentalism Project: A User's Guide," p. ix. That fundamentalists make use of the modern mass media or modern advertising techniques, as these scholars argue—or, by the same token, that villagers use genetically engineered seeds or cell phones—does not mean either group has jettisoned traditional discourses of legitimation in family or other quarters of life.

At times the views of these scholars seem more like ideological polemic than social analysis, as if they are saying fundamentalists have no claim to be the true carriers of tradition—we do. For instance, see Barr, *Fundamentalism*, where he writes, "It is not fundamentalism, but the mainstream of modern theology, including its involvement in critical biblical scholarship, that really stands in continuity with classical theology" (p. 184). For a fuller account of the pitfalls inherent in the traditional/modern dichotomy as used in studies of the developing world, see Ault, "Making 'Modern' Marriage 'Traditional.'" The belated recognition that change does occur within traditional societies at one point generated a minor growth industry among contemporary scholars documenting this and that "invention" of tradition. For example, see Eric Hobsbawm and Terence Ranger, eds., *The Invention of Tradition*.

12. These understandings of traditionalism, which recognize its deceptively innovative and amalgamating character, might alter the terms of debate among scholars about whether American fundamentalists are to be seen as traditionalists, harking back to America's distinct past, or primitivists, looking back to the first-century church for standards and teachings. See Hughes, ed., *The American Quest*, part 2, pp. 81ff., especially the discussion between Joel Carpenter and Mark Noll. Seeing traditionalism in these ways, we can understand how they can combine both in an amalgam conceived without history—time out of mind. For an earlier discussion of some of these issues, see pp. 157–59 above.

13. For example, the feminist movement of the 1960s and 1970s, with its critique of gender roles in family and personal life, cut a broader swath across the body politic in the United States than elsewhere. In France and England, for example, it was carried more narrowly in cosmopolitan intellectual circles, especially in Paris and London. At the time—in the late 1960s—the proportion of young people attending institutions of higher learning in the United States was several times higher than it was in Britain. In America historically, college students were prime consumers of rationalized schemes for family life. In its early days in the first half of the twentieth century, the sociology of the family largely consisted of how-to courses designed to give college students necessary guidance in marriage and family matters.

14. I mean *science* in the broadest sense of the term, including the human and social sciences, as Germans use the term *Wissenschaft*.

15. Noll, "The Image of the United States as a Biblical Nation, 1776–1865," in Hatch and Noll, eds., *The Bible in America*, p. 45. In the same volume, see also Nathan Hatch, "Sola Scriptura and Novus Ordo Seclorum." This claim to tradition is one reason fundamentalists, despite feeling themselves outsiders to an atheistic modern world, believe themselves to be true heirs of America's establishment. This is another one of the three paradoxes Marsden presents as vital to understanding American fundamentalism: that it sees itself as both outsider and heir to America's establishment tradition. Marsden, *Fundamentalism*, p. 6.

16. Joel Carpenter gives the following examples of fundamentalist practice regarding God's promise that his word would not return to him void. "They printed Bible verses on billboards, jackknife handles, and automobile spare tire covers; one naturalist wrote them on tags he tied to Canada geese." In Hughes, ed., *The American Quest*, p. 107.

17. Meeks, *The Origins of Christian Morality*, pp. 49 and 112.

18. Ibid., pp. 66ff. These problems arise in the scholarly understanding of other texts originating in oral performance. For ancient Greek works, see Ford, "The Inland Ship," and Havelock, *Preface to Plato*, chap. 10, especially pp. 182–86. I am indebted, here and elsewhere, to my friend and colleague Andrew Ford for pointing to these connections to the study of texts from the ancient world.

19. The historian George Marsden singled out ambivalence toward higher learning as another one of the three paradoxes defining American fundamentalism. Marsden, *Fundamentalism and American Culture*, p. 7.

20. Opposition to expert opinion in the interpretation of scripture and in favor of the common man's was very much part of the populist strain of revival in America's Second Great Awakening in the early nineteenth century. Armstrong, *The Battle for God*, pp. 87–91. For the prominence of such themes among American fundamentalists, see, for example, Carpenter, *Revive Us Again*, pp. 35ff., and for the case of Frank Norris, Hankins, *God's Rascal*, p. 173.

21. For this account of Baconian conceptions of science over and against those involving speculative hypotheses or theories, see Marsden, *Fundamentalism*, pp. 19–20, 55–56, 212–14; and also Bozeman, *Protestants in an Age of Science*, pp. 103ff.

22. For a good characterization of the ground rules of modern science, see Kaufman, *Methodology of the Social Sciences*. Whether "facts" in the human and social sciences, which depend on meanings of actors rooted in the cultures in question, can ever be framed in ways independent of observers' cultural backgrounds is extremely doubtful. For their part, Sharon and Frank Valenti told me that they saw science primarily as a means of learning about and demonstrating the nature of God, rather than a means of pursuing progress in life.

23. Brereton, *Training God's Army*, pp. 34 and 87.

24. On this pattern of change in fundamentalist theology, see Barr, *Fundamentalism*, pp. 161–62. Harding presents the example of racial segregation, among others, to show how change takes place surreptitiously within fundamentalism. She does not, however, present this process as intrinsic to tradition carried by the spoken word or consider the role of an interpretive community in contributing to those changes. Harding, *The Book of Jerry Falwell*, chap. 6, especially p. 180. Another of the many examples of change in fundamentalists' traditionalist discourse might be the fate of the Revised Standard Version of the Bible. Heralded by liberal Christians when it appeared in the 1950s as an improved edition grounded in historical and linguistic scholarship, it was condemned—and even ceremonially burned—by fundamentalists as "the Bible of the Antichrist." Yet a quarter of a century later, in 1978, a quite similar translation appearing as the New International Version became the version favored among many wings of the fundamentalist movement. See Boone, *The Bible Tells Them So*, p. 32. Griffith provides another example of how surreptitiously change was managed in Women Aglow, a conservative charismatic women's fellowship she studied, when women were first permitted under its constitution to serve as "advisers" on its international board. Griffith, *God's Daughters*, p. 155.

25. For these examples, see Marsden, *Fundamentalism*, p. 58.

26. See Numbers, *Darwinism Comes to America*, pp. 109ff. and 3ff. For a critical

review of the burgeoning literature debating Darwinian evolution from creationist and intelligent-design points of view, see Crewes, "Saving Us from Darwin."

27. The quotation is from Sandeen in Frank, *Less than Conquerors*, p. 73. In his useful account of dispensationalism, Frank writes that its appeal resided in "its rationalistic neatness and systematic comprehensiveness" giving to those using it "the key to all of history, handed down by God himself" (pp. 73–74). For a general account of dispensationalism, see Marsden, *Fundamentalism*, pp. 48–71, and the footnote, p. 242. See also Timothy Weber, *Living in the Shadow*.

28. Marsden points out these formal similarities between dispensationalism, on the one hand, and Darwinism and Marxism, on the other. Marsden, *Fundamentalism*, pp. 64ff.

29. Joel Carpenter, *Revive Us Again*, pp. 71ff., 89–109, and Appendix, p. 247. See also Marsden, *Fundamentalism*, p. 63, and Noll, *The Scandal*, pp. 132–37.

30. I recently found Karen Armstrong's characterization of fundamentalism as "new forms of faith to make the old traditions speak to them [believers] in their radically altered circumstances" as consistent with my own thinking here. See Armstrong, *The Battle for God*, p. 8.

Part Three

14 / To Film?

1. Michael Camerini's film *Dadi's Family* impressed me not only for its cross-cultural insight but also for its intimacy in portraying extended-family life in India. He went on to produce, among other things, a series of four programs for PBS on grass-roots agents of development, entitled *Local Heroes, Global Change*. (For these and other productions, see www.epidavros.org.)

2. This traditional doctrinal stand against political involvement was not as troublesome or difficult to overcome as some commentators think. See, for example, Boone, *The Bible Tells Them So*, p. 57. Though fundamentalists in the premillennial tradition always theorized that the world was bound to sink deeper into apostasy and unbelief, they nevertheless still hoped to be part of a revival extending the scope and influence of the true faith in America and beyond. Like their handling of issues of free will and determinism with respect to God's work in the world, they carried these theoretical inconsistencies lightly and felt no need to resolve them.

3. Given their limited connection to public groupings beyond family-based ones, it is all the more remarkable that these Shawmut River's families would give up their sons to risk their lives in national military service. It suggests how much their motivation depends upon the moral compulsion among men to sacrifice their lives, as a matter of male honor, to defend women and children in families. The unwarranted assumption that a lack of involvement in voluntary associations means social isolation and individualism underlies the widely influential analyses of Putnam, *Bowling Alone*, and before that, Bellah et al., *Habits of the Heart*. It is another one of the many ways intellectuals perceive the wider world through assumptions grounded in the taken-for-granted realities of their own family lives. See chap. 6, note 27 above.

4. For these dynamics in the creation of close-knit urban communities, see Suttles, *The Social Construction of Communities*.

5. For such an analysis, see Suttles, *The Social Construction of Communities*, and Kornblum, *Blue-Collar Community*.

6. This runs against the argument of Smith et al., "The Myth of Culture Wars," who suggest such ignorance is evidence that the culture wars never happened and were a media myth.

7. My coproducer, Michael Camerini, was and still is an independent filmmaker and cinematographer based in New York City (www.epidavras.org). Our principal editor, Adrienne Miesmer, was based in Cambridge, Massachusetts. Professor Donald Mathews, a historian of the religion of the South, was a third scholar consulting on the project, but Karen Fields and Nancy Jay played more critical roles. For Karen Fields's approach to the sociology of religion, see, first, her *Revival and Rebellion in Colonial Central Africa* and, later, her new translation of Emile Durkheim's *The Elementary Forms of Religious Life* with her remarkably substantive introduction to that volume. The approach of Nancy Jay, then a lecturer in social science and religion at Harvard Divinity School, is to be found in her book *Throughout Your Generations Forever.*

15 / Shooting

1. For schools being closed because of their practice of corporal punishment, see the *New York Times*, 3 and 30 June 1984. For the account of Janet Reno's decision regarding the Branch Davidian community in Waco, see Boyer, "Children of Waco," *The New Yorker* 71, no. 12 (15 May 1995): p. 42.

2. *Newsweek*, 16 July 2001, p. 42.

16 / Marriage

1. In this connection, see evidence about women lampooning men in all-women gatherings of Women Aglow in Griffith, *God's Daughters*, p. 155. Tensions around these categorical oppositions are bound to color, and give definition to, sexual desire itself.

2. Legitimating homosexuality would also raise tension on occasions of same-sex socializing prevalent in this social world. Recent debates over same-sex marriage, for example, seem too little informed about how opponents perceive this trend as actually threatening family life as they know it. See, for example, Jonathan Rauch's otherwise insightful article, in which he manages to convert President George W. Bush's stated objections to same-sex marriage into good reasons for actually *supporting* it. Why some people wholeheartedly identifying with Bush's view, including African-American church leaders, feel that gay marriage would threaten family life does not come into view at all in Rauch's piece. Better understanding such deeply rooted perceptions and feelings would help avoid our becoming hopelessly stuck in such a polarizing conflict. Rauch, "Power of Two," p. 13. For African-American church leaders' views that "gay marriage would contribute to the further erosion of traditional family structure in the black community," see Paulson, "Black clergy rejection," B1.

3. For the outburst from a Birthright activist about the word *sexuality*, see chap. 1, p. 4. Where sex is not seen as a necessary and important vehicle for intimacy in marriage and, instead, simply for procreation or for pleasure or recreation, it assumes less importance as an identity-forming, person-fulfilling practice. For example, it has been observed that working-class men may engage in homosexual acts—for example, truck drivers with homosexuals at truck stops—yet not see this as affecting their basic sexual identity. See Abraham Verghese, *My Own Country*, pp. 115–16. In this context, compare

Pastor Valenti's counsel to a man who has phoned him out of anxiety about his homosexual acts. See chapter 9, p. 144. "Just because you commit those acts," he had assured him, "doesn't mean you're a homosexual."

The same lack of importance of sex in marriage (apart from procreation) can be found in the propertied upper class, where extended-family ties cohere around family fortunes. It is manifest, for example, in the acceptance of a mistress or lover as a legitimate part of a stable configuration of marriage and family relationships. I remember an upper-class woman friend pointing out to me that her father's mistress even held signing privileges under his name at the very same country club to which she and her family belonged. For the propertied upper class, see also chap. 21.

According to Helen Horowitz, the new sexual frameworks (or discourses) elaborated in nineteenth-century America to guide and control sexual expression—such as Sylvester Graham's reform physiology or the free-love movement—were carried by the new urban middle class. These were not craftsmen, Horowitz writes, but, instead, employed clerks (who played more managerial roles at the time) and, at elite levels, doctors, writers, architects, engineers, etc. One of the more radical of these frameworks, she points out, placed sex at the core of one's being and held that sexual intercourse was natural as an expression of love, quite apart from the customary and communally sanctioned bonds of marriage. Helen Horowitz, *Rereading Sex*, pp. 87, 106, 121. For further discussion of these themes, see also my unpublished paper: Ault, "Sex, Love and Intimacy."

4. See Max Weber, *Economy and Society*, vol. 2, p. 604.

5. When marriage takes place within a vital extended-family constellation, there are often socially imposed restrictions on how autonomous and intimate a married couple might become. The classic study of this is Philip Slater, "On Social Regression." See also Georg Simmel on the qualities of two-person relationships as opposed to larger configurations of social relationships. Simmel, "The Isolated Individual."

6. See Stacey, *Brave New Families*. Stacey arrived at these conclusions by studying a feminist-minded administrator she met in an antipoverty agency in California's Silicon Valley, who then joined a charismatic church (pp. 28 and 34). See chap. 5, note 1.

7. In this regard, it is telling that Judith Stacey reports her evangelical Christian women as seeing feminism "as an autonomy text." Stacey, *Brave New Families*, p. 263. In making sense of her charismatic Christian women's acceptance of submission as part of God's plan for the family, Susan Rose concludes, "These women opt for intimacy and security over independence, and for community over individuality." Rose, "Women Warriors," p. 246.

8. For this conclusion about women in other conservative Christian congregations, see Stacey, *Brave New Families*; Rose, "Women Warriors"; Brasher, *Godly Women*; Manning, *God Gave Us the Right*; and Pevey et al., "Male God Imagery."

9. For an analysis of the forms of power available to women where families are embedded in kin-based networks, see Ault, *Class Differences in Family Structure*, chaps. 5 and 6. This pairing of factual powers in the face of formal authority seems the normal form taken by patrimonial authority underpinned by tradition, whether in relations between lord and peasant or in a modern household economy. Though subject to few limitations, in theory, the father's, or lord's, authority, according to Max Weber, is powerfully constrained, above all, by "the purely factual resistance against everything unwonted." Max Weber, *Economy and Society*, vol. 3, p. 1011. Or note, also, Gallagher's conclusion: "Husbands are expected to lead, but wives often find themselves getting the job done. In the end, being, not doing, is the essence of male leadership in evangelical homes." Gallagher, *Evangelical Identity*, p. 104.

10. Surprisingly enough, such an example actually occurred later in my fieldwork in one marriage at Shawmut River, where a husband, it was said, bought a rifle instead of a washing machine his family needed. (See p. 196.) This was recounted as reason for his wife to divorce him.

11. Themes of strong women needing to make room for men in the household come up repeatedly in the literature on marriage in conservative Christian families. See Rose, "Women Warriors," pp. 249ff.

12. John Rice in *The Home*, p. 102, observed in the 1940s that his fundamentalist women readers normally assumed that they should make decisions regarding home and family. And around Shawmut River, the normal running of a household was generally seen as women's doing.

13. Pohli, "Church Closets," p. 529.

14. Ibid.

Part Four

19 / "They've slandered my character!"

1. A husband and father's accountability and responsibility are key elements in powerful mechanisms of social control mediated by male honor. See Ault, *Class Differences in Family Structure*, chap. 6, "Gossip and Customary Controls over Family and Community Life."

20 / "Everybody could see it."

1. Some years later Scott Sanderson reported to me that he had recently read an article in a Christian magazine that had made him realize he and Sue might be more accurately described as "evangelical" rather than "fundamentalist."

2. For a discussion of the pastor's authority as arbiter of biblical interpretation, see Kathleen Boone, *The Bible Tells Them So*, p. 87.

21 / "The neck that turns the head"

1. See also chapter 7 on the Tatum scandal. It is hard to reconcile a close, realistic look at a congregation like Shawmut River with the view presented by some authors that fundamentalism represents an effort on the part of men to control women. If true, it would be hard to understand why women, who have historically made up the majority of fundamentalist congregations—including strong, intelligent women like Jean and Sharon—would be so invested in the faith and in the patriarchal models of authority it champions On the other hand, fundamentalism's aggressive insistence that men assume all visible positions of authority in the church, and its pride in championing a muscular Christianity appealing to men, as did figures as far apart as Billy Sunday and Frank Valenti, begs another, quite different, interpretation. When I once asked Pastor Valenti why he focused his energies more on winning husbands rather than wives to Christ, he responded quite simply, "because the women are much easier." It is not difficult to see why. For when we consider the pattern of change wrought in marriages by Shawmut River's ministry—focusing husbands more on family responsibilities and

bringing both spouses under a regime of biblical standards for marriage—it is more plausible to argue that fundamentalism is more attractive to women because it helps them control men. See also chap. 5, notes 3 and 5.

2. For evidence of families' greater involvement with a wife's kin, see evidence cited in Yanagisako, "Women-Centered Networks." Surveying relevant research in a number of advanced industrial nations, Yanagisako prefers to call such kin networks "women-centered." For more recent evidence about the prominence of women in "kinkeeping," see Gerstel, "The Third Shift," pp. 470 and 475. In 324 interviews with American wives and husbands, Gerstel found that wives' employment was associated with their substantially lower levels of "kinkeeping," especially for women "in more prestigious, time-consuming and lucrative jobs" (p. 475).

3. At Shawmut River and other conservative Christian churches, even though husbands are considered in God's plan for the family as leaders of a family's spiritual life, it is more often the case that wives exercise de facto leadership in first joining a congregation, and then bringing their husbands along afterward. In one ethnographic study of women in two charismatic Christian congregations in southern California, Brenda Brasher found that the vast majority of her subjects had been converted and begun attending these congregations before their husbands followed. Brasher, *Godly Women*, p. 111. For a fuller sociological account of cross-generational alliances among women where families are organized in and through kin-based networks, see Ault, *Class Differences in Family Structure*, chap. 5, especially pp. 273ff.

4. For further discussion of gossip at Shawmut River, see chapter 7, pp. 120ff. Gossip's ability to posit, tacitly, what "we know" or "we believe" in ways that are easy and unrestrained, uninterrupted by debate or interrogation, gives it that quality of pleasurable sociability and intimacy. Authentic gossip, of course, need not destroy reputations; it can build them, too. Moreover, it need not even affect reputations one way or another. It may be undertaken simply to enjoy, and further knit together, people sharing things in common as some we-group. Gossip, unlike rumor, is not normally conducted between strangers.

For a phenomenological analysis of gossip that explores how gossip works as a speech act, so that talk seen, according to the *Oxford English Dictionary*'s definition of gossip as "idle," "easy" and "unrestrained" and "groundless" is precisely the kind of talk that can affect reputations, see Ault, *Class Differences in Family Structure*, chap. 6, "Gossip and Customary Controls over Family and Community Life."

5. For the adversarial quality of men's talk described above on p. 63, see Tannen, *Gender and Discourse*, pp. 40ff. For the rapport-building nature of women's talk, see Tannen, *You Just Don't Understand*. The word *gossip* itself grew out of associations with very close-knit groups of women. Derived from the word *godsib*, gossip first meant "god kin"—like "godparent." But by the time it came to refer to a certain kind of talk, in sixteenth-century England, it had come to refer principally to a woman's close female kin, friends and neighbors invited to be present at her giving birth (*Oxford English Dictionary*, p. 310). Gossip's affinity to the feminine pole of traditional gender roles is evident in how some gay men embracing the feminine readily express their pleasure in practicing it—as a distinct benefit, perhaps, of their own gender identity.

6. We are reminded here of Susan Rose's observation that in domestic decisions made jointly by husband and wife, women "dominate the conversation." See Rose, "Women Warriors," p. 257.

7. It can be said that such a woman-controlled discourse overlaps considerably with those generated in various professions in which feminist-minded people, including men as well as women, are much involved—in the helping professions, for

example, or in academic life, not in, say, engineering, but especially in the humanities and social sciences.

8. For variations in power arrangements, recall that Sally Keener said of one church she attended that the pastor's wife "sort of ran the show indirectly," not something she or others said about the Valentis' regime at Shawmut River (chap. 4, p. 72). For a fuller analysis of authority and power in the context of family life, see Ault, *Class Differences in Family Structure*, chap. 5. For the case of the welfare mother given a hard time by Shawmut River's opinion makers, see chap. 5, note 1.

9. Among the impressive number of studies of conservative Christian communities that have appeared in the past decade, only one involved ethnographic research in a congregation with significant working-class membership, Brenda Brasher's insightful study of women in two charismatic congregations in southern California. Brasher, *Godly Women*. Brasher's study provides both evidence of this kind of women's power and other important lessons. Her key finding—and bold conclusion in a literature struggling to make sense of why conservative Christian women embrace patriarchal ideas of husbands' headship in family and church—is that, although women were "shut out of congregational authority, they still possess extraordinary power" (p. 75). Brasher attributes this power to an exclusively female discourse developed in "women's enclaves," that is, sex-segregated Bible studies and Sunday school classes (p. 64), through which, she says, women create "a symbolic alternative to overall congregational life" and, in moments of conflict and crisis, are able to shape church policy and, more generally, constrain a pastor's power by influencing "the way congregational winds were blowing" (pp. 78–79 and 85). This is very much in keeping with my observations at Shawmut River. Men may hold authority, Brasher concludes, but are "not actually in charge" (pp. 58–59).

Brasher's argument has been dismissed by one critic, who points out that, according to Brasher's own data, only one-fifth of the women in her more working-class congregation were participating in such women's enclaves to begin with (and only one-third in the more middle-class one). See Gallagher, *Evangelical Identity*, p. 13. What is missing in Brasher's account—and Gallagher's critique—is the wider context of women's *informal* discourse in the sex-segregated social life both within and around such congregations. At Shawmut River, for example, during two of the three years in which I did fieldwork, there were no formal women's groups, either Bible studies or prayer groups. But that did not mean that an exclusive domain of women's discourse did not exist *informally*. Or that such informal discourse was not given shape by preexisting, sex-segregated, family-based relationships. See above, chap. 6, p. 111.

But Brasher's study is of interest here as much for what it doesn't consider as what it does. Above all, I was surprised that Brasher did not inquire into her subjects' families of origin either as a foundation for women's discourse or an influence on their attitudes toward gender and family roles. This was especially puzzling since I was struck by how often important relations with relatives appeared in the conversion stories her subjects told, even in the unlikely environment of southern California, known for its rootless individualism. For instance, one church woman was moved to conversion by her brother and sister-in-law's lapse in faith (pp. 95–96); a second-generation Mexican-American woman found her daughter now learning Spanish while staying with her own mother (p. 17); and a blond-haired, blue-eyed surfer raised in a family of thirteen organized a "mini-industry of family, neighbors and friends" to search for her missing daughter and then found her way to faith by praying with a cousin (pp. 49–54).

I was even more puzzled, then, when Brasher made no reference to extended-family ties and, instead, even explained why her subjects first joined these churches by saying that during personal crises, they needed the "support of family or community" but often lived "far from where these resources were readily available to them" (pp. 30–31). I began to wonder whether these reported interactions with kin occurred over greater distances than they seemed or whether they were simply anomalies. Moreover, the fact that a sizable proportion of each congregation (one-third of the more working-class one) was from Mexican-American, African-American or Asian-American backgrounds heightened my suspicion that extended-family ties were present.

I was grateful to Professor Brasher, then, for clarifying the matter when I reached her by phone. No, she said, all these interactions among family had taken place locally in the everyday lives of her subjects. In fact, it had impressed her to find, in general, she said, that "their families were actually close-knit." But, she explained, "that was not a facet of their identity I was focused on. My focus was on authority, power and gender." Why an exploration of people's assumptions about gender and family roles wouldn't advise a consideration of their experiences in their families of origin still perplexed me. (How Brasher could then explain her subjects' coming to these churches as a result of their *distance* from family and community points again, perhaps, to the kind of perceptual problems I have been discussing here. As with Bill Moyers' film *The Vanishing Family*, discussed above, these perceptual problems are not simply individual but also have a collective character. See pp. 112–13 and chap. 6, note 29.)

Yet Brasher is not alone in this neglect. In another major study of conservative Christians attitudes toward gender and family, the research team carrying out the comprehensive survey upon which it was based made no inquiry into their subjects' families of origin (except whether they were religious or not). See Sally Gallagher, *Evangelical Identity*, and the wider study from which her data were drawn, in Smith et al., *American Evangelicalism: Embattled and Thriving*, Appendix D, pp. 258ff., especially p. 283.

In Brasher's own study, however, one can see how ignoring patterns of family relationships takes its toll on key parts of her argument. The real question, Brasher says quite boldly in her book, is why her fundamentalist women express no dismay or discontent with the patriarchal views their leaders enunciate about gender and family, and even express their acceptance of them (p. 126). These views include, according to her account: that the godly order of family and church requires different and complementary roles for men and women, in which men are "head" (p. 144); that abortion is *not* to be seen as an option for the ordinary married woman who unexpectedly becomes pregnant (p. 159); that a mother's work outside the home is not justified simply because of her own interest in such work (p. 162); that homosexuality is condemned and proposed legislation prohibiting sexual preference as a reason for discriminating in housing and employment is opposed (pp. 138 and 133). Despite her subjects' affirmation of all these traditional, essentialist and patriarchal teachings, Brasher concludes that these women are as much feminist as they are antifeminist. Why? Because, Brasher explains, they support equal pay for equal work and legislation against wife battery and marital rape (on these grounds, even Ronald Reagan and George Bush might qualify), and because one leader describes herself as a "feminist" because she (like Sharon Valenti, p. 258 above) says she doesn't agree with everything her husband, the pastor, teaches (though this pastor's wife adds, in an important qualification, that she is not "feminist" in the way "the world" views it [pp. 91 and 198]).

How, then, does Brasher explain her fundamentalist women's acceptance of the "disempowering" idea of male headship in family and church? What happens is this, she writes: Women come to these congregations and exploit "the same categorical gender differences men use to achieve sexual dominance" in order to create female enclaves, which give them some measure of power. Unfortunately, she says, "by luring active women to invest themselves in a congregational subsection they abet male dominance of overall congregational life. . . . Siphoning off the time and energies of some of the most talented congregational women from overall congregational life, they help keep women under the sacred canopy of Christian fundamentalism who might otherwise deem its gender biases unacceptable and either press for change or leave" (p. 112).

That is, according to Brasher, women coming to these congregations—women she otherwise deems "tradition-prone," holding "cardinal ideas" she, as "a committed feminist," disagrees with—might just as well react against their leaders' patriarchal teachings from feminist points of view. But why, then, have they been attracted to these churches to begin with? Why haven't they rejected their leaders' patriarchal teachings at the outset, or all along? Brasher also notes that the vast majority of women first come to these churches on their own and then bring their husbands to join afterward. How, then, are they actually "lured" into getting involved in women's enclaves to begin with? And bearing in mind, as mentioned above, that only a small fraction of church women (one-fifth in the more working-class congregation) participate in such enclaves to begin with, how do we explain the other four-fifths? Wouldn't a realistic consideration of subjects' preexisting attitudes toward gender and family formed in their families of origin, and inscribed in their ongoing "close-knit" family relationships, help us understand why the patriarchal teachings of their churches don't dismay these women or put them off, or why they find themselves readily at home in their traditional sex-segregated socializing?

Brasher is not alone in offering implausible, even self-contradictory, explanations for why conservative Christian women continue to embrace ideas of men's headship in family and church. For example, after demonstrating how malleable and adaptable conservative Christians' cultural "tool-kits" are—containing notions picked up here to do this and there to do that, in pragmatic fashion—sociologist Sally Gallagher explains evangelicals' persistent commitment to the idea of husbands' "headship" in family and church simply by the fact that this idea is a necessary boundary-marking symbol defining evangelicals as an embattled community in American life. Gallagher, *Evangelical Identity*. For cultural elements as "tool-kits," see p. 14 and passim, and for "headship," pp. 81–84 and 169–74. But how necessary and inflexible is the idea of husband's headship as one tool, among many, in their cultural "tool-kits"? And how distinctly "countercultural" and boundary defining is it to begin with, as Gallagher asserts? Is the idea that a man is the head of the household counter to American culture at large? Or to the culture of its working-class people? Or to the culture of Catholic immigrants, like Irish-, Polish-, Italian-, Croatian- and Hispanic-Americans? I do not think so. Furthermore, why are *new* converts to evangelicalism attracted to its family teachings to begin with, or at least not uncomfortable with them? (Manning makes a similar argument for her charismatic evangelicals, who were selected on the basis that they were all new to evangelicalism. Manning, *God Gave Us the Right*, chap. 7.)

Or, Gallagher argues, taking another tack, evangelicals embrace ideas of husbands' headship because it attaches to "other ideas about the nature of God and human beings" they already have—for example, that men are initiators and piercers, or that God, as father, is a source of authority, and so on (p. 172). Again, how distinctly *evangelical* are these ideas? Don't they and their equivalents have some resonance in the wider culture? Moreover, if these ideas, unlike other available tools, are so fixed and necessary, why do some evangelicals growing up with them shed them for more genuinely feminist views of family life? More important, perhaps, why the lion's share of

Gallagher's evangelical subjects report seeing feminism as a source of chaos, disorder and social breakdown, or something undermining their security as women, is not something that can be illuminated by an approach that ignores subjects' experience in and with their families of origin (see pp. 148 and 166–67).

For suggestive evidence on the importance of families of origin and their configuration within specific kinds of communities to explain support for conservative or liberal politics of the family, see Nancy Ammerman's findings about the social makeup of protagonists in battles between fundamentalists and moderates in the Southern Baptist Convention in the 1980s. On these findings in Ammerman's *Baptist Battles*, see chap. 6, note 14, above.

10. See also chap. 16, p. 252ff.

11. In the same vein, it is not uncommon in fundamentalist Baptist churches in the Baptist Bible Fellowship or Jerry Falwell tradition for sons or sons-in-law to succeed fathers as head pastors. For at least one possible dynamic involved in governing larger, family-based institutions, consider what two social scientists discovered about how traditional gender roles shaped conflict in an extended family in the wealthy business class of Mexico City. The family ran a number of businesses that functioned together informally as a conglomerate. Men held all positions of formal authority, but when conflicts arose between different branches of the same conglomerate, their commitment to face-saving honor made it difficult for them to handle them. Instead, conflicts were handled in the communicative work of family women, in which one elder woman played a critical role. The researchers observed her spending a good part of each day either on the phone or visiting with the wives or women relatives of the male parties involved. They, in turn, as wives, sisters or mothers would speak to the men involved, bringing collective pressure and sentiment to bear on the issue. See Lomnitz and Lizaur, "The History of a Mexican Urban Family." Some material was presented in an earlier paper by the authors at the Conference on Women and Development, Wellesley College, June 1–6, 1976. This pattern in a family-based enterprise involving sharply dichotomous gender roles, I would argue, may bear similarities to what occurs in churches like Shawmut River or other family-based institutions, such as fundamentalist colleges or Bible schools.

A grim account of Frank Norris' abusive attempts to make his son heir apparent to his fundamentalist empire can be found in Hankins's recent book, *God's Rascal*, pp. 128ff. Throughout the book, Norris' wife and mother, and any involvement they might have had with his ministries, are off the radar screen of this study. Professor Hankins explained that he was studying Norris' "public," not "private, life" (personal communication). Yet, upon the death of Norris' wife, during the tribute given her during Sunday-morning worship at their home church in Fort Worth, Texas, Louis Entzminger, a professor in Norris' then-thriving Bible Baptist Seminary and an organizational figure in the congregation, recounted for all those assembled "one experience I had with Mrs. Norris that I would like to mention." Up to that point, Entzminger explained, there had been much talk among Norris and his associates about founding a seminary, but always with the assumption that it would be located in Detroit. But, Entzminger recalled, "One day in 1939, in the early spring, Dr. Norris, Mrs. Norris and myself were present in his office. I looked at Mrs. Norris and said, 'I won't say this to Dr. Norris, I don't know what he thinks about it, but I'll say it to you, Mrs. Norris, that the place to build this great institution is in this church [that is, in Fort Worth] . . . I believe this is the place and this is the time.' She looked at me with a twinkle in her eye," he continued, "and said—I'll tell you the very words she said—'I think you've got something there,' and that was the beginning of the

Bible Baptist Seminary." On that occasion, Entzminger continued, Frank Norris said that he didn't have time to build a Bible institute himself, but he offered a piece of land and to do "everything in the world I can to back you up," to which Mrs. Norris said, "Amen!"

Entzminger said in conclusion, "And she encouraged me in every way." See transcript published as "Tribute to a Great Wife and Mother," *The Fundamentalist* (Fort Worth, Texas), 13 April 1927, pp. 3–4. Does this account suggest that the story of this church and its seminary is separable from Norris' "private life"? Where family is a key building block in institutional life, the distinction between "public" and "private" does not hold in ways many intellectuals assume. See chap. 6, above, pp. 102–104.

12. For Schlafly, see *Current Biography Yearbook*, 1978, pp. 360ff.; for Limbaugh, *Current Biography Yearbook*, 1993, p. 345ff.; and for Robertson, see Harrell, *Pat Robertson*, chap. 5. For another view of such alliances, see Berger and Berger, *The War over the Family*, pp. 38–39.

13. For the appeal of conservative stances on issues of gender and sexuality to Hispanic-American voters, see research reported in Adam Nagourney and Janet Elder, "Hispanics Back Big Government and Bush, Too," *New York Times*, 3 August 2003, p. 1.

14. For Norris' early support of the New Deal and his later reversal, see Hankins, *God's Rascal*, pp. 95ff. Other sources of division came into view at Shawmut River when a well-known right-wing author from a patrician background came to preach one Sunday. He arrived with his wife from New Hampshire dressed in the worn tweed jacket of a New England gentleman. But after the service during which he preached on conservative issues of the day, he and his wife begged off invitations to dinner and further socializing with Shawmut River's leadership and, to members' disappointment and dismay, hastily left.

15. See, for example, Gabriel Kolko, *The Triumph of Conservatism*.

16. I was pleased with the greater coherence provided by this way of interpreting the popular base of conservative pro-family politics: the way it enabled one to resolve apparent paradoxes and puzzles—such as women's support of patriarchal models of authority in church and family—and to make better sense of new-right enthusiasms that appeared, at first glance, to be contradictory, such as abortion and militarism. I was also pleased with the way it fit patterns in evidence gathered with other frameworks in mind. For example, the Bergers' use of new-class theory to interpret these conflicts in their *The War over the Family;* or Hunter's characterization of opponents in his *Culture Wars*, p. 302; or Ellis's evidence in *Social and Religious Factors* on the social backgrounds of protagonists in the fundamentalist/modernist controversies at the beginning of the twentieth century (see chap. 13, note 2); or studies discussed in chap. 6, note 14.

Luker notes that one of the measurable differences between pro-choice and pro-life activists she studied was that the latter had more children and had them earlier than the former. That is one way, of course, to facilitate the creation of extended-family ties across generations. Luker, *Abortion and the Politics of Motherhood*, p. 196.

17. Years later, to cite just one of many examples, an editor in a prominent publishing house in New York City told me that evenhandedness was not called for in the case of a book on fundamentalist Christians.

18. Richard Louv of the *San Diego Union*, for example, explicitly corrected such a misperception by quoting our exchange in an article he wrote about a public screening of *Born Again* at the La Jolla Museum of Contemporary Art. Louv, "In the Dark, the Fundamentalist Humanity Emerged," *San Diego Union*, 26 July 1987. For another

example from a sociologist, see chap. 21, note 9, and for further discussion, pp. 112–13, above.

19. Woolfolk, Review, *Contemporary Sociology: An International Journal of Reviews* 19, no. 1 (January 1990): pp. 159–60.

20. I have in mind here the approaches of Lawrence Kohlberg and James Fowler discussed in chapter 12, note 2. An erudite Korean theologian educated in Germany and the United States once told me the story of the wrenching adjustments he had had to make when he agreed to pastor a Korean immigrant congregation in Kansas City, Missouri. He noticed the congregation was respectful when he preached but seemed unenthusiastic, even unengaged. At some point, however, out of the sheer need to communicate more effectively with his flock, he began resorting to traditional metaphoric Korean language and began to notice some "Amens" and other signs of engagement and enthusiasm. He had learned how he needed to communicate with them. Now, as a distinguished professor at a theological school training pastors for ministry, he said he hopes he can help his students become "culturally amphibious"— that is, to be able to communicate effectively not only in "scholarly discourse," he said, but also in the discourse of ordinary church members' oral traditions. Interview filmed with Dr. Young Ho Chun for *Earthen Vessels*, produced for the Association of Theological Schools, 1994.

22 / "But what about you?"

1. Even though since that time, in 1988, the religious impulse seems to have become much more pronounced on American campuses, prejudices against Christianity—and faith, in general—still remain in academic life, as a number of stories I hear from friends and colleagues continually remind me. Sociology itself has its own sibling conflicts, perhaps, with fundamentalist Protestantism. They grew up together, emerging in the same historical period, at the end of the nineteenth and beginning of the twentieth century, as traditional legitimation of social life was eroded by urban industrial society and rationalist ones, such as sociology, emerged—including the very idea of culture itself as a way to understand social order. See Talcott Parsons, *The Structure of Social Action*. Fittingly enough, perhaps, a disproportionate number of presidents of the American Sociological Association in its early decades were the offspring of Protestant clergy.

2. This project, "An American Voyage," developed with a small grant from Trinity Grants, never found funding, in part because it did not satisfy the partisan interests of potential funders on either side of these conflicts at the time.

3. This account does not rule out the possibility of a more satisfactory feminist critique of gender relations in fundamentalist communities that would take into consideration those powers afforded women in certain kinds of social structures. Nor does it explore conditions under which certain conservative Christian ideas of gender and authority might become increasingly disadvantageous, even oppressive, to women— and indeed, perhaps, to men and entire communities: for instance, when a small church evolves into a large, bureaucratically governed one, making informal, family-based ties less relevant and thus making women's *formal* disenfranchisement more *substantively* disempowering. Instead, this account aims solely to better understand aspects of the popular conservative outlook on these issues—especially among conservative women—in the specific social settings in which they live.

4. See Kristin Smith, *Who's Minding the Kids?*, p. 5. Along another dimension, the

role of grandparents in raising children is estimated to have *increased* by 30 percent between 1990 and 2000. Kari Haskell, "When Grandparents Go into the Childcare Gap, Money Can Be Scarcer," *New York Times*, 30 November 2003, Region, p. 29. From their own experience of upward mobility and weakening family ties, many intellectuals imagine their own trajectory to represent the general trend. But their experience represents only a fraction of the population to begin with and, given their low birth rates, combined with the steady immigration of more traditional peoples, assumes no greater and greater significance in the makeup of the American people.

5. "Forum: Who Owes What to Whom?," *Harper's*, February 1991. For the southernization of America, see Carter, *The Politics of Rage*, p. 11. I cannot locate the *New York Times* reference, but by now a grassroots movement has emerged, including secular therapists and clergy of mainline churches, to help people work on marriage. Personal communication from Barbara Whitehead, author of *The Divorce Culture*. This tidal-like shift in American politics could partly explain why researchers taking the pulse of the body politic in the mid-1990s found culture-wars politics so little on people's minds. Smith et al., "The Myth of Culture Wars." But they are wrong, I believe, to conclude from that evidence that the culture wars have been a media myth. See chap. 7, note 1.

6. Even though evangelicalism in England shared with American fundamentalism many of the same theological and biblical ideas—and indeed invented some of them— it did not settle into the same popular militant critique of modern life that American fundamentalism did in the 1920s through the present. See Marsden, "Fundamentalism as an American Phenomenon," p. 222. Neither did it engage in the same militant defense of tradition in family life increasingly preoccupying conservatives on this side of the Atlantic. Tradition in family life has never been as undermined or challenged in England as it has been in the United States. See chap. 13, note 13.

For the middle-class status of the New Woman fundamentalists decried, see DeBerg, *Ungodly Women*, pp. 26–27, 37–39, and 117, where she writes: "In conclusion, if any social phenomenon made fundamentalists aware of how far from the middle-class mainstream they had slipped it was the flapper of the late 1910s and 1920s. She was the daughter of the middle-class urban establishment, and she, not the fundamentalists, carried the day." In considering the occupational and educational data DeBerg gives, it is necessary to bear in mind that in this period the job of clerk was quite different than it is today, requiring relatively more education and involving greater remuneration and prestige. See Harry Braverman, *Labor and Monopoly Capital*, pp. 293ff.

7. Hunter, *Culture Wars*, p. 298. Hunter goes on to consider other, more mixed, possibilities in the resolution of these conflicts (pp. 304ff).

8. A case in point is that the outcome of the United States' upcoming presidential election in November 2004—with its critical bearing on issues of international terrorism, occupation and war in Iraq and Afghanistan, and protracted economic recession—could conceivably be decided by conflicts over same-sex marriage.

9. If Diane Ravitch is correct, these struggles are, in certain ways, distorting and crippling good and sensible education in our public schools. See Ravitch, *The Language Police*.

10. Luker, *Abortion and the Politics of Motherhood*, pp. 55–62. Certain spaces for compromise also open up in traditionalist discourse, where people and the concrete circumstances of their lives matter more than abstract principles. See chap. 12, pp. 269ff. Such space for compromise is manifest in how some midwest jurors staunchly committed to capital punishment (including Bible-believing Christians) recently spared the life of a young man who had committed a heinous murder showing no respect for

life. It made a difference for them to hear the graphic and heart-wrenching details of his upbringing by an uncaring, drug-addicted mother, though, not unlike members of Shawmut River, they found it difficult to explain their actions to family and friends sharing their commitment to the death penalty. "Well," one juror resorted to saying simply, "you haven't been where I've been." See Kotlowitz, "In the Face of Death," *New York Times Magazine*, 6 July 2003, pp. 32ff., and quote on p. 50.

11. Those documentaries include portraits of youth-serving organizations in inner-city and rural Indiana, a series on African Christianity shot in a variety of church communities in Ghana and Zimbabwe, portraits of Episcopal parishes around the United States including an African-American one and one in California struggling with the challenges of becoming a bilingual (Spanish/English) congregation and a portrait of leadership and governance at Emory University in Atlanta, Georgia. (See James Ault Productions, www.jamesault.com). Observing responses to the latter, I was interested to see how many academics working in the area of higher education could not bear the upper-class men (and women) who served as trustees of that institution, disapproving morally of their good-old-boy reciprocities, their indirect ways of handling conflict and their southern folksiness. In fact, the different social worlds of trustees and professors tended to be one of the toughest divisions the president of Emory had to continually negotiate, one that came to a head with great regularity each year over decisions to award honorary degrees. The faculty tended to favor individuals known nationally or internationally for their contributions to specific fields, while the trustees preferred someone who had contributed broadly and in a multiplicity of ways to their local community. For more on these differences, see Ault, *Leading Out Print Resources*, pp. 37–42.

Epilogue

1. From conversation and e-mail communication with David Bergman. Bergman goes on to claim that his models for the atom and elementary particles "are consistent with experiments, without the inconsistencies in logic found in prevailing theories of modern physics." Bergman works independently, outside established creation science groups, "whose interest and success," he writes, "have been limited to less fundamental fields such as meteorology, biology, zoology, and geology." For Bergman's work and that of his colleagues in promoting what they call "common sense science," see their Web site: www.commonsensescience.org.

2. "The Holy Eucharist: Rite Two," *The Book of Common Prayer* (The Episcopal Church, 1977), p. 355.

3. Tape of a talk given by Frederick Buechner at the Trinity Institute's Twenty-first National Conference, "God with Us," January 1990.

4. Yet, in Buechner's next breath, he recounted the story of Jesus foretelling Peter's denying him three times before the cock crows, not an event taken to be "as random as rain."

BIBLIOGRAPHY

Ammerman, Nancy Tatom. *Baptist Battles: Social Change and Religious Conflict in the Southern Baptist Convention.* New Brunswick, N.J.: Rutgers University Press, 1990.
———. *Bible Believers: Fundamentalists in the Modern World.* New Brunswick, N.J.: Rutgers University Press, 1987.
Armstrong, Karen. *The Battle for God.* New York: Ballantine, 2001.
Arons, Stephen. "Book Burning in the Heartland." *Saturday Review,* 21 July 1979.
Ault, James M., Jr. "Class Differences in Family Structure and the Social Bases of Modern Feminism." Doctoral dissertation presented to the Department of Sociology, Brandeis University, 1981.
———. "Family and Fundamentalism: The Shawmut Valley Baptist Church." In *Disciplines of Faith,* edited by Raphael Samuels et al. London: Routledge and Kegan Paul, 1987.
———. *Leading Out Print Resources.* Northampton, Mass.: James Ault Productions, 1995.
———. "Making 'Modern' Marriage 'Traditional': State Power and the Regulation of Marriage in Colonial Zambia." *Theory and Society* 12 (1983).
———. "Sex, Love and Intimacy." Unpublished paper.
Barr, James. *Fundamentalism.* Philadelphia: Westminster Press, 1977, 1978.
Bartkowski, John P. *Remaking the Godly Marriage: Gender Negotiation in Evangelical Families.* New Brunswick, N.J.: Rutgers University Press, 2001.
Bell, Daniel, ed. *The Radical Right.* Garden City, N.Y.: Doubleday, 1963.
Bellah, Robert, et al. *Habits of the Heart: Individualism and Commitment in American Life.* Berkeley: University of California Press, 1985.
Bendroth, Margaret Lamberts. *Fundamentalism and Gender, 1875 to the Present.* New Haven, Conn.: Yale University Press, 1993.
Berger, Brigitte and Peter. *The War over the Family: Capturing the Middle Ground.* New York: Anchor Press, 1983.
Boone, Kathleen. *The Bible Tells Them So: The Discourse of Protestant Fundamentalism.* Albany: State University of New York Press, 1989.
Borg, Marcus J. *Meeting Jesus Again for the First Time.* San Francisco: HarperCollins, 1994.
Born Again: Life in a Fundamentalist Baptist Church, produced and directed by James Ault and Michael Camerini. Northampton, Mass.: James Ault Productions, 1987.
Bott, Elizabeth. *Family and Social Network.* 2d ed. New York: Free Press, 1971.
Boyer, Peter J. "Children of Waco." *The New Yorker* 71, no. 12 (15 May 1995).

Bozeman, Theodore Dwight. *Protestants in an Age of Science: The Baconian Ideal and Antebellum American Religious Thought.* Chapel Hill: University of North Carolina Press, 1977.

Brasher, Brenda. *Godly Women: Fundamentalism and Female Power.* New Brunswick, N.J.: Rutgers University Press, 1998.

Braverman, Harry. *Labor and Monopoly Capital: The Degradation of Work in the Twentieth Century.* New York: Monthly Review Press, 1975.

Brereton, Virginia Lieson. *Training God's Army: the American Bible School, 1880–1940.* Bloomington: Indiana University Press, 1990.

Brown, Karen McCarthy. "The Fundamentalist Control of Women." In *Fundamentalism and Gender,* edited by John Stratton Hawley. New York: Oxford University Press, 1994.

Buechner, Frederick. "God with Us." Talk recorded on tape at the Trinity Institute's Twenty-first National Conference, January 1990.

Carden, Maren Lockwood. *The New Feminist Movement.* New York: Russell Sage Foundation, 1974.

Carpenter, Joel A. "Contending for the Faith Once Delivered: Primitivist Impulses in American Fundamentalism." In *The American Quest for the Primitive Church*, edited by Richard T. Hughes. Urbana and Chicago: University of Illinois Press, 1988.

———. *Revive Us Again: The Reawakening of American Fundamentalism.* Oxford, England: University Press, 1997.

Carter, Dan T. *The Politics of Rage: George Wallace, the Origins of the New Conservatism, and the Transformation of American Politics.* New York: Simon & Schuster, 1995.

Cassell, Joan. *A Group Called Women.* New York: David McKay and Company, 1977.

CBS Reports: The Vanishing Family (CBS News, 1986), produced and directed by Ruth C. Streeter with Bill Moyers as executive editor.

Covington, Dennis. *Salvation on Sand Mountain: Snake Handling and Redemption in Southern Appalachia.* Reading, Mass.: Addison-Wesley, 1995.

Crewes, Frederick. "Saving Us from Darwin." *The New York Review of Books*, 4 and 18 October 2001.

Dayton, Donald W. "The Search for the Historical Evangelicalism: George Marsden's History of Fuller Seminary as a Case Study," and responses to it. *Christian Scholar's Review* 23 (September 1993).

DeBerg, Betty. *Ungodly Women: Gender and the First Wave of American Fundamentalism.* Minneapolis: Augsburg Fortress, 1990.

Dillistone, F. W. *The Christian Understanding of Atonement.* Philadelphia: Westminster Press, 1968.

Dudley, Carl, and David Roozen. *Faith Communities Today: A Report on Religion in the U.S. Today.* Hartford, Conn.: Hartford Institute for Religion Research, Hartford Seminary, 2001.

Dworkin, Andrea. *Right-Wing Women.* New York: Perigee Books, 1982.

Ellis, Walter Edmund Warren. "Social and Religious Factors in the Fundamentalist-Modernist Schisms Among Baptists in North America, 1895–1934." Doctoral dissertation presented to the University of Pittsburgh, 1974.

Epstein, Barbara. "What Happened to the Women's Movement?" *Monthly Review* 53, no. 1 (May 2001).

Evans, Sara. *Personal Politics.* New York: Random House, 1979.

Falwell, Jerry. *Strength for the Journey: An Autobiography.* New York: Simon & Schuster, 1987.

Fields, Karen E. *Revival and Rebellion in Colonial Africa*. Princeton, N.J.: Princeton University Press, 1985.

———. "Translator's Introduction: Religion as an Eminently Social Thing." In Emile Durkheim, *The Elementary Forms of Religious Life*. Translated with an introduction by Karen E. Fields. New York: Free Press, 1995.

FitzGerald, Frances. *Cities on a Hill*. New York: Simon & Schuster, 1986.

Fletcher, Joseph. *Situation Ethics: The New Morality*. Philadelphia: Westminster Press, 1966.

Flexner, Stuart, and Doris Flexner. *Wise Words and Wives' Tales: The Origins, Meanings and Time-Honored Wisdom of Proverbs and Folk Sayings Olde and New*. New York: Avon Books, 1993.

Ford, Andrew. "The Inland Ship: Problems in the Performance and Reception of Homeric Epic." In *Written Voices, Spoken Signs*. Edited by E. Bakker and A. Kahane. Cambridge, Mass.: Harvard University Press, 1997.

Fowler, James W. *Becoming Adult, Becoming Christian: Adult Development and Christian Faith*. San Francisco: Harper and Row, 1984.

Fox-Genovese, Elizabeth. *"Feminism Is Not the Story of My Life": How Today's Feminist Elite Has Lost Touch with the Real Concerns of Women*. New York: Doubleday, 1996.

Frank, Douglas. *Less than Conquerors*. Grand Rapids, Mich.: Eerdmans, 1986.

Gallagher, Sally K. *Evangelical Identity and Gendered Family Life*. New Brunswick, N.J.: Rutgers University Press, 2003.

Garfinkel, Harold. *Studies in Ethnomethodology*. Englewood Cliffs, N.J.: Prentice-Hall, 1967.

Gerstel, Naomi. "The Third Shift: Gender and Care Work Outside the Home." *Qualitative Sociology* 23, no. 4 (2000).

Gerstel, Naomi, Dan Clawson, and Robert Zussman, eds. *Families at Work: Expanding the Boundaries*. Nashville: Vanderbilt University Press, 2002.

Gold, Daniel. "Organized Hinduisms: From Vedic Truth to Hindu Nation." In *Fundamentalisms Observed*, edited by Martin E. Marty and R. Scott Appleby. Chicago: University of Chicago Press, 1991.

Gomes, Peter. *The Good Book: Reading the Bible with Mind and Heart*. New York: William Morrow and Company, 1996.

Griffith, R. Marie. *God's Daughters: Evangelical Women and the Power of Submission*. Berkeley: University of California Press, 1997.

Gusfield, Joseph. *Symbolic Crusade*. Urbana: University of Illinois Press, 1963.

Hankins, Barry. *God's Rascal: J. Frank Norris and the Beginnings of Southern Fundamentalism*. Lexington: University of Kentucky Press, 1996.

Harding, Susan Friend. *The Book of Jerry Falwell: Fundamentalist Language and Politics*. Princeton, N.J.: Princeton University Press, 2000.

Harrell, David Edwin. *Pat Robertson: A Personal, Religious and Political Portrait*. San Francisco: Harper and Row, 1987.

Haskell, Kari. "When Grandparents Go into the Childcare Gap, Money Can Become Scarcer." *New York Times*, 30 November 2003, Region, p. 29.

Hatch, Nathan O., and Mark A. Noll, eds. *The Bible in America: Essays in Cultural History*. New York: Oxford University Press, 1982.

Havelock, Eric Alfred. *Preface to Plato*. Cambridge, Mass.: Harvard University Press, 1963.

Heriot, M. Jean. "Perspectives on the Southern Baptist Convention as Expressed in Cypress Pond Baptist Church, 1985–1986." Unpublished paper, 1986.

Hill, Samuel S., ed. *Encyclopedia of Religion in the South*. Atlanta: Mercer University Press, 1984.

Hobsbawm, Eric, and Terence Ranger, eds. *The Invention of Tradition*. Cambridge, U.K.: Cambridge University Press, 1983.

Hofstadter, Richard. *The Paranoid Style in American Politics and Other Essays*. New York: Alfred A. Knopf, 1965.

———. "The Pseudo-Conservative Revolt—1955." In *The Radical Right*, edited by Daniel Bell. Garden City, N.Y.: Doubleday, 1963, pp. 63–80.

———. "Pseudo-Conservativism Revisited: A Postscript—1962." In *The Radical Right*, edited by Daniel Bell. Garden City, N.Y.: Doubleday, 1963, pp. 81–86.

Hoggart, Richard. *The Uses of Literacy*. New York: Oxford University Press, 1957.

Horowitz, Helen. *Rereading Sex*. New York: Alfred A. Knopf, 2002.

Hughes, Richard T., ed. *The American Quest for the Primitive Church*. Urbana and Chicago: University of Illinois Press, 1988.

Hunter, James Davison. *American Evangelicalism: Conservative Religion and the Quandary of Modernity*. New Brunswick, N.J.: Rutgers University Press, 1983.

———. *Culture Wars: The Struggle to Define America*. New York: Basic Books, 1991.

Ingersoll, Julie J. "'Traditional Family Values' in American Protestant Fundamentalism." *Contention* 4, no. 2 (winter 1995): 91–103.

Jay, Nancy. *Throughout Your Generations Forever: Sacrifice, Religion, and Paternity*. Chicago: University of Chicago Press, 1992.

Jones, Gareth Stedman. *Outcast London*. Baltimore: Penguin Books, 1971.

Kaufmann, Felix. *Methodology of the Social Sciences*. New York: Humanities Press, 1958.

Klatch, Rebecca E. *Women of the New Right*. Philadelphia: Temple University Press, 1987.

Klein, Patricia, et al. *Growing Up Born Again*. Old Tappan, N.J.: Fleming H. Revell Company, 1987.

Kohlberg, Lawrence. *The Philosophy of Moral Development: Moral Stages and the Idea of Justice*. San Francisco: Harper and Row, 1981.

Kolko, Gabriel. *The Triumph of Conservatism: A Re-Interpretation of American History, 1900–1916*. New York: Free Press of Glencoe, 1963.

Kopkind, Andrew. "America's New Right." *New Times*, 30 September 1977.

Kornblum, William. *Blue-Collar Community*. Chicago: University of Chicago Press, 1974.

Kotlowitz, Alex. "In the Face of Death." *New York Times Magazine*, 6 July 2003.

LaHaye, Tim. *The Battle for the Family*. Old Tappan, N.J.: Fleming H. Revell Company, 1982.

Liebman, Robert C. "Mobilizing the Moral Majority." In *The New Christian Right: Mobilization and Legitimation*, edited by Robert C. Liebman and Robert Wuthnow. New York: Aldine, 1983.

Lomnitz, Larissa Adler, and Marisol Perez Lizaur. "The History of a Mexican Urban Family." *Journal of Family History* 3 (1978): 392–409.

Luker, Kristin. *Abortion and the Politics of Motherhood*. Berkeley: University of California Press, 1984.

Manning, Christel J. *God Gave Us the Right: Conservative Catholic, Evangelical Protestant, and Orthodox Jewish Women Grapple with Feminism*. New Brunswick, N.J.: Rutgers University Press, 1999.

Marsden, George M. *Fundamentalism and American Culture: The Shaping of Twentieth-Century Evangelicalism, 1870–1925*. Oxford: Oxford University Press, 1980.

———. "Fundamentalism as an American Phenomenon: A Comparison with English Evangelicalism." *Church History* 46 (1977): 215–32.

———, ed. *The Fundamentals: A Testimony to Truth*. New York: Garland Publishing, 1988.

Marty, Martin E., and R. Scott Appleby, eds. *The Fundamentalism Project: A Study Conducted by the American Academy of Arts and Sciences*. 5 vols. Chicago: University of Chicago Press, 1991–1995.

———. "The Fundamentalism Project: A User's Guide" and "Conclusion: An Interim Report on a Hypothetical Family." In *Fundamentalisms Observed*, vol. 1 of *The Fundamentalism Project*. Chicago: University of Chicago Press, 1991.

Marx, Karl. *The Eighteenth Brumaire of Louis Bonaparte*. New York: International Publishers, 1935.

Mauss, Marcel. *The Gift: Forms and Functions of Exchange in Archaic Societies*. New York: Norton, 1967.

McLoughlin, William G. *Billy Sunday Was His Real Name*. Chicago: University of Chicago Press, 1955.

Meeks, Wayne A. *The Origins of Christian Morality: The First Two Centuries*. New Haven, Conn.: Yale University Press, 1993.

Nelkin, Dorothy. *The Creation Controversy: Science or Scripture in the Schools*. New York: Norton, 1982.

Nelson, Shirley. *Fair Clear and Terrible: The Story of Shiloh, Maine*. Latham, N.Y.: British American Publishing, 1989.

Niebuhr, H. Richard. "Fundamentalism." In *Encyclopedia of the Social Sciences*. New York: Social Science Research Council, 1931, 525–27.

Noll, Mark A. *American Evangelical Christianity: An Introduction*. Oxford: Blackwell, 2001.

———. *The Scandal of the Evangelical Mind*. Grand Rapids, Mich.: Eerdmans, 1994.

Numbers, Ronald L. *The Creationists*. New York: Alfred A. Knopf, 1992.

———. *Darwinism Comes to America*. Cambridge, Mass.: Harvard University Press, 1998.

Pagels, Elaine H. *Beyond Belief: The Secret Gospel of Thomas*. New York: Random House, 2003.

Parsons, Talcott. *The Structure of Social Action*. Glencoe, Ill.: Free Press, 1949.

Paulson, Michael. "Black Clergy Rejection Stirs Gay Marriage Backers." *Boston Globe*, 10 February 2004, B1.

Perlstein, Rick. *Before the Storm: Barry Goldwater and the Unmaking of the American Consensus*. New York: Hill and Wang, 2001.

Peshkin, Alan. *God's Choice: The Total World of a Fundamentalist Christian School*. Chicago: University of Chicago Press, 1986.

Pevey, Carolyn, et al. "Male God Imagery and Female Submission: Lessons from a Southern Baptist Ladies' Bible Class." *Qualitative Sociology* 19, no. 2 (1996): 173–93.

Pohli, Carol Virginia. "Church Closets and Back Doors: A Feminist View of Moral Majority Women." *Feminist Studies* 9, no. 3 (Fall 1983).

Putnam, Robert D. *Bowling Alone: The Collapse and Revival of American Community*. New York: Simon and Schuster, 2000.

Raboteau, Albert J. *Slave Religion: The "Invisible Institution" in the Antebellum South*. New York: Oxford University Press, 1978.

Rauch, Jonathan. "Power of Two: The President's Stealth Defense of Gay Marriage." *New York Times Magazine*, 7 March 2004, p. 13.

Ravitch, Diane. *The Language Police: How Pressure Groups Restrict What Students Learn.* New York: Alfred A. Knopf, 2003.

Rice, John. *The Home: Courtship, Marriage, Children.* Wheaton, Ill.: Sword of the Lord, 1945.

Rose, Susan. "Women Warriors: The Negotiation of Gender in a Charismatic Community." *Sociological Analysis* 48, no. 3 (1987).

Rowling, J. K. *Harry Potter and the Sorcerer's Stone.* New York: Scholastic Books, 1998.

Russell, C. Allyn. *Voices of American Fundamentalism: Seven Biographical Studies.* Philadelphia: Westminster Press, 1976.

Sandeen, Ernest. *The Roots of Fundamentalism: British and American Millenarianism, 1800–1930.* Chicago: University of Chicago Press, 1970.

Sasse, Connie R. *Person to Person.* Peoria, Ill.: Chas. A. Bennett Co., 1978.

Schlafly, Phyllis. *The Power of the Christian Woman.* Cincinnati, Ohio: Standard Publishing, 1981.

Schutz, Alfred. *Collected Papers.* Vols. 1, 2, and 3. The Hague: Marinus Nijhoff, 1967.

———. *The Phenomenology of the Social World.* Evanston, Ill.: Northwestern University Press, 1967.

Simmel, Georg. "The Isolated Individual and the Dyad." In *The Sociology of Georg Simmel,* edited by Kurt H. Wolff. New York: Free Press, 1950.

Slater, Philip E. "On Social Regression." *American Sociological Review* 28 (June 1963).

Smith, Christian. *American Evangelicalism: Embattled and Thriving.* Chicago: University of Chicago Press, 1998.

Smith, Christian, Sally Gallagher, et al. "The Myth of Culture Wars." In *Culture Wars in American Politics: Critical Reviews of a Popular Myth,* edited by Rhys Williams. New York: Aldine de Gruyter, 1997.

Smith, Kristin. *Who's Minding the Kids?* Current Population Reports, P70–70, U.S. Census Bureau, 2000.

Spong, John Shelby. *Rescuing the Bible from Fundamentalism: A Bishop Rethinks the Meaning of Scripture.* New York: HarperCollins, 1991.

Stacey, Judith. *Brave New Families: Stories of Domestic Upheaval in Late Twentieth Century America.* New York: Basic Books, 1990.

Stacey, Judith and Susan Elizabeth Gerard. " 'We Are Not Doormats': The Influence of Feminism on Contemporary Evangelicalism in the United States." In *Uncertain Terms: Negotiating Gender in American Culture,* edited by Faye Ginsburg and Anna Tsing. Boston: Beacon Press, 1990.

Stack, Carol B. *All Our Kin: Strategies for Survival in a Black Community.* New York: Harper and Row, 1974.

Stevick, Daniel. *Beyond Fundamentalism.* Richmond, Va.: John Knox Press, 1964.

Stout, Harry S. "Word and Order in Colonial New England." In *The Bible in America: Essays in Cultural History,* edited by Nathan O. Hatch and Mark A. Noll. New York: Oxford University Press, 1982.

Suttles, Gerald. *The Social Construction of Communities.* Chicago: University of Chicago Press, 1974.

Tannen, Deborah. *Gender and Discourse.* New York: Oxford University Press, 1994.

———. *You Just Don't Understand: Women and Men in Conversation.* New York: Random House, 1990.

Torrey, R. A., ed., et al. *The Fundamentals: The Famous Sourcebook of Foundational Biblical Truths.* Grand Rapids, Mich.: Kregel Publications, 1958.

Trimberger, Ellen Kay. "Women in the Old and New Left." *Feminist Studies* 5 (fall 1979).

Turner, Victor W. *Schism and Continuity in an African Society: A Study of Ndembu Village Life*. Manchester, U.K.: Manchester University Press, 1957.

Verghese, Abraham. *My Own Country: A Doctor's Story of a Town and Its People in the Age of AIDS*. New York: Simon and Schuster, 1994.

Walls, Andrew. Interview filmed with James Ault at Yale Divinity School, July 2001.

Weber, Max. *Economy and Society*. New York: Bedminster Press, 1968.

———. *Max Weber on the Methodology of the Social Sciences*. Translated and edited by Edward A. Shils and Henry A. Finch. Glencoe, Ill.: Free Press, 1949.

———. "Politics as a Vocation." In *From Max Weber: Essays in Sociology*, edited by H. H. Gerth and C. Wright Mills. New York: Oxford University Press, 1946.

Weber, Timothy P. *Living in the Shadow of the Second Coming: American Premillennialism, 1875–1982*. Chicago: University of Chicago Press, 1983.

———. "The Two-Edged Sword: The Fundamentalist Use of the Bible." In *The Bible in America: Essays in Cultural History*, edited by Nathan O. Hatch and Mark A. Noll. New York: Oxford University Press, 1982.

Whitehead, Barbara Dafoe. *The Divorce Culture*. New York: Alfred A. Knopf, 1996.

Woolfolk, Alan. "Review of *Born Again: Life in a Fundamentalist Baptist Church*." *Contemporary Sociology: An International Journal of Reviews* 19, no. 1 (January 1990): 159–60.

Woolsey, Suzanne H. "Pied Piper Politics and the Child Care Debate." In *The Family*, edited by Alice S. Rossi, Jerome Kagan, and Tamara K. Hareven. New York: Norton, 1978.

Yanagisako, Sylvia Junko. "Women-Centered Kin Networks in Urban Bilateral Kinship." *American Ethnologist*, vol. 4, 1977.

ACKNOWLEDGMENTS

A book that begins with a young scholar's postdoctoral research and, through his making a documentary film about the subject, becomes an altogether different book than originally imagined, accumulates an unusual trail of debts along the way. For funding the initial research for this book and believing in the importance of its subject, I would like to thank the American Council of Learned Societies, the Ford Foundation and the Pembroke Center for Teaching and Research on Women at Brown University.

I owe a profound debt to my teachers, especially, during graduate studies, Barrington Moore, Jr., at Harvard, and Egon Bittner at Brandeis. Each in his own inimitable way showed me and my fellow students not only how to think critically about social life, but also how to pursue sociological truth and its vital connections to human understanding, with passion, integrity, craft and art. My abiding thanks to both.

I also remember with gratitude my fellow students and other colleagues who, in sharing this peculiar journey, contributed so much to my own. In particular, among the many creative people who made the Brandeis Sociology Department and Cambridge, Massachusetts, such fruitful places to study during those years—including, for me, George Ross, Nancy Chodorow, Mahmood Mamdani and Fatima Mernissi—I must single out Karen Fields and the late Nancy Jay, who, as close friends and colleagues sharing the struggle to make important teachings our own, nourished me in so many ways. In addition, as consultants to our documentary film on the Shawmut River Baptist Church, they helped give that project the right direction.

The process of making a documentary film on Shawmut River deepened and extended the research underpinning this book and contributed in important ways to its shape. For sponsoring that project, I am grateful to Five Colleges, Inc.; for funding it, I would like to thank the National Endowment for the Humanities and the Massachusetts Foundation for the Humanities, and, at a later stage, the Corporation for Public Broadcasting. At CPB I am particularly grateful to Don Marbury, who helped shepherd our project successfully through the review process for finishing funds.

For sharing the experience of capturing something of life at Shawmut River on film, I would like to thank my thoughtful and creative collaborators in that effort: Audrey Zimmerman, Carol Ramsey, Cheryl Groff, and, above all, my coproducer and codirector, Michael Camerini, from whom I first began to learn the arts of *cinéma-vérité* filmmaking. Moreover, the process of shaping our raw footage into an effective film over many months in the editing room taught me much about the art of nonfiction storytelling and forever changed my approach to writing. For that and other things I am grateful to both Michael Camerini and our principal editor, Adrienne

Miesmer, as well as to other documentary filmmakers with whom I have since had the privilege to work: notably Lisa Jackson, Dirk Van Dall, Francis Kwakye, Tom Hurwitz, Jean Boucicaut and Kate Purdie.

I began writing this book with support from the Religion Division of the Lilly Endowment, then led by Robert Wood Lynn. I am grateful to Bob Lynn for believing in this book from the start and to the Lilly Endowment not only for that grant but also for gainful employment in a variety of projects over the years during which this book was written and rewritten. Susan Wisely, as director of evaluation at the Endowment, provided opportunities to develop my skills in ethnographic research, nonfiction writing and documentary filmmaking. Other film projects funded by the Endowment—on trusteeship and on leadership in higher education—also helped develop my skills as a producer and nonfiction storyteller. I am grateful to the Lilly Endowment for these opportunities, and also for the much-esteemed community of educators I met through that work, who enriched my life so much during those years.

Two other documentary projects contributed to this book in ways that show up in its pages. I am grateful, first, to the Association for Theological Schools under Jim Waits for the opportunity to produce *Earthen Vessels*, a documentary about issues facing theological education, which permitted me to explore cross-cultural issues in theology. I am also indebted to the Pew Charitable Trusts for funding a documentary film project on African Christianity (in progress) that enabled me to witness and explore connections between that branch of Christianity now exploding on the world stage and churches like Shawmut River. In that endeavor I have learned much, especially from Kwame Bediako and Andrew Walls.

Spirit and Flesh benefited greatly from close readings and criticisms of early drafts by a number of friends and colleagues. In particular, Shirley and Rudy Nelson went beyond the call of duty to pore over the entire manuscript at two critical stages to make important suggestions and criticisms. And it was Shirley, a gifted writer whose work I much admire, who gave me those clear and encouraging words of guidance that became my watchword while writing this book. After hearing the basic outlines of my story, she said simply, yet with enthusiasm and conviction, "Oh, that's easy! All you have to do is tell the truth!"

In the struggle to achieve this and other ends, I have been blessed with the wise counsel of my editor, Jane Garrett. I am grateful to her for seeing value in this book's interpretation and for helping deal with various issues with good sense and integrity. I am also indebted to the Alfred A. Knopf staff, who have steadily helped improve the manuscript in its later stages—especially Victoria Pearson and Barbara Grenquist, who carefully checked references and copyedited the manuscript.

I would also like to thank Fred Fierst for his generous and wise counsel and Jonathan Harr, Robert Cowden and, at Knopf, Anke Steinecke, for theirs. I am grateful to Howard Gallimore for doing some digging in the Southern Baptist Historical Library and Archives, to Naomi Gerstel for helpful conversation and references and to the research librarians of Smith College's Nielsen Library, who were, as always, of great help.

For reading and commenting on early versions of the manuscript, I give thanks to dear friends Ray Hughes, Alice Clemente, Rosa Ibarra, Cassandra Holden, Heidi Christensen, Nancy Goldstein, and Andrew Ford, as well as Rick Deutsch, Wayne Clymer, Esther Ashby Kane, Julie Talen, Joel Carpenter and Margaret Bendroth. Peggy Bendroth generously gave me good suggestions on my treatment of gender and fundamentalism, and guidance into the burgeoning literature on that subject. Joel Carpenter gave me encouragement and good advice on the relevant historiography on

American fundamentalism. And Andrew Ford, a classicist and old friend, illuminated issues regarding the ancient world and its texts, while always providing encouragement and inspiration. Indeed, our close circle of friends in Northampton, Massachusetts, where we first came together—Andrew, Martine, Heidi, Nancy, Bruce, Bob, Claudia, Kit, José and others—has always provided a warm and loving community for the life of the imagination and the pilgrim's spirit.

I would like to thank my former wife, Rachel Cartmell, for her support and encouragement during our years together. And I am grateful to our son, Henry, first, for his unflagging patience and good spirit even when his father seemed most hopelessly lost in thought, but, even more so, simply for his good company. I also thank Rosa Ibarra for her encouragement during some important years.

Most of all, I would like to thank my parents, Jim and Dorothy Ault, for their steadfast support, encouragement, counsel and love, and, especially, for showing me the way in life. With love and gratitude, I dedicate this book to them.

Finally, I want to thank the people of Shawmut River who shared their lives with me so graciously and intelligently, even when it was not convenient or comfortable to do so. What we shared—and continue to share—has enriched my life immeasurably. Even when tough issues arose regarding painful events recounted in this book, they showed the strength, courage and faithfulness to be there with me. For these and many other graces extending over the years, I will forever be grateful to them.

Northampton, Massachusetts
January 2004

INDEX

abortion, 66, 398*n*
  compromise measures on, 347–8
  demonstrations against, 5–6
  family obligation and, 91, 100–1, 107
  motherhood concepts and, 379*n*–80*n*
  pastoral message on, 48–9
  violent actions against, 345
academic discourse, 330–1
Aesop, 387*n*
African Americans:
  feminism of, 381*n*
  kinship networks of, 38, 112–13, 382*n*
  reciprocity among, 379*n*
  on same-sex marriage, 393*n*
  women's power in churches of, 316
African Christianity, 184–5, 404*n*, *see also
  non-Western Christianity*
AIDS, 94, 347
alcoholism, 251
All in the Family, 383*n*
altar call, 139
American Council of Learned Societies,
  11
American Sociological Association, 339,
  402*n*
Ammerman, Nancy, 375*n*, 380*n*, 381*n*
Amway, 101
angels, 184
apocalyptic outlook, 29
apostles, letters to early church by, 65,
  169, 211
  see also specific Bible books
Appleby, R. Scott, 389*n*–90*n*
Armstrong, Karen, 392*n*

Athol, Mass., sex-education conflict in,
  94, 104, 326, 378*n*
Atlantic Conference of the Evangelical
  Church, 332
atonement, 183–4, 385*n*, 388*n*
Augustine, Saint, 376*n*
Ault, Dorothy, 341, 380*n*
  religious background of, 14, 332–3,
  338
Ault, James, 338
  as Methodist minister, 13–15, 49, 153,
  333, 367
  politics of, 333
Ault, James, Jr.:
  academic career of, 3, 10, 11, 36, 38,
  94, 117, 127, 327
  antiwar activism of, 11, 18–19
  childhood of, 13–15, 49, 333
  documentary-film projects of, xii, 119,
  127–8, 141–3, 177, 179, 221–6, 310,
  340, 349, 366–8, 404*n*
  family background of, 13–15, 333,
  339, 367
  as father, 338, 352, 356
  feminist issues studied by, 10–11,
  36–8
  material aid to, 136–7, 176
  moral influence of Shawmut Church
  experienced by, 15–16, 289–90,
  348–9
  in new-left politics, 29, 36–7
  participant-observer research stance
  of, xii, 3–4, 15–16, 66–7, 68, 132–3,
  137, 240, 303, 372*n*–3*n*

Ault, James, Jr. (*continued*)
　proselytizing efforts toward, 74–6,
　　129–30, 132–3, 139, 222–3
　religious experience of, xi, xii, 13–14,
　　38–9, 49, 75, 132–3, 182, 222–3,
　　336, 337–40, 356, 367–8, 370

Bacon, Francis, 212, 215, 391*n*
Bakker, Jim, 57, 108
Bakker, Tammy, 57, 108
baptism, 160–1
Baptist Bible College (Springfield, Mo.),
　23–4, 30–1, 103, 306
Baptist Bible College East (Boston,
　Mass.), 31, 32, 147
Baptist Bible Fellowship (BBF), 199
　absolute pastoral authority in, 31, 127,
　　305
　autonomy of congregations in, 31, 54
　charismatic practices opposed by, 57
　establishment of, 31, 54, 109
　pastoral succession in, 400*n*
　plainspoken style of, 33
　schools affiliated with, 7, 31, 103, 306
　on Shawmut Church split, 300
Baptist fundamentalism, *see* fundamen-
　talism
Barr, James, 387*n*, 390*n*
Bartkowski, John P., 378*n*, 388*n*
Battle for the Family, The (LaHaye), 110
Beka Book Publications, 146, 149
Bellah, Robert, 392*n*
Bendroth, Margaret, 380*n*, 381*n*
Berger, Brigitte, 388*n*
Berger, Peter, 388*n*
Bergman, David, 356, 404*n*
Bible:
　as baseline source of authority, 210,
　　213
　change in interpretations of, 213–14,
　　391*n*
　common-sense approach vs.
　　scholarship on, 212, 391*n*
　composition of, 173, 211
　concordance of, 167
　dispensationalist interpretation of, 57,
　　60, 168, 215–16, 392*n*
　on drinking, 86, 186–7, 313
　family events recorded in, 210

family life guided by, 26–7, 49, 109–10
family stories in, 211
folk sayings from, 193–4, 195–6, 387*n*
Holy Spirit as source of, 166, 167, 173,
　187
inconsistencies within, 68, 154, 194–5,
　215
infallibility of, 15, 58, 59, 60, 173, 180,
　371*n*, 387*n*, 388*n*
King James version of, 48, 64, 165,
　166, 193, 194, 209, 373*n*, 387*n*
marriage guidance in, 86, 87, 88–9,
　92–3, 246–7, 250–1
memorization of, 193
New International Version of, 391*n*
Old Testament vs. New Testament, 47,
　168, 193
as proof, 173, 212
prophetic passages of, 28, 29, 60, 214,
　216
Revised Standard Version of, 39, 391*n*
salvation path in, 75, 129
on scientific lore, 214
small study groups on, *see* Bible-study
　groups supernatural events in, 180
tradition anchored in, 209–12, 213,
　217
translations of, 39, 64, 166, 194, 360*n*,
　373*n*, 387*n*, 391*n*
see also specific books of the Bible
Bible Baptist Seminary, 400*n*–1*n*
Bible Institute of Los Angeles, 213
Bible schools, 213
Bible-study groups, 60, 164–72
　doctrinal issues addressed in, 168–72
　evangelism in, 140, 155
　family-model intimacy of, 176–7
　interpretive guidance given in, 64,
　　375*n*
　prayer requests in, 174–5, 176, 177,
　　182, 222
　reading skills in, 165–6
Birthright, 3, 4, 94, 106, 107, 393*n*
Bittner, Egon, 331
Bob Jones University, 70, 151, 324, 360,
　362
Bono, Sonny, 249
Book of Common Prayer, 202
Boone, Kathleen, 375*n*

Borg, Marcus, 385*n*
Born Again:
  church members, reactions to, 298–9,
    334–5, 350–1
  cinéma-verité style of, 142, 232, 239,
    293, 366–7
  creative team of, 231, 293, 393*n*
  crew of, 233–4, 240–1
  editing process of, 293–4
  evenhandedness of, 328
  family life as focus of, 119, 229–31, 334
  funding of, xii, 127, 177, 222, 223–4,
    298
  liberals' responses to, 328
  marital breakup shown in, 231, 260–9,
    293, 334–5, 363
  new convert in, 293
  politics addressed in, 225, 226, 229
  prayer requests for, 177, 222
  producing/directing partnership of,
    221, 224, 231
  psychotherapeutic interpretations of,
    329–30
  public-television broadcast of, 127,
    293, 327, 350
  religious communities' reactions to,
    336–7, 350–1, 368
  review of, 330, 401*n*
  salvation effort in, 283–7, 288, 329–30
  Shawmut congregation cooperation
    on, 127–8, 141–3, 177, 223, 234,
    236–7, 239, 256, 260, 261, 282
  shooting of, 223–4, 239–41, 246, 260,
    265–6, 269–70, 274, 275, 278, 280,
    281, 287–8, 289
  sponsoring organization of, 224
  teenagers as subjects of, 241–5, 350–1
  worship services shown in, 246, 275–7,
    287
born-again experiences, 9, 16, 129–39,
  284–5
Boston Women's Health Collective, 37
Bott, Elizabeth, 372*n*
Bowling Alone (Putnam), 112, 382*n*
Branch Davidian community, 236
Brasher, Brenda, 375*n*, 377*n*, 396*n*,
  397*n*–9*n*
Bread and Roses, 37
Brereton, Virginia, 213

Brown University, women's studies
  center at, 11, 36, 37
Bryan, William Jennings, 59, 388*n*
Buechner, Frederick, 369, 404*n*
bureaucratic organizations, 100, 135,
  191, 199, 235–6, 347, 384*n*
Bush, George H. W., 117, 225
Bush, George W., 393*n*, 398*n*
business, government regulation of, 326

California, abortion rights history in,
  347–8
California, University of, at San Diego,
  327, 338
Calvinism, 212
Camerini, Michael, 224, 233–4, 240, 241,
  261, 266, 288, 293, 336, 392*n*, 393*n*
capitalism, 325–6
capital punishment, 100, 183, 201, 380*n*,
  403*n*–4*n*
Carpenter, Joel A., 59, 375*n*, 376*n*, 379*n*,
  381*n*, 389*n*, 391*n*
Carter, Dan T., 372*n*
Carter, Jimmy, 9
Catholic Church, ix, 4, 156, 160, 169,
  170, 171, 184
change:
  as restoration, 207, 208
  salvation as source of, 28
  traditionalist mode of, 213–14, 391*n*
charismatic (Pentecostal) Christians,
  56–7, 58, 68, 212, 215, 294, 309,
  343–4, 375*n*
Cher, 249
children:
  corporal punishment of, 26, 28, 234–7
  effects of divorce on, 343
  extended-family care of, 95, 113, 341,
    403*n*
  homeschooling of, 5, 151, 360
  independent legal rights of, 48, 49
chreiai, 211
Christ:
  necessary death of, 183–4, 385*n*
  Old Testament appearances of, 168
  reciprocal relationship with, 161,
    183–4
  second coming of, 29, 58, 60, 131, 226,
    371*n*

christenings, 162
Christian Academy:
  accreditation of, 119
  church split and, 301
  closing of, 359
  corporal punishment at, 234, 236–7
  curriculum of, 145–6, 147, 148–9
  in documentary film, 350, 351
  enrollment level at, 52, 145
  finances of, 53, 150, 224–5, 238
  opening of, 6, 53, 121
  principals of, 119, 121, 123, 358
  sports activities of, 77–8, 147, 149,
    227, 241, 260
  students of, 146–7, 355
  teachers at, 42–3, 69, 106, 119, 121,
    123, 124–5, 145, 148, 164, 238, 294,
    314, 358
Christian Broadcasting Network, 108
Christian Coalition, 6, 80, 228, 325, 343,
  361
Christian Law Association, 225
Christian music industry, 355
Christian Sociological Association, 339
Church, Andy, 256, 257
churches:
  belief maintained through attendance
    of, 130
  political influence of, 6–7
  see also fundamentalist churches
Church of England, 148–9, 215
Church of Nazarene, 20, 160, 368
cinéma-verité filmmaking, 142, 232, 239,
  293, 367
Clark University, 8
Clinton, Bill, 11–12, 343, 353
Clinton, Hillary Rodham, 353
CNN, 335
Collister, Alan, 336–7, 339
common culture, 189–94, 197, 204, 214
common sense realism, 212
common sense science, 356, 404n
communication styles, 330–1, 402n
communion, 137
communism, 99, 100, 252, 371n
Community Church of San Diego, 336,
  337–8
community engagement, 112, 382n
Congregationalists, 342

consciousness-raising groups, 37, 90,
  125, 322
conservative pro-family movement, xi–xii
  coalition building vs. political
    radicalism in, 343–4
  electoral impact of, 3, 11–12, 117, 228,
    325, 341–2
  family backgrounds and, 105–7
  historical populist roots of, 374n
  kin-based networks among members
    of, 95–109, 326–7, 341, 401n
  mainstream cultural impact of, 342–3,
    344
  media irrelevance in, 118, 383n
  mobilization of, 228
  in multiple religions, 10, 202, 203, 326
  new immigrants attracted to, 325
  rural/urban culture clashes and, 107–9,
    380n–1n
  as social conservatives, 371n
Constantine I (the Great), Holy Roman
  Emperor, 173
contraceptives, 107
Corinthians, First Book of, 187, 188,
  192, 251, 268, 306
Corinthians, Second Book of, 192, 266
corporal punishment, 26, 28, 234–7
corporate capitalism, 326
Corporation for Public Broadcasting,
  298
country music, 343
creationism, 119, 214, 388n
crucifixion, 369
culture, common, 189–94, 197, 204, 214
culture wars, 38, 345–6, 386n, 388n,
  389n, 393n, 403n

Dadi's Family, 392n
Dallas, 135
Daniel, Book of, 66, 214
Darwinism, 212, 216, 392n
death penalty, 100, 183, 201, 380n,
  403n–4n
DeBerg, Betty A., 375n, 378n, 403n
Degler, Carl, 110
democracy, 66, 321
Democratic Party, 325
  welfare policies of, 99, 100
  see also specific elections

Depression, 59, 325, 333
Deuteronomy, Book of, 187
Dillistone, F. W., 385*n*
Disciples of Christ, 210
dispensationalism, 57, 60, 168, 215–16,
    392*n*
divorce, 61, 91, 196–7, 251, 343, 352
drinking, prohibition of, 14, 86, 89,
    186–7, 188–9, 190, 267, 313
Durkheim, Emile, 393*n*
Dworkin, Andrea, 378*n*

earth, age of, 214
Ecclesiastes, 387*n*
Ecclesiastical Reformation, 148
education:
    in Bible schools, 213
    ethical issues addressed in, 343
    in evolutionary theory, 59–60, 118–19,
        145–6
    after high school, 356
    of homeschoolers, 5, 11, 360
    principle approach to, 146, 149
    school prayer and, 4–5
    on sexual behavior, 4, 5, 6, 94, 104,
        229, 249, 312, 326, 347, 361–2,
        378*n*, 403*n*
    see also Christian Academy; Liberty
        Baptist College
elders, 95–6, 101
elections:
    of 1964, 374*n*
    of 1968, 11, 374*n*
    of 1984, 117, 225
    of 1988, 228
    of 1994, 228
    of 2004, 403*n*
Ellis, Walter, 380*n*, 389*n*
Emmanuel United Evangelical
    Congregational Church, 332
Emory University, 404*n*
end times, 28, 29
England, evangelicalism in, 61, 375*n*,
    403*n*, Enlightenment, 185, 210, 369
En-psalm-bles, 45
Entzminger, Louis, 400*n*–1*n*
environmental preservation, 347
Ephesians, St. Paul's letter to, 301
    on drinking, 186

on marriage, 87, 88, 246–7, 250–1
Episcopalianism, 202, 367–8, 404*n*
Epstein, Barbara, 372*n*
equal rights amendment (ERA), 257, 258
evangelicalism, 72, 372*n*, 395*n*, 403*n*
    see also fundamentalism
Evangelical United Brethren, 332
Evans, Sara, 372*n*
evolution, 212, 216, 388*n*, 392*n*
    teaching of, 59–60, 118–19, 145–6

faith development, stages of, 386*n*
faith healing, 56, 215
Falwell, Jerry, 34
    in Bakker crisis, 57
    church congregation built by, 43, 52,
        54, 55, 58, 95, 108, 150, 153, 400*n*
    college education of, 24, 30– 1, 103,
        306, 325
    college operated by, xi, 7, 29–30, 31–2,
        45, 55, 119, 194, 307, 387*n*
    fundamentalist criticism of, 307, 353
    high school for pregnant teens run by,
        294–5
    Moral Majority organized by, xi, 6–7,
        31
    political influence of, 117, 226, 229,
        343, 353
    television/radio ministry of, 29, 32, 55,
        118, 151, 164
Family Forum, 5
family life:
    biblical relevance to, 26–7, 28, 49,
        109–10, 211
    chain of command in, 87, 88–9, 92,
        376*n*–7*n*, 394*n*, 396*n*, 398*n*, 399*n*
    church members' relationships
        modeled on, 95–9, 101, 112, 123,
        153–4, 323, 327
    class differences in, 112–13, 382*n*–3*n*
    conversion experiences and, 28, 397*n*
    division of labor within, 204, 205, 320,
        321–2
    English evangelicalism and, 403*n*
    extended networks of, 95, 96, 101,
        102, 103, 106–7, 113–14, 317,
        324–5, 326–7, 341, 342, 351, 352,
        381*n*, 383*n*, 397*n*–8*n*, 400*n*, 401*n*,
        403*n*

family life (*continued*)
  feminist critique of gender roles in,
    10–11, 91, 111–12, 202, 258, 321,
    322, 324, 345, 372*n*, 390*n*,
    399*n*–400*n*, 402*n*
  history of fundamentalist issues with,
    61
  individual-based social change vs.,
    344–6, 403*n*
  men's roles in, 88, 89, 90, 110, 246,
    250–2, 253–4, 255, 258–9, 320,
    394*n*, 395*n*
  reciprocal obligation in, 99, 100, 101,
    107, 205, 327, 341, 344
  rationalized schemes for, 209, 390*n*
  rural/urban differences and, 107–9,
    381*n*
  scholarship biases on, 10–11, 112–13,
    382*n*–3*n*
  unmarried grown children included in,
    102, 342
  women's prominence in kin networks
    of, 317–18, 396*n*
  see also marriage
fashion, 207–8
fasting, 177
Father Knows Best, 38
feminism:
  academic scholarship on, 36, 37–8
  autonomy as focus of, 253, 394*n*
  consciousness-raising groups of, 37,
    90, 125, 322
  fundamentalists' criticisms of, 90–2,
    229, 252–3, 257, 258, 322, 341,
    376*n*, 377*n*, 378*n*, 398*n*
  on gender roles within family, 10–11,
    91, 111–12, 202, 258, 321, 322, 324,
    345, 372*n*, 390*n*, 399*n*–400*n*, 402*n*
  homosexuality linked with, 252, 257
  neoevangelical movement and, 10,
    372*n*
  Second Wave of, 10–11, 345, 372*n*
  socioeconomic differences in appeal
    of, 10–11, 37, 103, 381*n*, 382*n*, 390*n*
Feminist Studies, 258
Ferraro, Geraldine, 117
fictive kinships, 98
Fields, Karen, 231, 393*n*
Finney, Charles, 176

FitzGerald, Frances, 108, 381*n*
Five College, Inc., 224
flappers, 344, 403*n*
Fletcher, Joseph, 389*n*
Florida, Baptist fundamentalist churches
  in, 357
Ford, Andrew, 391*n*
Fournier, Bill, 4, 5, 6, 7, 36, 37, 38, 326
Fournier, Karen, 4–5, 6, 7, 36, 38, 326
Fowler, James, 386*n*, 402*n*
Frank, Douglas, 392*n*
free enterprise, 326
Freud, Sigmund, 8
fundamentalism:
  as American phenomenon, 61, 375*n*,
    403*n*
  defined, 371*n*–2*n*
  English evangelicalism vs., 61, 375*n*,
    403*n*
  extended-family ties in institutions of,
    95–6, 324, 359, 400*n*
  foundational writings of, 183, 184,
    385*n*, 388*n*
  historical scholarship on, 58–61, 374*n*,
    375*n*
  language of, 133
  militant antimodernism of, 54, 59, 61,
    203, 403*n*
  moral absolutes of, 66, 94, 123, 131,
    154, 183, 190–200, 201, 202, 204,
    205–6, 207, 229, 328–9, 386*n*, 387*n*,
    388*n*
  origin of name, 59, 203
  other Christians, criticisms of, 368
  Pentecostal, 56–7, 58, 68, 212, 215,
    294, 309, 343–4, 375*n*
  popular vs. scholarly, 60, 387*n*
  rural/urban culture clashes and, 108–9,
    381*n*
  separatist impulse of, 54, 374*n*
  sociology's development and, 402*n*
  southern development of, 55, 108–9,
    357
  substitutionary atonement doctrine of,
    183–4, 385*n*
  tradition allied with, 203–17,
    389*n*–90*n*, 391*n*, 392*n*
fundamentalist churches:
  benevolent practices at, 134–7, 384*n*

congregation size of, 57–8
going forward in worship services at, 139, 368
independent status of, 31, 54, 304, 371*n*
invitation to salvation offered at, 137–40
masculine ideals of, 110–11
music styles of, 45–6, 68–70, 240–1, 359–60
names of, 56
pastoral authority in, 31, 93, 111, 127, 167, 302, 305–6, 309, 310–11, 320–1
personal atmosphere of, 49–51, 54–5, 323, 374*n*
political engagement in, 225–9
sermons in, 46–9
shared pastorates in, 95
size of, 57–8
splits in, 54–5, 359, 374*n*
stylistic uniformities of, 153
women's power in, 316–22, 396*n*, 397*n*, 402*n*
see also Shawmut River Baptist Church
fundamentalists:
anti-intellectualism of, 64, 212, 356, 375*n*, 391*n*
apostles' Epistles as source of doctrine focus of, 65, 376*n*
in Bible study groups, 60, 62–5, 164–72, 375*n*
on Bible translations, 39
cultural differences among, 70
evangelicalism vs., 72, 372*n*, 395*n*
evangelical responsibility of, 130–1
feminism criticized by, 90–2, 229, 252–3, 257, 258, 322, 341, 376*n*, 377*n*, 378*n*, 398*n*
government courts shunned by, 122
history of social conservatism of, 61
logical inconsistencies tolerated by, 131, 194–5, 384*n*, 387*n*
patriarchal authority supported by, 316, 318, 320–4, 395*n*, 397*n*, 398*n*–9*n*
popular misperceptions of, 141–3
spoken-word culture of, 151–3, 154
supernatural outlook of, 179–80, 184–5, 211, 213, 369, 371*n*

Fundamentalists Anonymous, 294
Fundamentals, The, 183, 184, 385*n*, 388*n*

Galatians, 136, 183
Gallagher, Sally K., 376*n*, 377*n*, 383*n*, 388*n*, 394*n*, 397*n*, 399*n*–400*n*
Garrett, Jane, 387*n*
General Regular Baptist Convention, 360
Genesis, Book of, 65, 87, 164–5, 166, 167–8, 174, 213, 214, 247, 253
geological catastrophism, 216
Gerard, Susan Elizabeth, 376*n*–7*n*
Gerstel, Naomi, 396*n*
giving, ethos of, 98, 134–7, 384*n*
gnomai, 211
God:
personification of, 50, 184
promises of, 168
going forward, 139, 368
Goldwater, Barry, 374*n*
Gomes, Peter, 376*n*
Good News, 333
Gordon, Sol, 4
gossip, 120–1, 124–6, 318–19, 320, 396*n*
Gouldner, Alvin, 389*n*
government programs, family reciprocity vs., 99–100, 134, 191
Graham, Sylvester, 394*n*
grandparents, children raised by, 341, 403*n*
Great Commission, 131
Griffith, R. Marie, 375*n*, 377*n*, 391*n*
Gund, Granny, 41, 73, 74, 96, 98, 126, 323
Gusfield, Joseph, 379*n*
Guyana, People's Temple mass suicide in, 311

hair styles, 207–8
Hankins, Barry, 400*n*–1*n*
Harding, Susan, 375*n*, 391*n*
Harper's, 343
Harry Potter books, 184, 386*n*
healing by faith, 56, 215
Hebrews, Book of, 207
helicopter design, 353–4
Henderson, Clarinda, 383*n*
Heriot, M. Jean, 381*n*

Heritage Baptist Church, 72, 74, 160, 363
Hinduism, 203, 389n
Hofstadter, Richard, 99, 371n, 379n
Hoggart, Richard, 386n
Holy Family Academy, 5, 6, 36, 38, 94, 326
Holy Spirit, 130–1, 132, 142
  Bible inspired by, 166, 167, 173, 187
  pastoral message as vehicle of, 46–7
  personification of, 138, 204
homeschooling, 5, 151, 360
homosexuality:
  as behavior vs. sexual identity, 144, 393n–4n
  biblical passages on, 71–2, 376n
  in Falwell's church, 353
  as feminist agenda, 252, 257
  fundamentalist criticism of, 65, 68, 70–2, 204, 248, 398n
  same-sex marriage and, 342, 393n
  sex education programs and, 361
Horowitz, Helen, 394n
House of Representatives, U.S., 228, 325, 343
housewives:
  cultural respect for, 257
  social isolation of, 103
Howell, George, 299
Hunter, James Davison, 345, 372n, 386n, 388n, 389n, 403n

idol worship, 171
"I Got You Babe," 249
individualism, 201, 392n, 397n
  American tradition of, 209, 210
  community obligations vs., 209, 343, 344–6
  moral absolutes vs., 205, 206, 328–9
  of television superheroes, 251
infant baptism, 160
intelligence, abstract discourse vs., 330–1
international terrorism, 346, 403n
invitation, 76, 137–40
Isaiah, Book of, 210

James, Book of, 62, 65, 169, 170, 174, 283
Jay, Nancy, 231, 388n, 389n, 393n
Jeff (C. Valenti's husband), 295, 296, 297, 298, 303, 304, 312, 351

Jehovah's Witnesses, 85–6, 160
Job, Book of, 214
John, Gospel According to, 9, 192, 284
Johnson, Lyndon, 12
Jones, Bob, Jr., 324
Jones, Bob, 111, 324
Jones, Jim, 311
Joy Circles, 62, 84, 89, 111
Judgment Day, 170

Kachudnis, Ben:
  anger exhibited by, 164, 230, 262, 270–2, 273, 274
  in Bible-study group, 164, 169, 172, 176, 178, 190
  church support of, 275–6
  as father, 163, 164, 176, 178, 264–5, 267, 268, 270, 271, 274, 275–6, 288, 293, 335, 363, 365, 366
  marital breakup of, 163, 164, 230, 250, 260–74, 293, 334–5, 363–4, 365–6
  religious practice of, 359
Kachudnis, Mikey, 262, 267–8, 270, 272–3, 276
Kachudnis, Pam, 250, 323, 359, 368
  church attendance of, 163–4, 268
  on documentary film, 261, 265, 334–5
  extramarital relationship of, 164, 230–1, 263, 266–7, 268
  jobs of, 164, 268, 364–5
  marital breakup of, 163, 230, 260–9, 270–1, 272, 274, 293, 334–5, 363, 365–6
  as mother, 163, 178, 260, 261, 262, 263, 264, 267–8, 288, 365
Keener, Dan, 117, 134
  background of, 73, 102
  church friend's reciprocity with, 97
  marriage of, 238, 275–6
  Ohio move of, 238, 294
  salvation experience of, 74–5
  as schoolteacher, 69, 145, 238, 358
Keener, Dave, 205, 225, 363
  background of, 42, 73, 74, 75
  Bible-study group of, 155
  church friends of, 65, 67–8, 275–6, 297
  as deacon, 42, 126, 138
  departure of, 294
  marriage of, 253, 256

on prayer requests, 79
proselytizing efforts of, 75
reciprocal relationships of, 98–9
salvation experience of, 74
as teacher in church school, 42–3, 69,
  145–6, 147, 241, 269, 294
Keener, Judy Waters, 196, 276
at Baptist Bible College, 52, 103–4
motherhood of, 104, 355, 358
Ohio move of, 238, 294
as schoolteacher, 53, 106, 145, 146,
  238, 358
in Shawmut church power circle, 106,
  126
Keener, Sally, 96, 126, 363, 383n, 397n
author's salvation sought by, 132–133
background of, 42, 73–4
Bible study of, 74, 155, 212
church friends of, 65, 67, 297
on church members' reciprocity, 78,
  97, 98–9
on elder care, 101, 205
on feminism, 92, 252, 253
on fundamentalist culture, 72–3
marriage of, 74, 253, 254, 256
mass media ignored by, 118, 150, 383n
as mother, 42, 43, 198
nursing career of, 42, 43, 73, 74
organ played by, 41, 69, 138
on public prayer, 181
on welfare programs, 99, 100
Kennedy, Edward M., 99
Kennedy, John F., 12
kin-based networks, 95, 96, 98, 108,
  112–13, 341, 378n–9n, 383n, 396n
King James Bible, 48, 64, 165, 166, 193,
  194, 209, 373n, 387n
Kings, First Book of, 47
Klatch, Rebecca E., 371n
knowledge class, 388n
Kohlberg, Lawrence, 386n, 402n
Kopkind, Andrew, 380n
Korean metaphoric language, 402n
Kornblum, William, 380n

LaHaye, Tim, 32–3, 110
Latino population, 325
Lauper, Cindy, 241
Laverne, Doug, 229, 294

background of, 156, 157, 162, 163,
  170–1
in Bible-study group, 154, 155–6,
  162–3, 164–6, 167, 169, 177, 178,
  182, 186, 189, 190, 204, 222
on church conflicts, 276, 279, 280,
  299, 300, 301, 302, 307, 310, 314
on documentary film, 234
later church involvement of, 358, 359
marriage of, 157, 158–9, 175, 248, 363
personality of, 156, 226, 384n
political involvement of, 226, 228
prayer life developed by, 181
religious faith of, 157–60, 161–2, 179,
  183, 188, 209, 212
work life of, 157, 175, 178, 205, 361,
  363
Laverne, Terry, 294
background of, 156, 162, 163
in Bible-study group, 154, 155–6,
  162–3, 166, 170, 171, 175, 176, 177,
  189, 190, 204, 362
on church-fellowship limitations, 229
marriage of, 156, 157, 158–9, 175, 248
religious commitment of, 160–1, 162,
  362–3
Shawmut church split and, 299, 301,
  307, 310, 314, 357–8
Lear, Norman, 294, 383n
Lennon, John, 387n
lesbian partnerships, 342
Leviticus, Book of, 65, 214
liberals, fundamentalist Christians
  distrusted by, 328, 329
liberal theology, 385n
Liberty Baptist College, 31–4, 70, 373n
campus of, 30
curriculum of, 31–3
development of, 29–30
music studies at, 45
name change of, 307, 353
pastors educated at, xi, 7, 30, 164,
  359
Liberty University, 307, 353
Limbaugh, Rush, 325, 329, 353, 360
Lincoln, Abraham, 210
Lincoln Square Baptist Church, 360–1
Little House on the Prairie, 251
Lord's Prayer, 50

Louv, Richard, 401*n*
love, as self-sacrificial duty vs. romance, 249, 268
Love Boat, 135
Lucifer, 184
Luke, Gospel According to, 183, 356
Luker, Kristin, 347, 379*n*–80*n*, 386*n*, 401*n*
lust, provocation of, 283–4
Luther, Martin, 44, 169, 203

Macbeth (Shakespeare), 269
Manning, Christel J., 377*n*, 399*n*
Margaret, "Aunt" (church member), 41, 50, 77, 78, 96–7, 117, 133–4, 137, 150, 323, 359
Mark, Gospel According to, 195
marriage:
  biblical guidance on, 86, 87, 88–9, 92–3, 246–7, 250–1
  couple privacy vs. extended-family ties in, 102–3, 106–7, 394*n*
  fundamentalist guidance on, 86–90, 92–3, 230–1, 334, 343, 395*n*–6*n*
  importance of sex in, 27, 394*n*
  pastoral counseling on, 42, 261–3, 264–9, 270–4
  of same-sex couples, 342, 393*n*, 403*n*
  self-sacrificial duty vs. romance in, 249
  women's subordination in, 87–9, 90, 246, 250, 253–6, 259, 376*n*–7*n*
  working on, 343, 403*n*
  see also family life
Marsden, George M., 58–9, 60, 375*n*, 376*n*, 390*n*, 391*n*, 392*n*
Marty, Martin E., 389*n*–90*n*
Marx, Karl, 37, 380*n*
Marxism, 216, 392*n*
Massachusetts Bay Colony, Puritan settlers in, 148
masturbation, 32
mathematics, theological symbolism of, 146
Mathews, Donald, 393*n*
Matthew, Gospel. According to, 122, 174, 387*n*
Mauss, Marcel, 385*n*
Meeks, Wayne, 211

men:
  adversarial conversational style of, 319–20
  church involvement of, 110–11, 381*n*, 395*n*
  in consciousness-raising groups, 36–7
  domestic responsibilities of, 88, 89, 90, 110, 246, 250–2, 253–4, 255, 258–9, 320, 394*n*, 395*n*
  honor of, 259, 319, 395*n*
  military service as duty of, 100, 101, 392*n*
  women's subordination to, 87–8, 89, 90, 92, 246–7, 250, 253–6, 259, 378*n*, 395*n*–6*n*
Mennonites, 233, 376*n*
Merton, Robert, 389*n*
Methodists, 20, 137, 160, 332–3, 375*n*
Miesmer, Adrienne, 293, 393*n*
militarism, 12, 100, 101, 201
miracles, 139, 180, 182
Mitch (Pam Kachudnis' boyfriend), 261, 262–3, 265, 266–7, 268, 269, 270, 271, 272, 365
modernism, militant opposition to, 54, 59, 61, 203, 403*n*
Mondale, Walter F., 117
Moody, Dwight L., 20, 215, 360
Moody Bible Institute, 45, 70
Moore, Raymond, 5
moral absolutes, 123, 201
  in concrete contexts, 190–200, 202, 204, 205–6, 386*n*, 387*n*, 388*n*
  doctrinal inconsistencies vs., 131, 154
  individual choice vs., 205, 206, 328–9
  motherhood as, 379*n*–80*n*
  pastoral counseling on, 32
  of reciprocal obligations, 183
  secular humanist rejection of, 66
  sex education as undermining of, 94, 229
  traditionalism and, 207
moral development, universal stages of, 386*n*.
Moral Majority, xi, 6–7, 31, 80, 117, 118, 229, 335, 343, 353
moral relativists, 102, 104–5, 197, 201, 206, 328, 329

Morgan, Robin, 382*n*.
Morgans (former church members),
    121–2, 123, 129
Mormonism, 203
morning message, 46–9
Morse, Ada, 120
    on author's Christianity, 222
    church influence of, 84, 128
    on church members, conflicts, 229, 294
    family background of, 106
    family influence wielded by, 317–18,
        354
    Florida move of, 352, 355
    on F. Valenti's counseling style, 32
    marriages of, 20, 21, 196
    on public prayer, 181
    religious practice of, 20, 23–4, 28–9,
        34, 318, 368
    Sandersons, friendship with, 67
    sex education opposed by, 4
    on Sharon and Frank's marriage, 22, 29
    Shawmut Church split and, 303, 305,
        309, 314
    on S. Valenti's faith, 297
    in Valenti business ventures, 354, 355
    on Vietnam War, 23
Morse, Tom, 23, 28–9, 354, 355
    career of, 21
    on charismatic Christians, 57
    church attendance of, 24, 34, 62
    on church finances, 279
    on church-town conflicts, 121, 181
    education standards of, 22, 120
    on family as organizational
        foundation, 101
    Florida move of, 352
    F. Valenti's ministry supported by,
        318
    on marriage, 255
    nursery project and, 276, 277
    Sandersons' friendship with, 67
    Shawmut Church split and, 300, 303,
        305, 309, 314
Mosher (Florida preacher), 89
Mosher, Mrs. (preacher's wife), 89, 90,
    111
motherhood:
    as women's duty, 100, 379*n*–80*n*
    see also parenthood

Moyers, Bill, 113, 398*n*
MTV, 241
Muilenberg, James, 14
music styles, 45–6, 68–70, 343, 355,
    359–60

Napoleon I, Emperor of France, 66, 214
National Association of Congregational
    Christian Churches, 342
National Education Association, 49
National Endowment for the
    Humanities (NEH), xii, 127, 141,
        142, 177, 221, 223–4, 225
National Organization for Women
    (NOW), 251
Nehemiah, Book of, 120
neoevangelical movement, 10, 372*n*
New Deal, 325, 333, 379*n*
New England, fundamentalist growth in,
    52
New Left, 12, 36–7, 344, 345
New Right, 3, 12, 118, 344, 371*n*
    see also conservative pro-family
        movement
New South, 55, 108, 109, 325
New Testament, 47, 168, 193
    see also Bible; *specific New Testament
        books*
Newtonian physics, 212, 215
New Woman, 61, 344
Niebuhr, H. Richard, 14, 109, 184
Nine to Five, 37
Nixon, Richard, 29
Noachian flood theory, 119, 214
Noll, Mark, 210
Non-Western Christianity, 184–5
Norris, J. Frank, 31, 54, 61, 108, 109,
    110–11, 325, 374*n*, 379*n*, 381*n*,
    400*n*–1*n*
Northampton, Mass., 342
Northridge (Temple Baptist) Church
    (Detroit), 108, 381*n*
NOW (National Organization for
    Women), 251
Numbers, Ronald L., 374*n*
nursing homes, 101

Oklahoma City, Okla., federal building
    bombed in, 236

old-fashionedness, 208, 389n
Old Testament, 47, 168, 193
  see also Bible; *specific old Testament books*
Old-Time Gospel Hour, The, 29, 32
Oral Roberts University, 324
oral tradition, 127, 151–3, 211–12, 327
  of Bible, 194, 211
  change accommodated in, 214
  common culture rooted in, 152–3,
    204, 208, 211, 216
  reading skills and, 165–6, 384n
  women's indirect shaping of, 320
organ donation, ix, xii
Our Bodies, Ourselves, 4, 5, 37, 91

parenthood:
  bag-of-flour exercise on, 378n
  as moral absolute, 379n–80n
  physical discipline methods of, 26, 28,
    234–7
Parents for Traditional Values, 326, 378n
Pascal, Blaise, 174
pastoral counseling, 32
Paul, Saint, 71–2, 87, 169, 187, 211, 301,
  311, 358, 376n
PBS, 127, 327, 335, 350
Pensacola Christian College, 146
Pentecostal (charismatic) Christians,
  56–7, 58, 68, 212, 215, 294, 309,
  343–4, 375n
People for the American Way, 294
People's Temple, 311
Peter (Terry Laverne's uncle), 169, 170,
  171
Peter, First Book of, 236
Peter, Saint, 404n
Philippians, 192, 273
phonics reading instruction, 165, 384n
physics, 212, 215, 356, 404n
Planned Parenthood, 5–6
polygamy, 215
postfeminism, 90, 377n
Potter, Harry, 184, 386n
prayer, 174–83
  answers found through, 178
  chains of, 180–1
  partners in, 150, 180
  personal relationship experienced in,
    50, 182–3

in schools, 4–5
  specificity of, 176
prayer life, 174
prayer requests, 78–9, 158, 174–5, 176,
  177, 222
Prayer Warriors, 177, 180
premillenial prophecy, 58, 60, 392n
Presbyterian theology, 58, 375n
Princeton school, 58
privacy, marital, 102–4, 106–7, 380n,
  394n
Progressive Era, 326
Promise Keepers, 88, 252
promises of God, 168
proof-texting, 173
Protestantism:
  denominational differences of, 375n
  fundamentalism vs. evangelicalism in,
    371n–2n
  fundamentalist roots in traditions of,
    58–9, 375n
  Reformation and, 44, 148, 169, 174,
    203, 210
  see also fundamentalism; *specific
    Protestant denominations*
Proverbs, Book of, 26, 27, 86, 120–1,
  234, 257, 373n
psychotherapy, pastoral counseling vs., 32
Puritans, 148–9, 168, 210
Putnam, Robert, 112, 382n, 392n

quilting tools, 354

racial segregation, 213–14, 391n
rapture, 28, 215
Rauch, Jonathan, 393n
Ravitch, Diane, 403n
reading skills, 165–6, 384n
Reagan, Ronald, 3, 12, 15, 117, 225, 228,
  398n
reciprocity, 97–9, 379n, 380n, 385n
  abuse of, 206
  Christ's death and, 161, 183–4
  extended-family relations and, 317
  family obligations as model of, 99,
    100, 101, 107, 205, 327, 341, 344
  moral absolute and, 183
  theology and, 182–5
Reed, Ralph, 343

Reformation, 44, 148, 169, 174, 203, 210
Reno, Janet, 236
Republican Party:
  congressional majority of, 228, 325,
    343
  social conservatives in, 11
reputation, gossip effects on, 125–6,
  318–19, 396n
revivalism, 58
Rice, John, 61, 395n
right-to-life groups, 3–4, 5–6, 106–7
Roberts, Oral, Jr., 324
Robertson, Pat, 6, 80, 108, 228, 229, 325,
  343, 344, 361
Robison, James, 32
rock music, fundamentalist criticism of,
  69–70, 249, 360
Rodeheaver, Homer, 333
Roger (Bible-study group visitor),
  186–90
Romans, Book of, 71–2, 75, 129, 159,
  169, 170, 192, 376n
Roosevelt, Franklin Delano, 325, 379n
Rose, Susan, 376n–7n, 382n, 394n, 396n
Rowling, J. K., 386n
Russell, C. Allyn, 374n
Russian Revolution, 216

salvation:
  of Abraham, 1.68
  baptism and, 160
  biblical steps to, 75, 129
  church service invitation to, 76,
    137–40
  Holy Spirit as instrument of, 130, 131
  reciprocity linked to, 161
  requirements of, 169–72
  sinner's prayer and, 129–30
same-sex marriage, 342, 393n, 403n
Sandeen, Ernest, 374n
Sanderson, Scott, 151, 256
  as assistant pastor, 63, 69, 144, 276,
    299, 300, 312, 320
  background of, 45, 70, 72, 96
  on Christian wives, 87
  church friends of, 65, 67, 297, 303
  on documentary film, 142, 237
  as evangelical vs. fundamentalist, 72,
    305, 395n

finances of, 68, 360
  on fundamentalist culture, 70, 249
  on gossip, 297–8
  homes of, 67, 125, 129, 300, 301
  on homosexuality, 70–1
  as interim pastor, 301
  as music minister, 40, 44–5, 46, 50,
    51, 63, 68–70, 144, 145, 310,
    359–60
  on public prayer, 181
  on Shawmut Church split, 299–300,
    301, 303, 307, 310–11, 320
  on Tatum's dismissal, 123–5, 126
  as teacher, 69–70, 145
Sanderson, Sue, 129, 160, 256, 364
  background of, 45, 72, 96
  on biblical guidance, 68
  children homeschooled by, 360
  church friends of, 65, 67, 303
  church music involvement of, 46, 50,
    51, 69, 160, 287, 297
  as evangelical vs. fundamentalist, 72,
    305, 395n
  on fundamentalist culture, 70
  on gossip, 297
  in new church community, 359
  on pastoral authority, 311
  Shawmut Church split and, 300, 301,
    307, 310, 313, 357
  as teacher, 69, 145
Satan, 57, 179, 184, 185, 204, 211, 249,
  251, 357–8, 369
Schiller, Johann Christoph Friedrich
  von, 389n
Schlafly, Phyllis, 91, 229, 325, 377n
science:
  biblical support of, 214
  of evolutionary biology, 59–60,
    118–19, 145–6
  fundamentalist ambivalence toward,
    212–13, 214–15, 216–17, 356,
    391n
  treating causes independent of God's
    actions, 369
  of physics, 212, 215, 356, 404n
  popular respect for, 209, 390n
  in school curricula, 59–60
Scofield, Cyrus Ingersoll, 215
Scofield Reference Bible (Scofield), 215

Scopes trial, 59, 374*n*, 388*n*
Scorby, Alexander, 151
second birth, 9
Second Coming, 29, 58, 60, 131, 226, 371*n*
Second Great Awakening, 391*n*
Second Wave feminism, 10–11, 345, 372*n*
secular humanism, 66, 68, 105, 127, 224, 328, 329, 361
self-sacrifice, 98, 100, 101, 206, 249, 327, 385*n*, 392*n*
sermons, 46–9
sewing tools, 354
sex education, 4, 5, 6, 45, 94, 104, 229, 249, 312, 326, 347, 361–2, 378*n*, 403*n*
sexes, social segregation of, 67–8, 111, 397*n*
sexual behavior:
    emotional intimacy in, 249, 393*n*
    in marriage, 27, 249, 394*n*
    pastoral counseling on, 32, 393*n*–4*n*
    pleasure vs. responsibility in, 107, 393*n*
    procreation as sole function of, 376*n*
    sexual identity vs., 144, 393*n*–4*n*
    see also homosexuality
Shawmut River Baptist Church:
    adult Sunday school of, 64
    attendance levels of, 40, 52, 58, 62, 130
    baptisms conducted by, 160–1
    benevolent ethos of, 134–7, 384*n*
    Bible study at, 62–5, 140
    civic relations with, 121, 143, 145, 231, 277
    deacons of, 42, 126–7, 128, 138, 312, 318
    development of, 51–3, 54, 308–9, 310, 349
    dispute resolution process of, 122, 303–4
    documentary film project on, xii, 119, 127–8, 141–3; *see also Born Again*
    establishment of, 44, 155
    evangelizing efforts of, 62, 75–6, 130–1, 132–3, 161–2, 282, 384*n*
    ex-Catholics as members of, 17, 51, 156

    family groups within, 43–4, 95, 101, 106, 111, 153, 155–6, 224, 226–7, 229, 231, 294, 314, 317, 323, 327, 330, 358, 359, 361
    female influence in, 84, 126, 128, 316–17, 318, 322, 323, 396*n*
    finances of, 42, 44, 52–3, 68, 78, 111, 150, 224, 225, 237–8, 276–80, 301, 302, 358
    gymnatorium built by, 39, 52, 53, 121, 133–4, 145, 157, 225, 238, 358
    insularity of, 226–8, 392*n*
    intimate and informal atmosphere of, 39, 41, 44, 47, 49–51, 104, 109, 154, 176, 204–5, 229, 323
    location of, 8, 52–3, 357
    marital counseling group of, 42
    mass media's irrelevance to, 150–1
    membership of, 39, 40, 42–4, 50–1, 53, 95, 381*n*
    men's involvement in, 110–11, 318
    music at, 39, 40, 46, 68–70, 144, 240–1, 275, 360
    new converts in, 231, 293
    nursery facilities of, 238–9, 276–7, 294, 306
    oral culture of, 151–3, 154, 204, 205, 327
    political involvement and, 48, 225–9, 256
    power elite of, 126, 128, 238, 256, 316
    preschool program of, 42, 77, 146, 150, 296
    replacement of pastors at, 299, 300, 301, 305, 306–7, 309, 310, 358, 359, 360
    salaries paid at, 68, 78
    school operated by, *see* Christian Academy
    sex segregation in social life of, 67–8, 111, 397*n*
    social support provided by, 77–9, 95–9, 132–4
    sociological perspectives on, 330, 339–40
    Southern Baptist churches vs., 357
    splits in, 54, 55, 111, 121–3, 153, 229, 231, 279, 280, 294, 299–306, 349, 357–8, 362

Sunday worship services at, 38–42, 44, 46–50, 62, 77, 78–9, 246, 287–8
teenagers of, 70, 147–8, 241–5, 295, 296, 312, 350, 359
unmarried congregants of, 117
Wednesday-evening services at, 62–4, 65, 95, 130, 275–6
weekly activities scheduled at, 10, 62
Shepperson, Mary, 261, 309, 365, 381*n*
background of, 77
church friendships of, 294
generosity of, 77–8
marriage of, 250, 253
motherhood of, 241, 242, 251
as prayer partner, 150, 180
as preschool teacher, 145, 150, 231, 250
Shawmut Church split and, 303
Shepperson, Pattie, 241–2, 243, 244
Shepperson, Paula, 242, 242, 243
sin:
accountability for, 296, 297
age of culpability for, 284–5
bad habits as, 289
as eternal, x–xi
homosexuality as, 71–2
as inescapable human condition, 71, 284, 297
of selfishness, 206
sinner's prayer, 71, 129–30, 160
situation ethics, 205, 206, 207
Slater, Philip, 394*n*
Smith, Christian, 383*n*, 393*n*
Smith College, 3, 224
smoking, 24, 89, 163–4, 176, 195, 242–3, 289
snake handling, 203
social change, individualism vs. family as basis of, 344–6
social connectedness, 112, 382*n*
social conservatives, 371*n*
see also conservative pro-family movement
social gospel ministries, 384*n*
sociology, Protestant fundamentalism's development and, 339, 402*n*
Sodom, destruction of, 71
Sonny and Cher, 249
Sonya Live, 335–6

South:
cultural influence of, 343
fundamentalist development in, 55, 108–9, 357
Southern Baptist Convention, 107, 353, 380*n*
spanking, 26, 28, 234–7, 242
Stacey, Judith, 376*n*–7*n*, 379*n*, 394*n*
Stack, Carol, 379*n*
status politics, 379*n*
Stevick, Daniel, 387*n*
Stewardship Banquet, 225
Strong, Brenda (Sam's wife), 281–4
Strong, Jean:
background of, 81, 86
in business, 82–3, 84, 326, 361, 362
church friendships of, 89, 97
church leadership and, 126, 298, 301, 303, 307, 310, 311, 313, 314–15, 316, 317, 319, 358, 359, 360
church split and, 311–16
on corporal punishment, 234
on documentary film, 330
evangelism of, 43, 79–80, 131, 281, 282, 288
family background of, 81, 105–6, 317
on feminist issues, 90–1, 92, 253
on gender roles, 90–1, 253–4, 255, 284
home of, 81–2, 83
leadership position of, 84, 87–8, 316–17
Lincoln Square Church joined by, 360–1
marriage of, 80–1, 83–5, 86–90, 92–3, 102, 111, 248, 254, 256, 284, 362
patriarchal authority endorsed by, 88, 253–4, 255, 395*n*
political activism of, 228
as preschool teacher, 255, 296, 313
religious experience of, 85–6
school management criticized by, 314
in women's church activities, 84, 90, 229
Strong, Phil:
background of, 83, 86
benevolence of, 137, 157
in Bible study, 63, 93
businesses of, 43, 44, 80, 82–3, 84–5, 312, 326, 361, 362

Strong, Phil (*continued*)
  on church finances, 44, 225, 238, 277, 278, 279
  church splits and, 122, 298, 301, 302, 303, 306, 307, 309, 310, 314, 358, 359
  death of father of, 199–200
  evangelism of, 43, 79–80, 131, 239, 281, 282, 284–5, 286–7, 288
  family of, 43, 79–80, 239, 294, 302, 317
  on F. Valenti's leadership, 276, 278, 279, 280, 299, 300, 302, 306, 311–12, 313, 315
  Lincoln Square Church joined by, 360–1
  marriage of, 80–1, 83–5, 86–90, 92–3, 158, 248, 256, 284, 362
  on pastoral authority, 93
  on personal prayer, 50
  political activism of, 228, 343–4, 361–2
  religious practice of, 79–80, 85–6, 88, 89, 2–39
  sex education opposed by, 361–2
  as spiritual mentor, 181, 283–5, 286, 361
  state Senate campaign of, 134–5, 199, 225–6, 227
  welfare proposal of, 134–5, 199, 387*n*–8*n*
Strong, Sam:
  background of, 83, 281
  on documentary film, 335
  marriages of, 281–3, 284, 293
  religious practice of, 359, 362
  salvation efforts of, 131, 281, 282, 285–7, 288, 293, 329, 334
  on Shawmut Church split, 362
substitutionary atonement, 183–4, 385*n*, 388*n*
Sullivan, Anne (welfare mother), 96, 97, 376*n*
Sunday, Billy, 111, 333, 395*n*
supernaturalism, 179–80, 184–5, 211, 213, 369, 371*n*
Swaggart, Jimmy, S7
swearing, 26, 86, 89, 289–90
Swindoll, Chuck, 118

Tatum, Bill, 119–25, 126, 128, 129, 181, 224, 256, 384*n*
Tatum, Sally, 124
television:
  evangelists on, 50, 117–18, 119, 141, 151
  fundamentalist criticisms of, 135, 251
temperance pledge, 14
Temple Baptist Church (Connecticut), 300
Temple Baptist (Northridge) Church (Detroit), 108, 381*n*
Ten Commandments, 169, 188
Tennessee Temple Baptist Bible College, 70, 86
terrorism, international, 346, 403*n*
testimony, 78
Thomas Aquinas, Saint, 376*n*
Thomas Road Baptist Church, 29, 34
Three's Company, 135, 251
Tillich, Paul, 14
"time out of mind," tradition and 208, 209
Timothy, First Book of, 300, 305, 311, 312
Timothy, Second Book of, 166, 187
tithes, 44
Titus, Book of, 311
tongues, speaking in, 56, 68, 145, 215
tradition, 203–17
  Bible as foundation of, 209–12, 213, 217
  changes accommodated in, 207, 208, 213–14, 391*n*
  as collective activity, 208
  in family life, 345, 403*n*
  oral transmission of, 127, 151–3, 194, 204, 208, 211–12, 214, 320, 384*n*
  as source of legitimation, 208, 389*n*
  timeless quality of, 207–9, 213, 216
  working class adherence to, 202
Tremont Temple, 108, 381*n*
Trinity Church (Wall Street), 335, 336, 339, 369
Turner, Tina, 241

Union Theological Seminary, 14, 15, 333
Unitarians, 210
United Church of Christ, 342

United Methodist Church, 333, 337

upper-class communities, family-based gender roles in, 324, 400*n*

Valenti, Christie, 65–6, 67, 234
  birth of, 21
  education of, 147, 294–5, 351
  jobs of, 351, 352, 356
  marriages of, 298, 351, 352
  motherhood of, 307, 351, 352, 356
  pregnancy of, 295–8, 299, 304, 305, 306, 312, 314, 315
  religious practice of, 244
  teen social life of, 241, 242, 245, 295, 303
  on television programs, 135–6

Valenti, Frank:
  on abortion, 48
  assistants to, 69, 164, 299
  on author's salvation, 129, 132, 222–3, 367
  background of, ix, 7, 9, 17–20, 21–2, 163, 228
  baptism conducted by, 160–1
  on biblical passages, 9, 47–9, 64, 159, 169, 170, 174, 186, 193–4, 196, 214, 299, 358
  born-again experience of, 9, 16, 24–6, 289, 293
  business ventures of, 352, 353–5, 356, 358
  on capitalism, 325–6
  on Catholic Church, 156
  charismatic practices opposed by, 57, 294, 302, 309
  on Christian education, 146, 147, 149, 212, 224, 355
  on church finances, 44, 78, 150, 224, 225, 237, 238–9, 276, 277–80
  church growth and, 52, 53–4, 97, 309, 358–9
  church splits and, 53–4, 80, 121–2, 123, 294, 299–317, 320, 321, 357, 358, 362, 374*n*
  church-state relations of, 121
  construction projects of, 53, 144, 148, 238–9, 276–7, 350
  on corporal punishment, 26, 28, 234
  creationism espoused by, 118–19, 214

  doctrinal criticisms of, 312–13, 316, 317, 319
  on documentary film, xii, 128, 141, 142, 143, 177, 233, 236, 237, 298–9, 330, 332, 334, 336, 350, 351
  on drinking, 186, 313
  education of, 18, 22, 29–30, 31, 32–5, 146, 302, 307, 350
  evangelizing efforts of, 34, 35, 129, 1, 32, 159, 163, 222–3
  on family life, 102, 112
  fatherhood of, 21, 26, 49, 295, 296, 297, 298, 300, 303, 304, 308, 312
  finances of, 32, 34–5, 53, 150, 225, 237, 238, 279–80, 302, 354–5, 356
  Florida move of, 307, 357
  on gender roles, 246–7, 248, 251–2
  on gossip, 120, 121, 126
  as grandfather, 351, 356–7
  helping relationships fostered by, 77–8, 97, 134, 135–7, 157, 163, 228
  on homosexuality, 65, 68, 144, 393*n* 4*n*
  hospital patient visited by, ix–x, xii
  housing proposal of, 277, 293
  humor used by, 47, 48, 63, 228
  injuries of, 19–20, 21, 177, 276
  intelligence of, 330
  invitation to salvation offered by, 76, 137–9, 288
  on liberal Protestant denominations, 15
  management skills of, 7, 276–7, 278, 279–81
  on marital relationships, 27, 246–7, 248, 249, 250–1, 255, 334
  marriage of, 21, 22–3, 25, 27–8, 34, 74, 86, 87, 90, 91, 149–50, 230, 247–8, 256, 257–8, 267, 293, 297, 317–18
  mechanical inventions developed by, 353–4, 358
  media appearances of, xi, 38, 226, 294, 335–56
  on men's place in church, 110, 111, 381*n*, 395*n*
  newcomers welcomed by, 38–9, 43, 50, 64, 117, 140, 145, 157, 228
  nursery construction project of, 238–9, 276–7, 306

Valenti, Frank (*continued*)
  office of, 8–9
  pastoral counseling of, 31, 144, 159,
    164, 230–1, 255, 261–3, 264–9,
    270–4, 334, 363, 368
  philanthropic goals of, 355, 356
  physical appearance of, ix, 9, 207, 208
  politics of, xi, 4, 21, 48, 49, 66, 225,
    226, 256, 257, 343, 353
  popular culture criticized by, 27, 250,
    251
  on prayer, 182
  resignation of, 299–300, 304, 312, 320
  return to ministry desired by, 356–7
  on salvation doctrine, 9, 129, 169–72,
    174
  on science, 214, 391n
  on secular humanists, 127, 328
  self-criticism of, 49, 51
  sermons of, 33, 46–9, 120, 176, 182,
    246–7
  on sexual behavior, 27, 32, 65, 67, 68,
    249
  Shawmut Church founded by, ix, 35,
    44, 52, 155, 279, 293, 308–9, 353,
    360
  on sin, x–xi, 71, 144, 170
  on situation ethics, 206
  smoking banned by, 163–4
  at Sunday worship, 40, 41–2, 43, 44,
    45, 46–52, 76, 77, 78, 95–6, 119, 288
  on televangelists, 118
  on university education, 127
  in Vietnam War, 17, 19–20
  Wednesday worship service led by,
    624, 275
  on working mothers, 198
Valenti, Joe, 17–18, 34, 35, 53, 122, 144,
  148, 309, 358, 359
Valenti, Kenny (Frank's brother), 17, 21,
  35
Valenti, Marie, 17, 34–5, 309, 358
Valenti, Sharon Waters, 62, 238
  on author's work, xii, 236, 356, 357,
    367
  background of, 20–1, 368
  benevolence of, 134, 135–7
  in Bible study, 63, 111, 155, 179, 210
  business ventures of, 352, 354
  on capitalism, 325–6
  church organization and, 44, 52, 126,
    256, 258, 307, 309, 318
  on church split, 299, 301, 305–6, 307,
    310, 314–15, 357
  on documentary film, xii, 141, 142,
    143, 236, 298–9, 334, 340, 351
  on education, 127, 356
  family ties of, 34, 102, 110, 308,
    317–18, 352, 355
  feminism disparaged by, 90–1, 92,
    229–30, 252, 257, 258, 322, 353,
    398n
  Florida move of, 307–8, 356
  on F. Valenti's ministry, 29, 33, 255,
    257–8, 276, 299, 300, 306, 308
  on gossip, 120–1
  as grandmother, 352, 355–6
  on indirect power of women, 316, 318,
    320, 323, 324
  at Liberty Baptist College, 30, 33, 34
  on Lucifer's fall, 184
  marriage of, 21, 22–3, 25, 27–8, 34, 74,
    86, 87, 90, 149–50, 230, 248, 254,
    256, 257–8, 259, 267, 293, 317–18
  on men, 110, 255, 316,318
  motherhood of, 21, 26, 34, 234, 248,
    294, 295, 296–7, 298, 303, 308, 312
  on pastoral authority, 305–6
  patriarchal authority endorsed by, 316,
    395n
  on Pentecostals, 57
  physical appearance of, 40
  on political issues, 21, 65, 256–7,
    325–6, 343, 353
  religious practice of, 24, 25, 30, 65,
    289, 293, 296–7, 308, 357
  on salvation, 200
  as schoolteacher, 6, 53, 145, 146,
    148–9, 314
  on science, 391n
  on secular humanists, 66, 104–5, 127,
    224, 328, 329, 356
  sex education opposed by, 4, 6
  Shawmut church founded by, 35, 44,
    52, 155, 293,.308–9, 353, 360
  smoking habit ended by, 24, 25
  at Sunday worship, 40–1
  welfare programs opposed by, 99, 134

in women's church activities, 84, 90, 120, 229

Valenti, Ted (Frank and Sharon's son), 355

Valenti, Timmy (Frank and Sharon's son), 21, 49

Valenti Enterprises, 352, 353, 355

values clarification, 94

Vanishing Family, The, 113, 398*n*

Vietnam War, 11, 18–20, 21, 75, 101

violence, as protest strategy, 345

virgin birth, 15, 59, 371*n*

Virgin Mary, 171

Waco, Texas, Branch Davidian community in, 236

Walden Street Commune, 36

Wallace, George, 11, 344, 372*n*, 374*n*

Walls, Andrew, 386*n*

Watergate tapes, 333

Waters, Judy, *see* Keener, Judy Waters

Weathermen, 345

Webber, Fred, 193

  background of, 164

  Bible-study led by, 164, 165, 166–8, 175, 194, 222

  on documentary film, 177

  on drinking, 186–7, 188–9

  marriage of, 248

  on prayer, 174, 176, 177, 178, 181–3, 223

Weber, Max, 37, 208, 249, 373*n*, 380*n*, 389*n*, 394*n*

Weber, Timothy, 374*n*

welfare programs, 99–100, 107, 134–5, 199, 201, 343, 379*n*, 385*n*, 387*n*–8*n*

Wesleyan holiness movement, 58

Wheaton College, 389*n*

Whitehead, Barbara, 403*n*

witnessing, 161–2

women:

  clothing restrictions on, 70, 72–3, 283–4, 353

  cross-generational cooperative relations of, 103–4, 111, 254, 317

  domestic life as sphere of, 103, 111, 254, 256, 257, 382*n*, 395*n*

  as flappers, 344, 403*n*

  gossip associated with, 319–20, 396*n*

  historical roots of fundamentalist views on, 61

  indirect power of, 316–23, 326–7, 397*n*, 402*n*

  moral authority of, 320

  motherhood as foremost duty of, 100, 379*n*–80*n*

  religious involvement initiated by, 381*n*

  subordinate position of, 87–8, 89, 90, 92, 246, 250, 253–6, 259, 376*n*–7*n*, 378*n*, 394*n*, 395*n*–6*n*

  in workforce, 91, 197–8, 391*n*, 398*n*

  see also feminism

Women Aglow, 375*n*, 391*n*

women's liberation movement, 10–11, 12, 251, 345, 372*n*

Worcester, Mass., 7–8, 109

Worcester City Hospital, ix working-class culture, 202, 386*n*

World Baptist Fellowship, 31

worldlies, 130

worldviews, opposition of, 201–2, 388*n*–9*n*

Yanagisako, Sylvia Junko, 396*n*

Young Ho Chun, 402*n*

ABOUT THE AUTHOR

James M. Ault, Jr., is a graduate of Harvard College, Brandeis University (Ph.D.), and the Mount Hermon School. After teaching at Harvard University and Smith College, he made his first film, *Born Again*, which won a Blue Ribbon at the American Film Festival and was broadcast nationally in the United States and abroad in 1987. Since then he has produced and directed a variety of educational and experimental documentary films for American foundations, including the Lilly Endowment, the Pew Charitable Trusts and the Episcopal Church Foundation. For the fall term of 2003, he held the William Spoelhof Chair at Calvin College, where he taught documentary filmmaking. He lives with his son, Henry, in Northampton, Massachusetts, where he continues to produce and distribute documentary films and videos (www.jamesault.com).

A NOTE ON THE TYPE

This book was set in Janson, a typeface long thought to have been made by the Dutchman Anton Janson, who was a practicing typefounder in Leipzig during the years 1668–1687. However, it has been conclusively demonstrated that these types are actually the work of Nicholas Kis (1650–1702), a Hungarian, who most probably learned his trade from the master Dutch typefounder Dirk Voskens. The type is an excellent example of the influential and sturdy Dutch types that prevailed in England up to the time William Caslon (1692–1766) developed his own incomparable designs from them.

Composed by Stratford Publishing Services
Brattleboro, Vermont
Printed and bound by Berryville Graphics
Berryville, Virginia
Designed by Virginia Tan